Library of
Davidson College

SAGE INTERNATIONAL YEARBOOK OF
FOREIGN POLICY STUDIES
I

Editorial Board

LJUBIVOJE ACIMOVIC
  Institute of International
  Politics and Economics
  Belgrade, Yugoslavia

MICHAEL BRECHER
  The Hebrew University
  Jerusalem, Israel
  and McGill University
  Montreal, Canada

ERNST-OTTO CZEMPIEL
  Goethe-Universität
  Frankfurt, GFR

WOLFRAM F. HANRIEDER
  University of California
  Santa Barbara, California USA

MICHAEL HAAS
  University of Hawaii
  Honolulu, Hawaii USA

CHARLES F. HERMANN
  Ohio State University
  Columbus, Ohio USA

JOHAN J. HOLST
  Norwegian Institute of
  International Affairs
  Oslo, Norway

MOHAMED KHAIRY ISSA
  Cairo University
  Cairo, Egypt

EDWARD L. MORSE
  Princeton University
  Princeton, New Jersey USA

KINHIDE MUSHAKOJI
  Sophia University
  Tokyo, Japan

RICHARD ROSECRANCE
  Cornell University
  Ithaca, New York USA

DIETER SENGHAAS
  Hessian Foundation for
  Peace and Conflict Research
  Frankfurt, GFR

ESTRELLA D. SOLIDUM
  University of the Philippines
  Quezon City, Philippines

DENIS STAIRS
  Dalhousie University
  Halifax, Nova Scotia, Canada

JANICE STEIN
  McGill University
  Montreal, Canada

YASH TANDON
  Institute for Development Studies
  Nairobi, Kenya

W. SCOTT THOMPSON
  Tufts University
  Medford, Massachusetts USA

LADISLAV VENYS
  Charles University
  Prague, Czechoslovakia

WILLIAM J.L. WALLACE
  University of Manchester
  Manchester, United Kingdom

SAGE INTERNATIONAL YEARBOOK OF FOREIGN POLICY STUDIES
VOLUME ONE

edited by

PATRICK J. McGOWAN
Program of International Relations
The Maxwell Graduate School of Citizenship and Public Affairs
Syracuse University

SAGE Publications Beverly Hills / London

Copyright © 1973 by Sage Publications, Inc.

All rights reserved. No part of this book may be reproduced or utilized in any form or by any means, electronic or mechanical, including photocopying, recording, or by any information storage and retrieval system, without permission in writing from the publisher.

For information address:

SAGE PUBLICATIONS, INC.
275 South Beverly Drive
Beverly Hills, California 90212

SAGE PUBLICATIONS LTD
St George's House / 44 Hatton Garden
London EC1N 8ER

Printed in the United States of America

International Standard Book Number 0-8039-0202-6

Library of Congress Catalog Card No. 72-98039

FIRST PRINTING

CONTENTS

Acknowledgements   7

Introduction
     PATRICK J. McGOWAN   9

Part One: CONTROVERSIES

1. On the Scope and Methods of Foreign Policy Studies
   MICHAEL HAAS   29

Part Two: THEORIES

2. Simulation in the Development of a Theory of Foreign Policy Decision-Making
   G. MATTHEW BONHAM and MICHAEL J. SHAPIRO   55

3. The PRINCE Concepts and the Study of Foreign Policy
   WILLIAM D. COPLIN, STEPHEN L. MILLS, and MICHAEL K. O'LEARY   73

Part Three: FINDINGS

4. The Relationship Between Public Opinion and Governmental Foreign Policy: *A Cross-National Study*
   MARTIN ABRAVANEL and BARRY HUGHES   107

5. The Impact of Defense Spending on Senatorial Voting Behavior: *A Study of Foreign Policy Feedback*
   STEPHEN COBB   135

6. Economic Interests and American Foreign Policy Allocations, 1960-69
   JOHN W. ELEY and JOHN H. PETERSEN   161

7. Foreign Policy Conflict Among African States, 1964-69
   RAYMOND W. COPSON 189

8. National Attributes and Foreign Policy Participation:
   A Path Analysis
   JAMES G. KEAN and PATRICK J. McGOWAN 219

Part Four: APPRAISALS

9. Public Opinion and Foreign Policy in West Germany
   RICHARD L. MERRITT 255

10. The Steps to War: *A Survey of System Levels, Decision Stages, and Research Results*
    KARL W. DEUTSCH and DIETER SENGHAAS 275

Part Five: BIBLIOGRAPHY

Bibliography of Recent Foreign Policy Studies, 1970-72
JAMES GREEN 333

ACKNOWLEDGEMENTS

Many people are due recognition for developing the idea of an *International Yearbook of Foreign Policy Studies* and for helping to produce this first volume. The members of the Inter-University Comparative Foreign Policy Project first saw the need. Professor James N. Rosenau of the University of Southern California was instrumental in making reality out of good intentions and Sara Miller McCune of Sage Publications has been creative and supportive in undertaking to publish the *Yearbook*. In establishing the editorial policy and organization of the *Yearbook* I have benefited greatly from the advice of the members of the editorial board, in particular, Professors Michael Haas, Charles F. Hermann, and Edward L. Morse. The suggestions of my colleagues at Syracuse University, Michael K. O'Leary and William D. Coplin, and Professor Philip Burgess of Ohio State University concerning format and content were invaluable. Members of the editorial board and a host of outside readers deserve credit for quickly and responsibly reviewing many manuscripts, without honorariums! James Green compiled the bibliography and did yeoman service as a copy and proof reader. Mrs. Sally La Mar and Mrs. Gloria Katz were, as always, efficient typists and editors of this editor's prose. Syracuse University was kind enough to grant me a semester's leave during which most of the work on this issue of the *Yearbook* was completed. Constance Greaser and Betsy Schmidt of Sage Publications were models of tact and efficiency in seeing the manuscript through to publication.

What merit this volume has, as the first in an annual series, is of course the result of the contributions of the chapter authors. It has been a rewarding experience to work with them as their editor. It is encouraging to know that there still are scholars who answer their mail, who meet deadlines, who follow style sheets, and who are at the same time creative thinkers and serious researchers. I gratefully acknowledge my debt to them and my admiration as well.

Finally, without the continued support and tolerance of my wife, Frouzandeh, this volume could not have been produced as painlessly as it was.

P.J.M.
Syracuse, New York
January 1, 1973

INTRODUCTION

PATRICK J. McGOWAN

Syracuse University

WHY THIS YEARBOOK?

This volume is the first in an annual series devoted to the systematic study of foreign policy. At present, no other scholarly publication focuses exclusively on the study of foreign policy as part of the social sciences. It is our intention that the *Sage International Yearbook of Foreign Policy Studies* should fill this gap in the literature and thereby sustain and give direction to the development of scientific studies of foreign policy.

We cannot present here the complete intellectual history of the emergence of a scientific approach to the study of foreign policy. Part of the story has already been told elsewhere and need not be repeated (Rosenau, 1971; McGowan and Shapiro, 1973). However, we must take note of several facts in order to understand why this new *Yearbook* of foreign policy studies has been launched at this time and why it has the editorial policy it does.

Political studies, particularly within the United States, underwent considerable change in the 1950s, although the intellectual foundations clearly had been laid before World War II. The so-called behavioral movement attempted to make political science a part of the social sciences with a stress on conceptualization, theory building, and systematic empirical procedures for establishing the truth content of theoretically derived hypotheses. At least within the United States this "revolution" has been accomplished and few political scientists are trained today without receiving a solid grounding in the theoretical and empirical methods of the various social sciences.

As the behavioral movement gained influence it began to affect areas of political science other than the study of American politics, which was its origin. A "new" comparative politics emerged in the late 1950s and early 1960s that claimed to be applying the rigorous methods of the social sciences to the study of politics outside the United States, particularly in the "non-Western" areas. The study of international relations and its subfields of international politics and foreign policy studies were in turn influenced by the behavioralists and by the new-style comparativists (compare Rosenau, 1961, to Rosenau, 1969). However, among the various fields of political science, the study of foreign policy has been more resistant to these changes in approach than any other field, with the possible exception of public administration.

The two disciplines that most shaped foreign policy studies, diplomatic history and international law, have proved fairly impervious to social scientific methods of research. Perhaps this is why the study of foreign policy began to manifest a comparative and therefore scientific orientation only in the late 1960s. In a survey of findings in the field of the comparative study of foreign policy, Shapiro and McGowan found only a handful of comparative studies published prior to 1963 (McGowan and Shapiro, 1973). On the other hand, during the five-year period 1966-1970, they identified one hundred and twenty-two articles and books that were clearly comparative-scientific studies of foreign policy (McGowan, 1972). Thus, while it is correct to say that much writing on foreign policy remains traditionally descriptive and oriented to making immediate policy recommendations to governments, by the 1970s a different approach to the study of foreign policy, distinguished by its attempt to ground itself in the empirical tradition of the social sciences, had emerged.

Many scholars are responsible for the emergence of the comparative study of foreign policy. Karl W. Deutsch of Harvard University has influenced a generation of scholars to collect carefully and to manipulate creatively "hard" data on nation-states and other units (e.g., Deutsch's sponsorship of the Yale Political Data Program, Russett et al., 1964). Johan Galtung and *The Journal of Peace Research* have encouraged rigorous research and a concern with fundamental value issues like peace and war, justice, and imperialism in the study of foreign policy. Charles A. McClelland broke new ground in the systematic collection of masses of data on the behavior of nation-states that has been followed up by many others (McClelland and Hoggard, 1969). James N. Rosenau made new theoretical advances in his many writings and edited books. Particularly important for the emergence of comparative studies of foreign policy was his essay on pre-theories and theories of foreign policy where he persuasively argued that "foreign policy analysis is devoid of general theory" and that until works were written which contained "explicit 'if then' hypotheses in which the 'if' is a particular form of internal factor and the 'then' is a particular type of foreign policy" (Rosenau, 1966: 32, 31), there would be little explanation and prediction in our field. The work of these men and others like them has established the intellectual foundations of our subject (see Jones and Singer, 1972, and McGowan and Shapiro, 1973, for surveys of this literature). Moreover, the scientific approach to the study of foreign policy is no longer a North American monopoly as this orientation has developed in and spread independently from Scandinavia to Europe and thence throughout the world.

By 1973 these advances have produced a growing community of researchers and policy analysts who need a forum for the publication of their research that shares their desire to develop further systematic studies of foreign policy. "Their" *Yearbook* should also be of interest to students of foreign policy who hold different beliefs but who wish to keep up with current research trends and, in particular, to specialists in international relations and comparative politics who share our orientation.

Readers of this first edition of the *Yearbook* deserve an explicit statement of what we plan to do with it so that they can decide to read it, to contribute to it, or to ignore it as their interests dictate. Our name has been chosen with care, so perhaps the most straightforward way to explain what we plan to do would be to discuss each concept in our *Sage International Yearbook of Foreign Policy Studies* title.

Foreign Policy

At present there does not exist an agreed-upon definition of foreign policy, nor do there exist well-known and validated typologies and scales of foreign policy behavior. Obviously, these problems are related. The study of foreign policy is clearly part of the broader field of international relations. An analogy may help at this point. If international relations is like economics, then international politics is like macroeconomics and foreign policy studies are like microeconomics. That is, within the field of international relations the subfield of international politics tends to focus on the structures and processes of the entire international political system in the way that macroeconomics deals with the aggregate behavior of whole national economies. The subfield of foreign policy analysis, on the other hand, focuses on the behavior of actors such as national governments and their representatives in the way that microeconomics tends to study the behavior of economic actors such as firms and consumers. Therefore, when we study "actors" and their behavior we are usually doing a foreign policy study, whereas when we study "systems" and their components, like alliances and international organizations, we are doing international political research.

A second comparison may also help. There is now a developing field of public policy studies which seeks to describe, explain, predict, and evaluate the outputs of governments and governmental agencies. One may well approach the systematic study of foreign policy from this direction, and if one does, then the comparative study of foreign policy can be viewed as an aspect of the broader field of public policy. Foreign policy could thus be defined as the actions of national or central governments taken toward other actors external to the legal sovereignty of the initiating governments. Foreign policy behavior in most instances must cross a national border or must link in an actor-target relationship the representatives of at least two separate and formally independent governments.

Most definitions of foreign policy therefore stress the special actors that engage in this behavior and the distinct aspects of that behavior. As the term is normally defined, only national governments and their agents make foreign policy although they may be influenced by—and seek to influence by their actions—a host of domestic, transnational, and international actors. Second, foreign policy behavior is almost invariably seen as purposive action designed to affect conditions external to the actor. If there is not a manifest intention to affect the external evironment of the nation-state we would not ordinarily consider the action to be foreign policy. However, foreign policy behavior may also exhibit intended or unintended consequences for the actor and unintended consequences for the environment.

Our *Yearbook* has therefore accepted as a working definition of foreign policy behavior the actions of national governments and their representatives toward explicit targets external to the society or societies under study. These actions may be verbal or physical; they may be manifested in single decisions, streams of events, or continuing allocations of men and materials. We intend to publish article-length papers that try systematically to describe, explain, predict, and evaluate such "foreign policy" behavior. We do not think that we have arrived at a perfect or final conceptual definition of our subject matter, nor do we intend to stipulate the ways in which foreign policy should be operationally measured. Indeed, we hope that our *Yearbook* will make a significant contribution to the further conceptualization and measurement of foreign policy behavior and the factors which influence it and are affected by it.

Studies

In truth, the major changes that have occurred during the last decade in the field of foreign policy studies have been methodological in nature. A growing number of specialists have come to accept a scientific paradigm in their work on foreign policy. But there is hardly any more agreement on what "scientific method" means than there is on what is meant by foreign policy. With respect to this controversy, we can only stipulate what we mean and the types of studies we intend to publish.

In our view, the study of foreign policy should be grounded in the empirical research traditions of the various social sciences, including post-behavioral political science. Such research will tend to be systematic in that it will try to elucidate the general rather than the particular. Scientific studies of foreign policy aim at making general explanatory statements about foreign policy behavior in the fashion that each social science seeks to make such statements about its own subject matter. A general explanatory statement is in the form:

> If a democracy lacks political unity, then its foreign policies will not be aggressive.

This is a general sentence, for it does not mention any proper names of countries or particular time periods. It applies to any democracy, past, present, or future. It is explanatory because it links two variable concepts, political unity and aggressive foreign policy. However, this sentence is not perfectly general for it applies only to the nation-state subclass of political democracies and to the foreign policy subclass of aggressive behavior. Scientific studies of foreign policy try to derive and validate such statements, and since they are primarily non-experimental, empirical studies of foreign policy will tend to be comparative (Zelditch, 1971).

We shall publish in our *Yearbook* research papers that have as their immediate or long-range objective the creation and testing of general explanatory sentences about foreign policy behavior. Such papers will frequently engage in systematic descriptions of foreign policy and its correlates. Many such papers will attempt to state and validate explanations of the causes and consequences of foreign policy behavior. Given the state of our knowledge, it will probably be infrequently that papers will attempt to predict future behavior, but we encourage this type of research. Finally, because foreign policy behavior is a part of human behavior, many papers will try to evaluate what we know about foreign policy in terms of explicit value concerns, such as peaceful conflict resolution or the more equitable distribution of resources among societies and their members.

Scientific studies of foreign policy are not wedded to a particular research technique like content analysis, survey research, or archival research. Scientific studies of foreign policy are not necessarily allied to any given political ideology. This approach can and has been used to defend the status quo and to attack it. Comparative studies of foreign policy do not presuppose a single type of research design; they may be cross-sectional, diachronic, or longitudinal. They may look at many cases statistically, or compare a few cases qualitatively, or even examine a single case in order to generate more general hypotheses or to explain why the case in question does not fit an already established pattern (Lijphart, 1971). Scientific studies of foreign policy can use as independent or dependent concepts measured attributes of units ranging from key individuals through to regional and international systems. The single unifying feature of systematic studies of foreign policy is their attempt to derive, validate, and evaluate general explanatory sentences about foreign policy. It is this type of research that we seek to publish in our *Yearbook*.

International

We intend to make this *Yearbook* a truly international forum for the analysis of foreign policy behavior. In our view there are good political and intellectual reasons for attempting to do this. National perspectives on research priorities and methods of research really do exist and a publication of our sort must reflect the realities of the contemporary international situation. Of particular importance is the present international distribution of scientific knowledge and the wherewithal to produce it. Most comparative and scientific research on foreign policy is both produced and consumed in North America and Western Europe. This is true even if the research is on the behavior and problems of the less developed states of the Third World. We therefore intend to try to redress this imbalance with this *Yearbook* by encouraging the publication of research by "non-Western" scholars on the foreign policies of their states and, indeed, on the external behavior of all states.

The primary intellectual reason for our attempt to make this a genuinely international *Yearbook* is the clearly ethnocentric nature of much research on foreign policy. Most specialists live in and do research on the more modern and powerful states of the Atlantic community. While scholars must be free to pursue their own interests, the result has been that most "theories" of foreign policy and much of the substantive research reflects a great-power bias. Very little theorizing and research have proved relevant to the needs of the less modern and less powerful states of Asia, Africa, the Middle East, and

Latin America. If we are concerned with developing a general science of foreign policy studies, then our work has been parochial rather than general.

In attempting to achieve this objective we have met with limited success so far. Our editorial board is genuinely international in composition. The majority of its members are citizens of countries outside North America. They are at work developing contacts and encouraging submissions from scholars outside the United States. Indeed, this is their prime job as members of the editorial board. However, in this first edition of the *Yearbook* we have not succeeded in publishing articles by many scholars working elsewhere than in the United States. Only one of our authors is not an American. In future editions we hope to rectify this imbalance. We therefore particularly encourage submissions by non-American authors.

Yearbook

A very reasonable question is why we have decided to launch a *Yearbook* instead of a new journal. Quite possibly we could have begun as a journal since both our publisher, Sage Publications, and members of the editorial board have considerable experience in publishing and editing journals. Nevertheless, we are persuaded that an annual volume of eight to ten articles is more suited to our needs than a quarterly journal which would publish anywhere from sixteen to thirty articles a year.

Because we will publish a maximum of ten articles in each edition, we hope that we will be able to achieve the highest possible standards of scholarship and writing style. Journals, with their quarterly publication deadlines, often do not have the time to devote to each manuscript that we have with our *Yearbook*. In addition, there is some question as to whether or not our field could support a journal devoted exclusively to scientific studies of foreign policy. Articles with this orientation already are published by the *Journal of Peace Research,* the *Journal of Conflict Resolution,* and the *International Studies Quarterly* as well as in some other journals. While none of these journals is primarily devoted to scientific-comparative studies of foreign policy, a journal of foreign policy studies would to some extent compete with these already established reviews. It might not be able to secure twenty-five high quality articles each year as the number of really good papers being written in our field that would be available to such a new journal is limited.

These are relatively peripheral reasons in any case. Yearbooks are, or at least they should be, different from quarterly journals. One would hope that a yearbook would be able to publish articles of some enduring worth. That is certainly our intention even though it may not yet be our achievement.

Second, yearbooks are freer to solicit articles and to commission papers on topics that need an in-depth study. While the same editorial standards must apply to such papers, including outside review, we can do this because of the greater flexibility of the yearbook format in comparison to a quarterly journal.

In our view, however, the primary reason for the establishment of this new *Yearbook* is that at present there is no journal or annual publication that covers the entire spectrum of foreign policy studies. As Michael Haas demonstrates in the first table of his article "On the Scope and Method of Foreign Policy Studies," no journal broadly represents all the possible purposes of foreign policy studies. He finds that "there is a division between three journals that are prescriptive, on the one hand, and five that have scientific orientations... on the other hand, with two journals cautiously clinging to the descriptive mode." We believe that Haas is correct in his evaluation of the state of the field of systematic studies of foreign policy. We therefore intend to meet the clear need for a review that represents all the various purposes of foreign policy studies. What are these objectives and to what extent has this first edition of our *Yearbook* dealt with each of them?

CONTENTS

It had been our intention to use this introduction to survey the current state of foreign policy studies and thereby to relate our new *Yearbook* to the future development of this field. Happily, Professor Haas has ably done part of the job for us in Chapter 1. We need only build upon what he has said.

We believe that there are five broad categories the *Yearbook* must cover if it is to achieve its overall objective which is to help advance the systematic study of foreign policy. We will annually publish articles that cover the areas of Development of the Field, Description, Explanation, Prediction, and Evaluation. It is our hope that the *Yearbook* will thereby make an important and unique contribution to the literatures of international relations and comparative politics.

Development of the Field

The format of a *Yearbook* is ideally suited to publishing essays that have as their major purpose the development of a field of inquiry. Such articles need not present new findings—which journals are so often expected to do—nor need they present new theoretical frameworks. Rather, they should discuss the scope and methods of foreign policy studies, appraise the state of our knowledge in certain areas, and suggest future research needs. Finally, they should inform us of the reliability and validity of our knowledge via the basic scientific process of replication.

Scope and Methods. We hope to be able to feature articles which attempt to define our field of inquiry and to discuss the various approaches and methodologies appropriate to the comparative-scientific study of foreign policy. In this edition of the *Yearbook* Michael Haas has contributed a wide-ranging survey of the state of our field. His essay focuses on "the multi-dimensional scope of the field of foreign policy studies" by classifying various aspects of the field in terms of its methodologies, its purposes, its theories, its principal research techniques, and its subjects of analysis. He concludes that there are few gaps in the literature and thus a substantial body of writings to be mastered. On the other hand, "the field lacks truly definitive studies within the various categories used herein to classify the field. It is the task of future foreign policy analysts to respond to this challenge." Such essays are analytical and prescriptive, therefore they will tend to be controversial—arguing what we are doing wrong or how we can do things better. It is for this reason that Part One of the *Yearbook* is entitled *Controversies.*

In future editions of this *Yearbook* we hope to include a variety of articles that address themselves to the types of issues raised by Professor Haas. What is it that we study? How can we best study foreign policy? What should we do with our knowledge once it is generated? These are some of the questions we shall investigate in these pages.

Appraisals. An essential aspect of the development of any field of inquiry is periodic stocktaking of the extent of our knowledge and the gaps that further research should try to fill. Surveys of findings, programmatic statements of needed research, critiques of existing theories and frameworks are among the types of essays that fall under the heading of appraisals. In this edition of the *Yearbook* we present two essays that can be classified as appraisals. Each is devoted to making the study of foreign policy a more cumulative discipline.

Richard L. Merritt examines the question of "Public Opinion and Foreign Policy in West Germany." He notes that public opinion polling has become very extensive in the Federal Republic since the end of the war. What possible use are these data and how can they contribute to the growth of systematic studies of foreign policy? Merritt surveys the types of data available and the research questions that can be asked of them. He concludes that "if we want to move beyond the parochial concern with policy formation in the United States in an effort to develop a valid model of such processes in the industrialized world, it will be imperative to focus more upon behavior in other countries." For example, he notes, "West Germany, as a country with well-developed surveying facilities and a rich data collection, may well be the place to begin." Certainly, if we are to develop valid models of the interaction of public opinion and foreign policy, we must indeed become more comparative—and Merritt usefully suggests how we can start this vitally needed job.

In their long essay on "The Steps to War," Karl W. Deutsch and Dieter Senghaas survey the findings of previous research on the outbreak of war in terms of two typologies of system-levels and decision-stages. They ask how we can develop a theory of war and peace since there is no scientific (i.e., falsifiable) theory of this type at present. Deutsch and Senghaas examine a vast array of literature in terms of explanatory levels ranging from the intra-psychic to regional and international systems. Although fully validated findings in this vital research area are few, they conclude that our pre-theories need to be revised. They note three needed areas of revision: (1) there was a basic change in the international political system around 1910, so basic that our knowledge of pre-1910 systems of behavior will not be much help in building models of contemporary foreign policy and international politics; (2) the assumption of rational behavior, so often made in studies of foreign policy, is unwarranted—particularly with respect to the steps leading to war between states; and (3) the behavior of nation-states appears to be far more internally determined than many theories suggest, thereby making a strong case for the comparative study of the domestic determinants of foreign policy behavior, including warfare.

In our view nothing can contribute more to the emergence of systematic studies of foreign policy than appraising types of essays such as those written by Merritt and by Deutsch and Senghaas for this first edition. It is because of this belief that Part Four of our *Yearbook* is entitled *Appraisals*. We intend to publish many more stocktaking essays. For example, in the second edition of our *Yearbook* we hope to have an essay that integrates a number of recent research efforts that have tried to establish empirically-grounded typologies of foreign policy behavior.

Replications. The purpose of replication is to examine the reliability and validity of previous research, to test its generality, and to extend the scope of previous findings by testing them in different time periods and with different sets of cases. One of the rare instances of replication in our field is the way Tanter (1966) and Wilkenfeld (1969, 1971) replicated the original research of Rummel (1963). In our view replications have been all too rare because they have not been rewarded in the fashion in which "original" research is normally rewarded. None of our journals specifically encourage the publication of replications, although obviously they will publish them upon occasion.

Our *Yearbook* will encourage replications since we feel that they are a basic part of the process of building a cumulative science of foreign policy studies. We do not have a replications section in this issue of the *Yearbook* but hopefully future editions will contain such a section. The editor and editorial board will especially welcome the submission of short (five to ten printed pages) research notes that report the results of replication studies.

Description

The second major category of the *Yearboook's* format is the publication of articles that engage in systematic descriptions of the patterns of foreign policy behavior around the world. Accurate and systematic description is the first stage of any scientific field of inquiry, although such descriptions usually presuppose some sort of paradigm or theoretical framework as a guide. Be this as it may, comparative systematic description is not well developed in our field, even though it is a basic requirement. Our *Yearbook* does not encourage the descriptive analysis of a single case unless it is undertaken to illuminate why the case in question does not fit a known pattern or to generate testable hypotheses which subsequently can be studied on a comparative basis. Ruling out all but these types of case studies leaves two basic forms of systematic description which our *Yearbook* strongly advocates.

Comparative Description. In most areas of inquiry on foreign policy we do not yet know what are the typical patterns and what are the atypical—that is, we have not measured means and variances in behavior and associated variables. By comparative description we mean the examination of two or more cases in order to validly and reliably describe foreign policy behavior.

In this edition of the *Yearbook,* Raymond W. Copson describes trends in "Foreign Policy Conflict Among African States, 1964-69." He finds that such conflict is declining over time and he asks why. Based upon an original data set of conflict events, Copson quantitatively describes the frequency of inter-state conflict by type, country, and region in Africa. He then proceeds to engage in the qualitative analysis of "conflict arenas" within Africa. He concludes that foreign policy conflict has not proven successful in achieving actor objectives in Africa—hence its decline. Thus, while his chapter is primarily descriptive, he does engage in explanatory analysis as well.

There are many possible types of systematic description. Indeed, much of the factor analytic studies of foreign policy behavior, for all their statistical sophistication, are nothing more than systematic description. We feel that such work is basic, however, and in our *Findings* part of each *Yearbook* we intend to publish innovative descriptive studies.

Correlation and Clustering. These two activities are merely names for quantitative description via the use of statistical routines such as correlation and regression analysis (correlation) and factor analysis (clustering). Every field of inquiry needs to know what is related to what and which variables are not related to each other under what conditions. The vast majority of published quantitative studies of foreign policy represent descriptions in the correlation and clustering mode. Our *Yearbook* encourages this type of research as part of the basic scientific activity of systematic description.

John W. Eley and John H. Petersen in their study "Economic Interests and American Foreign Policy Allocations, 1960-1969," present a correlational analysis of the relations between measured United States economic interests in foreign countries and official United States allocations of economic and military aid and diplomatic personnel. Their correlations are used to evaluate the explanatory power of two competing "theories" of American foreign policy—the neo-Marxist and the political-strategic. They find that neither framework fits the data perfectly and that neither time lags nor controls affect the relationships they have uncovered. Again, this study has explanatory elements in its evaluation of two competing explanatory sketches of United States foreign policy, but the primary contribution is the illustration of the possibilities of the systematic quantitative description of the foreign policy of a single country.

Explanation

Every science hopes to be able to explain what it studies. Frankly, we are not able to do this very well because explanation requires genuine theories and causal analyses to test propositions derived from these theories. Since our field does not have well-developed middle-range or general theories, we have had few causal analyses of foreign policy behavior. We intend to have the *Yearbook* make a positive contribution to the explanation of foreign policy behavior, which it can do by publishing two specific types of articles.

Theorizing. Part Two of the *Yearbook* is entitled *Theories.* This section will publish articles that are primarily conceptual and theoretical in orientation—but hopefully with some data analysis or direct application to empirical research. The justification for this section is that if foreign policy studies are to be firmly grounded in the empirical tradition of the social sciences, then the construction of testable theories of foreign policy is the ultimate objective of our entire enterprise. This edition of the *Yearbook* contains two articles that illustrate how simulation techniques and their related activities can further develop the level of our theorizing about foreign policy.

G. Matthew Bonham and Michael J. Shapiro have used simulation inductively to generate a model of the decision-making process. Based upon interviews with actual participants in a recent crisis decision, they have constructed a model of the psychological mechanisms involved in arriving at a foreign policy decision of some consequence. The simulation model is formal and can thus be applied to other situations. Eventually, their work will lead to better descriptions of the information-processing behavior of decision-makers and, hopefully, to the explanation of their behavior. If successful, they expect that their simulation can also be used in a prescriptive mode to recommend policy alternatives.

Simulation as an aid to the construction of theories of foreign policy can also be used deductively. In their essay on "The PRINCE Concepts and the Study of Foreign Policy," William D. Coplin and Michael K. O'Leary and their student, Stephen L. Mills, discuss how their deductively-generated programmed international computer environment (PRINCE) has generated a set of concepts and an approach that possibly have very fruitful application to comparative studies of foreign policy. In a long essay they present and defend an issue-based approach to the study of foreign policy and the concepts they utilize to study issues and issue outcomes—the issue position of each actor, each actor's power, the salience of the issue to the actor, and the affect relations among the concerned actors. They contrast their work with the long dominant "realist" approach to the study of international behavior and they indicate areas of empirical inquiry which they and others are undertaking within the PRINCE framework.

There are many ways to develop concepts and theoretical relationships besides simulations. Our *Yearbook* will continue to publish theoretical works, be they inductive or deductive; be they simulations, formal models, or operational typologies; be they highly general or middle range; be they abstract or directly policy-relevant. The one condition we shall impose upon the theoretical articles is that they be stated in such a fashion that they are either directly or indirectly operational and therefore, in some meaningful sense, testable (Blalock, 1968).

Trace Causation. Also treating the explanation of foreign policy behavior are empirical studies that test explicit hypotheses or that engage in some form of causal modeling within the framework of an explicit theory of foreign policy behavior. In cooking the proof is in the eating and in scientific research the proof is in the empirical findings! Our *Yearbook* therefore encourages the publication of studies that attempt to trace cause-and-effect relations among variables relating to foreign policy behavior. This edition contains three such studies in the Findings section.

Martin Abravanel and Barry Hughes attempt to determine the causal relationship between official foreign policy behavior and public opinion in their comparative study "The Relationship Between Public Opinion and Governmental Foreign Policy: A Cross-National Study." They very creatively combine two quite different data sets, one representing event interactions between states in Western Europe and two outside powers—the United States and the USSR—and the other representing the public-opinion attitudes of sampled citizens in these states. By the use of lagged correlation analysis they demonstrate that if there is a causal relationship present, it is where events influence attitudes and not vice versa. Their findings are summarized in a flow chart figure which is directly open to experimental study via simulations and small group experiments.

Stephen Cobb, a sociologist, focuses on a single case, the United States, in order to investigate the frequently-heard argument that a military-industrial complex determines United States foreign policy. This is a big question and Cobb narrows it down by asking what relationship, if any, exists between defense spending in states and senatorial voting on foreign policy issues. He measures military spending in a variety of ways and senatorial voting via a Guttman scale of "jingoism." He finds no support "for the contention that defense spending concentrations have a significant influence on the manner in which senators vote on issues in the area of foreign policy." Cobb's study is interesting in that it builds upon his earlier work and that of Bruce Russett (1970). He concludes that neither the pluralist nor the elitist interpretations of American political behavior fit this case and, based upon the writings of Lowi and Lieberson, Cobb suggests a fascinating alternative explanation of his findings.

In the final causal study in this volume, James G. Kean and the editor examine the relationships between the four national attribute variables of size, modernization, resources, and needs, and four measures of foreign policy behavior. Building upon considerable previous empirical research that has demonstrated a link between size and wealth (or modernization) and measures of foreign policy, they try to explain these findings by suggesting that they are statistically spurious. Size and wealth are related to the behavior of states because they are positively related to the intervening variables of resources and needs. The results of their study support this contention, but not conclusively.

Cobb's study, "The Impact of Defense Spending on Senatorial Voting Behavior," and the Kean and McGowan study of "National Attributes and Foreign Policy Participation" approach the status of replications, for they follow closely and build upon a great deal of previous empirical research. The Abravanel and Hughes paper, although it refers to a large literature, is extremely original in the questions it asks and the way in which it measures behavior and attitudes and relates them via lagged correlation analysis. The *Yearbook* will continue to feature such studies which trace causation, for this is a basic purpose of systematic studies of foreign policy.

Prediction

The fourth major objective must be to predict future patterns of foreign policy behavior and the likelihood of important events, such as the signing of a truce in Vietnam. In order to make predictions, however, one needs well-validated theories—unless one is willing to make crude projections from existing trends. Sometimes this is all the scholar can do, but as our field develops we will, hopefully, be able to make at least some modest theoretically-derived predictions. This edition of the *Yearbook* does not contain any articles that primarily engage in the predictive mode. We would like to publish such works and we encourage their submission, even the cruder types of trend analysis. After all, we must know where we are going and that is what predictions tell us—more or less reliably.

Evaluation

The fifth and final purpose of foreign policy studies is to evaluate the policies of governments and our systematic findings in the light of explicit value criteria. Not only do evaluative studies pass judgment upon current and past behaviors, but they can prescribe future behavior for governments and their opponents. Many prescriptive-evaluative studies will be undertaken by scholars and analysts with close connections to governments, for it is in the nature of their work to recommend "better" ways of doing what the governments want to do. On the other hand, studies by scholars and researchers outside any establishment will often be in the evaluative mode, for there is much to dislike and to wish to change in our area of study.

In this edition of the *Yearbook* we do not have an article that is primarily evaluative in nature. The Deutsch and Senghaas paper, "The Steps to War," clearly has an evaluative dimension. The authors do not like war; they would like to see it limited or eliminated as an element of foreign policy behavior. Their paper is thus in the tradition of peace research, even though they confine themselves to a careful analysis and classification of the literature concerning the outbreak of war.

In future editions of the *Yearbook* we hope to do better by publishing mainly evaluative studies of foreign policy behavior. We shall not specify a particular set of values on the basis of which evaluations and recommendations are to be made. It is quite likely that we shall publish studies by governmental officials who prescribe policies and studies by individuals completely outside any official governmental network who systematically criticize current policies. Our single condition with respect to publishing evaluative articles, beyond our usual concern for quality, is that the value basis of the evaluations and recommendations be perfectly explicit. Indeed, even in the cases where the article reports empirical findings, we hope that the authors address themselves to the policy implications of their findings, as this is one of the categories we are using to evaluate submitted manuscripts.

At the present time, no single publication in our field attempts to cover the five interrelated objectives of evaluation, prediction, explanation, description, and the development of the field itself. Our *Yearbook* will attempt to do this and to thereby make a significant and unique contribution to the growth of systematic studies of foreign policy. The fundamental assumption of this series is that the analysis of foreign policy should be grounded in the empirical tradition of the social sciences rather than the largely descriptive or prescriptive scholarship of the past. The *Yearbook* will encourage systematic studies of the causes and consequences of foreign policy behavior that develop the field of foreign policy analysis through theoretical, comparative, logical, quantitative, normative, mathematical, and qualitative forms of analysis. Only a careful reading of the pages that follow will determine if we have succeeded in this first effort to further develop the field of foreign policy analysis.

REFERENCES

BLALOCK, H. M., Jr. (1968) "The measurement problem: a gap between the languages of theory and research," pp. 5-27 in H. M. Blalock, Jr. and A. Blalock (eds.) Methodology in Social Research. New York: McGraw-Hill.
JONES, S. D. and J. D. SINGER (1972) Beyond Conjecture in International Politics. Itasca, Ill.: F. E. Peacock.
LIJPHART, A. (1971) "Comparative politics and the comparative method." American Political Science Review 65: 682-693.
McCLELLAND, C. A. and G. D. HOGGARD (1969) "Conflict patterns in the interactions among nations," pp. 711-724 in J. N. Rosenau (ed.) International Politics and Foreign Policy. New York: Free Press.
McGOWAN, P. J. (1972) "The future of scientific studies of foreign policy: an evangelical plea." Syracuse University Dept. of Political Science. (mimeo)
--- and H. B. SHAPIRO (1973) The Comparative Study of Foreign Policy: A Survey of Scientific Findings. Beverly Hills: Sage.
ROSENAU, J. N. (1971) The Scientific Study of Foreign Policy. New York: Free Press.
--- [ed.] (1969) International Politics and Foreign Policy. New York: Free Press.
--- (1966) "Pre-theories and theories of foreign policy," pp. 27-92 in R. B. Farrell

(ed.) Approaches to Comparative and International Politics. Evanston: Northwestern Univ. Press.

——— [ed.] (1961) International Politics and Foreign Policy. New York: Free Press.

RUMMEL, R. J. (1963) "Dimensions of conflict behavior within and between nations." General Systems Yearbook 8: 1-50.

RUSSETT, B. (1970) What Price Vigilance? The Burden of National Defense. New Haven: Yale Univ. Press.

——— et al. (1964) World Handbook of Political and Social Indicators. New Haven: Yale Univ. Press.

TANTER, R. (1966) "Dimensions of conflict behavior within and between nations, 1958-60." Journal of Conflict Resolution 10: 41-64.

WILKENFELD, J. (1971) "Domestic and foreign conflict behavior of nations," pp. 189-203 in W. D. Coplin and C. W. Kegley, Jr. (eds.) A Multi-Method Introduction to International Politics. Chicago: Markham.

——— (1969) "Some further findings regarding the domestic and foreign conflict behavior of nations." Journal of Peace Research 6: 147-156.

ZELDITCH, M. Jr. (1971) "Intelligible Comparisons," pp. 267-307 in I. Vallier (ed.) Comparative Methods in Sociology. Berkeley and Los Angeles: Univ. of California Press.

PART ONE

CONTROVERSIES

Chapter 1

ON THE SCOPE AND METHODS OF
FOREIGN POLICY STUDIES

MICHAEL HAAS
University of Hawaii

A Funny Thing Happened on the Way to My Lai

Half a decade ago a group of top-notch scholars assembled for a conference at the Institute for Advanced Studies in the Behavioral Sciences, Palo Alto. The purpose of the meeting, supported by funds from the Department of Defense, was to survey theoretical approaches to the study of international relations. In one session, devoted to the subject of foreign policy analysis under the title "Decision-Making and International Behavior," the audience of scholars listened to papers in which societal factors of countries were hypothesized to be related to particular styles of state behavior. So lopsided did this format appear to me at the time that I felt compelled to ask, "What ever happened to the analysis of foreign *policymaking*?" While the Pentagon was embarking on a controversial escalation of military force in Southeast Asia, I found it incredible that no person was willing to analyze the processing of information prior to decisions, as had been suggested by Snyder, Bruck, and Sapin (1963), nor was there a discussion of sources of perceptual confusion prior to decisions, as had been undertaken by North and associates (1963).

A more basic omission at the conference was any treatment of the morality of decisions in foreign policy, for that topic was supposedly to be the subject of a follow-up conference—on the application of scientific studies to policy questions in international relations—a conference which was never held! A comprehensive survey of the scope and methods of foreign policy analysis thus was too embarrassing an assignment for an American author during that period of the darkest hour of American foreign policy-making! It is for this reason that I issued my neotraditional (Haas, 1967) and multimethodological (Haas and Becker, 1970) pleas and hoped thereby that the decade of the 1970s would usher in a mood for change.

A period of change requires an analysis of the situation to be reconstructed. A mere listing of pertinent studies would be of little help. It is therefore the purpose of this essay to survey the multidimensional scope of the field of foreign policy analysis, using a variety of methods of classification, yet persistently posing the question, "What next?" The essay seeks to be comprehensive, not in terms of its bibliography, but instead in delineating the major facets of research into the nature of foreign policy.[1] The survey below classifies the field in terms of methodology, purposes of study, theories and paradigms, research methods, and subjects of analysis.

"Foreign Policy" and "International Relations"

The first type of foreign policy study is largely conceptual and *methodological*. Introspective studies about the field of foreign policy analysis are not only rare but also suspect. The rarity is due to the fact that the field called "foreign policy" is presumed without question to be a subcategory in the discipline of "international relations," and the methodology of the social sciences is relied upon without very much adaptation to the nature of foreign policy analyses. The reason such methodological essays are suspect is that there are so many schools of thought in the field that few scholars are perceived to be objective in discussing their own realm of inquiry. Nevertheless, five issues are crucial in foreign policy analysis.

The task of defining "foreign policy" as a field, first of all, has not been especially popular. Indeed, entire treatises containing major theoretical contributions to the field, whose titles contain the words "foreign policy," have failed to define this most basic concept in their own inquiry. One scholar insistently claims that the fields of "foreign policy" and "international politics" are identical (Gross, 1954). Another dismisses "foreign policy" as a concern for international relations from the viewpoint of only one actor; thus, the study of foreign policy is excluded from his effort to build a science of international relations (Wright, 1955). An intermediate position, stated by Sondermann (1961), has gained more widespread acceptance: "international relations" is composed of both "international politics" and "foreign policy," with the former concentrating on systems and processes, the latter on actors and individual decisions. The study of foreign policy thus focuses on the micro-components of international relations as dependent variables. Hence, studies on the United Nations belong to international politics unless there is explicit attention to policies pursued by particular states vis-à-vis the U.N.

Foreign policy analysis is as akin to history as to sociology, so the data of foreign policy studies will tend to come from documents and interviews with elites as well as from aggregate data and mass opinions. It is of course possible to cross back and forth along the nomothetic-idiographic continuum: a systemic variable may be related to a foreign policy choice, as when Israel contemplates developing thermonuclear weapons in response to the actions of its neighboring countries. If there is a high correlation between the wealth of a country and negative attitudes toward the United Nations (Vincent, 1968), what does this mean as regards a particular country on a particular issue, such as the attitude of China toward disarmament? Similarly, does a case study on a particular topic, say, the making of the peace treaty between Japan and the United States (Cohen, 1957), yield insights about foreign policy that can be generalized? This issue on the linkage between micro- and macro-analysis is especially vexing. Some of the methodological issues are discussed by Eulau (1969) but not specifically on the subject of foreign policy analysis.

A third methodological issue is whether the conduct of foreign policy really requires scientific analysis, whether decision-makers will settle for systematic policy analysis, or whether any empirical analyses at all are useful for those whose immediate responsibility it is to make foreign policy decisions. One tenet of the behavioralist approach in international relations is that the development of a *science* assists decision-makers in the long run. All too often those subscribing to this view seek rigor rather than research that has relevance to actual foreign policy options (Thompson, 1968). Moreover, the point is moot since no one has claimed that a full-fledged science of international relations or foreign policy exists today or will emerge in the very near future. Accordingly, exponents of *normative policy analysis* point out that foreign policy-making requires clarity in goals and in means for reaching those goals; no research is required but instead intellectual ratiocination. Foreign Minister Rajaratnam of Singapore has declared that his country opposes formation of a common market within Southeast Asia in view of these countries' low levels of economic development, he contemplates no further research.[2] Yet this is precisely where advocates of *systematic policy analysis* analysis would emerge: the view that there are certain necessary preconditions to the formation of a common market is an empirical question. One form of systematic policy analysis might be to codify existing knowledge on a particular subject, thus utilizing the efforts of those following the scientific approach, should any studies happen by accident to be relevant. Yet another task of systematic policy analysis might be to undertake new research to answer specific factual questions (Lasswell, 1956). This second group of studies would thus enter the body of literature in the field of foreign policy analysis, unless they are classified studies. Thus, the issue is whether research should be theory-oriented as in scientific analysis or problem-oriented as in systematic policy analysis. The choice between these forms of analysis is central to the methodology of foreign policy analysis.

A fourth issue is whether *foreign* policy analysis is different from other forms of public policy analysis. A field that erects boundaries around itself must have some justification for this act of self-parochialization. The facile answer, that the object of foreign policy is different from the object of domestic policy, is unsatisfactory from several points of view. Is a Chilean decision to expropriate a foreign corporation a domestic or a foreign policy decision? If there is no clear-cut answer to this question, we might say that the extent of foreign-versus-domestic involvement in a decision is a matter of degree. But even if the existence of an autonomous field called "foreign policy analysis" is based on matters of degree, there remains one unsupported factual premise: that foreign policy decisions differ in substantial ways from other decisions. In one study of decision-making processes, thirty-two decisions were coded along a domestic-foreign continuum by matters of degree in order to ascertain whether the foreign/domestic variable is a significant source of variation among approximately five dozen other variables (M. Haas, 1973: Part 2). The results indicate that there were seventeen independent sources of variation (factors) but none uniquely pulled together the foreign/domestic variable. If we cannot distinguish foreign policy from other types of policy, then we have no evidence to support the dichotomy between domestic intergovernmental relations and foreign intergovernmental relations, the latter an approximate definition of the province of "international politics." We may therefore expect that this fourth methodological issue may gnaw at the very foundations of the effort to develop a separate field for foreign policy analysis.

A fifth methodological question is whether there is a coherent body of knowledge about foreign policy. Surveys of findings (McGowan and Shapiro, 1973) and surveys on the *state of the discipline* serve this objective, such as the present essay.

In addition to these five main methodological dilemmas in foreign policy analysis, other issues are sometimes discussed, though they are matters that belong to the methodology of the social sciences, broadly conceived. Some issues may be raised because of obvious imbalances in the literature of current foreign policy analysis, though they are clearly correctible in time, and thus their explication will follow this survey of the field.

Purpose of Study

Methodological issues are intertwined with the various purposes for foreign policy studies. The aim of methodological studies is to promote the development of the field of study through an insightful and critical analysis.

A *descriptive* study seeks to establish facts, that is, to indicate in prose what is happening in the real world of foreign policy. A descriptive study may provide information relevant for policy-makers (Kent, 1970). Alternatively, the description may be of past events, to which the author either adds few of his own interpretations (Nicolson, 1961) or invokes a theoretical scheme to account for the facts (Wohlstetter, 1962).

Correlation is the purpose of studies that ascertain precisely how much one variable is related to another (Rieselbach, 1966). *Clustering,* a form of analysis that locates clumps of extremely highly intercorrelated measures, has been performed on decision-making cases (M. Haas, 1973), variables (Rummel, 1966), countries (Russett, 1967), but not on time-periods. When one ascertains which variables are determinants of others, the purpose is to trace *causation* (Weede, 1970).

Prediction is the objective of studies which extrapolate present trends into the future (Russett, 1965). One may also predict by noting various qualitative trends and then sketching forth a model of the future, as does Orwell's *1984* and C. Wright Mills' *The Causes of World War III*.

Prescription is a sixth aim of foreign policy studies. There is a sharp division today between studies that make policy recommendations within the framework of prevailing ideologies of foreign policy (Halpern, 1965) and those which are anti-establishmentarian and radical in orientation (Zinn, 1967).

When we code all articles appearing in ten leading journals that publish foreign policy studies, we find a fascinating distribution (Table 1). All journals publish articles that are of a descriptive nature, but no journal broadly represents all of the various purposes of foreign policy studies. There is a division between three journals that are prescriptive, on the one hand, and five that have scientific orientations (correlation, clustering, causation), on the other hand, with two journals cautiously clinging to the descriptive mode. A science of foreign policy thus has not yet been accepted as part of the mainstream of the field. A neotraditional bridge is required for traditional

TABLE 1
PURPOSES SERVED BY FOREIGN POLICY STUDIES, 1970[a]

Purpose of Study

Journals[b]	Development of the field	Description	Correlation	Clustering	Trace Causation	Prediction	Prescription	Foreign Policy Studies	Total Studies	Percent Foreign Policy Studies
FA		52(16)				3(1)	45(14)	(31)	(51)	61
IA(L)		73(16)					27(6)	(22)	(27)	81
IO	8(1)	54(7)	23(3)	8(1)		8(1)		(13)	(31)	42
ISQ	33(4)	33(4)	33(4)					(12)	(15)	80
JCR		60(3)	20(1)	20(1)				(5)	(22)	23
JIA		100(3)						(3)	(13)	23
JPR	9(1)	18(2)	46(5)	9(1)	18(2)			(11)	(19)	58
Orbis[c]	3(1)	58(22)			8(3)		32(12)	(38)	(50)	76
PRSP	20(2)	50(5)	30(3)	10(1)				(10)	(19)	52
WP	40(2)	60(3)						(5)	(21)	34

a. The figures represent percentages of all foreign policy studies for a given journal that serve one or more of the various purposes. Parenthesized figures refer to the number of articles falling into each category.
b. Key: FA, *Foreign Affairs;* IA(L), *International Affairs* (London); IO, *International Organization;* ISQ, *International Studies Quarterly;* JCR, *Journal of Conflict Resolution;* JIA, *Journal of International Affairs;* JPR, *Journal of Peace Research;* Orbis; PRSP, *Peace Research Society (International) Papers;* WP, *World Politics.*
c. Based on Volume 12.

scholars to embrace the scientific method, and a second bridge is needed lest scientific studies continue to be formulated without much reference to the unsolved practical problems of foreign affairs. Publication of the new *Bulletin of Peace Research Proposals* as a counterpart to the *Journal of Peace Research* may serve to distill policy implications from research in a separate journal, but the presence of two isolated subcultures of scholarship will evidently continue to develop until editorial boards of journals consciously seek to recognize the value both of opinions that are grounded empirically and of systematic studies on topics with relevance to policy questions, and this will occur when scholars themselves are more outward-looking in their orientations to the study of foreign policy.

Theories and Paradigms

Foreign policy studies may also be classified in accordance with the theoretical framework presupposed. Some studies may *propose* new frameworks (Snyder, Bruck, Sapin, 1963). Some essays are *critiques* of one or more frameworks (Jervis, 1969). What is of main interest here is the extent to which a framework is *applied* to a specific body of data or to a subject-matter domain. It is my view that all studies which do not make their theories explicit in fact do have implicit models of foreign policy; otherwise no analysis (as that word is defined conventionally) would be by definition possible. Yet another aspect of the effort to apply theoretical frameworks in analyzing foreign policy is the result expected from the study. If theory is applied properly, we should expect a *test* of the postulates of the theory. A second result is *serendipity*—that is, findings which emerge when we examine interrelationships between variables other than those testing the theoretical framework. It is worth mentioning that to date not a single exponent of a theory has disproved his own framework. Moreover, the bulk of findings in foreign policy analysis have been serendipitous (Table 2), thus enriching our factual information about foreign policy but contributing little to the development of a theoretical science of foreign policy. Three journals, in fact, are entirely a-theoretical. Two others display dissatisfaction with existing theories—either through critiques or by publishing new theoretical formulations. All of the remaining five journals publish essays that seek to test theories explicitly.

Although I have delineated nine major theoretical approaches to the study of international relations in an earlier essay (Haas, 1970), some of the theories tend to be more macro than micro in orientation. And some efforts to develop frameworks for the analysis for foreign policy are in fact eclectic, combining two or more of the main metatheories (Frankel, 1963; Jones, 1970; Scott, 1967; Wilkinson, 1969).

TABLE 2
THEORETICAL ORIENTATIONS OF FOREIGN POLICY STUDIES, 1970[a]

	Use of Theory				Framework Used							
Journals	Propose	Critique	Test	Seren-dipity	Cognitive Ration-alism	Genetic	Power	Decision-making	Strategy	Communi-cation	Field	System	Structural Functional
FA				100(31)	65(20)	3(1)	26(8)		6(2)				
IA(L)				100(22)	68(15)		27(6)			5(1)			
IO		8(1)	31(4)	62(8)	38(5)		15(2)			46(6)			
ISQ	16(2)	16(2)	25(3)	45(5)	33(4)			42(5)	8(1)	8(1)	16(2)		
JCR			40(2)	60(3)		40(2)		20(1)			40(2)		
JIA				100(3)	100(3)								
JPR	9(1)		46(5)	46(5)	9(1)	18(2)				9(1)	55(6)		9(1)
Orbis		3(1)		97(37)	37(14)	5(2)	45(17)		8(3)	5(2)			
PRSP	10(1)	10(1)	30(3)	60(6)	20(2)			20(2)	20(2)		30(3)	10(1)	
WP	40(2)			60(3)	60(3)					20(1)	20(1)		20(1)

a. For key, see Table 1.

Cognitive rationalism is the theory which depicts foreign policy decisions as the result of ends-means calculations: the aim of policies is to maximize goals of decision-makers. This theory has neither been explicated nor tested by an exponent, though it has been reviewed critically by Frankel (1963: ch. 12). Nonetheless, such works as Whiting's *China Crosses the Yalu* (1960) contain many serendipitous insights. Descriptive histories of foreign policies tend to be written in the manner prescribed by cognitive rationalist theory.

According to *genetic* theory a specific foreign policy choice is an inevitable consequence of preceding choices. Again, there is no explicit statement advocating this approach in the field of foreign policy analysis, but the Hegelian organismic analogy clearly guides Kahin and Lewis (1969) in their analysis of the history of American commitments to Southeast Asia leading up to President Johnson's decision to dispatch American troops in large numbers to defend the Saigon regime. Although there is no test of genetic theory in foreign policy studies, a study such as Kahin's and Lewis' does bring to light useful information. Studies of the socialization of children to international attitudes (e.g., Targ, 1970) and of the influence of age-group socialization on attitudes (e.g., Cutler, 1970) fall within the genetic paradigm. One may learn that a decision is not just a product of a rational discussion of objectives and means for reaching objectives, as assumed by the cognitive rationalist, but that past commitments constrain the full exercise of rationality among decision-makers. But there are other explanations for decision-making, so more theories are necessary.

Power theory postulates that the main aim of any foreign policy is to maximize the power of the state. In a contest between any two states, the one with superior power should win. Morgenthau (1967), eloquent developer of the theory, has failed to subject it to a scientific test because he regards its content as self-evident. As originally formulated by Morgenthau, the power approach was used to justify American intervention throughout the world in accordance with the superiority of the power of United States at the end of World War II. Morgenthau's opposition to American intervention in Indochina led him to modify his devotion to power theory.[3]

Decision-making theory holds that there is something about the process of locating the responsibility for a decision in a particular sphere of competence, of inputting communication and information to decision-makers, and of triggering a decision-maker motivationally that will determine the nature of the final decision. As developed by Snyder, Bruck, and Sapin (1963) and de Rivera (1968), this "something" is the entire structure of the decision-making process. Since each decision is likely to be made under unique combinations of circumstances, the theory is not really subject to falsification, and the only detailed application of the framework (Paige, 1968) yields serendipitous findings. Several scholars have used a more manageable set of variables from the framework to test subsidiary theories, though not the main theory itself (e.g., Hermann, 1969; Holsti, 1972). More recently, this writer (M. Haas, 1973: Part 2) reduces sixty-five variables from the decision-making approach into about fifteen factors, thereby indicating that the main types of variables in any decision-making analysis are not so numerous as has been thought previously. The factors are labeled Crisis, Bottlenecked, Clientele, Rationality, Watershed, Implementation Complexity, Successful, Unexpected, History-Mindedness, Pragmatism, Multi-Issue, Imperious, Consensus, Aggressiveness.[4]

Strategy theory analogizes foreign policy decision-making with choices in a game of poker; the player that most successfully outmaneuvers his opponent, often regardless of his power, is the victor. Strategic analysis began as a normative guide to policy-makers (Schelling, 1963), but tests of the theory have been undertaken by those disagreeing most vehemently with the recklessness of strategic analysis (Rapoport and Chammah, 1965). And there has been a reformulation of the strategic mode of analysis—to serve as a method for engineering arms races into peace races (Osgood, 1962). This newer normative thrust of strategy theory evidently made such an impact upon President Kennedy that Soviet-American de-escalation has progressed ever since 1963, when the theory of the peace race was first implemented (Etzioni, 1967).

Communication theory, developed from cybernetics by Karl Deutsch (1963), is cast in terms of methods at the disposal of decision-makers in steering their states. The postulates of this theory have proven difficult to unpack at the micro-level. In one study the concepts of loads, capabilities, and responses are applied to Anglo-American relations (Russett, 1963). A test of communication theory appears therein, but there has been little follow-up to test Deutsch's theory as it applies to foreign policy. At the macro-level, however, communication theory is transformed into integration theory, which has attracted considerable attention as a framework for analyzing the rise of regional international communities in which foreign policies are harmonized across a group of countries (Cobb and Elder, 1970; Deutsch et al., 1957; Etzioni, 1965; E. Haas, 1958; Nye, 1971).

Field theory places a decision-maker within a configuration of forces and pressures; a decision-maker, accordingly, gravitates in his decision toward the stronger influences. Often this approach is presented as a set of concentric circles, with the decision-maker in the innermost circle and other levels of analysis progressively enveloping each other, from individual variables, elites, the establishment, political-governmental, economic, social, and cultural variables, to policies of other states and systemic influences (McGowan and Shapiro, 1973: Ch. 2). Just as Snyder's decision-making approach contains a multiplicity of variables, so does the field approach; the former's apotheosis of *process* is similar to the latter's postulate that a given foreign policy is the composite effect of all *levels* operating simultaneously on the decision-maker. Field theory has been suggestively sketched by Rosenau (1971), but there is no specific empirical test of the major propositions. The framework has been chunked into smaller parts whenever it has guided empirical studies (Rosenau, 1969). Rummel (1965) and Galtung (1964) present more satisfying versions of field theory at the macro-level, inasmuch as they anticipate multi-level tests of the theory itself. The main difference between macro-level approaches and Rosenau's micro-level theory is that the latter is presented as a heuristic "pre-theory."

System theory is by definition an approach at the macro-level and thus should have little relevance to foreign policy. Such writers as Rosecrance (1963) present global histories of foreign policy in order to delineate power concentrations and the operation of regulatory mechanisms for maintaining a systemic equilibrium. At a slightly more micro-level, McClelland (1964) and McClelland and Hoggard (1969) trace sequences of events and interactions between states in order to determine patterns and cycles in foreign policy behavior, but the emphasis is on *action* more than on *policy*.

Although *structural-functional* theory might be used to analyze the foreign policy of national decision systems, thus far users of the theory have largely focused on such macro-level phenomena as the role of international organizations within the world polity (M. Haas, 1965; Gregg and Barkun, 1968; Tharp, 1971). Nonetheless, there are two formulations (Modelski, 1962; Rosenau, 1961), as yet untested, which have a structural-functional perspective. The postulate that functional specificity in foreign policy-making enables a country to manage conflict with other countries more effectively has been advanced by Goldman (1964, 1969) in a micro-level structural-functional framework that unfortunately has been overlooked in many surveys of foreign policy theory. Rosenau (1970) more recently has been developing a theory of adaptation. Since "adaptation" is one of the four categories in the structural-functional formulation of Parsons (1969), Rosenau is on the threshold of a major theoretical breakthrough for the study of foreign policy. Unfortunately neither framework has been tested, though there is one serendipitous application of structural-functionalism at the macro-level (M. Haas, 1973: Part IV).

Cognitive rationalism is the most common theoretical approach in foreign policy analysis (Table 2). Power theory is second in popularity. Among the new theories, there is no clear ordering of preferences, although macro-oriented theories (system and structural-functional) are rarely applied to a body of data. The power approach is common among political science journals. Interdisciplinary journals favor decision-making and field theories. In the aggregate, the journals present a rather balanced coverage of foreign policy in terms of theoretical presuppositions. What is needed for the future may thus be more comparisons between the various approaches, as Allison (1969) has attempted in his analysis of the Cuban missiles crisis of 1962. Two journals in Table 2 have encouraged multiple theoretical approaches, as evidenced by having sums of percentages over 100. Scholars are often critical of statesmen who apply only one model, sometimes quite rigidly, to their task in making foreign policy (Holsti, 1962). Should we not apply this criticism equally to scholars? It would appear, therefore, that there should be a trend toward comparative testing in order to advance the field. What this entails is testing critical propositions, that is, those in which the results serve simultaneously to support one competing theory and to discredit a rival approach. Theory seems limitless until it is brought to bear on data, and the limits of a particular theory are delineated in a test when one theory's support is another's invalidation. The function of eclecticism is to cause us to believe that all theories are true even when they are not, so comparative tests will lead us away from a facile, essentially nonscientific eclecticism.

Methods of Research

Foreign policy studies may also be classified by the methods used to collect data or information that is reported. A study that does not attempt to present a body of data may allude to certain facts or situations in a nonquantitative manner, but we are interested here in primarily quantitative research methods. The classification below is based on sources of data.

Content analysis, as described by North and associates (1963), has been used to analyze statements of decision-makers in order to discover their perceptual preoccupations (Holsti, 1972). What often distinguishes content analysis in foreign policy is that it is applied to the printed message, but much message content during a war may be broadcast over the radio. The analysis of wartime propaganda has concerned Lasswell (1938) and George (1959). Merritt (1966) demonstrates how symbols of "America" in the colonial press increased up to the outbreak of the war of independence against the British crown. Other quantitative studies of the press have been undertaken by Gamson and Modigliani (1971), Gould (1969), and Pool (1952).

Survey research is a common method used by scholars outside political science in analyses of foreign policy opinions. Buchanan and Cantril (1952) compare national stereotypes across approximately ten countries, based on information derived from interviews. Rosenberg, Verba, and Converse (1970) present findings about public opinion on the war in Vietnam. Other studies of public opinion have been undertaken by Almond (1965), Christiansen (1959), Cottrell and Eberhart (1948), and Murphy and Likert (1938). Merritt and Puchala (1968) have compiled results from polls on foreign policy among Western European countries. But the key to much of foreign policy is the attitude of elite groups. Interviews with elites form the basis for studies by Bauer, Pool, and Dexter (1963), Deutsch et al. (1967), Free (1959), Robinson (1967), and Rosenau (1962). Paul and Laulicht (1963) compare results of elite and mass opinions, finding some significant differences between the two samples. Earlier we mentioned two studies that were based on interviews of elites, but with contradictory findings (Gordon, 1969; Solidum, 1970). A primer on the methodological problems of interviewing and surveying persons in diverse cultures has been prepared by Ward and associates (1964), though other methods of analysis are treated in the same volume as well.

Roll-call voting is a third source of data. This form of analysis has been applied to discover which sections of a country support various foreign policies, as evidenced by votes cast by legislative representatives (Grassmuck, 1951). But the most prominent source of voting on foreign policy questions are roll-call votes in the United Nations (Alker and Russett, 1965; Hovet, 1960, 1963). The main purpose of the analysis is to identify bloc voting and membership in the various blocs.

A fourth source of data are events, that is, discrete occurrences of similar historical situations. In *events analysis* the effort is to code happenings so that one derives a listing that can be subjected to statistical or mathematical manipulations. The mathematical analyses of Richardson (1960a/b) are based on an enumeration of "deadly quarrels," that is, conflict situations between nations or subnational groups in which deaths result from the confrontation between the groups. Azar (1970) has described the method of event analysis in considerable detail. E. Haas (1968) and Nye (1971) use events data in order to ascertain the effectiveness of international organizations. Gamson and Modigliani (1971) trace the rise and fall of the cold war in terms of events and interactions.

Experiments are sometimes performed in order to learn about the processes of foreign policy decision-making. In contrast with abstract experimental games, as conducted by Rapoport and Chammah (1965), Guetzkow and associates (1963) have encouraged students of foreign policy to construct experiments in which the setting builds in components of the real world. Guetzkow's logic is that one can more easily generalize from a laboratory finding to the world outside the lab if the lab setting in fact simulates the real world. Brody (1963) and Hermann (1969) have used simulation to ascertain dynamics of foreign policy processes.

A systematic examination of archival documents for verbal meaning is known as content analysis. When governmental documents contain statistical information about a country, such as in statistical yearbooks, we refer to such figures as aggregate data. *Aggregate analysis* thus utilizes data that represent the entire territory and population of a country, regions within a country, or sets of countries. Russett and associates (1964) have prepared a compendium of data including some 75 variables across nearly all countries in the world; this source of data has been used in aggregate analyses by Russett (1965, 1967, 1970), and a methodological discussion has been prepared by M. Haas (1966) and Taylor (1968). Other aggregate analysts are Angell (1969), Cobb and Elder (1970), Deutsch (1953), Haas (1973), and Pincus (1965).

In addition to these six quantitative methods of analysis a very important source of data is *participant observation*. The field of foreign policy analysis is in considerable debt to practitioners and statesmen who have endeavored to record their observations in memoirs and analytic accounts of the processes and dilemmas of foreign policy decision-making. A bibliography of these books would be lengthy indeed, including such public leaders as Lord Grey (1926), Cordell Hull (1948), President Truman (1959), Roger Hilsman (1967), and Townsend Hoopes (1969). Retrospective accounts, however, may be so written that the author appears in a more favorable light than an objective account would portray. The methodology of historiography is therefore appropriate (North et al., 1963: Ch. 2). In the case of Woodrow Wilson, two scholars conducted an intensive psychological analysis (George and George, 1964), but much of the information was gleaned through content analysis as well as the participant observations of former associates of Wilson.

Just as all journals accept the need for descriptive studies, so too does nonquantitative analysis have a place throughout the entire field of foreign policy analysis (Table 3). Among quantitative methods, nearly all journals have at least one article that cites aggregate data for particular countries. Nevertheless, the same five journals that feature tests of hypotheses are the ones with data derived from the newer techniques of social science research. Experimental studies are quite rare, and no journal has all six forms of quantitative analysis within its pages.

Studies employing a variety of research methods are not common. Deutsch

TABLE 3
METHODS OF ANALYSIS IN FOREIGN POLICY STUDIES, 1970[a]

Journals	Non-quantitative Analysis	Content Analysis	Surveys	Roll-Call Voting	Event Analysis	Experiments	Aggregate Analysis
FA	97(30)						3(1)
IA(L)	87(17)						9(2)
IO	53(7)		23(3)	15(2)	8(1)		
ISQ	50(6)	16(2)	6(1)		6(1)	6(1)	6(1)
JCR	20(1)	40(2)		20(1)	20(1)		20(1)
JIA	33(1)						66(1)
JPR	27(3)		46(5)		9(1)		36(4)
Orbis	97(37)						3(1)
PRSP	10(1)	10(1)	20(2)		30(3)		30(3)
WP	80(4)						20(1)

a. For key, see Table 1.

and Edinger (1959) examine German foreign policy by looking at elite and mass opinion, aggregate data, and roll-call voting, but their aim is to describe rather than to test theory. When theories are tested comparatively, it will be essential to vary the data source systematically so that we can learn whether different theoretical images of foreign policy are specific to particular types of data. This is central to the resolution of micro-macro dilemmas. Fortunately, there are now repositories of such data for the convenience of those who wish to re-process the data used in existing studies (Tenter and Rosenau, 1970). The task ahead is to utilize some of the existing data in tests and re-tests of propositions. A general theory of foreign policy should pertain to perceptions, attitudes, preferences, events, behavior, and to aggregate phenomena. Critics of foreign policy practitioners often accuse leaders of considering too few of these phenomenal realms. A radical approach would insist on considering the total system in which foreign policy is located.

Subject of Analysis

Yet another way of classifying foreign policy studies is to look at the substance of what is being analyzed. Is the coverage in the field of foreign policy analysis well balanced or in fact overselective in the knowledge thus far derived?

Studies may differ in terms of the *country* whose foreign policy is examined. Most studies are unilateral in character, that is, devoted to the foreign policy of a single country (Hanrieder, 1967) or policies of an international organization (Miller, 1961). Some are bilateral (Reischauer, 1965) or trilateral (Appleton, 1961). Plurilateral relations, that is, between countries of a region or subregion of the world are not uncommon (Gordon, 1966), but truly multilateral and global studies tend to become transformed into world histories (Robertson, 1966) or analyses of the internal politics of an international organization (E. Haas, 1964). Even when the foreign policies of different countries are presented in separate chapters within a collection of essays (e.g., Macridis, 1967), the field of foreign policy analysis has consisted largely of *case studies* rather than of systematic *comparisons* across countries. Comparisons have been made of individual decisions (M. Haas, 1973; Paige, 1972) or of the policies of competing alliances (Holsti, North, Brody, 1968), but the only comparisons of policies of several dozen countries have been concerned with aggregated opinions on individual issues, such as votes in the United Nations (Alker and Russett, 1965), or decisions to enter war (Haas, 1973). This unimpressive range of studies is hardly adequate for developing a science of foreign policy, and for this reason there is a need for codifications of the knowledge derived from the various foreign policy studies, such as McGowan and Shapiro (1973) and Newcombe and Newcombe (1969).

The relevant journals publish studies on the foreign policy of individual countries and on regional foreign politics, and most present discussions of foreign policy that cover the globe (Table 4). It is the emphases that differ. Single-country studies are preponderant largely among journals that stress case rather than comparative analysis, as one might expect. Only three journals encourage area studies; two of these are case-oriented, the other prefers comparative studies. And three of the four journals with a majority or

TABLE 4
SCOPE OF COUNTRIES IN FOREIGN POLICY STUDIES, 1970[a]

Journals	Number of Countries					Focus of Analysis	
	1	2	3	Regional	Global	Case Analysis	Comparison
FA	39(12)	29(9)	3(1)	16(5)	3(1)	74(23)	3(1)
IA(L)	50(11)	9(2)	14(3)	14(3)	9(2)	86(19)	5(1)
IO	23(3)	8(1)		31(4)	31(4)	31(4)	62(8)
ISQ	16(2)	8(1)	8(1)	8(1)	16(2)	16(2)	67(8)
JCR	40(2)			20(1)	40(2)	40(2)	60(3)
JIA	33(1)			33(1)		33(1)	
JPR	36(4)			18(2)	36(4)	55(6)	36(4)
Orbis	45(17)	8(3)	5(2)	35(13)	3(1)	76(29)	11(4)
PRSP	20(2)			10(1)	60(6)	20(2)	70(7)
WP	60(3)			20(1)		60(3)	20(1)

a. For key, see Table 1.

plurality of global studies feature mostly comparative modes of analyses. The five journals in which hypotheses are tested rank as the five journals with the largest percentage of comparative studies. What Table 4 does not reveal, however, is that most of the single-country studies focus on the United States, the home country of most of the journals, thus skewing our knowledge in the field of foreign policy case studies and also revealing a sampling bias that is unavoidable, given the number of foreign policy scholars in each country around the world.

Foreign policy studies may also be classified by the type of *issue* that is explored. Some analyses are multi-issued in focus (e.g., Needler, 1966), but foreign policy is so multifaceted that most scholars do not claim to cover all sorts of issues in their treatises. Examples of specialized studies include those focusing on cultural relations (Useem and Useem, 1955), on diplomacy (Nicolson, 1954), economic relations (Magdoff, 1969), ideological disputes (Zagoria, 1963), legal disputes (McDougal and Burke, 1962), military policy (Halperin, 1967), and political maneuvering by states to maximize their power (Chomsky, 1970) or to ensure the survival of the state (Butow, 1954).[5]

Closely related to foreign policy issues are the types of *decisions* emerging from decision-makers. In a study of 32 decisions, Haas (1973) attempts to develop an empirical typology of types of decisions. Through factor analysis and cluster analysis, three types of decisions are derived empirically.[6] The *importance* of a decision in terms of either low- or high-priority (tactical or strategic) values for a country is the first type of decision (Robinson, 1960, vs. Finer, 1964). The method of *resolving* foreign policy differences is a second basis for classification, distinguishing between those handled in institutionalized or ad hoc channels (Robinson, 1967, vs. Abel, 1966). The third category pertains to *consequences* of decisions, that is, whether the decision-making country or the object of the decision is stabilized or destabilized (Vatcher, 1958, vs. Batchelder, 1961). Since any given decision may be dichotomized in all three ways, there are at least eight possible composite types. So-called crisis decisions, for example, are strategic, are handled outside institutional channels, and seek sometimes to stabilize or to destabilize (Hermann, 1969; Holsti, 1972).

Problems of foreign policy in the ten journals tend to be primarily political in character (Table 5). Nevertheless, there is a wide coverage of other types of issues in the various journals. Military questions rank second, with cultural and legal issues of lesser significance. The ranking of issue priorities appears to follow closely the perceptions of superpowers, whereas for the less developed countries it is my impression—as supported by Alker and Russett (1965)—

TABLE 5
ISSUES IN FOREIGN POLICY STUDIES, 1970[a]

Journals	Cultural	Diplomatic	Economic	Ideological	Legal	Military	Political
FA		3(1)	10(3)	6(2)	10(3)	39(12)	32(10)
IA(L)		18(4)	23(5)			18(4)	41(9)
IO	8(1)	15(2)	8(1)	8(1)	8(1)	15(2)	38(5)
ISQ		16(2)	8(1)	8(1)		25(3)	46(5)
JCR	20(1)	20(1)			20(1)		40(2)
JIA			67(2)				33(1)
JPR	27(3)	18(2)		9(1)		27(3)	18(2)
Orbis	3(1)	8(3)	5(2)	3(1)	8(3)	32(12)	37(14)
PRSP		10(1)				60(6)	40(4)
WP			20(1)	20(1)			60(3)

a. For key, see Table 1.

that economic issues are of major importance. The primacy of economic issues among poorer countries is a proposition that can be tested through comparative analysis. Certainly a discipline whose priorities do not correspond to those of the world around it will fail to serve its obvious clientele.

Conclusion

We may now turn to questions of imbalance in the coverage of foreign policy studies. What is most striking is the cleavage between journals regarding the role of science and the role of public policy studies. Such a division will stultify the field if it continues very much longer. There is still a low awareness of theoretical orientations and quantitative methods as well as a need to go beyond protean theories so that critical tests can be made of the relevance of abstract formulations in improving our comprehension of factors that control foreign policy directions. Causal analysis has hardly begun in the field, and many theories virtually lie dormant while data are brought to bear on marginal propositions. Surely serendipity can no longer prevail even among journals that accept the need for scientific analyses. The coverage of foreign policy studies in terms of numbers of countries and topics investigated seems rather broad at first glance, but even though we have no precise scale of priorities against which to compare the present distribution of attention (as recorded in Tables 4 and 5) economic issues have not received the type of consideration that Adam Smith, Marxists, and have-not countries might insist.

The most complacent statement that can be made about the field of foreign policy analysis, accordingly, is that there are few gaps in the scope or methods of study. There is, in other words, a substantial body of literature with which a novice must become familiar. The most pessimistic conclusion is that the field still lacks truly definitive studies within the various categories used herein to classify the field. It is the task of future foreign policy analysts to respond to this challenge.

NOTES

1. The references will seek to be exhaustive of the important books in the field, with the exception of collections of readings. For a bibliography on the vast article literature, see McGowan and Shapiro (1973) and the combined references in the author's forthcoming *Behavioral International Relations*.

2. Rajaratnam's views are succinctly presented by Tan (1970).

3. This conclusion is based on a conversation with Johan Galtung in the summer of 1966. See also Morgenthau (1969).

4. Three other variables were included in the analysis as measures of data quality control. These reduced to 2 factors independent of the remaining 15.

5. For a longer list of issues, see Lindberg and Scheingold (1970: Ch. 3).

6. Nine factors and 4 clusters are derived in the first-order analysis. The threefold typology presented here is a composite summary of the higher-order factors and clusters.

REFERENCES

ABEL, E. (1966) The Missile Crisis. New York: Bantam.
ALKER, H. R., Jr. and B. M. RUSSETT (1965) World Politics in the General Assembly. New Haven: Yale Univ. Press.
ALLISON, G. T. (1969) "Conceptual models and the Cuban missile crisis." American Political Science Review 63 (September): 689-718.
ALMOND, G. A. (1965) The American People and Foreign Policy. New York: Praeger.
ANGELL, R. C. (1969) Peace on the March. Princeton: Van Nostrand.
APPLETON, S. (1961) The Eternal Triangle? East Lansing: Michigan State Univ. Press.
AZAR, E. (1970) "Analysis of international events." Peace Research Review 4 (November): 1-113.
BATCHELDER, R. C. (1961) The Irreversible Decision. New York: Macmillan.
BAUER, R. A., I. de S. POOL, and L. A. DEXTER (1963) American Business and Public Policy. New York: Atherton.
BRODY, R. A. (1963) "Some systemic effects of the spread of nuclear weapons technology: a study through simulation of a multi-nuclear future." Journal of Conflict Resolution 7 (December): 663-753.
BUCHANAN, W. and H. CANTRIL (1952) How Nations See Each Other. Urbana: Univ. of Illinois Press.
BUTOW, R.J.C. (1954) Japan's Decision to Surrender. Stanford: Stanford Univ. Press.
CHOMSKY, N. (1970) At War with Asia. New York: Vintage.
CHRISTIANSEN, B. (1959) Attitudes Toward Foreign Affairs as a Function of Personality. Oslo: Oslo Univ. Press.
COBB, R. W. and C. ELDER (1970) International Community. New York: Holt, Rinehart & Winston.

COHEN, B. C. (1957) The Political Process and Foreign Policy. Princeton: Princeton Univ. Press.
COTTRELL, L. S., Jr., and S. EBERHART (1948) American Opinion on World Affairs in the Atomic Age. Princeton: Princeton Univ. Press.
CUTTLER, N. E. (1970) "Generational succession as a source of foreign policy attitudes: a cohort analysis of American opinion, 1946-66." Journal of Peace Research 7, 1: 33-48.
DE RIVERA, J. H. (1968) The Psychological Dimension of Foreign Policy. Columbus, O.: Merrill.
DEUTSCH, K. W. (1963) The Nerves of Government. New York: Free Press.
——— (1953) Nationalism and Social Communication. Cambridge, Mass.: MIT Press.
——— and L. J. EDINGER (1959) Germany Rejoins the Powers. Stanford: Stanford Univ. Press.
——— R. C. MACRIDIS, and R. L. MERRITT (1967) France, Germany and the Western Alliance. New York: Scribner's.
ETZIONI, A. (1967) "The Kennedy experiment." Western Political Quarterly 20 (June): 361-380.
——— (1965) Political Unification. New York: Holt, Rinehart & Winston.
EULAU, H. (1969) Macro-Micro Political Analysis. Chicago: Aldine.
FINER, H. (1964) Dulles over Suez. Chicago: Quadrangle.
FRANKEL, J. (1963) The Making of Foreign Policy. New York: Oxford Univ. Press.
FREE, L. A. (1959) Six Allies and A Neutral. Glencoe: Free Press.
GALTUNG, J. (1964) "A structural theory of aggression." Journal of Peace Research I, 2: 95-119.
GAMSON, W. A. and A. MODIGLIANI (1971) Untangling the Cold War. Boston: Little, Brown.
GEORGE, A. (1959) Propaganda Analysis. Evanston, Ill.: Row, Peterson.
——— and J. GEORGE (1964) Woodrow Wilson and Colonel House. New York: Dover.
GOLDMAN, R. M. (1969) "A transactional theory of political integration and arms control." American Political Science Review 63 (September): 719-733.
——— (1966) "A theory of conflict processes and organizational offices." Journal of Conflict Resolution 10 (September): 328-343.
GORDON, B. K. (1969) Toward Disengagement in Asia. Englewood Cliffs, N.J.: Prentice-Hall.
——— (1966) The Dimensions of Conflict in Southeast Asia. Englewood Cliffs, N.J.: Prentice-Hall.
GOULD, L. N. (1969) the ENDC and the Press. Stockholm: Almqvist & Wiksell.
GRASSMUCK, G. L. (1951) Sectional Biases in Congress on Foreign Policy. Baltimore: Johns Hopkins Univ. Press.
GREGG, R. W. and M. BARKUN [eds.] (1968) The United Nations System and Its Functions. Princeton: Van Nostrand.
GREY, E. (1926) Fallodon Papers. Boston: Houghton-Mifflin.
GROSS, F. (1954) Foreign Policy Analysis. New York: Philosophical Library.
GUETZKOW, H., C. F. ALGER, R. A. BRODY, R. C. NOEL, and R. C. SNYDER (1963) Simulation in International Relations. Englewood Cliffs, N.J.: Prentice-Hall.
HAAS, E. B. (1968) Collective Security and the Future International System. Denver: University of Denver Social Science Foundation.
——— (1964) Beyond the Nation State. Stanford: Stanford Univ. Press.

––– (1958) The Uniting of Europe. Stanford: Stanford Univ. Press.
HAAS, M. (forthcoming, 1974) International Conflict. Indianapolis: Bobbs-Merrill.
––– (forthcoming, 1973) Behavioral International Relations.
––– (1970) "International relations theory," pp. 444-476 in M. Haas and H. S. Kariel (eds.) Approaches to the Study of Political Science. San Francisco: Chandler.
––– (1967) "Bridge-building in international relations: a neotraditional plea." International Studies Quarterly 11 (December): 320-338.
––– (1966) "Aggregate analysis." World Politics 19 (October): 106-121.
––– (1965) "A functional approach to international organization." Journal of Politics 27 (August): 498-517.
––– and T. L. BECKER (1970) "The behavioral revolution and after," pp. 479-510 in M. Haas and H. S. Kariel (eds.) Approaches to the Study of Political Science. San Francisco: Chandler.
HALPERIN, M. H. (1967) Contemporary Military Strategy. Boston: Little, Brown.
HALPERN, A. M. [ed.] (1965) Policies Toward China. New York: McGraw-Hill.
HANRIEDER, W. H. (1967) Contemporary Military Strategy. Boston: Little, Brown.
HERMANN, C. F. (1969) Crises in Foreign Policy. Indianapolis: Bobbs-Merrill.
HILSMAN, R. (1967) To Move a Nation. Garden City, N.Y.: Doubleday.
HOLSTI, O. R. (1972) Crisis, Escalation, War. Montreal: McGill-Queen's.
––– (1962) "The belief system and national images: a case study." Journal of Conflict Resolution 6 (September): 244-252.
––– R. C. NORTH, and R. A. BRODY (1968) "Perception and action in the 1914 crisis," pp. 123-158 in J. D. Singer (ed.) Quantitative International Politics. New York: Free Press.
HOOPES, T. (1969) The Limits of Intervention. New York: McKay.
HOVET, T. (1963) Africa in the United Nations. Evanston, Ill.: Northwestern Univ. Press.
––– (1960) Bloc Politics in the United Nations. Cambridge, Mass.: Harvard Univ. Press.
HULL, C. (1948) The Memoirs of Cordell Hull. New York: Macmillan.
JERVIS, R. (1969) "The costs of the quantitative study of international relations," pp. 177-217 in K. Knorr and J. N. Rosenau (eds.) Contending Approaches to International Politics. Princeton: Princeton Univ. Press.
JONES, R. E. (1970) Analyzing Foreign Policy: London: Routledge & Kegan.
KAHIN, G. McT. and J. W. LEWIS (1969) The United States in Vietnam. New York: Dial.
KENT, G. (1970) "Foreign policy analysis: Middle East." Peace Research Society Papers 14: 95-112.
LASSWELL, H. D. (1956) The Decision Process. College Park: University of Maryland Bureau of Governmental Research.
––– (1938) Propaganda Techniques in the World War. New York: Smith.
LINDBERG, L. N. and S. A. SCHEINGOLD (1970) Europe's Would-Be Policy. Englewood Cliffs, N.J.: Prentice-Hall.
McCLELLAND, C. A. (1964) "Action structures and communication in two international crises: Quemoy and Berlin." Background 7 (February): 201-215.
––– and D. G. HOGGARD (1969) "Conflict patterns in the interactions among nations," pp. 711-724 in J. N. Rosenau (ed.) International Politics and Foreign Policy. New York: Free Press.
McDOUGAL, M. S. and W. T. BURKE (1962) The Public Order of the Oceans. New Haven: Yale Univ. Press.

McGOWAN, P. J. and H. B. SHAPIRO (1973) The Comparative Study of Foreign Policy. Beverly Hills: Sage.
MACRIDIS, R. C. [ed.] (1967) Foreign Policy in World Politics. Englewood Cliffs, N.J.: Prentice-Hall.
MAGDOFF, H. (1969) The Age of Imperialism. New York: Monthly Review Press.
MERRITT, R. L. (1966) Symbols of American Community, 1735-1775. New Haven: Yale Univ. Press.
--- and D. J. PUCHALA [eds.] (1968) Western European Perspectives on International Affairs. New York: Praeger.
MILLER, R. I. (1961) Dag Hammarskjold and Crisis Diplomacy. Dobb's Ferry, N.Y.: Oceana.
MILLS, C. W. (1958) The Causes of World War III. New York: Simon & Schuster.
MODELSKI, G. (1962) A Theory of Foreign Policy. New York: Praeger.
MORGENTHAU, H. J. (1969) A New Foreign Policy for the United States. New York: Praeger.
--- (1967) Politics Among Nations. New York: Alfred A. Knopf.
MURPHY, G. and R. LIKERT (1938) Public Opinion and the Individual. New York: Harper.
NEEDLER, M. C. (1966) Understanding Foreign Policy. New York: Holt, Rinehart & Winston.
NEWCOMBE, H. and A. NEWCOMBE (1969) Peace Research Around the World. Oakville: Canadian Peace Research Institute.
NICOLSON, H. (1961) Diplomacy. New York: Oxford Univ. Press.
--- (1954) The Evolution of the Diplomatic Method. London: Constable.
NORTH, R. C. et al. (1963) Content Analysis. Evanston, Ill.: Northwestern Univ. Press.
NYE, J. S. (1971) Peace in Parts. Boston: Little, Brown.
OSGOOD, C. E. (1962) An Alternative to War or Surrender. Urbana: Univ. of Illinois Press.
PAIGE, G. D. (1972) "Comparative case analysis of crisis decisions: Cuba and Korea," in C. F. Hermann (ed.) International Crisis. New York: Free Press.
--- (1968) The Korean Decision. New York: Free Press.
PARSONS, T. (1969) Politics and Social Structure. New York: Free Press.
PAUL, J. and J. LAULICHT (1963) In Your Opinion. Clarkson: Canadian Peace Research Institute.
PINCUS, J. A. (1965) Economic Aid and International Cost Sharing. Baltimore: Johns Hopkins Univ. Press.
POOL, I. de S. with H. D. LASSWELL, D. LERNER et al. (1952) The "Prestige Papers." Stanford: Stanford Univ. Press.
RAPOPORT, A. and A. M. CHAMMAH (1965) Prisoner's Dilemma. Ann Arbor: Univ. of Michigan Press.
REISCHAUER, E. O. (1965) The United States and Japan. New York: Viking.
RICHARDSON, L. F. (1960a) Arms and Insecurity. Chicago: Quadrangle.
--- (1960b) Statistics of Deadly Quarrels. Chicago: Quadrangle.
REISELBACH, L. N. (1966) The Roots of Isolationism. Indianapolis: Bobbs-Merrill.
ROBERTSON, C. L. (1966) International Politics Since World War II. New York: John Wiley.
ROBINSON, J. A. (1967) Congress and Foreign Policy-Making. Homewood, Ill.: Dorsey.
--- (1960) The Monroney Resolution. New York: McGraw-Hill.

ROSECRANCE, R. N. (1963) Action and Reaction in World Politics. Boston: Little, Brown.
ROSENAU, J. N. (1971) The Scientific Study of Foreign Policy. New York: Free Press.
――― (1970) The Adaptation of National Societies. New York: McCaleb-Seiler.
――― [ed.] (1969) Linkage Politics. New York: Free Press.
――― (1962) National Leadership and Foreign Policy. Princeton: Princeton Univ. Press.
――― (1961) Public Opinion and Foreign Policy. New York: Random House.
――― (1960) The Nomination of "Chip" Bohlen. New York: McGraw-Hill.
ROSENBERG, M. J., S. VERBA, and P. E. CONVERSE (1970) Vietnam and the Silent Majority. New York: Harper & Row.
RUMMEL, R. J. (1966) "Some dimensions in the foreign behavior of nations." Journal of Peace Research 3, 3: 201-224.
――― (1965) "A field theory of social action with application to conflict within nations." General Systems Yearbook 10: 183-211.
RUSSETT, B. M. (1970) What Price Vigilance? New Haven: Yale Univ. Press.
――― (1967) International Regions and the International System. Chicago: Rand-McNally.
――― (1965) Trends in World Politics. New York: Macmillan.
――― (1963) Community and Contention. Cambridge, Mass.: MIT Press.
――― H. R. ALKER, Jr., K. W. DEUTSCH, and H. D. LASSWELL (1964) World Handbook of Political and Social Indicators. New Haven: Yale Univ. Press.
SCHELLING, T. C. (1963) The Strategy of Conflict. New York: Oxford Univ. Press.
SCOTT, A. M. (1967) The Functioning of the International Political System. Englewood Cliffs, N.J.: Prentice-Hall.
SNYDER, R. C., H. W. BRUCK, and B. SAPIN [eds.] (1963) Foreign Policy Decision Making. New York: Free Press.
SOLIDUM, E. D. (1970) The Nature of Cooperation Among the ASEAN States as Perceived Through Elite Attitudes. Ann Arbor: University Microfilms.
SONDERMANN, F. A. (1961) "The linkage between foreign policy and international politics," pp. 8-17 in J. N. Rosenau (ed.) International Relations and Foreign Policy. New York: Free Press.
TAN, A.H.H. (1970) "The role of Singapore in regional cooperation in southeast Asia." Presented to the SEADAG Regional Development Seminar, East-West Center, Honolulu, July.
TANTER, R. and J. N. ROSENAU (1970) "Field and environmental approaches to world politics: implications for data archives." Journal of Conflict Resolution 14 (December): 513-526.
TARG, H. R. (1970) "Children's developing orientations to international politics." Journal of Peace Research 7, 2: 79-98.
TAYLOR, C. L. [ed.] (1968) Aggregate Data-Analysis. Paris: Mouton.
THARP, P. A., Jr. [ed.] (1971) Regional International Organizations. New York: St. Martin's.
THOMPSON, K. W. (1968) "The internationalist's dilemma: relevance and rigor." International Studies Quarterly 12 (June): 161-173.
TRUMAN, H. S. (1959) Memoirs. Garden City, N.Y.: Doubleday.
USEEM, J. and R. H. USEEM (1955) The Western-Educated Man in India. New York: Dryden.
VATCHER, W. H. (1958) Panmunjom. New York: Praeger.

VINCENT, J. E. (1968) "National attributes as predictors of delegate attitudes at the United Nations." American Political Science Review 62 (September): 916-931.
WARD, R. E. with F. BONILLA, J. S. COLEMAN, H. H. HYMAN, L. W. PYE, and M. WEINER (1964) Studying Politics Abroad. Boston: Little, Brown.
WEEDE, E. (1970) "Conflict behavior of nation-states." Journal of Peace Research 7, 3: 229-235.
WHITING, A. S. (1960) China Crosses the Yalu. Stanford: Stanford Univ. Press.
WILKINSON, D. O. (1969) Comparative Foreign Relations. Belmont: Dickenson.
WOHLSTETTER, R. (1962) Pearl Harbor. Stanford: Stanford Univ. Press.
WRIGHT, Q. (1955) The Study of International Relations. New York: Appleton-Century-Crofts.
ZAGORIA, D. S. (1963) Sino-Soviet Conflict, 1956-1961. New York: Atheneum.
ZINN, H. (1967) Vietnam: The Logic of Withdrawal. Boston: Beacon.

PART TWO

THEORIES

Chapter 2

SIMULATION IN THE DEVELOPMENT OF A THEORY OF FOREIGN POLICY DECISION-MAKING

G. MATTHEW BONHAM
The American University

MICHAEL J. SHAPIRO
University of Hawaii

Over the past fifteen years increasingly sophisticated theoretical frameworks have been applied to the study of human behavior in the form of computer simulations of individual and social processes. Beginning with models of human problem-solving (Newell and Simon, 1963), the simulation of individual cognitive processes has been extended to verbal learning behavior (Feigenbaum, 1963) and belief systems (Abelson and Carroll, 1965). Social scientists have developed computer simulations of group interaction (Hare, 1961), processes in formal organizations (Cyert and March, 1963), and resource allocation in city government (Crecine, 1969). In addition, a number of simulations of voting behavior have been designed and used to predict election outcomes in a community fluoridation referendum (Abelson and

AUTHORS' NOTE: A revised version of a paper delivered at the International Studies Meeting, Dallas, March 1972, this research was supported by a grant from the Institute of International Studies, University of California, Berkeley.

Bernstein, 1963), a Wisconsin primary (McPhee, 1961), and the 1960 and 1964 Presidential elections (Pool, Abelson, Popkin, 1965).

Except for Crisiscom, a simulation of information processing by decision-makers in an international crisis (Pool and Kessler, 1965), and TEMPER, a complex model that was developed to make forecasts about cold-war conflict behavior (Abt and Gorden, 1969), there are few examples of the application of computer simulation to the study of international politics. Recently, however, work has begun on a number of simulations that promise to advance our ability to predict and explain international behavior. Zinnes, Van Houweling, and Van Atta (1972) are testing a simulation of balance-of-power systems; Alker and Greenberg (1973) have developed a computer simulation of U.N. decision-making that uses a precedent logic to predict U.N. involvement in international conflicts; Leavitt (1971) has developed models of interstate alliance formation, maintenence, and dissolution; Tanter (1971) is working on CACIS, a model of international conflict behavior.

The purpose of this paper is to illustrate the role of theory in computer simulation of international relations by (1) describing the theoretical foundations of a simulation of foreign policy decision-making that is coherent with social-psychological perspectives on attitude formation and decision-making, and (2) showing how the simulation model contributes to the theory-building enterprise. In the first part of the paper we will describe the main elements of the simulation: the way beliefs of decision-makers are represented, the operations of the cognitive and choice processes, and the theoretical propositions that are embedded in the model. In the second part of the paper we will discuss the simulation as a contribution to theory in international relations—as an advancement of knowledge about the behavior of decision-makers and as a device for improving beliefs about international relations that are held by policy specialists.

THEORETICAL FOUNDATIONS OF THE SIMULATION

The major theoretical presupposition of our model is that beliefs of foreign policy decision-makers are central to the study of decision outputs and probably account for more of the variance than any other single factor. Beliefs represent both the congealed experiences of the decision-maker and his expectations about the decision environment. In the decision-making process, beliefs act like templates for channeling information and for relating possible policy options to perceptions about the intentions and behavior of other nations, and also to the policy objectives of the decision-maker. (For further discussion of our theoretical approach, see Shapiro and Bonham, 1973.)

Representation of Beliefs

Beliefs of decision-makers are represented in the simulation as a map of causal linkages among three types of concepts. "Affective" concepts refer to the policy objectives or interests of the actors in the international system; "cognitive" concepts denote beliefs about actions that occur in the international system; and "conative" concepts indicate possible alternatives from which the decision-maker selects policy recommendations. The linkages between concepts are represented as arrows which carry either a positive or negative sign in order to distinguish the direction of the causal relationship perceived by the decision-maker, and, in some instances, a "p" to indicate that the linkage is somewhat problematic. Taken together, the concepts and the causal linkages between them form a "cognitive map" of the decision-maker's belief system. It is this cognitive map which allows a decision-maker to relate an event or a series of events to policy alternatives and policy objectives. For example, a participant in one of the political games we have used to study decision-making processes made the following statement about a crisis that had developed in the Middle East:

> It would appear to me that the continuous occupation of Arab territories by Israel is precisely this causal factor that makes the Arab regimes open to proffers of Soviet military aid and brings more and more Soviet penetration into the Middle East, therefore bringing us all to a sort of brink in the world situation. It tends to polarize more the situation, and it tends to make the Arab states more dependent on the Soviet Union.

This statement was coded as part of his cognitive map and is shown in Figure 1 as a structure consisting of six concepts linked together by five positive arrows.

This representation of beliefs of decision-makers reflects the proposition that decision-makers tend to believe that international events are causally related and thus try to infer causal relationships underlying events and the actions of other nations, even when there is little or no evidence of a causal nature. Jervis (1970: 29) has observed this tendency in his study of the use of signals and indices by foreign policy decision-makers. This proposition is also supported by research on attribution phenomena in social psychology, which holds that a person's motivation to exercise control over his environment is related to his attribution of causal relationships to the behavior of others (Abelson and Reich, 1969; Kelley, 1971; Kanouse, 1971).

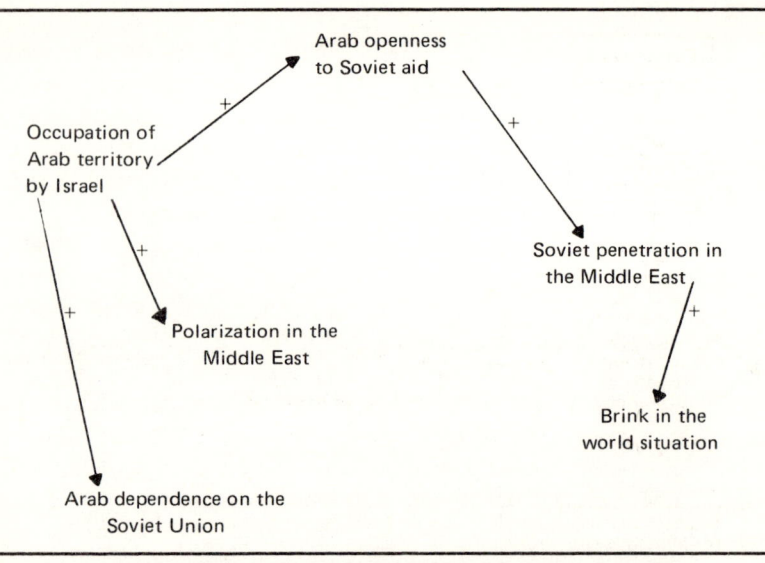

Figure 1: A DIGRAPH FROM THE TRANSCRIPT OF A POLITICAL GAME

Amplification of Beliefs and Search for Explanations

Four processes are invoked in the simulation model when a decision-maker is confronted with a new international situation that requires a response from his government: the amplification of beliefs, the search for an explanation, the search for policy options, and the choice of a policy (Figure 2).

During the *amplification of beliefs process,* the decision-maker attempts to put the new international situation into the context of his experiences. This is a process of bringing together various components of the situation with his existing beliefs about the nations and actions involved so that the decision-maker can define the situation. It is similar to the cognitive problem that Abelson (1968: 136-139) has simulated with his ideology machine, which makes novel events understandable by referring them to a structure that has interpreted them in the past: a set of beliefs about past events which are stored at different levels of abstraction.

At the amplification of beliefs stage of the simulation, concise statements describing new international developments are fed into the model to activate concepts in the decision-maker's belief system. When an event exemplifying a concept is received as an input, that particular concept is "highlighted" and this information is stored in the model's memory. After all concepts directly pertaining to a new international situation have been highlighted, the simulation searches for additional concepts that would be highlighted by

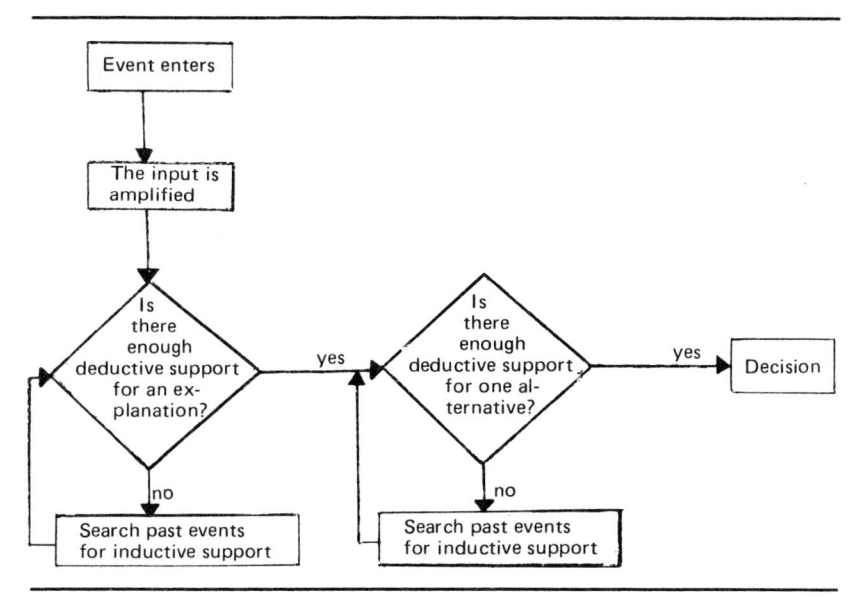

```
                    ┌──────────────┐
                    │ Event enters │
                    └──────┬───────┘
                           │
                           ▼
                    ┌──────────────┐
                    │ The input is │
                    │  amplified   │
                    └──────┬───────┘
                           ▼
              ╱╲                     ╱╲
             ╱  ╲                   ╱  ╲
            ╱ Is ╲                 ╱ Is ╲
           ╱there ╲               ╱there ╲
          ╱ enough ╲    yes      ╱ enough ╲   yes    ┌──────────┐
         ╱deductive╲────────────╱deductive╲─────────▶│ Decision │
         ╲ support ╱            ╲ support ╱          └──────────┘
          ╲for an ╱              ╲for one╱
           ╲ex-  ╱                ╲alter-╱
            ╲plan╱                 ╲nat?╱
             ╲ ╱                    ╲ ╱
              │no                    │no
              ▼                      ▼
     ┌──────────────────┐   ┌──────────────────┐
     │ Search past events│   │Search past events│
     │for inductive support│ │for inductive support│
     └──────────────────┘   └──────────────────┘
```

Figure 2: SIMPLIFIED FLOWCHART OF FOREIGN POLICY DECISION-MAKING PROCESSES

implication (i.e., those that are reachable from the initially highlighted concepts). Once causal paths have been followed from initially highlighted concepts, the decision-maker has an amplified set of concepts which is a subset of his conceptual overviews of the international environment. This subset is then utilized in the subsequent phases of the decision process.

The amplification of beliefs process of the simulation can be illustrated with a cognitive map that we constructed from notes of interviews with fifteen foreign policy specialists in the Departments of State and Defense and members of the National Security Council staff who participated in the Jordanian crisis of September 1970. In the interviews, which were conducted about eighteen months after the crisis, the participants were asked to discuss: (1) events that preceded the Jordanian crisis, such as the American peace initiative, the cease-fire agreement between Egypt and Israel in August 1970, and the conflict in Jordan between the Palestinian commandos and King Hussein; (2) likely responses of the major actors in the Middle East, especially the United States, the Soviet Union, Israel, and Egypt; and (3) interests of the United States and other countries that were affected by the crisis. Responses of the foreign policy specialists to these questions were used to make the cognitive map of the Jordanian situation shown in Figure 3. Although this map is only a fragment of the cognitive systems of the specialists who were interviewed, it does portray, in highly simplified form, how these specialists perceived the Jordanian crisis.

In a simulation of the Jordanian crisis using the cognitive map shown in Figure 3, the amplification of beliefs process would begin with receipt of information about the use of Syrian land forces in the conflict between the Palestinian commandos and King Hussein's troops, urgent messages from King Hussein asking for help, and intelligence reports about a partial mobilization

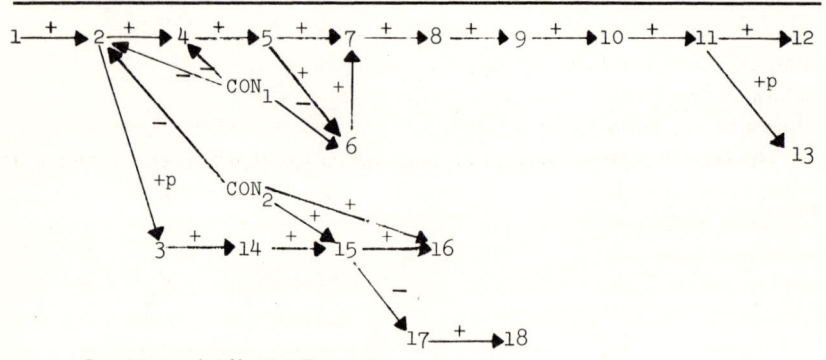

Cognitive and Affective Concepts

1. Syrian intervention in Jordan.
2. Threat to viability of Hussein's regime.
3. Hussein's regime is overturned.
4. Israeli concern about protecting her borders.
5. Israeli occupation of part of Jordan.
6. Egypt resumes fighting.
7. Arabs ask Soviet Union for help.
8. Soviet pilots fly for Egypt and Syria.
9. Some Soviet planes are shot down by Israel.
10. Soviet Union loses face and prestige.
11. Soviet Union escalates conflict with Israel.
12. Security of Israel is threatened.
13. United States-Soviet confrontation.
14. Jordanian government under radical control.
15. Radicalism in moderate countries, e.g., Lebanon and Saudi Arabia.
16. United States loses friends in the Middle East.
17. Presence of moderate governments in the Middle East.
18. American economic interests in the Middle East.

Conative Concepts

CON$_1$ United States provides air cover and Israel intervenes from air only.
CON$_2$ United States intervenes militarily to support Hussein.

Figure 3: SIMPLIFIED COGNITIVE MAP OF AMERICAN POLICY SPECIALISTS WHO PARTICIPATED IN THE JORDANIAN CRISIS OF SEPTEMBER 1970

in Israel and the movement of Israeli forces near the area of the fighting. Because of their relevance to the incoming information, three cognitive concepts in the map would be immediately highlighted: Concept 1 (Syrian intervention in Jordan), Concept 2 (threat to viability of Hussein's regime), and Concept 4 (Israeli concern about protecting her flank). The amplification of beliefs process also involves the discovery of additional concepts besides those directly highlighted, so the model would search for concepts that should be highlighted because they are connected to initially highlighted concepts by causal paths. Accomplishing this for Figure 3, the model would find all other cognitive concepts in the map are highlighted by implication, although many other concepts pertaining to the Middle East (which are not shown in this particular map) would not be activated by the Jordanian crisis.

The second decision-making process, *search for explanations,* is somewhat more involved than the first process. As noted in the flowchart (see Figure 2), a simulated decision-maker must determine whether he possesses an adequate explanation of what has occurred. An explanation in our model consists of the arrows or "paths" connecting a set of two or more highlighted concepts. The initial concept in an explanatory path is most often an actor's intention or motivation. The path is a sequence from intention concept to the consequence or set of consequences that were initially inputted in the amplification of beliefs phase of the decision process. Once new information has activated concepts in a decision-maker's cognitive system, the model searches for arrows between highlighted concepts and isolates them for further processing.

The first two processes, amplification and search, are a representation in the model of the proposition that decision-makers tend to fit incoming information into their existing theories and images (Jervis, 1968: 455). The crucial role of images in international relations has been discussed by Boulding (1956, 1959). More recently Jervis (1968, 1972) has analyzed effects of images on information processing by policy-makers and has illustrated this proposition with numerous historical examples; meanwhile, Holsti (1962) and Finlay et al. (1967) have tested it in a study of former Secretary of State John Foster Dulles (see also Axelrod, 1972).

In our interviews with foreign policy specialists who participated in the Jordanian crisis, we found evidence of the role of images in information processing. For example, when American specialists learned that Syria, a country supplied with military equipment by the Soviet Union, was using its tanks in Jordanian territory, they suspected that the Soviet Union was behind the Syrian action. This inference reinforced a global-strategic interpretation of the situation: that the crisis was a test of American strength in the Middle East and might upset the Soviet-American balance in this crucial area. The suspicion that the Syrians were acting with the positive agreement of the Soviet Union, which was largely refuted by subsequent events, probably resulted from an image of the Soviet Union as a government that supported the Egyptian violations of the cease-fire agreement a month earlier during the "misslie move-up," and a nation that retains tight control over the use of its military equipment even when provided to its closest allies, such as members of the Warsaw Pact.

At the operational level amplification-and-search processes are accomplished by treating the cognitive maps of decision-makers as directed graphs or "digraphs" and using the rules of digraph theory for making calculations. Digraph theory, a formal system with elaborate rules for moving about in a network of interrelated elements, provides an inference structure that is convenient for both representing the elements in a cognitive structure and calculating cognitive processes. Calculation is greatly facilitated because the inventors of digraph theory have worked out the relationships between digraphs and matrix algebra, so it is possible to manipulate relationships between and among elements. The set of rules (axioms, primitives, theorems, etc.) which constitute the theory of directed graphs is far too elaborate to treat here (see Harary et al., 1965; Harary, 1961). We shall simply note, as we proceed, those rules which directly pertain to the explication of our model of foreign policy decision-making. For example, we use the idea of "reachability" in the amplification-and-search calculations. In digraph theory reachability suggests that concepts connected by paths to initially highlighted concepts will also be highlighted. Thus, if concept V_1 in digraph D (Figure 4) is initially highlighted, then the other three concepts, V_2, V_3, and V_4, which are reachable from V_1, would be highlighted by implication. The search for additional concepts is accomplished in the computer by constructing a *reachability* matrix as a basic input for the simulation and then checking relationships in the matrix.

When a decision-maker possesses only one explanation for a policy situation, the simulation goes on to the next stage, search for alternative courses of action. If there is more than one explanation in his cognitive

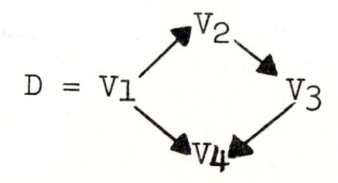

Figure 4.

system, the model selects the one with the most "deductive support." For our purposes deductive support is defined as the number of logically independent reasons that reinforce an explanation, and it is calculated by counting the number of separate paths comprising a given explanation. However, in cases where more than one decision-maker is being represented, it is possible that a number of explanations, each with considerable deductive support, will be isolated and stored by the model for the alternative-searching and policy-choice processes.

For example, the cognitive map shown in Figure 3 contains two explanations of the Jordanian crisis. One explanation, the causal path consisting of Concepts 1-2-3-4-5-6-7-8-9-10-11-12-13, focuses on the implications of the crisis for a possible confrontation between the United States and the Soviet Union in the Middle East. This explanation, which was articulated by nearly all the policy specialists whom we interviewed, stems from the belief that the occupation of additional Jordanian territory by Israel, as a consequence of the Israeli desire to protect her border in the event of the removal of King Hussein in Jordan, would lead to a resumption of fighting by Egypt, requests for help from the Soviet Union, greater military involvement of the Soviet Union in the situation, an appeal from Israel for American aid, and the possibility of a superpower confrontation. The other explanation portrayed in Figure 3 was given largely by specialists in the Department of State who work in the Bureau of Near Eastern and South Asian Affairs. This explanation, which consists of Concepts 1-2-3-14-15-17-18, focuses on the crisis more as a conflict between Arabs which may have implications for future American relations with Middle Eastern countries. According to this explanation, the Syrian intervention increases the probability that Hussein might be replaced by a radical regime, a development which would strengthen radicalism in countries like Lebanon and Saudi Arabia, put pressure on moderate governments, and possibly threaten U.S. economic interests in the area.

This subroutine of the simulation model follows directly from the proposition that decision-makers tend to rely on explanations that are supported by several logically independent reasons. This is stated in this form by Jervis (1973), who notes that it is an application of consistency theories and is compatible with theories dealing with avoidance of psychological conflicts (Kelman and Baron, 1968; Abelson and Rosenberg, 1958; Abelson, 1968). In addition, research on cognitive complexity provides some evidence for this proposition (Bieri, 1955; Driver, 1962; Schroder et al., 1967).

A decision-maker's belief system is usually dense enough for him to find an explanation for a policy situation, but there are occasions when he lacks an adequate explanation for an event or series of events. If there is not any explanation in a decision-maker's belief system with sufficient deductive support, then the model begins searching for inductive explanatory support, as indicated in the flowchart. The decision-maker scans his memory and attempts to find similar past events which might provide an explanation for the current situation, such as the 1967 war in a simulation of the Jordanian crisis. During the search the relevance of historical events is determined for the decision-maker by the categories or constructs through which he views the international system.

The logic of the inductive search process (in both the explanatory and choice of an alternative phases) is similar to the precedent search in Alker and Greenberg's model of U.N. decision-making (Alker and Greenberg, 1973). The search of past events scans the stored events and initially chooses the event with the most concepts in common with the current situation. If more than one event has the same number of shared concepts, the most recent event is selected. The search then proceeds lexicographically. If the explanatory or choice of alternative rule in the first historical event leads to a selection from among two or more possible paths, the search is ended. If the first event selected does not successfully continue or terminate the decision process, a second one is selected, using the same decision rules, and so on, until a past event is found that overcomes the uncertainty that led to the inductive search process.

The inductive search process of this part of the model is responsive to the proposition that decision-makers, in the absence of firm beliefs about new events, tend to rely on previous experience. Writers on foreign policy have often made reference to the significance of historical events in shaping images and decisions. This position has been stated succinctly in Holsti et al. (1968: 125):

> Essentially, then, it is by projecting past experience into the future that human beings make decisions; and statesmen, in this respect, are not exceptions. Foreign policy decisions, like other human decisions, imply not only an abstraction from history, but also the making of "predictions"—the assessment of probable outcomes.

Effects of historical events have been studied by Deutsch and Merritt (1965), and Jervis (1968: 470-472) has analyzed how decision-makers analogize from historical experience. Furthermore, the proposition is a basic assumption of the CASCON (Beattie and Bloomfield, 1969) and CACIS (Tanter, 1971) models.

Search for Options and Policy Choice

The next decision-making process is the *search for an acceptable course of action*. Once various alternative explanations of the situation have been sorted out, the decision-maker searches for alternative policies with which to respond. To accomplish this he follows the explanatory paths from the policies he might select (conative concepts) to the objectives he feels are at stake in the situation (the affective concepts), and calculates which alternative or combination of alternatives will result in the maximum net gain in objectives.

The signs of the causal linkages (as well as the probability weightings) in the decision-maker's cognitive map are important at this point in the process, because the model must calculate how each policy alternative will affect every policy objective to which it is connected by an explanatory path. At the operational level, we used a *signed* digraph, which takes into account whether relationships between concepts are positive or negative. The signed digraph is converted into an adjacency matrix which preserves the signed relationships. This kind of matrix, which is called a *valency* matrix, makes it possible to determine whether there is a positive or negative path from a specific conative concept to one or more affective concepts (Harary et al., 1965).

The search for policy options that are embedded in a decision-maker's explanation of a situation is a procedure supported by the proposition that decision-makers tend to consider policy options that are part of their explanations of events. At this point in the decision process, a policy-maker looks for options that he thinks will give him some control over events in the international system. He believes that the choice of a policy that is part of his understanding of a situation will lead to changes in events, which as a consequence will have a favorable impact on his policy objectives. This proposition is similar to the notion of an "isomorphism of experience and action"–first introduced by Asch (1952) and since discussed extensively by Campbell (1963)–which holds that a person's views of the world and his tendency to respond to the world are essentially equivalent.

In the example of the Jordanian crisis the cognitive map shown in Figure 3 contains two conative concepts or possible policy alternatives for controlling the situation. The first alternative, indicated on the map as "CON_1," would consist of a coordinated military operation with the United States using its Sixth Fleet to safeguard Israel's rear and flanks, while Israel attacked Syrian tank forces from the air only. This alternative would have the advantage of helping to insure the preservation of Hussein's government and reducing Israel's concern about protecting her borders without occupying territory (and thus triggering an Egyptian reaction and possible Soviet intervention). The second alternative, shown on the map as "CON_2," would be a policy of direct American military intervention to protect King Hussein from the Syrians and the Palestinian commandos. This alternative might remove the threat to the viability of Hussein's regime, at least in the short run, but it would have the consequence of strengthening radical elements, weakening other moderate governments, and further eroding American influence in the Middle East.

As in the case of the explanatory phase of the decision process, when a decision-maker finds that he is ambivalent about possible alternatives or none seem to be adequate, he reflects on relevant historical experiences in an attempt to adduce additional concepts which will lead to an acceptable alternative. In the Jordanian crisis, for instance, a decision-maker might recall the joint Anglo-American use of military force in 1958 to support the governments of Jordan and Lebanon.

The *choice of a policy option* from among a number of possible alternatives is the final decision-making process in our simulation. There are, of course, a variety of decision models one can employ to deal with the trade-offs involved in this calculus. For our simulation we employ a lexicographic decision calculus which assumes that the decision-maker first uses his most important policy objective to see if the alternatives affect it differently. If this objective does not distinguish between alternatives, he then moves to his second objective, and so on, until he gets to an objective that distinguishes one alternative as better than the others.

In the simulation the choice process is operationalized as follows: A valency matrix is used to trace the connections between policy options and policy objectives, and then the model invokes a lexicographic decision calculus. To decide whether a particular policy objective distinguishes among two or more policy alternatives, the model takes into account not only the sign of the relationship but also the number of paths involved. For example, there may be three positive paths from a particular policy alternative to a given policy objective, whereas other alternatives have only one or two positive paths to the same objective. After a policy option is selected, the model recycles by adjusting the decision-maker's cognitive system to take into account any new or strengthened causal linkages, and stores information about the decision situation for future reference.

We can illustrate this process by returning to the example of the Jordanian crisis. Most of the policy specialists whom we interviewed agreed that the United States has four major groups of policy objectives in the Middle East. Group 1 objectives—the highest ranking policy values for these officials—

consist of the avoidance of a confrontation between the United States and the Soviet Union through the containment of conflicts in the Middle East which might escalate. Group 2 objectives—policy values which rank second—focus on the limitation of Soviet influence in the Middle East, which can be achieved by preserving moderate governments. Group 3 objectives—or the third ranking policy values—are all related to the security of Israel. Finally, Group 4 objectives—the lowest ranking policy values for these policy specialists—consist of American economic interests, such as oil, investments and trade, and access to air and sea routes.

In the Jordanian crisis all of these objectives were perceived by the policy specialists as being threatened. As shown in Figure 3, the possibility of fighting between the Soviet Union and Israel (Concept 11) would jeopardize the security of Israel (Concept 12) and might lead to a confrontation between the United States and the Soviet Union (Concept 13). Moreover, the replacement of Hussein with a radical regime (Concept 14) would encourage radical elements in other countries (Concept 15), harm moderate governments (Concept 17), and threaten American economic interests in the Middle East (Concept 18).

In a simulation of the Jordanian crisis, the model, at this stage, would compare the effectiveness of the two policy alternatives, CON_1 (an Israeli air action supported by the United States) and CON_2 (direct U.S. military intervention in Jordan) for helping the United States to control the situation and reducing the threat to American policy objectives. In this example, both alternatives would eliminate the threat to Group 1 objectives (avoidance of a confrontation between the United States and the Soviet Union by reducing the threat to the viability of Hussein's regime (Concept 3) and thus reducing Israeli concern about protecting her borders (Concept 4). However, CON_1 is clearly superior for reducing the threat to Group 2 objectives (limitation of Soviet influence by preserving moderate governments), because it would help to preserve Hussein's regime without strengthening radicalism (Concept 15) and consequently harming moderate governments (Concept 17), as would CON_2. Furthermore, while both alternatives would reduce the threat to Group 3 objectives (security of Israel), the use of CON_1, unlike the use of CON_2, would not harm American economic interests in the Middle East (Concept 18).

The prediction that CON_1 would have been chosen over CON_2 by the United States had the situation deteriorated is supported by press reports (The New York Times, Oct. 8, 1970) and our interviews with American policy specialists. While members of the National Security Council staff did not want to speculate about what the President might have done, other specialists believed that it was highly unlikely that CON_2 would have been used. For example, one high official said that the United States would not have used its tanks and air power in Jordan, "not even in the wildest scenario."

THEORY DEVELOPMENT

Although research on foreign policy decision-making has been cognizant of recent advances in theory-construction, no comprehensive framework has been developed which would allow for the explanation as well as the description of responses by decision-makers to international events. The model outlined above incorporates hypotheses about cognitive processing and rational choice behavior in a computer simulation of decision-making. The simulation utilizes information about the beliefs of decision-makers concerning (1) possible international events, (2) their ability to influence these international events, and (3) the consequences of various policy options for foreign policy objectives in order to explain and predict choice behavior.

Will our model of foreign policy decision-making contribute to the development of theory in international relations? First, through the application of propositions from cognitive process research, there may result a better appreciation of the role of psychological factors in foreign policy decision-making. Our model was derived from cognitive process theory and is being used to explore the behavior of political decision-makers in the international system. This application of cognitive process theory to international politics will help us to learn how much of the behavior of foreign policy decision-makers can be explained by psychological mechanisms. Second, by constructing a computer model of decision-making, we are combining a number of hypotheses in a rigorous and formal system. This serves not only as an integrating device for a body of knowledge, but also adds up to a theory of decision-making that has predictive power. While no single hypothesis can be expected to account for all evidence, a number of interrelated hypotheses, by explaining different aspects of behavior, provides a framework for making predictions about decision-makers. Third, the collection of data for running the simulation may help to increase our understanding of how information processing by governmental officials in actual decision situations, such as international crises, lead to policy decisions. In order to determine the degree to which the model can be generalized we have collected primary data from the government officials in the United States and from two small countries, Austria and Finland, which occasionally play the role of buffers in European politics. Cognitive maps and rankings of objectives obtained in these interviews should provide us with much information about relationships between perceived policy options, beliefs about international events, and policy objectives.

Another possible contribution of the simulation to the development of theory is more policy-oriented; it is an attempt to advance and improve the theories about international politics held by the decision-makers we are trying to study. Our discussion of decision-making has been grounded in a view of the policy-maker as an "applied scientist" or a person who is concerned about applying his knowledge of causal relations in order to exercise control over his environment. Both scientists and policy-makers try to develop theories from ambiguous data and must interpret information in light of those theories. We are interested in using our simulation to help policy specialists improve their theories about international politics by translating their verbal theories into causal models which can be more easily restructured. Furthermore, we want to use the simulation to illuminate the kinds of information processing and choice behavior which could be employed to achieve conflict resolution decisions that are less costly in terms of human lives and resources. By confronting simulated decision-makers with current and future international situations, we can predict some of their responses and explore likely effects of new commitments and policies. Ultimately, we want to be in a position to make machine-aided policy recommendations that are congruent with the way real decision-makers use concepts and justify choices.

REFERENCES

ABELSON, R. P. (1968) "Psychological implication" in R. P. Abelson et al. (eds.), Theories of Cognitive Consistency: A Source Book. Chicago: Rand McNally.
——— and A. BERNSTEIN (1963) "A computer simulation model of community referendum controversies." Public Opinion Quarterly 27: 93-122.
ABELSON, R. P. and J. D. CARROLL (1965) "Computer simulation of individual belief systems." American Behavioral Scientist 8: 24-30.
ABELSON, R. P. and C. M. REICH (1969) "Implicational molecules: a method for extracting meaning from input sentences." Prepared for the International Joint Conference on Artificial Intelligence, Washington, D.C. (mimeo)
ABELSON, R. P. and M. J. ROSENBERG (1958) "Symbolic psychologic: a model of attitudinal cognition." Behavioral Science 3: 1-13.
ABT, C. C. and M. GORDEN (1969) "Report on project TEMPER," in D. G. Pruitt and R. C. Snyder (eds.), Theory and Research on the Causes of War. Englewood Cliffs, N.J.: Prentice-Hall.
ALKER, H. R. and W. J. GREENBERG (1973) "The U.N. Charter: alternative pasts and alternative futures," in J. D. Ben-Dak (ed.), Simulation Yearbook. New York: Gordon and Breach (forthcoming).

ASCH, S. E. (1952) Social Psychology. Englewood Cliffs, N.J.: Prentice-Hall.
AXELROD, R. (1972) "How people make sense out of a complex world." Berkeley: University of California Department of Political Science. (mimeo)
BEATTIE, R. R. and L. P. BLOOMFIELD (1969) CASCON: Computer-Aided System for Handling Information on Local Conflicts. Cambridge: Center for International Studies, ACDA/SEC-141, Vol. 2.
BIERI, J. (1955) "Cognitive simplicity-complexity and predictive behavior." Journal of Abnormal and Social Psychology 51: 263-268.
BOULDING, K. E. (1959) "National images and international systems." Journal of Conflict Resolution 3: 120-131.
--- (1956) The Image. Ann Arbor: Univ. of Michigan Press.
CAMPBELL, D. T. (1963) "Social attitudes and other acquired behavioral dispositions," in S. Koch (ed.), Psychology: A Study of a Science, Vol. 6. New York: McGraw-Hill.
CRECINE, J. P. (1969) Governmental Problem-Solving: A Computer Simulation of Municipal Budgeting. Chicago: Rand McNally.
CYERT, R. M. and J. G. MARCH (1963) A Behavioral Theory of the Firm. Englewood Cliffs, N.J.: Prentice-Hall.
DEUTSCH, K. W. and R. C. MERRITT (1965) "Effects of events on national and international images," in H. C. Kelman (ed.), International Behavior. New York: Holt, Rinehart & Winston.
DRIVER, J. (1962) Conceptual Structure and Group Processes in an Inter-Nation Simulation. Ph.D. dissertation. Princeton University Department of Psychology.
FEIGENBAUM, E. A. (1963) "The simulation of verbal learning behavior," in E. A. Feigenbaum and J. Feldman (eds.), Computers and Thought. New York: McGraw-Hill.
FINLAY, D. J., O. R. HOLSTI, and R. FAGEN (1967) Enemies in Politics. Chicago: Rand McNally.
HARARY, F. (1961) "A structural analysis of the situation in the Middle East in 1956." Journal of Conflict Resolution 5: 167-178.
HARARY, F., R. Z. NORMAN, and D. CARTWRIGHT (1965) Structural Models: An Introduction to the Theory of Directed Graphs. New York: John Wiley.
HARE, A. P. (1961) "Computer simulation of interaction in small groups." Behavioral Science 6: 261-265.
HOLSTI, O. R. (1962) "The belief system and national images." Journal of Conflict Resolution 6: 244-252.
HOLSTI, O. R., R. C. NORTH, and A. BRODY (1968) "Perception and action in the 1914 crisis," in J. D. Singer (ed.), Quantitative International Politics: Insights and Evidence. New York: Free Press.
JERVIS, R. (1973) Perception and International Relations (forthcoming).
--- (1970) The Logic of Images in International Relations. Princeton: Princeton Univ. Press.
--- (1968) "Hypotheses on misperception." World Politics 20: 454-479.
KANOUSE, D. E. (1971) "Language, labeling, and attribution." New York: General Learning Press.
KELLEY, H. H. (1971) "Attribution in social interaction." New York: General Learning Press.
KELMAN, H. and R. BARON (1968) "Inconsistency as a psychological signal," in R. P. Abelson et al. (eds.), Theories of Cognitive Consistency. Chicago: Rand McNally.

LEAVITT, M. R. (1971) A Computer Simulation of International Alliance Behavior. Ph.D. dissertation. Northwestern University Department of Political Science.

McPHEE, W. N. (1961) "Note on a campaign simulator." Public Opinion Quarterly 25: 184-193.

NEWELL, A. and H. A. SIMON (1963) "A program that simulates human thought," in E. A. Feigenbaum and J. Feldman (eds.), Computers and Thought. New York: McGraw-Hill.

POOL, I. de S., R. P. ABELSON, and S. POPKIN (1965) Candidates, Strategies, and Issues: A Computer Simulation of the 1960 and 1964 Presidential Elections. Cambridge: MIT Press.

POOL, I. de S. and A. KESSLER (1965) "The kaiser, the tsar, and the computer." American Behavioral Scientist 8: 31-38.

SCHRODER, H. M., M. J. DRIVER, and S. STREUFFERT (1967) Human Information Processing. New York: Rinehart & Winston.

SHAPIRO, M. J. and G. M. BONHAM (1973) "Cognitive processes and foreign policy decision-making." International Studies Quarterly (forthcoming).

TANTER, R. (1971) "A computer aided conflict information system (CACIS)." Ann Arbor: University of Michigan Department of Political Science. (mimeo)

ZINNES, D., D. VAN HOUWELING, and R. VAN ATTA (1972) "International system structure and the balance of power propositions: a computer simulation study." Evanston: Northwestern University Simulated International Processes Project. (mimeo)

Chapter 3

THE PRINCE CONCEPTS AND THE STUDY OF FOREIGN POLICY

WILLIAM D. COPLIN
STEPHEN L. MILLS
MICHAEL K. O'LEARY

International Relations Program
Syracuse University

INTRODUCTION

The purpose of this essay is to explore the potential utility of a framework for the study of foreign policy based upon a set of concepts which were originally developed in the construction of PRINCE—a programmed international computer environment.[1] Although the model on which PRINCE is based was developed as a heuristic educational device, we have come to believe that it may be useful for both policy analysis and the theoretical

AUTHORS' NOTE: This paper is a product of a research and educational project surrounding the development of PRINCE, a programmed international computer environment. That project has been supported by funds from the ESSO Foundation on Higher Education, the Voluntary International Cooperation Project of the University of Michigan, the NASA Program, and the International Relations Program of Syracuse University. We are indebted to a number of colleagues for the general development of the project including Dale Dean, Julian Friedman, John Handelman, John Hodgson, William Leogrande, Patrick McGowan, Howard Shapiro, and John Vasquez.

study of foreign policy. We shall argue the usefulness of these concepts quite independently of their application in the specific simulation format represented by PRINCE. In other words, one need not accept the methodological approach of computer simulation to use PRINCE concepts for understanding foreign policy behavior or for evaluating the policy implications of various strategies. In fact, our hope is that neither those who support nor those who attack simulation methods prejudge the PRINCE concepts. We want the usefulness of the concepts to be the criteria of evaluation rather than whether or not a particular methodological technique is employed.

In addition, we feel that the contemporary study of foreign policy has been permeated by the concepts developed most extensively by Hans Morgenthau.[2] The systematic studies of the 1960s and early 1970s have assumed that foreign policy behavior can be viewed in terms of some type of dimension relating directly or indirectly to the so-called struggle for power among states. The most obvious manifestation of this tendency has been that almost every theoretical proposition tested in the foreign policy literature has contained a dependent variable that either expresses the conflict concept (e.g., war-peace, conflict-cooperation) or focuses on state A influencing state B (e.g., the relationship between votes in the United Nations and some other inter-state relationship). In fact, a recent survey of empirically-based foreign policy theory (McGowan and Shapiro, 1973) identified 118 propositions, and in 94 the dependent or independent variable (or both) referred directly or indirectly to dimensions of foreign policy behavior relating to war-peace questions and to the struggle for power. Although there are some works (to be noted later) which have looked beyond the war-peace dimension in the systematic study of foreign policy, the Morgenthau *Weltanschauung* continues to serve as the theoretical underpinnings for most studies.

In contrast, the PRINCE concepts focus on a dependent variable that is drawn from another tradition. Unfortunately, it is a tradition which has not significantly found its way into systematic foreign policy studies. Instead of trying to explain politics as the struggle for power among individuals or groups, this tradition seeks to study politics from the perspective of policy analysis. It focuses on how and why policy outcomes occur, rather than how and why political actors seek to dominate each other. In short, the PRINCE concepts constitute a different set of theoretical questions from the Morgenthau framework because they are focused on policy outcomes in the transnational setting rather than on a struggle for power among states.

In this paper, the PRINCE concepts will be presented as a set of ideas that focuses on the study of foreign policy with a perspective which is different from, if not competitive to, the concepts of the realist school. Our aim is to present the PRINCE concepts in such a way that they can be understood as a framework that could substantially alter the kinds of theoretical questions asked by students of foreign policy as well as the types of data collected and interpretations made. To accomplish this aim, the essay is divided into five parts: (1) a presentation of the PRINCE concepts, (2) an illustration of the kinds of theoretical questions that might be asked using the concepts, (3) a discussion of some theoretical and empirical reasons which suggest that the concepts are at least a plausible alternative to the Morgenthau paradigm, (4) a brief description of the agenda for research suggested by the concepts, and (5) examination of some of the policy implications that might grow out of research using the concepts.

THE BASIC PRINCE CONCEPTS

Accepting David Easton's (1965) definition of politics as the processes leading to the authoritative allocation of values, the PRINCE concepts focus on the competition among actors over specific policy outcomes. The essential analytical units that have evolved out of this focus are issues and actors. Issues are defined as *a proposed allocation of values which can be achieved only through collective action,* and the actors are *those individuals, groups and/or institutions which determine whether or not the collective action occurs.* Instead of viewing international politics as the struggle for power among states, our conceptual framework looks at the bargaining among all kinds of actors over proposed foreign policy outcomes.

The basic analytical structure that focuses on issues and actors introduces a level of complexity into the study of foreign policy that is not contained in the Morgenthau paradigm. The latter deals only occasionally with subnational forces and dyadic and polyadic forces among states. But the PRINCE framework adds to the concern of the scholar the relationship of these factors vis-à-vis a wide agenda of issues. As we shall see, this complexity requires that we include some concepts which heretofore have not been part of foreign policy studies, and also that we revise radically some concepts which have been used.

In this section, we will define the four central PRINCE concepts: (1) issue position, (2) power, (3) salience, and (4) affect. We will include in our definition some suggestions on possible empirical referents for these concepts. In addition, we will illustrate how the four concepts can be hypothetically applied to the issue of the United States' declaring a twelve-mile limit for its territorial seas.[3]

Issue Position

Issue position is a two-dimensional concept. The first dimension is the differentiation among support, opposition, or neutrality toward a proposed issue-outcome. In our example, we will take the United States adoption of the policy of a twelve-mile limit as an issue-outcome. The second dimension of issue position is the certainty with which the actor holds its favorable or unfavorable stance on the issue. Our practice has been to combine these two dimensions into a single symbolic notation. Whether the actors favor or oppose the issue as stated is indicated by a plus or minus sign, respectively. An integer from 1 to 10 is used to indicate the certainty with which the actor holds its position. A 10 indicates a position of certainty; a 1 indicates a very uncertain position. (Those who feel more comfortable with probabilities are invited to divide the absolute value of all scores in this and subsequent discussions by 10, so that a +1 becomes a .1 and a 10 becomes 1.0.) Neutrality is represented by a zero. In this analysis actors may be any type of political institution which influences the foreign policy-making process. In our illustration, we could conceivably identify hundreds of actors including the government of the Soviet Union, special interest groups within the United States, and international pressure groups such as the International Council of Scientific Unions.[4] Table 1 lists some of the actors and their possible issue positions.

Empirical referents for issue position can be found in the verbal and non-verbal behavior of official representatives of the groups and institutions attempting to influence the foreign policy outcome. Content analysis of public statements and writings as well as budget decisions can be used to determine the issue position of foreign policy actors. Because the empirical referents are likely to be ambiguous, a great deal of care must be exercised in

TABLE 1

ILLUSTRATIVE ISSUE POSITIONS OF ACTORS CONCERNING THE ADOPTION BY THE UNITED STATES OF A TWELVE-MILE TERRITORIAL LIMIT

Actor	Issue Position
Defense Department	−10
State Department	1
U.S. fishing interests	0
Latin American coastal states	10
Underdeveloped states	4
Western European states	−8
Other developed states	−4
International organizations concerned with territorial rights	7

assigning issue positions to actors. In some cases, scholars who have specialized in the study of a particular actor can be consulted to provide estimates of the issue positions of those actors.

Power

Power is, of course, a widely used concept in both domestic and international political studies. The variety of definitions for this key concept is a well-known, if not notorious, aspect of political science. In our formulation, an actor's power is conceived as being specific to each issue-outcome under consideration. Power is assigned to each actor on a specific issue by answering the following questions: If the actor under consideration fully mobilized all his resources within realistic limits, and if no other actor interfered, what is the likelihood that the issue under consideration would be resolved? If the answer is that the actor could certainly resolve the issue by himself, in the absence of opposition, then he is assigned a 10. If there is no possibility of his resolving the issue himself, he is assigned a zero. More moderate levels of capabilities are assigned integers ranging between 0 and 10.

Because the twelve-mile limit issue demands compliance among official governmental actors, and in particular actions by U.S. governmental officials, they have substantially more power than other actors. Table 2 provides an illustration of the distribution that might be expected for power on the twelve-mile issue. Remember the level of analysis at which we have chosen to cast our example: we are concerned with predicting whether or not the United States government accepts the twelve-mile limit; not whether such a rule becomes universally accepted.

TABLE 2
ILLUSTRATIVE POWER OF ACTORS CONCERNING THE ADOPTION BY THE UNITED STATES OF A TWELVE-MILE TERRITORIAL LIMIT

Actor	Power
Defense Department	6
State Department	4
U.S. fishing interests	3
Latin American coastal states	2
Underdeveloped states	1
Western European states	3
Other developed states	1
International organizations concerned with territorial rights	1

Empirical referents for the power concept depend upon the kind of issue in question. Traditional measures of power such as Gross National Product and military expenditures are rarely satisfactory by themselves unless the issue involves large-scale military encounters. Additional factors such as legal and/or institutional authority as well as technical knowledge and functional competence must also be considered. The complexity of the concept suggests that some type of expert judgment be used to supplement more traditional "hard" measures of power.

Salience

The third PRINCE concept is salience, which we have defined as the importance of an issue to each actor. Salience can be interpreted differently for different sets of actors. But in this case, we evaluate salience in terms of the percentage of time spent on the issue in question by the top leaders of each institutional actor. We have scaled salience, like power, ranging from 0 to 10 to indicate issues of least to most salience, or importance, for each actor. Using the range of 0 to 10, Table 3 presents the salience values for the twelve-mile issue.

Empirical referents for the salience concept depend primarily on the kind of actor. Terms like preference, utilities, or priorities are most descriptive of the concept of salience. When applied to individuals, these terms are relatively clear and can be obtained through normal questionnaires and interview procedures. When applied to groups or institutions, the concept implies some collective sense of priority and importance, and therefore raises questions of empirical complexity. Generally, we have distinguished between levels of salience in terms of what segments of the group or institution are mobilized. Low salience conditions exist when only low-level officials of the group or

TABLE 3
ILLUSTRATIVE SALIENCE OF ACTORS CONCERNING THE ADOPTION BY THE UNITED STATES OF A TWELVE-MILE TERRITORIAL LIMIT

Actor	Salience
Defense Department	8
State Department	4
U.S. fishing interests	9
Latin American coastal states	6
Underdeveloped states	2
Western European states	4
Other developed states	3
International organizations concerned with territorial rights	7

institution are directly involved. High salience conditions exist when the entire membership is mobilized and/or the leaders of the group or institution devote a great deal of time to the issue. Evidence on the level of salience can be obtained by looking at publications of the group or institutions (e.g., frequency with which the issue is mentioned). Traditional interviewing and questionnaire techniques may also be given to the rank and file as well as to the leaders, although as the actor becomes larger the costs increase and the accessibility to leaders decreases. Because there are substantial difficulties in obtaining such data, we again suggest surveying scholars who have specialized in the behavior of the actor under consideration.

Affect

The fourth concept in the PRINCE framework—affect—describes the general political relationship among the actors; that is, the degree to which actors are likely to cooperate with each other on any randomly selected issue. In other words, the concept is not issue-specific. Unlike the other three concepts, it can be expressed in an actor-by-actor rather than an actor-by-issue matrix. Affect is the closest of the four concepts to the traditional Morgenthau paradigm concept of alliance, although it departs from Morgenthau because it can apply to groups and institutionals across national boundaries.

Table 4 indicates the affect values among the actors for our illustrative example. The values range from +10 for positive affect to −10 for negative affect. The matrix can be read as the degree to which the actor in the row "feels" friendship for the actor in the column which intersects with that row. Hence, according to Table 4, the State Department registers a −5 toward the Department of Defense while the Department of Defense registers a −4 toward the State Department.

Empirical referents for the affect concept depend upon the types of individuals, groups, and institutions involved. As one goes up the scale of formality, the types of techniques alter from direct observation of interaction, as for example Alger (1968) has performed on representatives at the United Nations, to a study of official statements and actions that is usually covered by events data (Azar, 1970). Leavitt (1968) and Kegley (1971) have used multi-dimensional scaling techniques to measure the affect variable. Because the concept is similar to the Morgenthau construct much of the empirical work of the 1960s can be used at least for affect among states and blocs of states. These techniques may also be applied to determine affect for sub-national and transnational institutions.

TABLE 4
ILLUSTRATIVE AFFECT FOR ACTORS INVOLVED IN THE ADOPTION BY THE UNITED STATES OF A TWELVE-MILE TERRITORIAL LIMIT

	Defense Department	State Department	Fishing Interests	Latin American Coastal States	Under-Developed States	Western European States	Other Developed States	International Organization Concerned With Territorial Rights
Defense Department	X	−4	0	−8	−2	+4	−3	−5
State Department	−5	X	0	−2	+1	+4	−2	+2
U.S. Fishing Interests	+2	+2	X	−10	−3	+2	+1	0
Latin America Coastal States	−3	−1	−10	X	+5	−3	−3	−1
Underdeveloped States	−3	−3	−3	+4	X	−3	−3	0
Western European States	−2	−2	+1	−3	+1	X	−1	0
Other Developed States	−3	−3	+1	−3	+1	−1	X	0
International Organization Concerned with Territorial Rights	+1	+1	+1	+1	+1	+1	+1	X

SOME THEORETICAL QUESTIONS SUGGESTED BY THE PRINCE CONCEPTS

The basic focus of issue and actor plus the four concepts just outlined constitute the major elements of the PRINCE conceptual framework for the systematic study of foreign policy. To elaborate on the logic of the framework, we will present in this section some basic theoretical questions that can be explored with the PRINCE concepts.

One of the most obvious questions is a specification of the conditions under which a given issue is likely to be resolved. Since an issue exists when there is disagreement among the relevant actors on the desirability of a particular policy outcome, a scholar who accepts the PRINCE framework is forced to ask how we know when there is likely to be sufficient consensus so that an outcome can take place.

One answer to that question is to formulate a procedure for calculating the probability of issue resolution. Issue position, as we indicated above, can be thought of as the probability that an actor holds a position favoring or opposing the outcome; power may be thought of as the probability that an actor has capabilities to bring about its preferences; and salience may be thought of as the probability that an actor will be inclined to bring to bear its capabilities to effect its preferences. To assess the relative political forces favoring and opposing an outcome, we can combine these three variables. One method is to multiply the value of the three variables for each actor, to add the products for all actors on the issue (taking account of positive and negative products derived from issue position), and to convert them into a probability range.[5] If the sum of the products is equal to zero, this would tell us that the favoring and opposing forces are exactly balanced and that a resolution is highly unlikely. A zero result further tells us that if the issue is resolved, there is a 50-50 chance that the issue will be resolved either positively—that is the outcome will be achieved—or negatively—that is, the outcome will become a dead issue. If the sum of the products is either positive or negative, it would indicate a greater probability that the issue will be resolved in accordance with the positive or negative sign. A sample of these calculations is presented in Table 5 for our hypothetical issue of U.S. policy favoring the twelve-mile limit. The sum of the products is −395, indicating a greater likelihood that the issue will become a dead issue than that it will actually become policy. This sum is then normalized into a probability range by dividing by 8,000 (8, the number of actors in the example, times 1,000, the maximum contribution which any one actor can make to the outcome). The resulting number (rounded) is −.05. This tells us two things: (1) the absolute value, .05, is the probability that the issue will be resolved; (2) the

TABLE 5
ILLUSTRATIVE CALCULATION OF ISSUE RESOLUTION FOR ADOPTION OF A TWELVE-MILE LIMIT BY THE UNITED STATES

Actors	Issue Position	x Power	Salience	Product
Defense Department	−10	x 6	x 8 =	−480
State Department	1	x 4	x 4 =	16
U.S. fishing interests	0	x 3	x 9 =	0
Latin American coastal states	10	x 2	x 6 =	120
Underdeveloped states	4	x 1	x 2 =	8
Western European states	−8	x 3	x 4 =	−96
Other developed states	−4	x 1	x 3 =	−12
International Organizations concerned with territorial rights	7	x 1	x 7 =	49
			TOTAL	−395
		Normalized to account for possible range		−.049

signed number, −.05, is the extent over .50 that the issue is likely to be negatively resolved. Thus the figures can be interpreted to mean that in our illustration there is only one chance in twenty that the issue will be resolved (in other words, nineteen chances out of twenty that it will continue to be an issue). Furthermore, in the event (highly unlikely in this case) that the issue is resolved, the probability is slightly better than half (.55 to .45) that it will be inclined toward negative resolution.

The purpose of the illustration is to indicate the relatively formalized way in which the PRINCE concepts can suggest a meaningful answer to the theoretical question of the probable disposition of an issue. Another theoretical question that is suggested by the conceptual framework is an outgrowth of the first question. It concerns the conditions under which an actor is likely to change its issue position. One answer to this particular question has evolved from the development of the PRINCE computer simulation.[6] We will present some of the essential propositions on this question not because we think they represent definitive answers but because we feel they illustrate how the question is conceptualized in PRINCE terms.

In that model, issue position, power, salience, and affect are used to predict the issue positions of actors. More specifically, we employ the issue position of all actors at time "t" along with power, salience and affect of all actors at time "t." Simply stated, each actor is considered to be a reference actor, in social psychological terms, for each of the other actors. This relationship can be summarized in the following four propositions.

(1) An actor moves closer to the issue positions held by those other actors which it considers to be positive reference groups, and it moves farther from the issue positions of those actors which it considers to be negative reference groups.

(2) An actor will be more likely to move toward or away from the policy position of another to the extent that the affect felt by the actor toward the other tends toward extreme ranges, that is, when affect is strongly negative or positive.

(3) An actor will be more likely to move toward or away from a reference actor the higher the salience of that issue to the reference actor.

(4) The higher the salience of the issue for the actor in question, the more extreme will be its moves toward or away from other reference actors.

Applying this model to the data appearing in Tables 2-5, we would be led to predict that the position of the Defense Department is unlikely to be much less negative during the immediate future. The reason for this is that the only actor for which the Defense Department has a positive affect (the Western European States) also has an extremely negative issue position. Those actors which support the positive resolution of the issue are not "friends" of the Defense Department and therefore exert "pressure" to increase the issue difference between themselves and the Department. Similar predictions can be made for each of the actors in our example.

However, it is necessary to qualify this prediction by indicating the assumed conditions in this simple illustration. First, it is assumed that the other actors do not change their issue positions. Second, it assumes that power, salience, and affect remain constant during the period of influence. Both of these assumptions are unlikely to hold in any actual situation. They certainly have to be circumvented in any empirical research. Indeed, one of the functions of the complete PRINCE model (of which the above is a small part) and related research is to provide testable propositions about how actors mutually influence one another's issue position changes, and how changing values over time may be generated for salience and affect. (In all our work we have been content to let power remain a constant, since we have been dealing with relatively short time-frames—up to a year—within which we assume power is unlikely to change.) Within these limits of simplifying assumptions, we believe that the model described above is a plausible guide to help predict the changing foreign-policy issue positions of international actors.

Hopefully, the discussion in this section has illustrated some of the theoretical questions contained in the PRINCE framework. It has also been intended to help clarify the nature of the concepts and some of their logical interrelationships. In latter sections of the essay, we will describe the research and policy implications of the framework. Before doing that, however, we need to discuss the reasons for our considering the PRINCE conceptual framework to be a plausible alternative to the intellectual constructs of Morgenthau.

ON THE PLAUSIBILITY OF THE PRINCE PARADIGM

The purpose of this section is to indicate the plausibility of the PRINCE framework in two relatively distinct ways. We will first show the degree to which the PRINCE concepts build on existing work in the social sciences, including the field of international relations. We will next indicate some preliminary empirical analysis which we believe supports the idea of incorporating the PRINCE concepts into the study of foreign policy.

Theoretical Support

Despite its relatively unconventional treatment of foreign policy, the PRINCE framework does nevertheless correspond to some aspects of previous systematic and traditional studies in the field of foreign policy as well as in the social sciences more generally. We have no intention of claiming pristine uniqueness for the PRINCE concepts. On the contrary, we will indicate the degree to which the PRINCE concepts are supported by some elements of the existing literature.

The focus on issues as proposed allocations of values and the issue positions of relevant actors has received little careful attention in the foreign policy literature. The prime attention, as stated earlier, has been on conflict and cooperation as dependent variables. Perhaps the most well-known possible exception to this general trend is the work of James Rosenau in using what he terms "issue areas" as a classification device for the analysis of foreign policy behavior (Rosenau, 1966, 1967). However, Rosenau does not seem to conceive of specific allocation of values as issues which states pursue. Instead, his concept of "issue-areas" appears primarily intended to point out that there are different power struggles, involving different sets of actors, occurring around the world simultaneously. Indeed, his work since that time, however innovative in some respects, appears well within the tradition of viewing the behavior of states in non-issue, single-dimensional terms (Rosenau, 1970).

A less well-known but in the long run more important exception to the exclusion of the concern for issues in foreign policy research is the work of Michael Brecher et al. (1969). This article presented a framework for research that integrates the differences between issues into its data collection and hypothesis testing in contrast to Rosenau and those who have used Rosenau's framework in their research. Unfortunately, except for other work by Brecher (1972), the framework has not been extensively applied in systematic studies of foreign policy. Therefore, its substantial emphasis on issues has not had the impact it deserves in the foreign policy analysis literature.

There has, however, been a growing literature in policy analysis outside the foreign policy field that is extremely germane in this respect. The concerns of this literature closely match what we have termed issue outcomes and issue positions. Robert Dahl's work (1961) was path-breaking in this respect and has been followed by studies in a variety of fields (Bouma, 1970; Forward, 1969; and Polsby, 1963). Froman's (1968) discussion of the concept of issue catalogues and variety of uses was developed outside the field of foreign policy.

Closely related to the emphasis on issues in the study of politics is the movement toward social indicators (Bauer, 1966). Social indicators frequently measure the consequences of the political process surrounding the outcome of issues and therefore, constitute a critical dependent variable extremely relevant to the PRINCE concepts. In the foreign policy field, the results of some works on indicators is beginning to appear. The unpublished work of Bobrow (1971) as well as Burgess and others have made similar arguments. The PRINCE framework essentially tries to formalize the focus on the forces that shape and the conditions that result from the policy process.

Second, there is some support in the literature of the use of actors as a primary focus for the study of foreign policy. Those who study foreign policy have frequently cited sub-national actors such as interest groups and bureaucratic factions as important influences in the foreign policy-making process (Cohen, 1959; Haas and Whiting, 1956; Milbrath, 1967). Unfortunately, they have not considered transnational groups and institutions as an inherent part of the influence process.

However, recent developments suggest that such actors may soon be integrated into the theoretical models of foreign policy scholars. The appearance of an issue of *International Organization* edited by Nye and Keohane (1971) devoted completely to transnational actors has helped in this respect. At the foreign policy level, Rosenau's discussion of penetration

(1966) has also highlighted the importance of transnational actors in the formulation of foreign policy. While there has been no empirical research within a framework accepting the role of transnational actors in the foreign policy process, recent developments in the literature suggests that such a framework is needed.

At a more general level, the notion of actors as conceived within the PRINCE framework can be traced to the group theories of Bentley (1949) and Truman (1951). Although some scholars mistakenly assume that the group theory tradition focuses solely on the interplay of interest groups, a careful reading of the works of Bentley and Truman reveals a more generic definition of group. Calling on scholars to "examine the quantities that have been in play to produce the given results," Bentley (1949: 202) has laid the groundwork for a conception of the policy process that suggests we identify the actors that bargain with each other over the outcome of a particular issue. The tendencies of this brand of research are to combine the generic notion of actor with the traditional political science framework. In our work we are especially concerned with combining this trend with the emphasis on sub-national and transnational groups for the study of international relations. This is why we have given the notion of actor a major role in the PRINCE framework.

On the subject of power, there is an impressive quantity, if not quality, of work on which to draw. It is perhaps one of the surest indicators of the state of foreign policy studies that one of the most widely used concepts is also one of the most lacking in consensus as to its meaning. In the hopes of minimizing any further confusion, we can at least indicate our position relative to others who have studied the subject.

In the first place, we have adopted a conception of power as capabilities to achieve relatively specific outcomes. We think of an actor's power over issue-outcomes rather than an actor's power over another actor—although the relative power of two actors will influence their relationship. Insofar as we are talking of military or economic outcomes, the indicators we would use to measure power are the same as those traditionally used in the Morgenthau paradigm: national wealth, military forces, and the like. However, we see states as being concerned with many other issues besides military-economic issues. And in these cases other sources of capabilities will be more important. In this regard we find support in the work of Brecher and his colleagues discussed earlier. They comparatively studied foreign policy behavior with the conclusion, in their words, that "the much-publicized view that the maximization of power, defined as military and economic capability, is the chief motivating factor in state behavior is invalid" for the eight states they studied (Brecher et al., 1969: 93).

Their study further concluded that in the minds of the elites of the states they studied, capabilities were clearly evaluated in issue-specific terms. Military and economic capability were ranked important by elites in the military and economic issue areas, respectively. But these two forms of capability were ranked far down the scale of importance in other areas of foreign policy (Brecher et al., 1969: 93).

The idea of issue-specific power is not new to the social science literature outside foreign policy studies. In fact, it is the core question in the debate between the pluralist and the power elite schools, centered most prominently around community power studies (Dahl, 1961; Polsby, 1963; Banfield, 1961). The pluralist argues that there are several elites corresponding roughly to functional issues, while the power elite school maintains there is one elite cutting across a variety of issue. Although the debate has continued for sometime in the area of domestic politics, it has scarcely even begun in the international relations field. The reason for this is the dominance of the Morgenthau paradigm discussed at the beginning of the essay. While some synthesis between the two viewpoints might be appropriate for the study of foreign policy, there is clearly a need to introduce the idea so that the forces of scholarly synthesis can begin.

Unlike the concepts of issues, actors, and power, the concept of issue salience has not appeared in the literatures of either international relations or foreign policy. The reason for this is also found in the Morgenthau framework which contains an implicit assumption that issues are either questions of power politics and therefore overwhelmingly important, or not related to the so-called power struggle and therefore irrelevant. The bulk of the quantitative and non-quantitative literature has accepted this distinction by concerning itself almost entirely with questions of war and peace and by sharply distinguishing between security and functional issues.

In contrast, the PRINCE framework assumes that there are gradations of importance across a variety of issues and that the behavior of actors in the foreign policy-making process is related to the importance they attach to particular issues. Although this viewpoint has been ignored in the international relations and foreign policy literature, it has been recognized in other areas of the social sciences. Studies of domestic political processes that have employed the concept of agenda-building (Cobb and Elder, 1971) have clearly recognized the importance of issue salience. Much of the application of welfare economic concepts has also dealt with salience through the concept of preferences (Black, 1968). Coleman's work on collective decisions (1963, 1966, 1970) has clearly focused on the importance of salience in a way very similar to the PRINCE concept. Finally, a major body of literature in the area of social psychology has included the concept of salience as a major factor in attitude change (e.g., Sampson and Insko, 1964).

Finally, the concept of affect is already central to the international relations and foreign policy literature. In fact, the Morgenthau assumptions about the monolithic nature of the power struggle and the ebb and flow of hostility and friendship have played, in our view, a disproportionately large role in that literature. In the PRINCE framework, affect relates the ebb and flow of general political relationships among states which acts as an input into the predictive model on issue positions. In fact, affect is viewed as a mechanism through which friendship and hostility are registered in the bargaining that occurs among actors across a variety of issues.

Not only has the traditional literature given a major place to the concept of affect, but most of the major new approaches to the study of international relations have done the same. The applications of economic theories focusing on the question of collective and non-collective goods (Olson, 1966; Russett and Sullivan, 1971; Burgess and Robinson, 1969) are basically concerned with the dynamic evolution of general political relationships between states. Similarly, the work of psychologists concerned with international relations from the perspective of two-person games has focused on factors generating trust and distrust among states (Rapoport, 1963; M. Deutsch, 1958). Riker's (1962) work on coalition theory has done the same. Finally, much of the quantitative work such as the Singer-Small (1967) studies of alliance and war, the Stanford studies of the First World War (North, 1967), and McClelland's World Event Interaction Survey (WEIS) project (1968) have taken as their major question the ebb and flow of friendship and hostility among states.

To say that the PRINCE concept of affect is compatible with one of the major Morgenthau concepts as it has permeated the traditional and non-traditional study of international relations, however, is not to say that it plays the same theoretical role in the PRINCE framework as it does in the Morgenthau framework. On the contrary, there is a clear-cut difference in the way the concept is employed in the two frameworks. The Morgenthau framework uses the affect variable as both a dependent and an independent variable with affect at "t" predicting affect at "t+1." The PRINCE framework also suggests that affect can be used as both types of variables, except that the other PRINCE variables (viz., issue position, power, and salience) play an intervening role. Table 6 illustrates this difference between the Morgenthau and the PRINCE frameworks. The Morgenthau framework ignores the variables that influence changes in affect over time and therefore tends to assume either some type of Richardson process or a static set of conditions. The PRINCE framework sees the issue position, power, and

TABLE 6
AFFECT IN THE MORGENTHAU AND PRINCE FRAMEWORKS

Morgenthau Framework	
Time t	Affect of Actor i and Actor j
Time t + 1	Affect of Actor i and Actor j
PRINCE Framework	
Time t	Affect of Actor i and Actor j
Time t + 1	Issue Position, Power and Salience of Actor i and Actor j
Time t + 2	Affect of Actor i and Actor j

salience of any two actors across all issues as important intervening variables.

We feel that the theoretical literature suggests that the PRINCE concepts have some plausibility even though they mark a fairly radical departure from the existing concepts and assumptions that now prevail in the foreign policy field. While some of the concepts have yet to occupy a central place in the systematic study of foreign policy, they are well developed in other social science fields that have contributed to the study of foreign policy in the past.

Empirical Support

Our aim in this brief section is to indicate the degree to which some rudimentary empirical findings that we have generated tend to support the PRINCE conceptual framework. We are by no means claiming that these findings are anything more than rough indications that further research employing the PRINCE framework is warranted. Nevertheless, we feel it is worthwhile to present the evidence at this time as part of a general discussion of the PRINCE concepts.

If the PRINCE framework has some validity, the major difference that we might assume it would make in cross-national and time series studies is related to the role of issues and their salience. By not controlling for issues and the relative levels of salience that might occur in different issues, many studies may be producing null-hypotheses findings as an artifact of their aggregation procedures. To test this idea, we attempted to see if acts sent by states had different patterns when one controlled for issue. Using a coding scheme on WEIS data developed by O'Leary and Shapiro (1972), we calculated the mean value of influence attempts sent from one country to another. The mean was then calculated, controlling for issues.

The material presented in Table 7 is by no means complete in listing all dyads. Nevertheless, it shows that some issues do make a statistically significant difference in the distribution of WEIS acts for some dyads. Even given the limited sample used in this table, it is clear that in some dyads

TABLE 7
TEST OF THE ROLE OF ISSUES IN DISTRIBUTION OF WEIS VARIABLES

Actor	Target	Overall Mean*	Sample Mean**	Issue
United States	N. Korea	−2.1	−5.8	1 ***
			−3.1	4
Egypt	United States	−2.4	−4.6	1
			− .9	2 ***
			− .6	3 ***
			−1.0	5
			−3.0	6
Israel	Egypt	−7.9	−8.3	1 ***
			−2.6	3 ***
			−1.0	4 ***
Chinese People Republic	United States	−4.6	−5.1	1 ***
			−5.2	4

* Average value of the influence attempts sent from actor to target across all issues.

** Average value of the influence attempts sent from actor to target on the issue listed. For each dyad, some issues had 2 or fewer acts and were therefore not listed.

*** A statistical test was run to answer the question, "Are the acts on this issue a random sample of acts in this dyad?" Those issues marked *** are significantly nonrandom at the .05 level.

Issue Definition
1 Vietnam
2 Use of troops in Middle East
3 Search for peace in Middle East
4 Territorial rights
5 Economic aid
6 Military aid and arms sales

controlling for issues would generate indices significantly different from those aggregated across all issues.

This finding suggests the possibility that much of the empirical work using general conflict-cooperation coding schemes have come up with little or no significant relationship, either statistical or substantive, between the independent and dependent variables because they did not control for issues. While we cannot be sure of this speculation, it is certainly plausible, particularly given the results in Table 7.

More careful investigation of this matter would require reworking many previous studies. Because there are few instances in which the scholar has included issue-categories in his research, the reworking would involve recoding or collecting new data. Fortunately, there are some studies which can be usefully reviewed without such extensive reworking. We will look at two of them in this section: the Gamson-Modigliani (1971) study of Soviet-American interactions and the Abravanel-Hughes study which appears as Chapter 4 of this volume. The purpose of looking at these studies is to provide some additional evidence on the plausibility of the PRINCE framework.

Gamson and Modigliani studied American-Soviet interactions from 1946 to 1963 by classifying reports of actions appearing in The New York *Times*. Through an analysis of these interactions, the authors identified five stages in Soviet-American relations, which they describe in the following manner:

Phase I: January 1946 to March 1947—Varied Soviet responses and belligerent Western actions. The first phase runs from the beginning of the cold war to the announcement of the Truman Doctrine and is characterized by Soviet vacillation and Western belligerence.

Phase II: April 1947 to December 1950—Mutual hostility. Each side becomes increasingly convinced of the other's aggressive designs and hostile exchanges take place over many issues and in many areas.

Phase III: January 1951 to September 1956—Wary accommodation. Truce negotiations begin in Korea, marking an easing of tension, yet each coalition continues to see the other as expansionist and untrustworthy.

Phase IV: October 1956 to October 1962—Entangling alliances and hostility. Acts on both sides tend to be refractory though the Soviet bloc does react in a conciliatory fashion, even in the face of Western hostility.

Phase V: November 1962 to November 1963—Detente. Few interactions analyzed after the Cuban missile crisis, but the few actions noted reflect mutual accommodation.

In this fashion Gamson and Modigliani analyze undimensional conflict and cooperation patterns between the two countries and come up with an analysis based on changing patterns over time. However, as Figure 1 indicates, there does not seem to be such a clear pattern over time.

Figure 1 should be read in the following manner. The upper right-hand corner indicates instances when both states sent refractory acts to each other during the year. The lower left-hand corner indicates when both states sent cooperative acts during the year. The lower right indicates an asymmetry with the United States sending the refractory acts. It is difficult to find any systematic pattern in Figure 1 in terms of clusters of years.

We have surmised that what has been happening is not so much an overall change in the relationship between the two countries, but rather that different issues have become more important with the passage of years. It is the change in the political agenda, or to use PRINCE terms, issue-salience, by

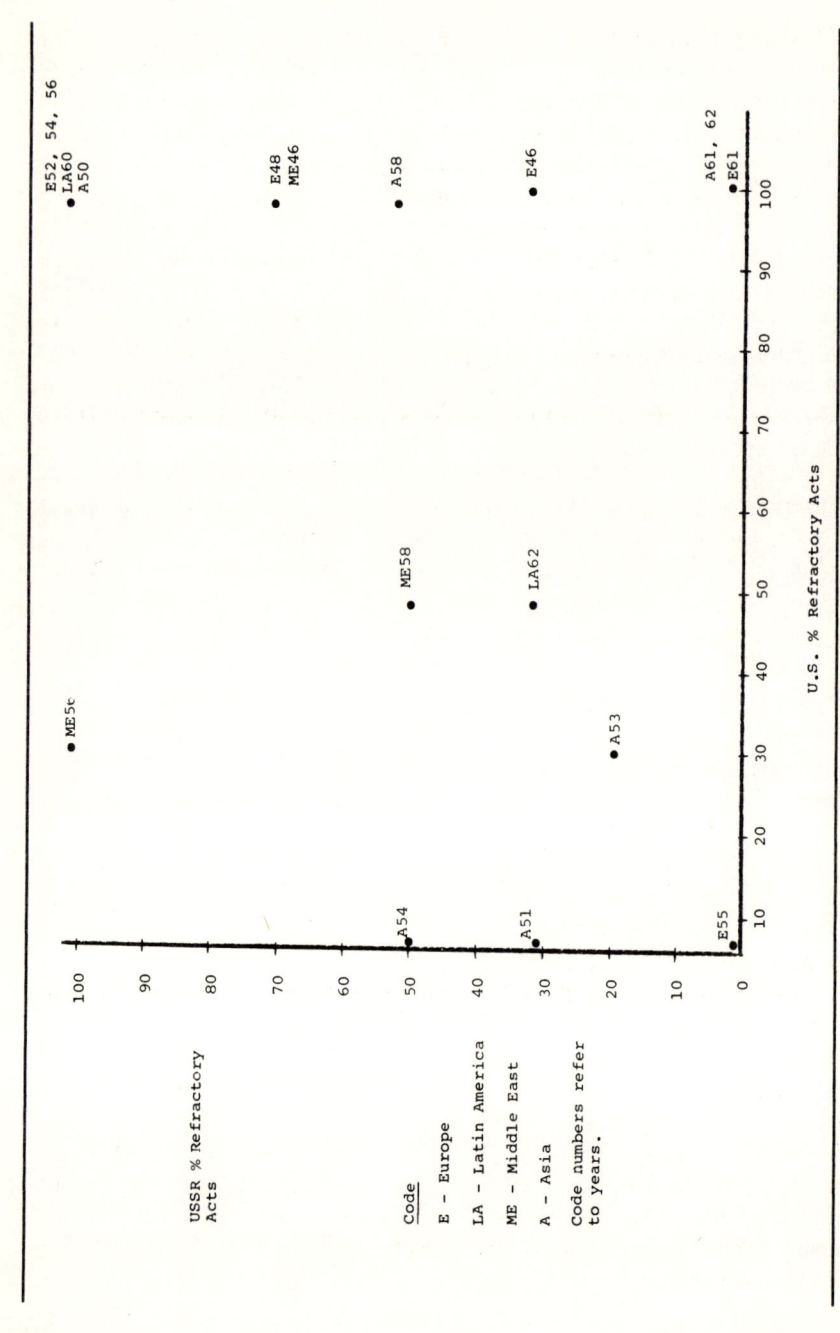

Figure 1: PATTERNS OF REFRACTORY ACTS SENT BETWEEN THE UNITED STATES AND THE SOVIET UNION FROM 1946-1963

the United States and the Soviet Union which accounts for changes in the patterns of relationships. We surmise that the relationship on a given issue may remain constant, but that the frequency of interaction concerning an issue leads to the setting of an overall pattern. As different issues increase in importance, along with their characteristic interaction patterns they produce more interactions and thus set the pattern for the general relations between the two countries. Gamson and Modigliani do not code for issues, but they do code for geographical area of interaction, which may be taken as a rough indicator of issue areas. Figure 2 shows the pattern of interaction over time in Europe. It shows that in every year but one (1955) the United States sent refractory acts irrespective of the acts sent by the Soviet Union. It seems to us likely that a more detailed attention to the issues being dealt with by the two countries might have led to a testing of more complex propositions about United States-U.S.S.R. interactions.

Turning from the development of theory involving dyadic interactions between the two superpowers to the essay by Abravanel and Hughes (Ch. 4 below), we can see the application of PRINCE concepts to building theory about the relationship between public opinion and foreign policy. The article is relevant to the PRINCE framework because it tries to relate foreign policy actions to public attitudes. However, the theoretical structure of the article ignores issues and draws an analogy that supports the Morgenthau paradigm. That analogy relates the findings of the Survey Research Center that party identity is more important than policy issues in voting behavior, a finding that itself is becoming increasingly questioned (Pomper, 1972). The authors assume that foreign policy behavior can be related to public attitudes most effectively by dimensionalizing the public's view in terms of general affect toward other states. Hence, the authors correlate affect levels of the publics of various European states with the affect of foreign policy acts the European states have taken toward each other.

Among other things, they find a correlation between the two variables that is produced primarily by the role of the Soviet Union as a statistical outlier (Ch. 4: 117). When the Soviet Union is removed, the correlations fall below normal significance levels. The role of issues and salience can be used to explain this finding. For cooperative acts, as reported in Table 1 (Ch. 4: 117-8), the correlation magnitudes increase over time, and for the conflictual events the correlation magnitudes decrease over time—particularly after 1963. Based on that trend, and on the conclusions we can draw from the Gamson and Modigliani study that issues become more complex and the threat from the Soviet Union toward Europe less dominant, the Soviet Union does not produce the outlier effect in which the publics of European states register

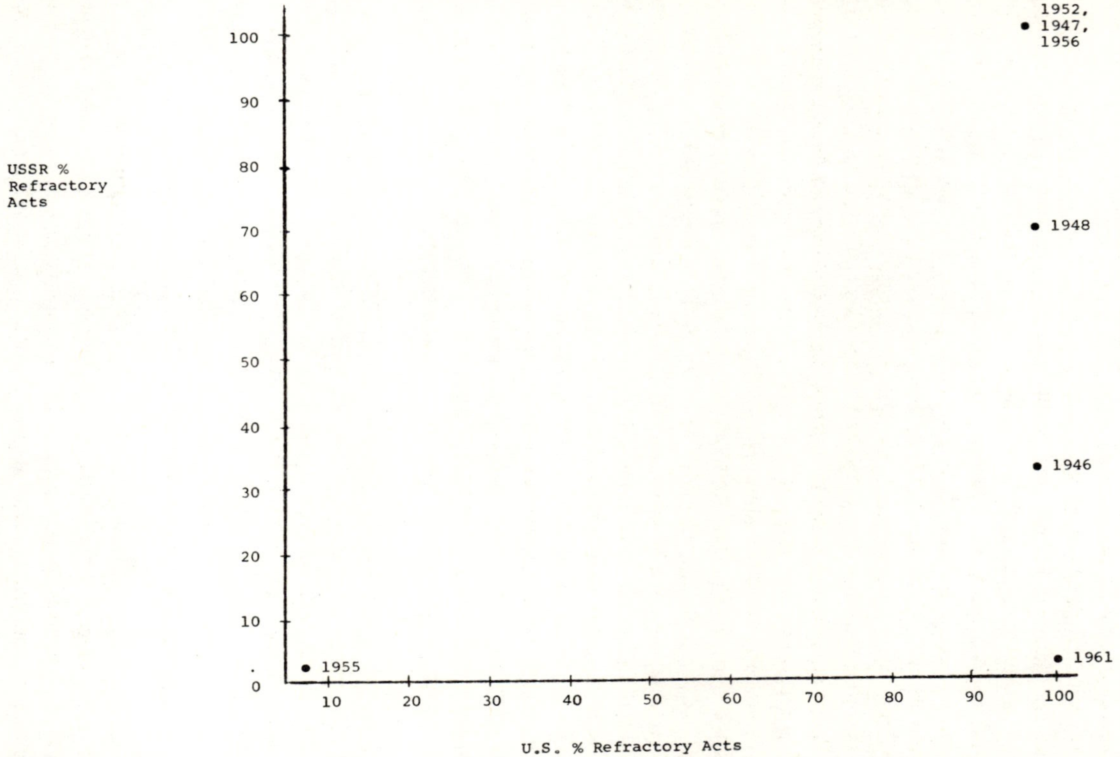

Figure 2: U.S.-SOVIET INTERACTIONS IN EUROPE

affect levels symmetrical to Soviet conflict actions. Similarly, with the East-West conflict in European issues lessening in importance, the cooperative acts of the Soviet Union are more clearly perceived by the publics, thus accounting for the higher correlations.

While this explanation of the pattern in the data is not the only one that could be made, it is, we feel, plausible. It is, therefore, suggestive that consideration of issues and their salience as distinct from country affect is helpful in providing explanatory and predictive theory to fit the data. Certainly, it could be valuable if it were integrated into the general theoretical framework that Abravanel and Hughes used in analyzing their data.[7]

At this stage in our research, we can only provide prima facie arguments of the theoretical utility of the PRINCE framework. We have tried to show that the framework has its roots in existing theoretical work in the social sciences even though the strength of the Morgenthau paradigm has precluded its extensive use in the systematic study of foreign policy. We have also attempted to show that some evidence can be found in empirical data generated by other scholars who have not shared the PRINCE framework as well as data specifically generated to test the PRINCE concepts. In making these arguments, we have implicitly accepted the idea that the addition of PRINCE variables to empirical foreign policy theory will provide sufficient benefits in terms of predictive and explanatory power to offset the loss of parsimony that the introduction of such variables would require. The appeal of Morgenthau's theory to empirical theorists has been the parsimony it provided by allowing theorists to generalize without considering issues and heterogeneity within states. However, we believe that the empirical theory of the 1960s in the foreign policy areas attests to the conclusion that we have reached—the Morgenthau paradigm creates such highly aggregated concepts that most of the foreign policy behavior which empirical theorists might want to study is either missed, or cannot possibly be explained or predicted from the independent variables derivable from the available theoretical assumptions.

RESEARCH WITHIN THE PRINCE FRAMEWORK

Perhaps the most efficient way to communicate the nature of our ongoing work is to suggest some of the empirical propositions with which we have concerned ourselves and the data problems we have been faced with. The four propositions concerning issue-position change to which we previously referred are one of the primary sources of testable hypotheses. Among the more promising are the following:

(1) The higher the salience of an issue for a state, the less likely it is to change its issue position.

(2) If a state does change its issue position on a high salience issue, it will change in an extreme fashion.

(3) The lower the salience of an issue for a state, the more it will tend to make frequent, but minor, changes in issue position.

(4) The more numerous the relatively highly salient issues which are considered in the interactions between two states, the more their affect will tend to be moderate, that is, neither extremely friendly nor extremely unfriendly.

(5) Conversely, the fewer the high salience issues of concern for a pair of countries, the more their affect will tend to be either highly friendly or highly unfriendly.

Our research on the PRINCE concepts has so far been of the most tentative nature. It has consisted largely of conducting secondary analyses of other empirical works (as suggested by our comments earlier). We have also attempted to read and reread the more traditional students of foreign policy to discover any similarities between our own thinking and their work. The field of political science, especially the debates over issue-specific power in the community power studies, has also been useful. Other social sciences, such as the social psychologists' concern with cognitive dissonance and sociology's studies of roles and reference groups, have also strongly influenced our thinking.

But these efforts are clearly of the most preliminary, foundation-laying nature. The utility of the framework certainly must be judged by the research it helps produce. Accordingly, we are spending an increasing portion of our time on empirical studies—ranging from large-scale events data analyses to case studies using the PRINCE concepts—which either directly test or at least throw more light upon the relationship we have concerned ourselves with.[8]

As one part of our empirical work, we will continue to undertake the coding of events data in order to capture the dimensions of issue position and salience. Although there is a serious lack of reliable data and a frequent over-representation of certain types of data inherent in events data (Azar, 1970), there is adequate data-making potential to warrant the issue-coding of events data.

Finally, because the coding of events data is so costly and is inherently limited, we are in the process of developing techniques to collect expert-generated data. We have recently developed an instrument which shows some capacity to generate reliable data. We hope to develop a reliable instrument so that we can collect, on a time series basis, the issue position, salience, power, and affect of actors in the foreign policy making process.[9] Although we are aware of the inherent difficulties in developing procedures to create expert-generated data sets, there appears to be little alternative if we are going to adequately test the PRINCE framework.

POLICY IMPLICATIONS OF THE PRINCE FRAMEWORK

The probability—not to mention the desirability—that a given academic approach will have an influence upon policy making is always difficult to assess. Our work has been so rudimentary that it would be premature to suggest any profound policy implications we think it might have. However, for many of the same reasons that we think the PRINCE concepts are a plausible aid to foreign policy research, we believe that they will be of greater value to the policy-maker than the research now dominated by the Morgenthau paradigm.

Evidence for this position can be obtained by studying a supplemental volume of *World Politics* (Spring 1972) edited by Raymond Tanter and Richard H. Ullman entitled "Theory and Policy in International Relations." Intended to "bridge the gap between the community of policy-makers and the community of theorists," the volume begins by admitting that there is little communication between the two communities and that almost everyone agrees "by and large, the policy-makers have not missed much" (1972: 2). Although the editors hint that the reason for this may be the increasing technical nature of foreign policy studies and the lack of social-science training on the part of the policy-makers, a serious look at the works in the volume indicate that the problem may not be the language and background of the two communities. Rather, the problem as we see it may very well be the highly abstract kinds of questions asked by the scholars which in part is a product of the continued implicit reliance on the Morgenthau framework. Except for the Allison-Halperin essay, the discussions are aggregated at the national level with both evaluation of foreign policy output and explanatory statements looking at neither sub-national nor transnational pressures. Even the essay by Morse entitled "Crisis Diplomacy, Interdependence, and the Politics of International Economic Relations"—which emphasizes the interdependence of the United States and the international economy—is focused on the struggle among nations for economic control. Virtually every essay except the one by Allison and Halperin adopts the general Morgenthau paradigm.[10]

Asking monumental questions that lead to causal modeling of conflict patterns between NATO and the Warsaw Pact (Tanter and Ullman, 1972) or the long-range interaction of resources, technology, and population on international conflict (Choucri and North, 1972) cannot lead to the critical policy-making questions that have to be dealt with. These questions concern the day-to-day and week-to-week decisions that constitute the domain of most policy-makers in authority rather than the month-to-month and year-to-year and—in the case of the Choucri-North essay—the decade-to-decade broad decisions that occupy the attentions of these and most other scholars. When the broad long-term questions are not asked, the focus is placed on crisis decisions—which again assumes that importance of the national interest in life-or-death war-peace situations. Both the broad questions and the crisis questions are inherent in a world view that sees foreign policy as the struggle for power among states.

Research based on the Morgenthau paradigm may have some utility, but that utility is limited by the access scholars have to the top-level decision-makers involved in crisis decisions and to the broad scope of influences that might shape policy over a long period of time. The market is highly limited for research that uncovers the kinds of general relationships posited in the essays in the Tanter-Ullman volume. Although proponents of social-science methods frequently cite the utility of the methods as distinct from the findings, there is clearly little that can be done until some relevant substantive findings are presented in a conceptual framework that is likely to be understood by foreign policy-makers at all levels of the decision-making hierarchy.

Although the kinds of quantitative research guided by the Morgenthau paradigm are too highly aggregated to be of general interest to the policy-maker, the research suggested by the PRINCE concepts is not. By studying foreign policy as a process in which values are allocated through the interaction of a variety of actors, the PRINCE framework posits a dependent variable that any policy-maker attempts to shape every day of his life. In addition, the framework becomes easier to apply as one moves to more concrete and perhaps mundane levels. The imminent threat of war or the existence of a crisis or the evaluation of long-range national policy is not required by the PRINCE concepts. Instead, the PRINCE concepts, especially issue position, appear to be the conceptual basis for the kinds of intelligence and monitoring activities that foreign policy actors—whether they be governmental agencies, transnational organizations, or pressure groups—need to perform.[11] In short, the PRINCE framework calls for the conceptual decomposibility of the world, which is required in order for the policy-maker to use foreign policy research in the way that an engineer uses physical science research.

In order for any of these potentialities to be realized, of course, it is a necessary if not sufficient condition that the empirical research mentioned above bear some intellectual fruit. It is for this reason that we are continuing our work, and that we hope for communications from others who are similarly inclined.

NOTES

1. Information on PRINCE can be obtained from authors at the International Relations Program, Syracuse University. The program and player materials are now in use at approximately 25 colleges and universities throughout the U.S.

2. We are referring here to the so-called "realist" school whose most important scholarly figure is Morgenthau. That school is extensively discussed in Thompson (1960). Morgenthau's most influential and generic work is clearly *Politics Among Nations*, which was originally published by Alfred A. Knopf in 1948 and has gone through four editions since then. For a systematic presentation of this viewpoint, see Handelman and Vasquez (1972).

3. The choice of this particular issue is arbitrary. It is made purely for heuristic reasons. The data used in the example are also provided only for heuristic reasons although we hope that they do not misrepresent reality too greatly. However, the work of Robert Friedheim and Joseph Kadane (1972) has generated data that could be analyzed within the PRINCE framework.

4. Given limited resources, there is always the problem of choosing the most important actors—as these might be defined. This is one of the main methodological problems of applying the PRINCE concepts, and it is an aggregation problem not unusual in this type of research. The decision of the scholars in most quantitative studies to deal only with states as actors solves that particular aggregation problem to some extent, but it has led to theoretical and other methodological problems which, we believe, are more severe.

5. This particular formula is one of the more obvious and simple ways to use the PRINCE concepts as a predictive instrument. It is provided for illustrative purposes since we have no basis for assuming that there is a linear multiplicative relationship among the three variables. Further heuristic applications of the predictive utility of the PRINCE concepts are discussed extensively in Coplin and O'Leary (1972).

6. For a full discussion of all the theoretical relationships in PRINCE, see Coplin, Mills and O'Leary (1971).

7. These comments on the Abravanel-Hughes essay should not be viewed as general criticisms. In fact, we feel that their essay is clearly one of the most important attempts in the comparative foreign policy literature to relate domestic political variables to foreign policy variables over a period of time. Instead, our comments should be viewed solely as a defense of the PRINCE concepts.

8. Issue-coded data collection has been supported in part by the Voluntary International Cooperation Project of the University of Michigan. Information on available data can be obtained from the authors.

9. An instrument to generate data on the PRINCE variables has been developed and a primary report written (Leogrande, 1972). A set of eight experts on two different countries generated data on salience and issue position. The interjudge reliability was .73, .81 for salience and issue position for one of the countries, and .81 and .75 for salience and issue position on the other country.

10. The Allison-Halperin (1972) essay can be viewed as a departure from the Morgenthau paradigm because it focuses on sub-national actors as an everyday and acceptable part of the foreign policy process. However, until it integrates sub-national actors from other states and transnational actors, the framework can be viewed only as a partial approach to foreign policy analysis.

11. Because the PRINCE concepts allow actors at a variety of levels into the theoretical framework, they can be used by any of those actors as well as other actors that have access to the ones posited in the framework. This contrasts sharply with the theoretical frameworks in the Tanter-Ullman book, which can be used only by national actors and in some cases only with the United States.

REFERENCES

ABRAVANEL, M. and R. HUGHES (1973) "The relationship between public opinion and governmental foreign policy: a cross national study," in P. J. McGowan (ed.) Sage International Yearbook of Foreign Policy Studies I. Beverly Hills: Sage.

ALGER, C. F. (1968) "Interaction in a committee of the United Nations General Assembly," pp. 51-84 in J. D. Singer (ed.) Quantitative International Politics: Insights and Evidence. New York: Free Press.

ALLISON, G. and M. HALPERIN (1972) "Bureaucratic politics: a paradigm and some policy implications," pp. 40-80 in R. Tanter and R. Ullman (eds.) Theory and Policy in International Relations. Princeton: Princeton Univ. Press.

AZAR, E. (1970) "Analysis of international events." Peace Research Reviews 4 (November).

BANFIELD, E. C. (1961) Political Influence. New York: Free Press.

BAUER, R. [ed.] (1966) Social Indicators. Cambridge: MIT Press.

BAUER, R. A., I. de S. POOL, and D. A. LEWIS (1964) American Business and Public Policy. New York: Atherton Press.

BENTLEY, A. (1949) The Process of Government. Bloomington: Principia Press. (First published in 1908.)

BLACK, D. (1968) "The elasticity of committee decisions with alternation in member's preference schedules," pp. 102-113 in B. M. Russett (ed.) Economic Theories of International Politics. Chicago: Markham.

BOBROW, D. B. (1971) "Analysis and foreign policy choice: some lessons and initiatives." Presented at the annual meeting of the American Political Science Association.

BOUMA, D. H. (1970) "Issue-analysis approach to community power: a case study of realtors in Kalamazoo." American Journal of Economics and Sociology 29, 2 (April): 241.

BRECHER, M. (1972) The Foreign Policy System of Israel: Setting, Images, Process. New Haven: Yale Univ. Press.

BRECHER, M., B. STEINBERG, and J. STEIN (1969) "A framework for research on foreign policy behavior." Journal of Conflict Resolution 13.

BURGESS, P. M., R. W. LAWTON, and T. P. KRIDLER (1972) "Indicators of international behavior: an overview and re-examination of micro-macro designs." Prepared for the annual convention of the International Studies Association, Dallas.

BURGESS, P. M. and J. A. ROBINSON (1969) "Alliances and the theory of collective action: a simulation of coalition processes," pp. 640-653 in J. N. Rosenau (ed.) Foreign Policy and International Politics. 2nd ed. New York: Free Press.

COBB, R. W. and C. ELDER (1971) "The politics of agenda-building : an alternative perspective for modern democratic theory." Journal of Politics 33: 892-915.

COHEN, B. (1950) The Influence of Non-Governmental Groups on Foreign Policy-Making. Boston: World Peace Foundation.

COLEMAN, J. S. (1970) "Political money." American Political Science Review 64 (December): 1074-1088.

--- (1966) "Foundations for a theory of collective decisions." American Journal of Sociology 71 (May): 615-627.

--- (1963) "Comments on 'On the concept of influence'." Public Opinion Quarterly 27 (Spring): 63-82.

COPLIN, W. D., S. L. MILLS, and M. K. O'LEARY (1972) A Description of the PRINCE Model. Syracuse University International Relations Program.

COPLIN, W. D. and M. K. O'LEARY (1972) Everyman's PRINCE: A Guide to Understanding Your Political Problems. North Scituate: Duxbury.

CHOUCRI, N. and R. NORTH (1972) "Dynamics of international conflict: some policy implications of population resources and technology," pp. 80-123 in R. Tanter and R. Ullman (eds.) Theory and Policy in International Relations. Princeton: Princeton Univ. Press.

DAHL, R. A. (1961) Who Governs: Democracy and Power in an American City. New Haven: Yale Univ. Press.

DEUTSCH, M. (1958) "Trust and suspicion." Journal of Conflict Resolution 2: 267-279.

EASTON, D. (1965) A Systems Analysis of Political Life. New York: John Wiley.

FORWARD, R. (1969) "Issue analysis in community power studies." Australian Journal of Politics and History 15, 3.

FRIEDHEIM, R. L. and J. B. KADANE (1972) "Ocean science in the UN political arena." Journal of Maritime Law and Commerce 3: 473-502.

FESTINGER, L. (1950) "Informal social communication." Psychological Review 57: 271-282.

FROMAN, L. A., Jr. (1968) "The categorization of policy contents," in A. Ranney (ed.) Political Science and Public Policy. Chicago: Markham.

GAMSON, W. and A. MODIGLIANI (1971) Untangling the Cold War. Boston: Little Brown.

GRIFFITH, B. C. and N. C. MULLINS (1972) "Coherent Social Groups in Scientific Change." Science 177 (September): 959-963.

HAAS, E. B. and A. S. WHITING (1956) Dynamics of International Relations. New York: McGraw-Hill.

HANDELMAN, J. and J. VASQUEZ (1972) PRINCE Research Study 8. Syracuse University International Relations Program (October).

KEGLEY, C. W. (1971) Toward the Construction of an Empirically Grounded Typology of Foreign Policy Output Behavior. Ph.D. dissertation. Syracuse University International Relations Program.

KLINEBERG, F. L. (1941) "Studies in measurement of the relations among sovereign states." Psychometrika 6: 335-352.
LEAVITT, M. R. (1968) Towards the Development of an Empirical Index of Hostility and Friendship Between States. Master's thesis. Wayne State University.
LEOGRANDE, W. (1972) "Systematic analysis of expert-generated data: report of a pilot project." PRINCE Research Study 1. Syracuse University International Relations Program.
MILBRATH, L. (1967) "Interest groups and foreign policy," pp. 231-252 in J. Rosenau (ed.) Domestic Sources of Foreign Policy. New York: Free Press.
McCLELLAND, C. A. (1968) "Access to Berlin: the quantity and variety of events, 1948-1963," pp. 159-187 in J. D. Singer (ed.) Quantitative International Politics: Insights and Evidence. New York: Free Press.
McGOWAN, P. J. and H. B. SHAPIRO (1973) The Comparative Study of Foreign Policy: A Survey of Scientific Findings. Beverly Hills: Sage.
MORGENTHAU, J. (1967) Politics Among Nations. 4th ed. rev. New York: Knopf.
MORSE, E. (1972) "Crisis diplomacy, interdependence and the politics of international economic relations," pp. 123-151 in R. Tanter and R. Ullman (eds.) Theory and Policy in International Relations. Princeton: Princeton Univ. Press.
NORTH, R. C. (1967) "Perception and action in the 1914 crisis." Journal of International Affairs 21, 1: 103-122.
NYE, J. S. and R. O. KEOHANE (1971) "Transnational relations and international organization." Special issue of International Organization (summer).
O'LEARY, M. K. and H. SHAPIRO (1972) Instructions for Issue-Coding WEIS Acts. Syracuse University International Relations Program.
OLSON, M. (1966) The Logic of Collective Action. Cambridge: Harvard Univ. Press.
POLSBY, N. (1963) Community Power and Political Theory. New Haven: Yale Univ. Press.
POMPER, G. M. (1972) "From confusion to clarity: issues and American voters, 1956-1968." American Political Science Review 66 (June): 415-429.
RAPOPORT, A. (1963) "Formal games as probing tools for investigating behavior motivated by trust and suspicion." Journal of Conflict Resolution 7: 570-579.
RIKER, W. H. (1962) The Theory of Political Coalitions. New Haven: Yale Univ. Press.
ROSENAU, J. N. (1970) "Foreign policy as adaptive behavior: some preliminary notes for a theoretical model." Comparative Politics 2 (April): 365.
--- (1967) "Foreign policy as an issue-area," pp. 11-50 in J. N. Rosenau (ed.) Domestic Sources of Foreign Policy. New York: Free Press.
--- (1966) "Pre-theories and theories of foreign policy," pp. 27-93 in R. B. Farrell (ed.) Approaches to Comparative and International Politics. Evanston: Northwestern Univ. Press.
RUMMEL, R. J. (1968) "The relationship between national attributes and foreign conflict behavior," pp. 187-215 in D. J. Singer (ed.) Quantitative International Politics: Insights and Evidence. New York: Free Press.
RUSSETT, B. M. and J. D. SULLIVAN (1971) "Collective goods and international organization." International Organization 25: 845-865.
SAMPSON, E. E. and C. A. INSKO (1964) "Cognitive consistency and performance in the autokinetic situation." Journal of Social Psychology 65: 184-192.
SINGER, J. D. and M. SMALL (1967) "National alliance commitments and war involvement, 1815-1945." Peace Research Society (International) Papers 5: 109-140.

TANTER, R. and R. ULLMAN [eds.] (1972) World Politics: Theory and Policy in International Relations. Princeton: Princeton Univ. Press.
THOMPSON, K. W. (1960) Political Realism and the Crisis of World Politics. Princeton: Princeton Univ. Press.
TRUMAN, D. (1951) The Government Process. New York: Alfred A. Knopf.
WALTZ, K. N. (1959) Man, State and War. New York: Columbia Univ. Press.

PART THREE

FINDINGS

Chapter 4

THE RELATIONSHIP BETWEEN PUBLIC OPINION AND GOVERNMENTAL FOREIGN POLICY: A CROSS-NATIONAL STUDY

MARTIN ABRAVANEL
BARRY HUGHES
Case Western Reserve University

Political scientists have often employed the term "linkage" to denote the pattern of association between governmental institutions, policies, and actions, on the one hand, and popular values, beliefs, and attitudes, on the other.[1] Especially since the advent of systematic survey research, a sizable body of empirical research has accumulated on the nature of this relationship. Partly for reasons relating to data quality and comparability, however, many of these investigations have been restricted in scope.[2] The purpose of the present study is to examine citizen-government linkages by taking advantage of two time-series data sets, one dealing with foreign policy (the actions of one nation toward another), and the second dealing with citizen attitudes (the views of the citizens of one nation toward another). We feel that an important contribution can be made to the study of linkages when the investigation takes place within the context of a prolonged time period and when it involves comparison over a number of different political systems.

THE STUDY OF LINKAGES

The relationship between mass opinion and foreign policy behavior has been examined with at least two distinct questions framing the research: (a) what constrains perception and interpretation? and (b) who influences whom?

In the first instance, the question is asked: what political, social and/or psychological categories help to explain divisions of mass opinion as they apply to foreign policy affairs?[3] This is the problem of cues and constraints on opinion, and approaches to its study take the form of correlating mass attitudes and beliefs with objective and subjective characteristics of the individual. The direction of influence is not the key question in these studies; it is assumed that attitudes are formed and modified primarily as a result of personal predispositions and environmental stimuli such as party identification, social and economic status, interest, education, knowledge, alienation, anxiety, etc. While the findings of these studies vary somewhat, it is clear that whether or not a citizen supports the foreign policies of his government depends considerably upon the characteristics and experiences of the individual.

In the second approach to the study of opinion-policy linkages, the question is usually phrased as follows: does mass opinion set direction for, or limits on, a nation's foreign policy behavior (and on a nation's decision-makers) or does a government's foreign policy shape the direction and content of mass attitudes? Research into this subject has taken a number of different forms, with one group of scholars looking into the correlation between mass attitudes and national policy, and a second group looking into the correlation between mass attitudes and elite (decision-maker) attitudes.[4]

It is reasonable to suggest that the nature of the relationship between public sentiment and foreign policy is still an unresolved issue. Warren Miller and Donald Stokes, for example, found that American legislators are not "instructed delegates" when it comes to the issue of foreign affairs. "On the question of foreign involvement," they report (1963: 49), "there is no discernible agreement between legislator and district whatever." Yet Milton Rosenberg (1965: 285) argues that while national elites have control over the shaping of public opinion on issues of foreign policy, attempts at policy alteration are in turn influenced or at least constrained by the very public opinion that they have sought to create and control.

In sum, I have suggested that, in the area of foreign relations, elitists' perceptions of the opinions of publics (whether these be specialized and articulate pressure groups or the "mass public" itself) tend to have some effect upon policy processes, and particularly that at times they do *constrain* and limit the shaping and execution of policy innovations.

He is quick to add, however, that "the extent to which policy processes are controlled by such perceptions has hardly been assessed in any systematic studies" (1965: 285).

In an ambitious and resourceful attempt to tie the various pieces of this puzzle together—public attitudes, elite attitudes, and foreign policy—Sophia Peterson found that although "American mass opinion seems aloof from the influence of conflictual events," there is a positive correlation between American elite and mass attitudes toward the target of these events, in this case the Soviet Union. She concludes (1971: 30) as follows:

> It should be emphasized that the evidence cannot support the position that no matter what attitude, at a given moment, was expressed by decision-makers, the public would emulate it; nor can we assume that a spectacular event might not affect mass opinion. What the evidence does bear out is that over an extended period of time, the foreign-policy elite probably can influence the general evaluative orientation of the public towards a very salient target.

Even though many of the major issues of the linkage problem continue to generate divisions among scholars, research into the two areas outlined above—that dealing with the correlates of opinions and that dealing with the question of influence—offer many useful guideposts to the student of citizen support of foreign policy. In the American context, at any rate, some tentative conclusions seem warranted:

(1) A majority of the public tends to support the general tenets of national policy relating to foreign affairs. (Oscamp, 1965; Gamson and Modigliani, 1966; Campbell and Cain, 1965; Rogers et al., 1967; and Rosi, 1965).

(2) Depending upon time period, circumstances, and issue, foreign policy sometimes generates enough disagreement to place the level of popular support for specific policies or actions at a very low level. (Belknap and Campbell, 1951-52; Mueller, 1971; and Miller, 1967).

(3) The level of general or specific support does not, however, always reflect the perceived success of failure of policies, nor does it always reflect the outcome of events in international relations.[5]

Research into the linkage between citizen attitudes and foreign policy has benefited from the various approaches and techniques applied to this subject.

Yet it is clear that the literature is lacking in a number of important respects: the scope of the research, the time perspective, the consistency and quality of data, and the lack of differentiation between response objects. While all these problems are closely related to one another, each presents a different challenge.

With regard to the problem of scope, most studies gather data from a single nation, and in more cases than not that nation is the United States.[6] While some more eclectic scholars draw upon data from two or more countries (or refer to investigations carried on in other countries), comparability is a major obstacle (on comparability, see Davis and Verba, 1960; Almond and Verba, 1963; and Przeworski and Teune, 1970). It cannot be denied that the linkages under consideration may reflect political, cultural, and social setting; yet cross-national research requires substantial resources. The collection of propositions from isolated, single-nation endeavors or re-analysis of independent surveys constitutes a first step; truly cross-national research represents a second-level accomplishment.

Second, most studies analyze the relationship between international relations and public attitudes at one point in time, especially after important international events, during an election campaign, or whenever opinion surveys happen to be conducted (exceptions are Bobrow and Cutler, 1968; Caspary, 1970; Davis and Verba, 1960; and Richman, 1970). Again the problem of resources and of the comparability of research over time present impediments to the researcher. In the field as a whole, most of the more ambitious cross-national studies of political attitudes or predispositions have utilized data gathered from a single cross-sectional survey, and where attempts have been made to go beyond this, the consistency problem emerges as paramount.[7]

Consistency and quality of data, then, present a third limitation in the literature. As far as survey research is concerned, differences in sampling methods, question wording, and survey purpose make comparison either across nations or over time at best tenuous. With regard to the analysis of foreign policy behavior, comparison rests upon the construction of measures that are consistent across the events under consideration and sensitive to the nuances of international relations. Until recently there has been little effort exerted to develop such measures.

Finally, there has been a noticeable failure to distinguish between response objects—i.e., whether or not an obtained association between foreign policy and citizen attitudes is short-ranged and contingent upon a particular external object (the recency of an attention-getting event, the stimulus of an electoral campaign, etc.) or is part of a longer-range "set" or "mood" of the public under investigation. Numerous political scientists and social psychologists have observed a basic stability of political attitudes even in the face of changing external stimuli (Key, 1964: 253-257; Berelson and Steiner, 1964; Deutsch and Merritt, 1965). This datum, combined with the knowledge that most citizens are neither very concerned about nor cognizant of foreign policy affairs, makes it necessary to separate long-term orientations of mass publics from short-term reactions to and evaluations of specific stimuli.

Although we cannot hope to overcome all the limitations outlined above, we wish to make a beginning. Accordingly, we shall study the problem of citizen support of foreign policy stance by analyzing data from Britain, France, Italy, and West Germany for the period 1954 to 1964. In addition, we have chosen to view the linkage concept both in its long-term and in its short-term contexts.

Short-term ("specific") support taps the degree to which the citizenry of a nation is sensitive to shifts in its government's policy toward a foreign nation. This is measured by the degree to which these shifts are accompanied by a corresponding shift in public opinion. Easton has written that support "will increase or decline depending upon the way in which the members interpret the consequences of the various outputs of the system" (Easton and Dennis, 1969: 61; Easton, 1965). It can easily be added that such interpretation depends upon knowledge of these outputs and a "belief system" that is flexible enough to respond to them. Whether or not large numbers of the general public within any system respond to periodic changes in foreign policy behavior should first be ascertained. It then may be determined to what degree this sensitivity to policy affects the level of support for these policies.[8]

Long-term ("diffuse") support taps the degree to which the citizenry is in tune with the more general policy stance of its government. This is measured by the degree to which the basic direction of policy (or action) toward a foreign nation is congruent with the basic orientation of public attitudes. Certainly long-term support also depends upon some knowledge of the programs and activities of government at various points in time; yet this facet of support, in Easton's terms, refers to more generalized trust and confidence and is "not contingent on any *quid pro quo;* it is offered unconditionally" (Easton and Dennis, 1969: 63). Especially in a policy area as remote from most people as foreign policy, long-term support is heavily relied upon by those in authority.

Based on these general remarks, we shall state more precisely the hypotheses to be tested in this study.

Hypotheses 1 and 2 follow directly from our previous discussion:

(1) *Support as congruence.* In the long run, the nature (conflictual or co-operative) and intensity of interactions between two nations will be congruent with the nature and intensity of attitudes held by the people in each nation toward the other nation. The relationship should be moderately strong.

(2) *Support as sensitivity..* In the short run, shifts in the nature and intensity of interactions between nations will tend to occur coincidently with shifts in the nature and intensity of attitudinal affect between the corresponding peoples. The relationship should be weak.

The third hypothesis, regarding the direction of relationship between attitudes and events, predicts that changes in attitudes, if any, occur subsequent to changes in behavior patterns between nations. This hypothesis does not rule out the influence of public opinion in the establishment of foreign policy, especially among selected or special-interests publics and in the long run, but it does assume that in the majority of cases, the aggregated "opinion" of the entire adult population in any country represents the dependent rather than the independent variable.

(3) *Direction of relationship.* In the short run, shifts in the nature and intensity of interactions between nations will tend to occur prior to shifts in the nature and intensity of attitudinal affect between peoples.

In order to test these hypotheses, we turn to a more detailed discussion of the measurement of "citizen attitudes" and "foreign policy behavior."

MEASURING CITIZEN ATTITUDES AND FOREIGN POLICY BEHAVIOR

In addition to the problems that we have outlined above, investigations into the relationship between government policies and citizen attitudes encounter the further difficulty of operationalizing the broad concepts of "public attitudes" and "foreign policy." In this regard we have chosen to make use of two time-series data sets that we believe are well-suited for the study of supportive linkages. The first of these data sets measures public affect toward foreign nations, and the second measures various types of interaction between pairs of governments.

Attitudinal Data

Since 1952 the United States Information Agency has been engaged in an ambitious program of cross-national survey research directed at gauging public *evaluations* of important international issues and public *feelings* about other nations. Issue-related survey questions, of course, are specific to particular circumstances and time periods, and the public attitudes they elicit are as likely to reflect the unique characteristics of these issues as they are some more general notion of public sentiment. Furthermore, a comparison of public response to two different issues must take into consideration differences in the wording of survey questions, the ultimate effect of which is very difficult to determine.[9]

Feelings about foreign nations, on the other hand, tend to exist over an extended period of time, both before issues arise and long after they are forgotten.[10] In addition, the wording of survey questions tapping the dimension of public affect for foreign nations need not be changed as the issues and events of international politics change. As a result, using the notion of affect toward nations as a barometer of public support for its government's policies toward these nations gives us a consistently worded index of both long-term trends and short-term shifts in attitude.

One question that can provide us with a general measure of citizen affect has been asked on each of the U.S.I.A.'s surveys conducted since 1954. It reads as follows:

Question: Please use this card to tell me your feelings about various countries. First (the United States/ the Soviet Union/ Britain/ France/ West Germany/ Italy). Second ... etc.

Responses: Very favorable (very good) opinion; Favorable (good) opinion; Fair (neither good nor bad) opinion; Unfavorable (bad) opinion; Very unfavorable (very bad) opinion.

This simple, non-directive question taps a very diffuse collection of attitudes toward other nations. Its apparent drawback is that it does not refer to an explicit set of national characteristics or attributes and therefore we have no way of knowing which symbols and associations serve as referents to the respondent prior to his expression of feelings. It is, however, *because* the sole cue lies in the name of the nation and *because* it asks about the person's "feelings" that we believe this question to be of particular value for our study.

Most research into public opinion has shown that specific knowledge of international affairs, be it the political activity of other nations or the foreign policy of one's own nation, is quite limited. On the other hand, most people are aware of and hold general feelings about foreign nations, especially those which for various reasons are salient to many of their fellow countrymen and to their government. We would hypothesize that these general feelings often serve as a lens through which people view interactions among nations, filtering perceptions and constraining beliefs. The relative stability of these feelings, and their acquisition early in one's lifetime, serve as evidence in support of this hypothesis.

If we are correct, then this central, anchoring dimension of people's images of the international environment ought to be considered a key measure of public confidence in or dissatisfaction with national policies and behavior toward other nations. We can draw an analogy with evidence from the study of American voting behavior (see Campbell et al., 1960; Abravanel, 1971). In predicting a person's vote, for example, it is (statistically) less significant to know that he agrees with a candidate's policy on a specific issue, like civil rights, than to know that he likes the Republican Party and dislikes the Democratic Party, or that he changed his basic affections from Democrat to Republican at some time in the past. Support for a party, measured by votes, is highly correlated with affection for the party. We would contend that positive identification with a foreign nation, like positive identification with a political party, also gives structure to a person's other opinions and behavior. In the study of citizen attitudes toward foreign policy (i.e., policy toward other nations), the U.S.I.A.'s non-directive question dealing with likes and dislikes of foreign nations can serve as an important indicator of the level of public support for these policies.

We shall make use of the U.S.I.A. surveys that were conducted repeatedly between 1954 and 1965, with a primary focus on four nations: Great Britain, France, Italy, and West Germany. The question measuring affect was put to citizens in each of these nations, with the referent being each of the remaining three countries plus the United States and the Soviet Union. Although there are a possible twenty dyads of nations for which we have attitudinal data, three were excluded from the study because of incomplete data over the eleven-year period.[11]

Events-Interaction Data

Foreign policy behavior consists of many diverse actions, including state visits and meetings, agreements and treaties, exchanges of notes, United Nations votes, economic, military, and technical aid, and military action or threats of action. A nation's foreign policy posture toward another nation consists of a combination of all these things, and judgments made about the relations between two nations on the basis of a selected number of such actions is likely to be incomplete and inadequate.

It was partly in search of a composite measure of international interaction that events-interaction data were developed. In constructing an index of foreign policy behavior, it is necessary to weight different actions, making the assumption, therefore, of some underlying dimension. Most international actions can be placed along dimensions of co-operation and conflict, and accordingly scales have been developed to assign intensity values to the various types of international actions. By summing over a period of time (day, week, month, or year), one can obtain a composite measure of co-operation or conflict between any two nations.

The technique for collecting events-interaction data involves culling from newspaper indexes, or other chronologies of events, all cases of interaction between nations. The events are then ranked (either by the investigator or by judges) on dimensions of conflict or co-operation according to predetermined guidelines. The individually weighted events can then be combined to form a general index of co-operation or conflict.[12]

The source of events for the present study is *Keesing's Contemporary Archives*. It has been noted frequently by users of events-interaction data that no source is complete in its coverage of events (Azar, 1970). For instance, *Keesing's* as a British publication is likely to report actions involving Britain somewhat more fully than events in which other nations are involved. Comparison of *Keesing's* data with data from *The New York Times Index* and *Facts on File* over a two-year period, however, showed that *Keesing's* did contain nearly all events that involved clear-cut action as opposed to official speeches or government statements. Although *Keesing's* did not adequately report speeches of decision-makers that were directed at other countries, in our scale these speeches were not included as events. For our purposes, events are restricted to occurrences clearly involving "action." As an obvious consequence, among the four Western European nations we found only low levels of conflict; that is, few conflictual actions occurred.

In sum, events-interaction data offer a measure of general foreign policy behavior with high face validity. It remains to be discussed just how the events data can be juxtaposed with the attitudinal data in order to test our hypotheses.

TESTING PROCEDURES

We have mentioned the problem of response objects in the study of public support for foreign policy, and as we have argued, these have not generally been treated independently. The first response object involves a nation's basic foreign policy stance toward specific nations. Our interest here is in the degree of long-term attitude-policy congruence. For instance, United States behavior toward the Soviet Union is much less co-operative and much more conflictual than United States behavior toward the United Kingdom. Similarly, the attitudes of American citizens are more favorable toward Great Britain than toward the U.S.S.R. It would be difficult indeed for the United States government to begin pursuing a foreign policy based on as high a level of cooperation with the Soviet Union as with the British without *some* attitudinal change.

By comparing our attitudinal data and events data, we can examine the degree to which there exists a general congruence between foreign policy directed at particular nations and feelings toward these nations. If congruent, the correlation between these two data types—across our seventeen dyads in each time period—should be quite high. In order to test this hypothesis, the events data were summed on the dimension of co-operation into yearly intervals and compared with the relevant surveys.[13] The attitudinal summary measure consists of the sum of those respondents who felt "good" and those who felt "very good" toward another nation.

In order to test the first hypothesis we correlated the events data measure with the attitudinal measure across the seventeen dyads for each year from 1954 to 1965.[14] The correlations are presented in the following section. A number of variations of the two summary measures were tried, but few changed the correlations substantially and none raised them. It was felt, for instance, that it might be useful to look at the relationship between "bad" attitudes and conflict within the events data. It was also felt that it might be useful to compute a value of net co-operation based on co-operation minus conflict, and to correlate this with a net measure of attitudinal affect (favorable feelings minus unfavorable feelings). Still other variations consisted of weighting "very good" or "very bad" feelings more heavily than "good" or "bad" opinions (to incorporate the factor of "intensity") or to weight conflict more heavily than co-operation in computing the net co-operation measure. As noted, none of these variations increased the magnitude of the correlation coefficients.

The second hypothesis concerns the short-term association between attitudes and foreign policy behavior. It should be clear that the foreign policy of the United States toward the Soviet Union can be generally consistent with American public opinion, while day-to-day variations in policy which deviate from the more basic orientation may not affect public attitudes. In order to test the sensitivity hypothesis we make use of the longitudinal dimension of our data. Our basic question is whether or not changes in the level of co-operation between two nations give rise to modifications in public regard for the participating nation.[15]

In testing the third hypothesis we introduce the problem of causality. Fortunately, the best indicator of causal relationship (although by no means proof of it) is temporal precedence. Our procedure for suggesting the direction of causality is to compute correlations allowing feelings to lag six months, one year, eighteen months, two years, or even four years behind events. Similarly, we allowed events to lag up to four years behind attitudes. In this way we hope to explore further the issue of citizen-policy linkages.

DATA ANALYSIS

Event-Attitude Congruity

We can look first at long-term congruence between levels of attitudinal affect and event interaction. The cross-sectional correlations displayed in Table 1, relating the amount of cooperation between pairs of nations to the level of favorable feelings held by the public in the acting nation,[16] suggest a surprisingly strong relationship over the seventeen dyads for a one-year period. Two different treatments of the events data (a yearly average and a running average over three-year periods) were correlated with two different treatments of the attitudinal data (a simple sum of all good and very good attitudes, and an intensity measure weighting very good responses twice as heavily as the good responses). It appears from Table 1 that the measure used is largely irrelevant.

TABLE 1

PEARSON PRODUCT MOMENT CORRELATIONS OF CO-OPERATIVE EVENTS INTERACTION DATA AND FAVORABLE PUBLIC OPINION DATA.
N=17 NATION-DYADS

Approach	1955	'56	'57	'58	'59	'60	'61	'62	'63	'64	'65	Average
1	.19	.24	.28	.41	.32	.73	.50	.69	.72	.70	.42	.49
2	.28	.26	.28	.37	.37	.60	.63	.69	.73	.79	.58	.51
3	.16	.20	.21	.29	.24	.56	.40	.62	.69	.63	.32	.39
4	.22	.22	.21	.28	.26	.52	.55	.60	.68	.74	.50	.43
Average	.21	.23	.24	.34	.30	.65	.52	.65	.71	.72	.46	.46

Approach 1: Very good plus good attitudes versus co-operative events
Approach 2: Very good plus good attitudes versus moving average co-operative events
Approach 3: Twice very good plus good attitudes versus co-operative events
Approach 4: Twice very good plus good attitudes versus moving average co-operative events

None of the correlations in Table 1 takes on negative value, and the lowest positive coefficient is .16. The correlations range to a high of .79, with an average value of .46.[17] There can be little doubt that the general level of cooperation within these seventeen dyads reflects, or is reflected by, the level of good feelings among the mass public. The results obtained with correlating bad feelings and conflict behavior are more striking (see Table 2). In this case the average correlation is .67, with a range whose upper limit is .90.[18]

There is a very obvious reason why these correlations are high: four of the dyads contained attitudes toward and relations with the Soviet Union. Feelings about the Soviet Union were consistently and strongly unfavorable at the same time that cooperation with the U.S.S.R. was low and conflict was high. These four dyads represent extreme points to which the Pearson product moment correlations reacted very "positively." It is thus interesting (and informative) to look at the correlations for nations whose actions and attitudes vary to a lesser degree.

Table 3 correlates positive feelings with co-operation with the four dyads in which the Soviet Union was the target eliminated from the calculations. The differences are dramatic. Similar results can also be seen in Table 4 which presents correlations of negative feelings and conflict, but which again omits the four U.S.S.R. dyads. In neither Table 3 nor Table 4 is there any relationship between nation-affect and foreign policy behavior. This is not surprising since differences in policy orientations among the European nations are, relatively speaking, not very substantial. A uniformly high rate of cooperative actions characterized all dyads, and differences in level appear largely determined by the proximity and size of the nations involved.

TABLE 2

PEARSON PRODUCT MOMENT CORRELATIONS OF CONFLICTUAL EVENTS INTERACTION DATA AND UNFAVORABLE PUBLIC OPINION DATA. N=17 NATION-DYADS

Approach	1955	'56	'57	'58	'59	'60	'61	'62	'63	'64	'65	Average
1	.85	.76	.40	.87	.81	.45	.63	.87	.70	.28	.17	.62
2	.77	.84	.68	.87	.90	.67	.70	.85	.81	.65	.29	.73
3	.86	.75	.38	.88	.81	.41	.61	.88	.72	.31	.15	.61
4	.79	.86	.67	.88	.90	.64	.68	.85	.82	.67	.29	.73
Average	.82	.80	.53	.88	.86	.54	.66	.86	.76	.48	.23	.67

Approach 1: Very bad plus bad attitudes versus conflict events
Approach 2: Very bad plus bad attitudes versus moving average conflict events
Approach 3: Twice very bad plus bad attitudes versus conflict events
Approach 4: Twice very bad plus bad attitudes versus moving average conflict events

TABLE 3
PEARSON PRODUCT MOMENT CORRELATIONS OF CO-OPERATIVE EVENTS INTERACTION DATA AND FAVORABLE PUBLIC OPINION DATA.
N=13 NATION-DYADS

Approach	1955	'56	'57	'58	'59	'60	'61	'62	'63	'64	'65	Average
1	−.50	−.19	−.38	−.47	.17	.30	−.17	.22	.57	.37	−.14	−.02
2	−.51	−.27	−.39	−.43	−.15	.26	.10	.17	.50	.59	.05	−.01
3	−.43	−.18	−.38	−.51	.12	.23	−.29	.18	.55	.30	−.23	−.06
4	−.48	−.25	−.37	−.43	−.20	.17	−.01	.08	.46	.54	−.02	−.05
Average	−.48	−.18	−.38	−.46	−.02	.24	−.09	.16	.52	.45	−.09	−.03

Note: For an explanation of the four approaches see Table 1.

Differences in attitudes are more substantial, with the French and Germans manifesting a good degree of attitudinal distance, and with the British feeling much less positive toward the Italians than the Italians felt toward the British.

To this point we have been examining data relevant to the first hypothesis that suggested a general congruence between public opinion and foreign policy behavior. Tables 1 and 2 show convincingly that major differences in interstate interaction patterns are highly related to similar differences in patterns of nation-affect. Tables 3 and 4 show that where policy differences between nations are less dramatic, the frequency of conflict or cooperation is unrelated to the factor of public esteem for target nations.

Event-Attitude Sensitivity

We turn to a second set of questions. To what degree is the public sensitive to discrete events and to changes in foreign policy, and conversely, how responsive are policy changes to public opinion?

TABLE 4
PEARSON PRODUCT MOMENT CORRELATIONS OF CONFLICTUAL EVENTS INTERACTION DATA AND UNFAVORABLE PUBLIC OPINION DATA.
N=13 NATION-DYADS

Approach	1955	'56	'57	'58	'59	'60	'61	'62	'63	'64	'65	Average
1	.00	.48	.11	−.01	.61	−.03	−.11	−.19	−.00	−.17	.04	.07
2	−.44	.33	.17	.25	.42	.06	−.09	−.08	−.06	−.14	−.00	.04
3	.00	.44	.10	.08	.53	−.03	−.17	−.21	.02	−.15	−.05	.06
4	−.40	.29	.15	.25	.34	.03	−.15	−.14	−.05	−.13	.00	.02
Average	−.22	.39	.13	.14	.48	.01	−.13	−.16	−.02	−.15	.02	.04

Note: For an explanation of the four approaches see Table 2.

Table 5 lists longitudinal correlations between the level of cooperation within individual dyads, and the frequency of favorable attitudes toward the target nation within the acting country. These Pearson product moment correlations were computed using yearly intervals for aggregation over the 1955-65 period. Linear trends in the data have been removed by computing yearly changes in the two data types (first differences). In addition to correlating attitudes and events from year to year, lag correlations were introduced allowing both events and attitudes to lag up to two years.[19]

A small average correlation (.26) is obtained between events and feelings when no lag is present, and, as displayed in Table 5, no other average correlation is higher than this. A glance at this table reveals little consistency in these correlations from dyad to dyad, since they range from −.17 to .74. Moreover, the fact that the only meaningful average correlation occurs with zero time lag means that we have no basis for suggesting the direction of relationship.

TABLE 5

PEARSON PRODUCT MOMENT CORRELATIONS OF *YEARLY CHANGE* CO-OPERATIVE EVENTS-INTERACTION DATA AND *YEARLY CHANGE* FAVORABLE PUBLIC OPINION DATA. N=11 YEARS (1956-65)

Dyad	−2	−1	0	1	2
WG-FR	.02	−.39	.08	.05	−.50
IT-FR	.19	.23	−.17	.49	−.55
BR-FR	−.16	.16	.26	−.26	.21
FR-WG	.33	−.56	.24	−.54	.29
IT-WG	.40	−.06	−.04	−.32	.38
BR-WG	.38	−.54	.53	−.10	−.29
FR-BR	.08	−.39	.32	−.18	.11
WG-BR	−.40	−.07	.49	−.04	−.50
IT-BR	.00	.03	.20	−.31	−.43
FR-US	.13	−.17	.65	−.01	−.54
WG-US	.17	−.29	−.02	.44	−.36
IT-US	−.45	.47	.22	−.43	−.42
BR-US	−.15	−.40	.10	.19	−.05
FR-SU	.17	.30	.36	−.42	−.21
WG-SU	−.48	.18	.18	−.06	−.61
IT-SU	.15	−.02	.24	.00	.28
BR-SU	.69	−.57	.74	−.52	.16
Average	.02	−.12	.26	−.12	−.18

Column header (spanning −2 to 2): Lag in years of events behind attitudes

Note: The following abbreviations are used: Britain=BR; France=FR; West Germany=WG; Italy=IT; United States=US; Soviet Union=SU.

TABLE 6
PEARSON PRODUCT MOMENT CORRELATIONS OF YEARLY CHANGE CO-OPERATIVE EVENTS INTERACTION DATA AND YEARLY CHANGE FAVORABLE PUBLIC OPINION DATA. N=11 YEARS (1955-65)

	Lag in years of events behind attitudes			
Dyad	−1.5	−.5	.5	1.5
WG-FR	−.28	.21	.29	−.37
IT-FR	−.37	.35	−.11	−.09
BR-FR	−.51	.89	−.73	.33
FR-WG	.05	−.08	−.17	.21
IT-WG	.56	−.56	.14	.06
BR-WG	−.69	.18	.23	−.48
FR-BR	−.92	.87	−.59	.33
WG-BR	−.49	.68	.19	−.68
IT-BR	−.40	.45	−.32	.01
FR-US	−.24	.89	−.10	−.19
WG-US	−.17	−.15	.22	−.05
IT-US	.12	.32	−.08	−.69
BR-US	−.52	.19	.11	−.07
FR-SU	.14	.63	−.40	−.12
WG-SU	.10	−.03	.22	−.65
IT-SU	.55	−.52	.69	−.14
BR-SU	−.33	.37	−.41	.47
Average	−.20	.28	−.05	−.12

In a further attempt to study direction, we computed correlations with a minimum lag of six months rather than one year. These are presented in Table 6. Again, there is only one suggestive (if small) average correlation: that of .28 *when attitudes are lagged six months behind events.* This is an indication that where sensitivity exists at all, *attitudes respond to events.* As indicated, it should not be generalized from this data that public opinion does not constrain policy. It can only be argued that events (and by implication foreign policy) do not respond to fairly small shifts in nation-affect.

Dyadic Differences

The extent to which individual country dyads deviate from the average requires further discussion. Two aspects of Tables 5 and 6 are especially important in this regard.

(1) *Differences in dyadic correlations between Tables 5 and 6.* If both the zero-lag correlations in Table 5 and the six-month lag correlations in Table 6 characterize the dyads, then correlations for any given dyad should be similar in those two columns of Tables 5

and 6. If they differ substantially, this will suggest a large amount of instability or error in the data.

(2) *Extreme differences between correlations for different dyads.* In Table 6 variation among dyads even exceeds that found in Table 5—they range from −.56 to .89. If it is not possible to explain some of this variation, we will again be forced to question the stability and validity of the data.

Although there are some fairly dramatic changes in correlation level between the dyadic scores in the center column of Table 5 and those in the second column of Table 6, in general the same rank order of correlations are found in both tables. The Spearman rank order correlation is .54, and the Kendall's Tau for the two rank orderings is .30. Since both measures are significant at $p < .05$ (given an N of 17), it appears that there is enough stability in these data to warrant our proceeding to examine variation among dyads. Yet we cannot ignore the presence of instability since this will have a number of consequences.[20] One such result is that the correlations presented above are almost certainly lower than those which would accurately describe the relationship between feelings and events. Furthermore, in trying to explain the variability among correlations, we will obviously be hindered by such large error components. Notwithstanding these caveats, it will be useful to attempt to explain the differences among dyads.

One might first hypothesize that support levels vary in some consistent and meaningful way among "acting countries" whereby countries differ in the degree to which policy change is mirrored by attitude change regardless of the targets of these changes. When the dyads are classified into four groupings on the criterion of acting country, it becomes evident that there is substantial between-country variation. Table 7 presents the four groupings (for both zero lag and six-month lag) and presents the average correlation for each acting country.

It is of interest that the highest average correlations are for France and Britain, the two nations of the set with the longest uninterrupted histories of democracy. That Almond and Verba (1963) classify the British as high on scales of both input and output cognition and affect may be especially noteworthy, for these correlations suggest that interest in public affairs and sensitivity to national policy is related to the more basic linkages between citizen and system. To carry the argument one step further, between the West Germans and the Italians, the correlations are higher for the former. In this regard Almond and Verba found considerable output cognition and affect for the Germans while noting almost total alienation within the Italian "political

TABLE 7
PEARSON PRODUCT MOMENT CORRELATIONS FROM TABLES 5 AND 6, GROUPED BY ACTING STATE AND AVERAGED

France		Great Britain		W. Germany		Italy	
No Lag	6 Mths	No Lag	6 Mths	No Lag	6 Mths	No Lag	6 Mths
.65	.89	.74	.89	.49	.68	.24	.45
.36	.87	.53	.37	.18	.21	.22	.35
.32	.63	.26	.19	.08	−.03	.20	.32
.24	−.08	.10	.18	−.02	−.15	−.04	−.52
						−.17	−.56
.39	.58	.41	.41	.18	.13	.09	.01

culture." Where between-nation differences are significant, then, the implication is that attitude-policy linkages in the American context would be more similar to our findings in the case of Britain than in the case of Italy.[21]

It takes only a glance at Table 7, however, to realize that between-country differences account for only a small part of the total variation among dyads. The ratio of between-to-within country variations is .51, suggesting no significance for country as an explanatory variable. Yet given the instability of the correlations noted earlier, and assuming that such instability might come close to averaging out over the four or five dyads in which each country is involved, it is obvious that between-country differences are important, even if not statistically significant.

We can hypothesize at least two other general explanations that may account for some of the dramatic differences among dyadic correlations, especially those differences that occur within each acting country with regard to various target nations.

First, the public (within a single country) may be more "set" in its response to some target nations than to others. Within most cultures we find that there are some nation-objects that are more rigidly stereotyped (either favorably or unfavorably) than others, possibly as a result of longstanding friendship or longstanding hostilities. Attitudes toward these nations are hardly likely to vary in response to relatively minor fluctuations in policy. Consider, for instance, American attitudes toward the Soviet Union, French attitudes toward Germany, or Israeli attitudes toward Egypt. Such an attitudinal set would obviously *decrease* correlations between nation-affect and inter-nation events.

Alternatively, however, differences between dyadic correlations may be accounted for by the concept of salience. In this case we would argue that (assuming no difference in attitudinal set) the more salient a dyad, the more likely that people of one of the nations will respond to governmental behavior toward the second nation. Based on any number of prior "causes," saliency of particular nations would be a function of visibility, news reporting, interest, and so forth. These factors facilitate information flow which in turn may stimulate attitude formation and change.

In one sense, attitude set and salience may represent opposite tendencies. Yet it seems reasonable to hypothesize that all possible combinations of the two variables can occur, so that, for example, citizens in country A may be very "set" in their attitudes toward a very salient foreign country, B, and toward a much less salient country, C. The remaining two logical possibilities also appear reasonable.[22] These concepts, independently or together, may help to explain the high degree of variability among dyadic correlations.

These hypotheses can be tested if we can devise measures of the fixity of attitudinal set and of the salience of specific foreign nations. Since set implies little change or movement of attitudes, we will examine the degree to which the aggregate feelings of a country for its dyadic counterpart varied over the twelve-year period. For instance, within the German population the largest percentage of those who felt "very good" toward France was 6 per cent in 1963, and the smallest percentage was 1 per cent occurring in six different years. The difference between the two extremes is 5 per cent. This, added to the variation in percentage of those feeling "good" toward France (32 per cent), "bad" (28 per cent), and "very bad" (8 per cent), gives a final total of 73 per cent. Ranking third among the seventeen dyads, this represents a high level of variability.

Developing a measure of salience is more difficult.[23] Although a rough measure could be built on subjective determinations, it is very difficult to judge, for example, whether the Germans or the Americans are more salient for the French. It would be even more difficult to compare the salience of the Germans to the British as opposed to the salience of the Italians for the French.

A major component of the importance of one country to another is the rate of interaction between countries. Pairs of nations whose relationships are characterized by a high level of cooperation or conflict are likely to consider each other important. There are certainly important exceptions to this— Chinese-American relations are an obvious example. Yet within the European context, the closest parallel to the U.S.-China example (where nations are artifically separated) is probably West Germany and the Soviet Union. If we include conflict in our discussion of interaction, moreover, we can partially overcome even this problem. Consider, for instance, a measure of saliency for each dyad based on the highest level of cooperation over the twelve-year period plus the highest level of conflict. On this measure, the two most salient dyads are Britain-Soviet Union and France-Soviet Union. Clearly then, the four nations in our data set frequently interact across ideological barriers, and thus we judge these interactions to constitute one index of saliency.

Although rate of inter-nation transactions is not a completely satisfactory measure of a nation's salience for a second nation, it has one particular advantage that should be noted. The events data are gathered from stories appearing in newspapers throughout the world, and this partially reflects the journalist's notions of importance. These conceptions may well be shared by (or imparted to) the general public.

Table 8 is a presentation of the dyadic correlations (an average of the correlations with no time lag and with six-months lag) as they relate to our measures of salience and set. The dyads were ranked on each of the two measures, and for the sake of presentation these ranks were grouped into three categories representing "high," "medium," and "low" values of each variable. We can see in this table that there is some relationship between the variables and the correlations, and we should particularly underscore the fact that all three of the negative correlations fell into the lower right-hand corner of the table—as they should according to our previous expectations. There is little other support for our hypotheses in this table.

As a second test of our explanatory hypotheses, correlation coefficients were computed between the ranked correlations (again averages of zero lag and six-months lag) and the ranked set and salience measures. The Spearman rank order correlations are −.31 and .26 respectively. (Kendall's tau correlations are −.13 and .13.) These correlations are in the predicted direction but are not significant.

The average correlations are used here because there is little reason to assert the superiority of either the set of correlations obtained with no lag or

TABLE 8

		Attitudinal Set	
Salience	12-17 (low)	6-11 (medium)	1-5 (high)
1-5 (high)	BR-SU (.56) FR-SU (.50) WG-FR (.15)	FR-WG (.08)	BR-US (.15)
6-11 (medium)	WG-BR (.59)	BR-FR (.53) IT-FR (.26)	BR-WG (.37) FR-BR (.60) IT-WG (−.30)
12-17 (low)	IT-BR (.33)	FR-US (.77) IT-SU (−.14) WG-SU (.08)	IT-US (.27) WG-US (−.08)

that obtained with attitudes lagging six months behind events. The major argument to distinguish them, however, is that we would expect attitudes to respond to events rather rapidly. Thus we are inclined toward the correlations obtained with no lag. When these coefficients are ranked, and rank order correlations computed to relate them to the measures of attitudinal set and salience, the Spearman rank correlations climb to −.38 and .37 respectively. (The taus are −.24 and .17.) Given an N of 17, the correlation with attitude set is significant at $p < .1$.

These correlations do not allow us to reject the null hypothesis implied by our set and salience explanations. Nevertheless, the correlations consistently support the explanations. We could not have expected much higher correlations given the instability of the data as documented earlier. If a more accurate procedure could be developed for relating attitudes and events, not only might the relationships with attitudinal set and nation saliency increase but the explanatory power of country differences would almost certainly be much greater.

SUMMARY

Our intention has been to expand upon the literature dealing with linkages between public opinion and foreign policy by departing from previous studies in two respects. First, we have introduced time series data. This has allowed us to distinguish between short-term change and long-term congruency in the attitude-policy relationship. Second, to deal with the variability of the relationship between popular beliefs and foreign policy, our investigation was built on a total of seventeen dyads of nations. In exploring the conditions underlying observed variability, we have focused upon differences between countries, upon attitudinal stability, and upon country saliency. Our findings can be summarized as follows:

(1) In the short run, changes in attitudes and shifts in policy are correlated at a relatively low level. And to the degree that a short-term relationship can be found, it is the public that responds to government action rather than vice versa. While the relationship between the two is probably greater than the average correlation of .28 reported above, our finding is consistent with other research which indicates that a relatively small segment of the public normally relates to governmental behavior. The portion of the public which is concerned with foreign policy has been called by Almond the "attentive public" (including those who are opinion makers).[24] Our correlation between attitudes and events varia-

bility is small not only because this portion of the public is small but because we are dealing with an even smaller subset—the attentive public which responds to government action by changing attitudes in the direction corresponding to that action.

(2) When the objects of governmental policy and citizen attitudes are the major countries of Western Europe plus the United States and the Soviet Union, a high level of congruency between behavior and belief is visible. Major differences in national policy orientations are reflected in equally large differences in public affect. Whereas in the short run few people are even aware of most government foreign policy actions, let alone responsive to those actions in changing attitudes, in the long run a process of diffusion of opinion takes place. Media and interpersonal communications certainly are more effective in reaching a wide portion of the public over a long period of time than they are immediately following an event.[25]

(3) Three variables were examined and found to affect the strength of relationship between policy and beliefs: country differences, set, and salience. Country differences, although not statistically significant, exist and affect the relationship in a relatively interesting fashion. The relationship is high in France and Britain, low in Germany, and even lower in Italy. Attitudinal "set" decreases the degree to which a public responds to governmental behavior, and country saliency increases the degree to which a country's population reacts to the cues present in its government's behavior toward other nations.

In conclusion, we find Figure 1 a useful summary of the linkage between governmental action and immediate public attitude change. The individual is the unit of analysis in the diagram. The flow chart presents a series of conditions which must be met if the individual is to change his attitude in correspondence with the governmental action. Clearly these conditions are met infrequently. Over time, the attitudes of a wider public will change, either in response to especially salient events or to the influence of other people.

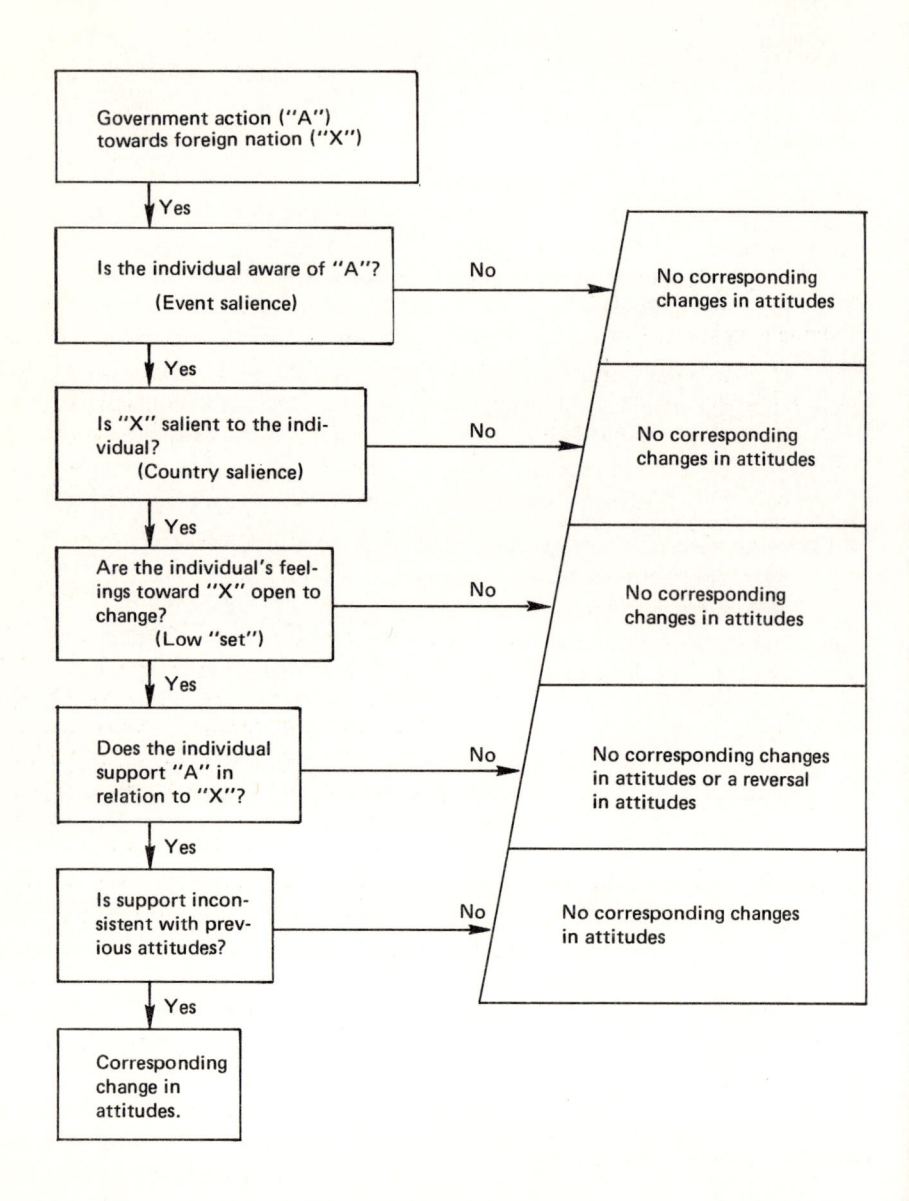

```
                    Government action ("A")
                    towards foreign nation ("X")
                              │
                              ▼ Yes
                    ┌─────────────────────┐     No      ┌──────────────────┐
                    │ Is the individual   │────────────▶│ No corresponding │
                    │ aware of "A"?       │             │ changes in       │
                    │ (Event salience)    │             │ attitudes        │
                    └─────────────────────┘             └──────────────────┘
                              │
                              ▼ Yes
                    ┌─────────────────────┐     No      ┌──────────────────┐
                    │ Is "X" salient to   │────────────▶│ No corresponding │
                    │ the individual?     │             │ changes in       │
                    │ (Country salience)  │             │ attitudes        │
                    └─────────────────────┘             └──────────────────┘
                              │
                              ▼ Yes
                    ┌─────────────────────┐     No      ┌──────────────────┐
                    │ Are the individual's│────────────▶│ No corresponding │
                    │ feelings toward "X" │             │ changes in       │
                    │ open to change?     │             │ attitudes        │
                    │ (Low "set")         │             │                  │
                    └─────────────────────┘             └──────────────────┘
                              │
                              ▼ Yes
                    ┌─────────────────────┐     No      ┌────────────────────────┐
                    │ Does the individual │────────────▶│ No corresponding       │
                    │ support "A" in      │             │ changes in attitudes   │
                    │ relation to "X"?    │             │ or a reversal          │
                    │                     │             │ in attitudes           │
                    └─────────────────────┘             └────────────────────────┘
                              │
                              ▼ Yes
                    ┌─────────────────────┐     No      ┌──────────────────┐
                    │ Is support incon-   │────────────▶│ No corresponding │
                    │ sistent with prev-  │             │ changes in       │
                    │ ious attitudes?     │             │ attitudes        │
                    └─────────────────────┘             └──────────────────┘
                              │
                              ▼ Yes
                    ┌─────────────────────┐
                    │ Corresponding       │
                    │ change in           │
                    │ attitudes.          │
                    └─────────────────────┘
```

Figure 1: THE RELATIONSHIP BETWEEN A FOREIGN POLICY ACTION AND PUBLIC ATTITUDE CHANGE TOWARD THE TARGET NATION

NOTES

1. The term has also been used in other contexts and with other meanings. For instance, Rosenau (1969) used the term to denote the relationship between domestic and foreign politics.

2. Precisely for these reasons, Key (1964: 411) commented that "discussion of public opinion often loses persuasiveness as it deals with the crucial question of how public opinion and governmental action are linked." On the subject of linkages, see Norman R. Luttbeg (1968).

3. For examples of this approach, see Black and Gergen (1963), Davies (1952), Robinson (1967), Willick (1970), Rogers et al. (1967), McClosky (1967), Belknap and Campbell (1951-52), Lott and Lott (1963), Smith (1961), Halle (1966), and Kuroda (1964).

4. See, for example, Miller and Stokes (1963), Rosenberg (1967), Buchanan and Cantril (1953), Almond (1960), Rosenau (1961), Rosenberg (1965), Rosi (1965), Epstein (1964: 142-146), Mueller (1971), Richman (1970) and for a general discussion of the issue, Key (1964: 551-558).

5. Oscamp (1965) reports a tendency to evaluate favorably actions attributed to one's own country while judging the very same actions unfavorably when they are attributed to another country. Katz and Piret (1963) find that foreign policy failures attributed to the President often result in public approval of the President.

6. Most of the research cited above utilizes data gathered from a single nation or from a limited segment of its population. See, however, many of the chapters in Kelman (1965) which combine focused studies with the findings of diverse secondary sources. Scott (1965), for example, analyzes surveys conducted independently in a number of different countries and integrates his findings with published research from an additional set of countries. Other exceptions include Davis and Verba (1960), Buchanan and Cantril (1953), Lerner and Gorden (1969).

7. Cross-national studies of general interest to the political scientist include Almond and Verba (1963), Dennis et al. (1968), Buchanan and Cantril (1953), Cantril (1965), Converse and Dupeux (1966), Alford (1963), Davis and Verba (1960), and Lambert and Klineberg (1967). Of the above examples, only Alford and Davis-Verba utilize a time dimension, and these studies are distinguished from the remainder in that they re-analyze data originally conducted by various polling agencies for purposes other than their use by these researchers.

8. Rosenau (1961), among others, reports that public knowledge of foreign affairs is generally very low, and this of course would serve to reduce any correlation between shifts in policy and shifts in public opinion. Among the many reasons for such a relative lack of public information on the subject of international affairs is the fact that newspaper space allocated to foreign affairs constitutes no more than 5 to 8 per cent of the total space in American newspapers (see Cohen, 1963). These facts should be considered in the interpretation of our findings as presented since we do not distinguish among the general public on the criterion of international affairs knowledge.

9. On the subject of question wording, see, for instance, the discussion in Mueller (1971: 367-368).

10. See Deutsch and Merritt (1965) and Lambert and Klineberg (1967). The first study, using aggregate comparisons over time, finds that large segments of the Western European population hold semi-permanent feelings toward foreign nations, while the

second study documents the existence of attitudes (and stereotypes) toward foreign countries in young children.

11. Survey data regarding French, British, and West German feelings toward Italy are available for only five of the eleven years. It was impossible to extend the study beyond 1965 because the USIA substantially reduced the number of its surveys in some subsequent years. For a discussion of USIA data-collection procedures, see Merritt and Puchala (1968).

12. The present study uses a 30-point scale developed by Moses et al. (1967).

13. Only cooperative actions are used in testing our hypotheses because of the low level of conflict among the four Western European nations. The number of events involved in the analysis differed very substantially for each dyad and for each year. To give some idea of the N here, we identified more than 9,000 events (many multilateral) for 26 nations over a 20-year period.

14. When more than one attitudinal survey was taken in the period of a year, the surveys were averaged.

15. It should be noted that although one-year intervals are useful in examining the general level of congruence between attitudes and events, they are less useful for the study of short-term sensitivity. In fact, even one-half year intervals may conceal a considerable amount of shorter range change. In testing this hypothesis it would be desirable to introduce intervals as short as a month, but unfortunately the U.S.I.A. surveys are not conducted as regularly or as frequently as this would require. For an analysis usefully employing much shorter time periods see Richman (1970).

16. Because of the symmetry in the events data, the level of cooperation is the same for acting and target nations. The level of good feelings does vary between actor and target nations.

17. Average correlations will be used in this section to provide summary descriptions of lists of correlation coefficients. Such averages lack any statistical meaning in terms of relationship.

18. Attempts were made to combine into net indices the positive and negative measures of events and attitudes, so as to obtain an overall correlation. It was not found possible, however, to build a combination measure so that the obvious correlation between the two data types remained. It is for this reason, and because of the scarcity of conflictual events in many dyads, that the study will rely primarily upon the two positive measures.

19. Table 5 shows lags of no more than two years because none of the larger lag periods proved to be of any particular interest in interpreting our findings. Richman (1970) has also contrasted "long term" with "short term" relationships. His procedure is similar, but the interested reader should refer to his very imaginative paper.

20. Instability is hardly unexpected since we are aggregating data into yearly periods. Moreover, the surveys in a year vary in number and chronological relationship to major international events which more generally affect public opinion. It would be ideal if we could manage to conduct a "pre-survey," note the occurrence immediately afterward of a salient international event, and follow this with a second survey. Unfortunately, we are not likely to find this possible.

21. Unfortunately, Almond and Verba did not include France among the countries studied, for numerous scholars have struggled to characterize the French political culture with much less evidence (and often, with more impressionistic evidence) than is applied in the Five Nation study. Although affect toward authorities and government seems to

be generally negative in the French context, there may be a tendency to accept the policies and decisions of the executive and particularly of the bureaucracy. This, coupled with more interest in foreign policy than, for example, in Italy, might help to explain the fairly high correlations noted above. See Ambler (1971: 47-71).

22. In fact, the Spearman rank order correlation between the two measures is only $-.37$. Kendall's tau is $-.29$.

23. See Merritt (1968). Merritt's measure of salience is based upon the percentage of a population which characterizes its feelings toward another nation as either good or bad. Specifically, his measure is total responses minus twice the sum of "don't know" and neutral responses, over total responses. His measure does not correlate positively with ours. In fact, Spearman's r equals $-.34$.

24. Almond (1960). James Rosenau stresses the variability of this public by writing of "attention publics" (1961: 27-37).

25. The second step of the "two step flow" process obviously can involve many "steps," with the steps often separated by some length of time. See Katz and Lazarsfeld (1955).

REFERENCES

ABRAVANEL, M. (1971) Affect, beliefs, and international affairs: Soviet-American competition and the national images of mass publics. Ph.D. Dissertation. University of Wisconsin.
ALFORD, R. (1963) Party and Society. Chicago: Rand McNally.
ALMOND, G. A. (1960) The American People and Foreign Policy. New York: Praeger.
--- and S. VERBA (1963) The Civic Culture. Princeton: Princeton Univ. Press.
AMBLER, J. (1971) The Government and Politics of France. New York: Houghton Mifflin.
AZAR, E. (1970) "Analysis of international events." Peace Research Reviews 4 (November): 28-35.
BELKNAP, G. and A. CAMPBELL (1951-52) "Political party identification and attitudes toward foreign policy." Public Opinion Quarterly 15 (Winter): 601-623.
BERELSON, B. and G. STEINER (1964) Human Behavior. New York: Harcourt, Brace.
BLACK, K. W. and K. GERGEN (1963) "Public opinion and international relations." Social Problems 11 (Summer): 77-87.
BOBROW, D. and N. CUTLER (1968) "Time oriented explanations of national security beliefs: cohort, life-state and situation." Peace Research Society (International) Papers 8.
BUCHANAN, W. and H. CANTRIL (1953) How Nations See Each Other. Urbana: Univ. of Illinois Press.
CAMPBELL, A., P. CONVERSE, W. MILLER, and D. STOKES (1960) The American Voter. New York: John Wiley.
CAMPBELL, J. T. and L. S. CAIN (1965) "Public opinion and the outbreak of war." Journal of Conflict Resolution 9: 318-329.
CANTRIL, H. (1965) Patterns of Human Concerns. New Brunswick, N.J.: Rutgers Univ. Press.
CASPARY, W. R. (1970) "The 'mood theory': a study of public opinion and foreign policy." American Political Science Review 64 (June): 536-547.
COHEN, B. (1963) The Press and Foreign Policy. Princeton: Princeton Univ. Press.

CONVERSE, P. and G. DUPEUX (1966) "Politicization of the electorate in France and the United States," Ch. 14 in A. Campbell et al. (eds.) Elections and the Political Order. New York: John Wiley.

DAVIES, J. C. (1952) "Some relations between events and attitudes." American Political Science Review 46 (September): 777-789.

DAVIS, M. and S. VERBA (1960) "Party affiliation and international opinions in Britain and France, 1947-1956." Public Opinion Quarterly 24: 590-604.

DENNIS, J., L. LINDBERG, D. McCRONE, and R. STIEFBOLD (1968) "Political socialization to democratic orientations in four Western systems." Comparative Political Studies 1: 71-101.

DEUTSCH, K. and R. MERRITT (1965) "Effects of events on national and international images," pp. 132-187 in H. C. Kelman (ed.) International Behavior. New York: Holt, Rinehart & Winston.

EASTON, D. (1965) A Systems Analysis of Political Life. New York: John Wiley.

--- and J. DENNIS (1969) Children in the Political System. New York: McGraw-Hill.

EPSTEIN, L. (1964) British Politics in the Suez Crisis. Urbana: Univ. of Illinois Press.

GAMSON, W. and A. MODIGLIANI (1966) "Knowledge and foreign policy opinions: some models for consideration." Public Opinion Quarterly 30 (Summer): 187-199.

HALLE, N. H. (1966) "Social position and foreign policy attitudes." Journal of Peace Research 3: 46-74.

KATZ, E. and P. F. LAZARSFELD (1955) Personal influence. New York: Free Press.

KATZ, F. and F. PIRET (1963-64) "Circuitous participation in politics." American Journal of Sociology 69: 367-373.

KELMAN, H. C. (1965) International Behavior. New York: Holt, Rinehart & Winston.

KEY, V. O., Jr. (1964) Public Opinion and American Democracy. New York: Alfred A. Knopf.

KURODA, Y. (1964) "Correlates of the attitudes toward peace." Background 8: 205-214.

LAMBERT, W. and O. KLINEBERG (1967) Children's Views of Foreign Peoples. New York: Appleton-Century-Crofts.

LERNER, D. and M. GORDEN (1969) Euratlantica: Changing Perspectives of the European Elites. Cambridge: MIT Press.

LOTT, A. J. and B. E. LOTT (1963) "Ethnocentrism and space superiority judgments following cosmonaut and astronaut flights." Public Opinion Quarterly 27: 604-611.

LUTTBEG, N. R. [ed.] (1968) Public Opinion and Public Policy. Homewood, Ill.: Dorsey.

McCLOSKY, H. (1967) "Personality and attitude correlates of foreign policy orientation," pp. 51-109 in J. C. Rosenau (ed.) Domestic Sources of Foreign Policy. New York: Free Press.

MERRITT, R. (1968) "Visual representation of mutual friendliness," pp. 111-141 in R. Merritt and D. Puchala (eds.) Western European Perspectives on International Affairs. New York: Praeger.

--- and D. PUCHALA (1968) Western European Perspectives on International Affairs. New York: Praeger.

MILLER, W. E. (1967) "Voting and foreign policy," pp. 213-230 in J. Rosenau (ed.) Domestic Sources of Foreign Policy. New York: Free Press.

--- and D. E. STOKES (1963) "Constituency influence in Congress." American Political Science Review 57 (March): 45-56.

MOSES, L., R. BRODY, O. HOLSTI, J. KADANE, and J. MILSTEIN (1967) "Scaling data on inter-nation action." Science 156 (May): 1054-1059.
MUELLER, J. E. (1971) "Trends in popular support for the wars in Korea and Vietnam." American Political Science Review 65 (June): 358-375.
OSCAMP, S. (1965) "Attitudes toward U.S. and Russian actions: a double standard." Psychological Reports 16: 43-46.
PETERSON, S. (1971) "International events, foreign policy-making, elite attitudes, and mass opinion: a correlational analysis." Delivered at the twelfth annual convention of the International Studies Association (March).
PRZEWORSKI, A. and H. TEUNE (1970) The Logic of Comparative Social Inquiry. New York: John Wiley.
RICHMAN, A. (1970) "Public opinion and foreign affairs: the mediating influence of educational level." Delivered at the sixty-sixth annual convention of the American Political Science Association (September).
ROBINSON, J. P. (1967) "World affairs information and mass media exposure." Journalism Quarterly 44 (Spring): 23-30.
ROGERS, W. C., B. STUHLER, and D. KOENIG (1967) "A comparison of informed and general public opinion on U.S. foreign policy." Public Opinion Quarterly 31 (Summer): 242-252.
ROSENAU, J. N. (1969) Linkage Politics. New York: Free Press.
--- (1961) Public Opinion and Foreign Policy. New York: Random House.
ROSENBERG, M. J. (1967) "Attitude change and foreign policy in the cold war era," pp. 111-159 in J. Rosenau (ed.) Domestic Sources of Foreign Policy. New York: Free Press.
--- (1965) "Images in relation to the policy process: American public opinion on cold-war issues," pp. 278-334 in H. C. Kelman (ed.) International Behavior. New York: Holt, Rinehart & Winston.
ROSI, E. J. (1965) "Mass and attentive opinion on nuclear weapons tests and fallout, 1954-1963." Public Opinion Quarterly 29 (Summer): 280-297.
SCOTT, W. (1965) "Psychological and social correlates of international images," pp. 71-103 in H. C. Kelman (ed.) International Behavior. New York: Holt, Rinehart & Winston.
SMITH, P. A. (1961) "Opinions, publics, and world affairs in the United States." Western Political Quarterly 14: 698-714.
WILLICK, D. H. (1970) "Foreign affairs and party choice." American Journal of Sociology 75 (January): 530-549.

Chapter 5

THE IMPACT OF DEFENSE SPENDING ON SENATORIAL VOTING BEHAVIOR: A STUDY OF FOREIGN POLICY FEEDBACK

STEPHEN COBB
Tennessee State University

For the past several years, one of the major controversies in sociology has concerned the question of how national policy is determined and by whom. Many authors have suggested that the foreign and domestic policy of the United States may be unduly influenced by what some have termed a "military-industrial complex" (Mills, 1956; Cook, 1962; Lens, 1970). At its most basic level, the theory of the military-industrial complex maintains that a combination of industrial interests and military officers work together with high executive branch officials to insure that the level of defense expenditure remains high.

According to this theory, the career interests of the high military officers lead them to support a large military establishment. Under conditions of peace and a small military machine such as we have had throughout much of

AUTHOR'S NOTE: *The author wishes to thank Nancy Hendrix Cobb for her support and her critical readings of earlier drafts of this paper; also Richard A. Peterson, Leo Rigsby, and John McCarthy for their time and suggestions. A greatly revised paper based on this same data is scheduled to appear in* Testing the Theory of the Military-Industrial Complex, *edited by Steven Rosen and published by D. C. Heath in 1973.*

the history of this country, the opportunities for advancement and satisfying careers are severely limited for the professional officer. The officer corps has repeatedly been the "victim" of massive cutbacks in defense spending at the termination of the various conflicts in which the United States has participated.

The theory suggests that the economic dependence of some private firms on government contracts for war materiel leads them to work with military officers to keep up the level of defense spending. It is suggested that at least part of the reason for the relative absence of the traditional drop in defense expenditures after World War II was the liaison of military officers and potential or actual defense contractors or persons whose firms could expect to benefit from heavy defense spending.[1]

One hypothesis which may be derived from the notion of a military-industrial complex is that members of Congress are being pressured into voting for high levels of defense spending and aggressive foreign policies by their defense-oriented constituents. Firms dependent on defense expenditures are hypothesized to be generating public support and lobbying directly for foreign policies and levels of defense spending which will insure their prosperity. As Turner (1951) has noted, congressmen are usually quite responsive to the major organized members of their constituencies. Bolton (1966) has shown that the economic size of defense firms, especially in some areas, is sufficient to classify them as "major" and powerful constituents.

There have been a number of empirical studies of the relationship between defense spending and congressional voting in several areas. Cobb (1969 and 1972a) has studied this relationship in the House of Representatives. He found almost no evidence that concentrations of defense spending had an influence on how members of the House voted on a series of foreign policy issues labeled the Jingoism scales. The only exception to this lack of relationship occurred among representatives with a great deal of seniority and, to a lesser degree, among those who were members of important House committees such as Ways and Means or Armed Services.

Investigations into this relationship have also been performed for the United States Senate. Gray and Gregory (1968) found there were small but statistically significant (Tau) correlations between their measure of defense spending based on total military spending as a percentage of total income in a state and two of their five voting scales. Correlations of $-.14$ (in the expected direction) were found between defense spending and their scale of "liberalism" and between defense spending and their scale entitled "foreign aid-test ban." Three other scales, including one labeled "cold war-ethnocentrism," were not significantly related to defense spending. They used votes from the 88th Congress (1963-64).

Russett (1970a) investigated the relationship between several different measures of defense spending and several scales of Senate voting.[2] He was concerned with the 87th Congress (1961-62) and the 90th Congress (1967-68). For the 87th Congress he constructed three separate Guttman scales covering somewhat different content areas which he called "General Defense," "Military Assistance," and "Aerospace." For the 90th Congress he constructed four scales entitled "General Defense," "NASA," "Gun Control," and "Arms Sales."

For the 87th Congress, Russett found that his General Defense scale was significantly correlated with only one of the five measures of defense spending he used. Using a rank-order correlation (Kendall's tau), he obtained a figure of .14 (in the expected direction) between this scale and Department of Defense military payrolls index.[3] When he controlled for region, his only significant correlation disappeared, leaving no significant correlations between defense spending and the general-defense scale of Senate voting. When controlled for party, the correlation between Defense Department military payrolls increased to .21 and a formerly non-significant correlation between Defense Department civilian payrolls and general defense became significant (.13).

There were other significant correlations between various measures of defense spending and his other two scales, military assistance and aerospace. However, the direction of the correlations presented an unstable pattern in that it would be in the expected direction (postive) in one instance and in a direction conflicting with Russett's hypothesis in another. Perhaps the most consistent finding was that prime contract awards showed no correlation with any scale under any controlled or uncontrolled conditions.

For the 90th Congress, Russett found somewhat more impressive evidence of a relationship between defense spending and voting. He found that both military and civilian Defense Department payroll indices showed significant or near-significant (if relatively small) relationships with the General Defense scale. This pattern held up under uncontrolled conditions and when party or region was controlled. The correlations range from .11 to .28. Again, he found no relationship between prime contract allocation and voting on the General Defense scale. He also found no relationship between three other measures of defense spending and voting on this scale. Several of his defense spending measures were correlated with NASA voting. The figures ranged from below .10 to .17 (in the expected direction). There were considerably fewer correlations between spending and the Arms Sales scale (ranging from below .11 to .14). The relationships were somewhat higher between various measures of spending and voting on the Gun Control scale (ranging up to

−.27) but were not consistent in direction. He concludes (Russett, 1970a: 75):

> *Clearly, Department of Defense expenditures for military installations go to support and reinforce if not to promote a set of hawkish and strongly anti-communist postures in American political life.*

Later (1970a: 77) he adds:

> The correlations are not, it must be noted, astonishingly high—nor did our original expectations, which recognized the data handicap of using heterogeneous states as units of analysis and identified the probable sources of many deviations from the simplest expectations, anticipate very high correlations.

In short, though his pattern of correlations appears rather weak and somewhat inconsistent, he concludes that there is support for the hypothesis that defense spending concentrations do affect the voting of United States senators. His results and the results of Gray and Gregory contradict those of Cobb to the degree that the limited pattern of significant correlations in the former studies is taken as support for the basic hypothesis of these studies. In this paper, we shall investigate the relationship between Senate voting and defense spending and try to resolve the discrepancies between the previous studies.

THE JINGOISM SCALES

We have constructed two separate scales of roll-call votes in the United States Senate. Based on the universe of roll-call votes from the first session of the 89th Congress (1965) and the first session of the 90th Congress (1967), we have been able to develop two five-item Guttman scales which we interpret to reflect dimensions of jingoism analogous to those reported in Cobb (1969, 1972a).

The years 1965 and 1967 were chosen because defense spending data were readily available for those years and because there were votes on relevant issues in the Senate with sufficient variance to allow us to attempt to construct a Guttman scale. Further, it was of some interest to correlate the analysis of the Senate with the earlier analyses of the House (Cobb, 1969, 1972a) in order to eliminate differences in years as a possible source of different findings.

Investigation of the relationship between defense spending and voting is perhaps more difficult in that states are very large and heterogeneous. It is unlikely that a state will be as dependent on any one industry as can be the

TABLE 1
THE 1965 SENATE JINGOISM SCALE

Number	Issue	Difficulty[a]
CQA 155[b]	Young Amendment to reduce $124,370,000 Defense Dept. Civil Defense funds to $97,190,000 as passed by the House[c]	15%
CQA 28	Foreign relations committee amendment to reduce Arms Control and Disarmament agency funds from $40,000,000 to $20,000,000	41%
CQA 12	Appropriations committee move to strike House prohibition of Food for Peace sales to Egypt and substitute a somewhat less restrictive clause	49%
CQA 90	Miller amendment to prohibit aid to any country more than 1 year behind in its payment of U.N. assessments unless President determines and reports otherwise	67%
CQA 29	Passage of bill authorizing $20,000,000 for the Arms Control and Disarmament Agency	84%

The coefficient of reproducibility is .944

a. Difficulty is measured by the percentage of all senators who voted in a non-jingoistic manner. All signs of intent were used including voting, pairing, the announcement of preference, and responses to the CQA poll.
b. CQA refers to the Congressional Quarterly Almanac.
c. Yea votes on items 1, 3, and 5 were considered non-jingoistic while negative votes on items 2, and 4 were considered non-jingoistic.

case in some congressional districts. However, there are a number of reasons for studying the Senate, including that body's historic concern with foreign and defense policy. Even today the Foreign Relations Committee is accorded the highest prestige. The Senate shares with the House the power of the purse. The cost of foreign and defense policy today is very great. This increases the potential importance of the legislature in the conduct of foreign affairs and increases the need to understand voting patterns on these issues.

The Democrats and the Republicans could be scaled together in both 1965 and 1967. We interpret this to mean that members of both parties view these issues as representing points along the same dimension and that they felt that the particular issues were ordered along that dimension in one particular array.

MEASURING DEFENSE SPENDING

We have computed six measures of defense spending, one of which was based on Pentagon-supplied figures on defense-created jobs and one of which

TABLE 2
THE 1967 SENATE JINGOISM SCALE

Number	Issue	Difficulty[a]
CQA 91	Selective Service Act of 1967. Morse amendment to permit a registrant to be represented by a lawyer when appearing before his draft board[b]	21%
CQA 106	Selective Service Act of 1967. Adoption of the conference report extending draft and forbidding the institution of a lottery	24%
CQA 156	Tower amendment restoring authorization of Department of Defense revolving funds for arms sales aid	49%
CQA 46	Mundt move to prevent pending consular treaty with the Soviet Union from taking effect until the President determined that U.S. troops were no longer needed in South Vietnam or that U.S. troop removal was not being hampered or delayed by Soviet military aid to North Vietnam	72%
CQA 79	Amendment declaring that Congress would provide all necessary support to U.S. servicemen fighting in Vietnam and that Congress supported (1) persons trying to bring about an honorable settlement in Vietnam and (2) persons trying to convene an international meeting to plan an end to the war	79%

The coefficient of reproducibility is .94

a. Difficulty is measured as the percentage of all senators who voted (or paired, announced, etc.) against the jingoistic vote.
b. A yea vote on issues 1 and 5 was considered non-jingoistic. Nay votes on all other issues were considered non-jingoistic.

was based on 1964 fiscal-year data, and which will both be correlated with the 1965 Jingoism scale; and four of which were based on fiscal 1967 data, and which will be correlated with the 1967 Jingoism scale. It would be preferable to have to compute only one accurate measure of defense spending, reflecting jobs generated in an area as a percentage of total employment or similar figure for each year of the study. This has not been possible because the Pentagon will not release detailed and accurate data on things like sub-contracting, which would make the computation of such figures possible. These data are not available because of security considerations and because the government desires to protect the proprietary information of the companies which furnished it to the government in confidence.

The first measure, called "Defense Involvement" or DI, is defined as the total value of all Defense Department prime contracts allocated to a state as a percentage of the total value added by manufacture in that state.[4] The value of the prime contracts is divided by this measure of industrial activity because the impact of a contract of a given size would vary depending upon how large a percentage of the state's economy it constituted.

An important defect involved in using prime contract data as an indicator of defense spending concentrations is that approximately 50 per cent of all prime contracts on the average are in turn sub-contracted out to another firm. These sub-contracting firms may be, but often are not, in the same state as the firm to which the contract was originally let. Therefore, knowing where a prime contract is allocated is not the same as knowing where the money involved is actually spent and has its impact. It is possible that public announcements of contracts by important political figures may help to overcome this difficulty to some extent by making the senator and his constituents feel dependent on these contracts even when a part is to be sub-contracted out of the state. Bolton (1966: 17) discusses these problems in greater detail.

$$DI = \frac{\text{Prime Contract Value--Fiscal 1964}}{\text{Value Added by Manufacture}}$$

Cobb (1969) discusses other types of error which may be expected when using prime contract and value added by manufacture statistics. The measures used in his article are analogous to the first two measures of defense spending we utilize in this paper.

The second measure of defense spending is defined as total number of defense generated jobs in a state divided by the total state work force. It is entitled "Defense Dependency" or DD.

$$DD = \frac{\text{Total State Defense Generated Jobs}}{\text{Total State Work Force}}$$

Buehler (1967) reports a defense-dependency score by states which we have utilized. His figures for DD include work done on all prime contracts over $10,000, all military and civilian employment at defense installations, and an estimated 12 per cent of the total indirect employment generated in everything from raw materials to finished product manufacture (DOD Bulletin, 1966). It includes sub-contracted work only at the top 400 companies (in terms of defense contract allocation) surveyed. This measure is based on data gathered by the Pentagon's Economic Information System's Plantwide Economic Report and Individual Project Report Program, which were begun in 1966.

The next measure of defense spending is based on the allocation of military prime contracts for the fiscal year 1967. It is entitled "Defense Involvement (military)" or DIM and is defined as the total value of military prime contracts allocated to a state as a percentage of the total value added by manufacture.

$$DIM = \frac{\text{Military Prime Contracts–Fiscal 1967}}{\text{Value Added by Manufacture}}$$

The defects in this measure are similar to those discussed with regard to DI. Prime contracts are often sub-contracted out in whole or part and our data do not contain information on this sub-contracting. Therefore, this measure does not indicate as well as might be hoped where defense spending actually becomes wages and profits. The problems associated with the use of "value added by manufacture" are present. It should be noted that unlike DI, which is based on both military and civil functions prime contracts together, DIM is based only on the military prime contract.

There is another source of error in this indicator. The numerator is taken from the fiscal year in question (fiscal 1967) while the denominator comes from the 1963 Census of Manufactures. If, for example, all areas did not grow at an equal rate between 1964 and 1967, some error would be introduced.[5] Due to the short period of time involved, the error is likely to be minimal.

The second measure of defense spending is called "Defense Involvement (civilian)" or DIC. DIC is the total value of civil functions prime contracts as a percentage of the total industrial activity, again measured by "value added by manufacture" in the state.

$$DIC = \frac{\text{Civil Functions Prime Contracts–Fiscal 1967}}{\text{Value Added by Manufacture}}$$

The problems associated with this measure are approximately the same as were discussed with reference to DIM. The reason for creating a separate index based on civil functions contracts was to determine if the absence of correlations between prime contracts and voting found in certain studies (Cobb, 1969, 1972a) was attributable to the fact that civil functions prime contracts might be less visible or dramatic in their impact on a district and hence serve to reduce the correlation between spending and voting.

The third measure of defense spending is called "Defense Dependency (military)" or DDM. It is defined as the total military payroll in a state as a percentage of the total income of that state.

$$DDM = \frac{\text{Total Military Payroll–Fiscal 1967}}{\text{Total Income}}$$

The figure for the total income of the state is based on the 1960 census figures. The military payrolls are taken from Pentagon data furnished for fiscal 1967. If income has grown unevenly among the states, some error will be introduced.

The final measure of defense spending is called "Defense Dependency (civilian)" or DDC. This is defined as the total Department of Defense payrolls in a state paid to civilian employees as a percentage of the total income of the state.

$$DDC = \frac{\text{Total Civilian Payroll--Fiscal 1967}}{\text{Total Income}}$$

The difficulties with this measure are the same as those experienced with DDM. The advantage of separating the two kinds of payrolls again hinges on the possibility that military payrolls have a more obvious impact on a district. The shopkeeper who lives by the trade of uniformed military personnel is perhaps somewhat more likely to be aware of the source of his prosperity than is the merchant whose customers are civilian employees of the Department of Defense.

FINDINGS

Table 3 lists a series of correlations between defense spending (DI and DD) and the 1965 Senate Jingoism scale under various controlled conditions. None of the correlation coefficients shown in Table 3 are significant at the .05 level. Party and region (coded as a series of dummy variables) were expected to show a strong relationship with voting on our scales (Turner, 1951). Therefore, it was conceivable that the effects of these variables might

TABLE 3
CORRELATIONS BETWEEN 1965 SENATE VOTING AND
MEASURES OF DEFENSE SPENDING
N=99

Correlation type[a]	DD	DI	Criterion[b]
Uncontrolled	-.029	.074	-.197
Controlled for Region[c]	-.040	.038	-.195
Controlled for Party[c]	-.072	.058	-.195
Controlled for Region and Party	-.120	.007	-.193

a. All correlations, except when otherwise noted, are product-moment.
b. The criterion level is the level a correlation must attain to be statistically significant at the .05 level.
c. Coded and entered by means of dummy variables.

have been obscuring a small but statistically significant relationship between DI and 1965 Jingoism or DD and 1965 Jingoism. However, Table 3 shows that even when controls are imposed, in no case does the relationship between spending and voting reach the level of statistical significance.[6]

Half of the small correlations found in Table 3 do not have the expected sign. From the method of construction of our scales of Senate voting it is clear that the correlation between spending and voting should be strongly negative if our hypothesis of a relationship is true. In the case of the relationship between 1965 Jingoism and DD, the correlations are in the expected direction though not statistically significant. In the case of the relationship between 1965 Jingoism and DI, the correlation coefficients are both statistically non-significant and in the wrong direction. Even if they were significant, they could hardly be viewed as confirmation of our hypothesis. Were we to find significant, positive correlations we would be forced to conclude that the more dependent a senator is on defense spending, the less likely he is to vote for belligerent, jingoistic foreign policies. While extremely interesting, if a pattern of such correlations were found it would not constitute support of our original hypothesis.

Therefore, we find in Table 3 no support for the hypothesis that the votes of United States senators on the foreign and defense policy issues listed in our 1965 Jingoism scale are influenced by the amount of defense spending in their districts. This result does not really contradict the findings of Russett for 1961-62. He finds few significant correlations in the expected direction between his various measures of defense spending and his scales, especially the important General Defense scale (Russett, 1970a: 72).

Table 4 reports a series of correlations between defense spending measures based on 1967 data and voting on the 1967 Senate Jingoism scale. For the Senate as a whole, only two of the correlations are significant at the .05 level.

TABLE 4

CORRELATIONS BETWEEN 1967 SENATE VOTING ON JINGOISM SCALE AND SEVERAL MEASURES OF DEFENSE SPENDING WITH CONTROLS
N=99

Correlation Type	DIM	DIC	DDM	DDC	Criterion
Uncontrolled	.138	.165	−.036	−.007	−.197
Controlled for Region	.145	.247*	.002	−.021	−.195
Controlled for Party	.083	.107	−.107	−.081	−.195
Controlled for Party and Region	.065	.210*	−.021	−.059	−.193

*Statistically significant.

These two significant relationships are between dependency on civil functions prime contracts and voting controlled for region and controlled for region and party. These two significant correlations are not in the expected direction. The interpretation would have to be that a senator from a dependent state would be less likely to vote for jingoistic foreign policy measures. This would not support our hypothesis. Russett found no instances of significant correlations between prime contract allocation and voting either in 1961-62 or 1967-68.

All the correlations between prime contract data and voting are in a direction which does not confirm our hypothesis. Seven of eight correlations between defense spending measures based on 1967 payrolls (DDM and DDC) are in the expected direction. None, however, are statistically significant. Therefore, we find no support in Table 4 for the hypothesis that the votes of United States senators on foreign policy issues studied are influenced by the amount of defense spending in their states. The findings of Table 4 are in partial disagreement with the findings of Russett. He, too, found no relationship between voting and prime contract allocation. He did, however, find a series of small but significant rank-order correlations between voting and spending measures based on payrolls of the Department of Defense.

When entered in this order, region makes the largest contribution to the explanation of variance in the 1965 Jingoism scale. Party explains a

TABLE 5

VARIANCE EXPLAINED IN SENATE VOTING ON THE JINGOISM SCALE BY INDEPENDENT VARIABLES IN A GIVEN ORDER
N=99

Variable	Per Cent of Variance	Sign
1965		
Party affiliation	6.2	−
Region represented	20.9	
DI	0.0	
Party affiliation	6.2	−
Region represented	20.9	
DD	1.0	−
1967		
Party affiliation	10.7	−
Region represented	14.7	
DIT	0.5	+
Party affiliation	10.7	−
Region represented	14.7	
DDT	0.0	

substantial portion of the total explained variance though it is not as powerful as region. When DI is added, no additional variance in the Jingoism scale is explained. Though not surprising in view of the pattern of correlations found in previous tables, it reinforces and vividly demonstrates those findings.

In another part of the same table, the addition of DD after the entering of party and region explains an additional per cent of the variance in the 1965 Jingoism scale. It is consistent with Russett's findings to have a larger effect for a jobs-based measure of defense spending than for prime contracts. The effect in this table, though present, is not large.

The bottom half of Table 5 reports the results of a similar regression computation explaining variance in the 1967 Jingoism scale using 1967 defense spending, party, and region figures. Party and region are again entered first and the variance they explain is listed. The correlations reported in previous tables indicate that separate computation of DIM and DIC would not be productive. DIT, the measure of defense spending used in part of Table 5, is a composite of DIM and DIC representing total military and civil functions prime contracts in a state as a percentage of the value added by manufacture in that state. Party explains almost 11 per cent of the variance in 1967 Jingoism while region explains about 15 per cent. DIT explains only an additional one-half of 1 per cent.

At the bottom of Table 5 the final computation is reported. DDT is the total dependency on both military and civilian payrolls measured as a percentage of total state income. DDT adds no additional variance to that explained by party and region. This finding is not consistent with Russett's findings in that he found that payroll-based spending indices (such as our DDM, DDC, and DDT) were better able to explain voting than prime contract-based indices (such as our DIM, DIC, and DIT). While the spending figures in our study for 1965 and 1967 are not perfectly comparable, the findings reported at the bottom of Table 5 appear to be somewhat inconsistent with the findings reported at the top of that table. In short, while DIT did show a small effect on 1967 Jingoism, this table gives little support to the contention that there is a relationship between defense spending and foreign policy voting by senators.

We hypothesized that membership on a powerful committee or high seniority would be related to spending and voting and would serve to obscure the relationship between voting and spending (Cobb, 1972a). We therefore correlated DI and DD with the 1965 Jingoism scale under controlled conditions. The partial correlations and the zero-order relationship for comparison are reported in Table 6. None of the correlations obtained were significant at the .05 level. Table 7 reports the results of similar tests for the 1967 data.

TABLE 6
CORRELATIONS BETWEEN SENATE VOTING ON 1965 JINGOISM AND MEASURES OF DEFENSE SPENDING
N=99

Correlation Type	DI	DD	Criterion
Uncontrolled	.074	−.029	−.197
Controlled for membership[a] on important committees	.069	−.032	−.195
Controlled for seniority	.071	−.050	−.195

a. For the purposes of this study, the important committees are Appropriations, Foreign Relations, and Armed Services.

In this table, the correlations between DIC and voting on the 1967 Jingoism scale and DIM and Jingoism are larger than those reported between DI and the 1965 Jingoism scale. However, they, like those between DI and 1965 Jingoism, are not in the expected direction and, hence, do not confirm the hypothesis. The only significant correlation in Table 7 (between DIC and 1967 Jingoism controlled for seniority) is not in the expected direction. Tables 6 and 7 do not lend much support to the original hypothesis.

It could be hypothesized that those senators whose power and seniority were especially needed to pass defense and foreign policy would be especially likely to be rewarded with the allocation of defense spending to their states if they voted jingoistically. Cobb (1972a) has demonstrated such a pattern in the House of Representatives. We have divided our sample into two groups—those with high seniority and those with less. In this manner we hoped to uncover any relationship between spending and voting that might be occurring in only one of the groups. The results are reported in the first part of Table 8 and do not lend support to the original hypothesis for the 1965 Jingoism scale and the measures of spending shown. The correlations between DI and Jingoism (1965) remain small and in the direction opposite to that expected. While the

TABLE 7
CORRELATIONS BETWEEN SENATE VOTING ON 1967 JINGOISM SCALE AND VARIOUS MEASURES OF DEFENSE SPENDING

Correlation Type	DIM	DIC	DDM	DDC	Criterion
Uncontrolled	.138	.165	−.036	−.007	−.197
Controlled for membership on important committee	.139	.169	−.003	−.040	−.195
Controlled for seniority	.135	.205*	−.005	−.51	−.195

*Statistically significant but not in the expected direction.

TABLE 8

CORRELATIONS BETWEEN SENATE VOTING ON 1965 JINGOISM SCALE AND MEASURES OF DEFENSE SPENDING

Power Group	N	DI	DD	Criterion
Whole Senate[a]	99	.074	−.029	−.197
Senior members	54	.069	−.033	−.268
Non-senior members	45	.036	−.116	−.294
Powerful committee members[b]	54	.138	.071	−.268
Non-powerful committee members	45	.000	−.127	−.294

a. Mean number of terms in the Senate for this group is 3.97 (almost 24 years). The mean for the non-senior group is 1.61 terms (almost 10 years).
b. Member of the Appropriations, Foreign Relations, or Armed Services Committees.

correlation between spending and voting was higher and in the expected direction among the non-senior members of the Senate, the coefficients are not statistically significant. It should be noted that the correlation which was higher was not the figure which was expected to increase.

The Senate was also divided by committee membership. Those senators who were members of powerful committees might be expected to be especially likely to be rewarded for jingoistic voting. The correlations reported in the second part of Table 8 do not support this belief and therefore provided no support for the original hypothesis.

Table 9 reports the results of similar tests with the 1967 defense spending and voting data. The correlations based on prime contract measures of defense spending are not significant and are positive. Most of the correlations based on payroll measures of spending are in the expected negative direction. However, only one of them is statistically significant. It is somewhat

TABLE 9

CORRELATIONS BETWEEN SENATE VOTING ON 1967 JINGOISM SCALE AND MEASURES OF DEFENSE SPENDING
N=99

Power Groups	N	DIM	DIC	DDM	DDC	Criterion
Whole Senate	99	.138	.165	−.036	−.007	−.197
Senior members	54	.145	.193	−.018	−.126	−.268
Non-senior members	45	.063	.222	−.130	−.499*	−.294
Powerful committee members	54	.217	.196	−.031	.005	−.268
Non-powerful committee members	45	.057	.134	−.050	−.012	−.294

*Statistically significant

TABLE 10
MEAN CHANGE IN DI-DIT[a] BY CHANGES IN JINGOISM
N=99

Group	N	Mean Change
Those who became LESS jingoistic	29	.111
Those who stayed the SAME in jingoism	31	.083
Those who became MORE jingoistic	39	−.003
Total Sample	99	.057

a. Change = 1967 DIT−1964 DI.

surprising to find that the correlation between the 1967 Jingoism scale and a spending measure based on civilian payrolls is larger than that between 1967 Jingoism and military payrolls. This correlation appears to be essentially random and generates little confidence in the original hypothesis in the face of the lack of significant correlations in most of the other attempts.

Before attempting to draw final conclusions, we shall examine two tables which make use of the limited over-time changes possible with our data. For Table 10 we have divided our sample into three approximately equal groups on the basis of a comparison between their 1965 Jingoism and their 1967 Jingoism scores. The first group is comprised of those whose Jingoism scores went up between 1965 and 1967.[7] This indicates that the senator became less jingoistic in his voting between those years. The second group is comprised of those whose scores remained the same, while the final group had scores which decreased, indicating that they were voting in a more jingoistic manner. If our original hypothesis is true, we should expect to find that those senators who became more jingoistic should have a greater increase in dependence on defense spending than the other groups. That is, we would expect that as a man became more jingoistic, he would be rewarded by the allocation of more military funds to his state.

Inspection of Table 10 indicates that this expectation is not supported by the data. What effect there is operates in a manner contrary to our expectations. Those whose voting became less jingoistic were on the average more dependent on defense spending. Those who became more jingoistic in their voting were on the average slightly less dependent on defense spending in their areas. Those whose voting had remained the same had become more dependent upon defense spending, though to a lesser degree than those who became less jingoistic. This pattern lends little support to contention that military spending concentrations influence senators to vote more jingoistically.

Table 11 is an attempt to determine whether senators with high seniority

TABLE 11
MEAN CHANGE IN DI BY POWER GROUPS[a]

Power Group	N	Mean Change in DI
Whole Senate	99	.045
Senior senators	54	.037
Non-seniors	45	.046
Members of powerful committees	54	.053
Non-members of such committees	45	.031

a. Change=1967 DIM−1964 DI. This measure will probably underestimate changes slightly.

or those who are members of powerful committees are more likely over-time to see jingoistic voting rewarded by increases in defense spending in their states sufficient to increase the dependence of those states on that spending. The findings again lend little support to the original hypothesis. Those who are members of powerful committees are more likely to increase their dependence on defense spending than those who are not members of such committees. However, those with high seniority are actually increasing their dependence on defense spending less than those with less seniority. The first result supports the original hypothesis while the latter does not.

CONCLUSIONS

The findings reported in this paper do not support the contention that defense spending concentrations have a significant influence on the manner in which senators vote on issues in the area of foreign policy. Our findings support the conclusions reached by earlier studies of the House (Cobb, 1969, 1972a) but conflict with at least the interpretations of the findings of the earlier studies of the Senate (Gray and Gregory, 1968; Russett, 1970a).

Russett (1970b) has suggested a number of reasons why our results have differed. We have discussed these differences in detail elsewhere (Cobb, 1972b). A major difference between the studies of the House (Cobb, 1969) and the Senate (Russett, 1970a) was the length of the Guttman scale employed as the dependent variable. In both the earlier House study and the present study of the Senate, we have used small carefully designed scales measuring what we have termed "jingoism." Russett uses much longer scales. We feel, and Russett (1970b) then agreed, that the overlap of items was such that it was likely that we were measuring about the same dimension.

Many of the other differences cited by Russett have been eliminated in the present study. This is a study of the Senate as was Russett's work, for example, and our later year is approximately the same as his later year. A major difference that remains with regard to the statistic employed to ascertain the relationship between spending and voting remains in this paper as it did in the earlier study of the House. We have used the product-moment correlation with its assumptions of linearity and interval level of measurement while Russett uses the Kendall's tau with its rank-order assumptions.

Russett states: "The distribution of military spending impacts by state is notably skewed, with a few states such as Alaska emerging as extreme outliers. Under these conditions, with interval correlations, the outliers exert extreme influence on the presence or absence of an apparent relationship."

Statistically his contention has merit but examination of Figures 1 and 2 would indicate that elimination of the highly dependent states would not materially affect the correlation except to raise the strength of the relationship necessary to attain statistical significance.

Russett also objected to the use of the product-moment statistic on the basis of a refusal to assume a linear relationship between spending and voting. This is a valid fear in that certain curvilinear relationships of high strength

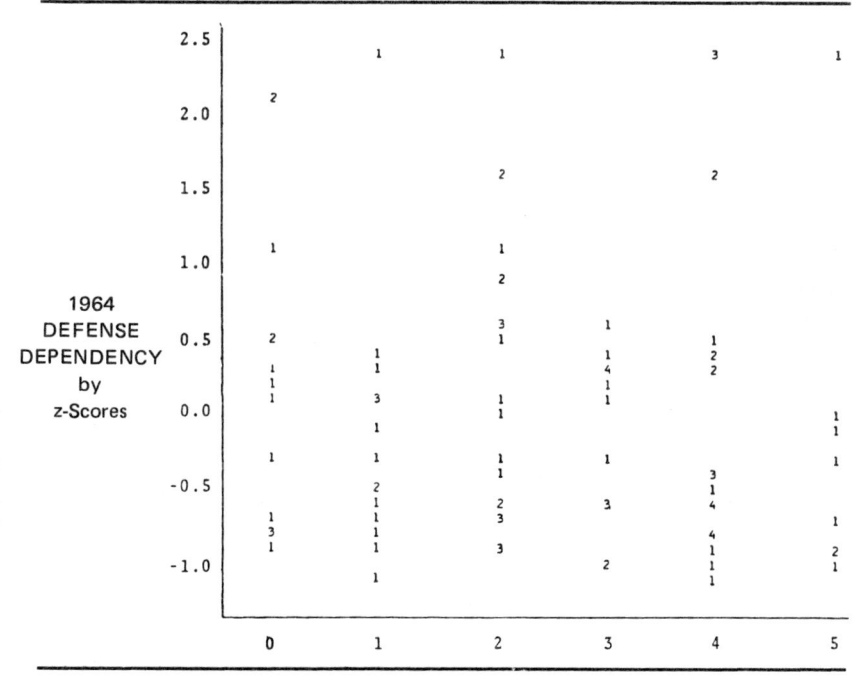

Figure 1: POSSIBLE VALUES ON 1965 JINGOISM SCALE

[152]   FINDINGS

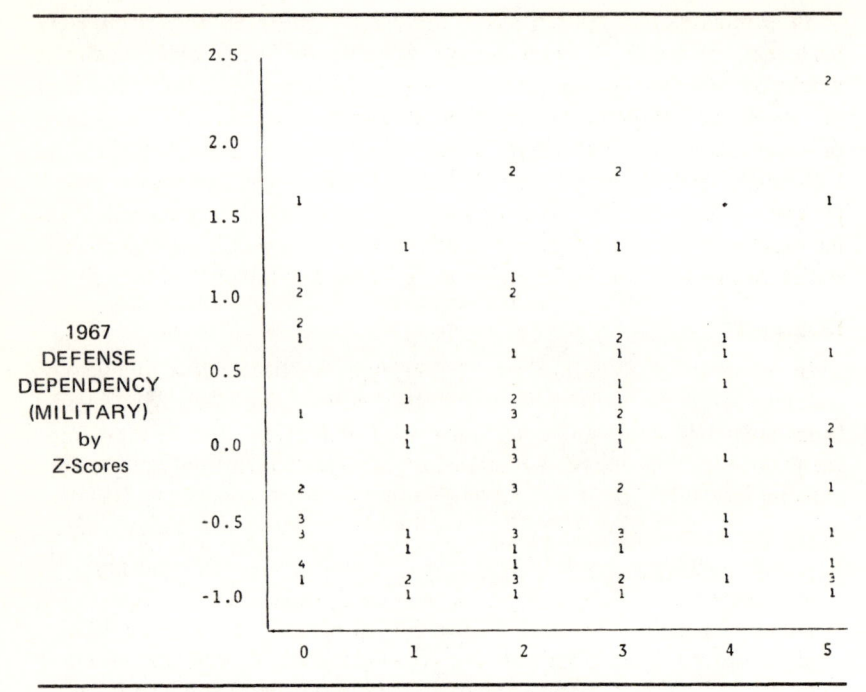

```
                    2.5

                                                                            2
                    2.0
                                              2           2
          1.5       1                                            •          1
                              1                           1
                              1               1
          1.0       2                         2
1967                2
DEFENSE             1                1        2           1
DEPENDENCY 0.5                                1           1
(MILITARY)                    1      2        1
    by              1                3        2
          0.0                 1      1        1                             2
Z-Scores                      1      3                    1                 1
                    2                3        2                             1
         -0.5       3                                     1
                    3         1      3        2           1                 1
                              1      1        1
                    4                1                                      1
                    1         2      3        2           1                 3
         -1.0                 1      1        1                             1

                    0         1      2        3           4                 5
```

Figure 2: POSSIBLE VALUES ON 1967 JINGOISM SCALE

may result in a product-moment correlation near zero because of the assumption of a non-existing linear relationship. Examination of Figures 1 and 2 reveals no pattern of curvilinear relationship between spending and voting such as would have been obscured by the use of the product-moment correlation.

He also indicates a fear that a relationship between spending and voting may exist up to a certain degree of dependence after which increments of dependence do not result in increased concern by the senator for his constituents. A senator might fear or respect a large defense contracting firm just as much as a *very* large defense company. Figures 1 and 2 lend no support to this contention, either.

Finally, there are a number of difficulties inherent in the use of non-parametric statistical methods which are discussed by Cohen (1965: 119). He notes, after a substantial discussion of the issues involved, that "since the premises which underlie the current widespread use of non-parametric methods are generally false, they be relegated to those restricted and infrequent circumstances where they are uniquely appropriate."

In summary, *our figures reveal neither a significant nor a consistent pattern of correlations between defense spending and foreign policy voting.* It would perhaps not be too inaccurate to say that our results differ less than our respective interpretations of them. An eight-ounce glass with four ounces of water can be called half-empty or half-full. Perhaps we are calling that glass half-empty while Russett calls it half-full. In any event, we suggest that a pattern of results this inconsistent and weak, especially if it is dependent for its existence on the somewhat controversial choice of a non-parametric statistical method, is insufficient evidence to support the original hypothesis.

Discussion

In a recent article, Lieberson (1971) expands the range of models of societal governance beyond the traditional "elitist" and "pluralist" notions. In his study of military-industrial linkages, he finds that neither of these ideas adequately fits the data and that a third is suggested. He first sketches the older models (1971: 562):

> On the one hand, the elitists argue that a relatively small group of people representing a relatively narrow range of interests determines national policy across a range of domains including foreign affairs, military spending, and major domestic programs. By contrast, the pluralist school views national decision-making as a process influenced by a broad and diverse array of interest groups with no group or set of groups powerful enough to consistently dominate the national political system.

Lieberson first shows that the elitist argument has some merit by pointing out the large number of retired military officers working for defense contractors, by showing the coordination among corporations, and by showing that the vast bulk of the enormous American defense expenditure goes to a relatively small number of corporations.

However, he goes on to show that few of these large companies are heavily dependent—in percentage terms—on defense spending. He notes that civil functions spending is a more efficient generator of corporate income than military spending and that most industries would gain under disarmament (with a compensating budget increase in non-defense areas). Under these circumstances, it would not seem wise for any broad-scale corporate elite to push for high levels of defense spending.

The pluralist approach fares no better. If the system is thought to be pluralist, it becomes difficult to explain this continued high level of defense spending when the majority of major corporations would gain from disarmament (with compensating non-defense increases) and when military spending is less efficient than civilian for the generation of corporate income.

Lieberson suggests a third alternative approach which he labels the "hypothesis of compensating strategies." He states: "Military spending can be explained by a high level of interest on the part of one segment of American business accompanied by a relative lack of concern on the part of the other segments of industry" (Lieberson, 1971: 578). He feels that industrial concerns will concentrate their efforts in areas which benefit them most directly. They will ignore small losses in other areas in order to concentrate their forces in areas more relevant to their concerns. Industries like aircraft manufacture, ordnance production, and electronics design and construction would suffer considerable losses if armaments spending were to decline precipitously. They will be likely to work to see continued high levels of defense spending.

Melman (1970) carries this idea one step further. He notes that certain defense related industries not only have a "high level of interest" in defense spending, but actually have become part of a super-organization called the "state-management." He believes that the old idea of a military-industrial complex as a loose coordination of businesses, civilian bureaucracies, and military officers based on mutual interests has been superseded. He states that since the early sixties the Pentagon has treated most defense contractors as if they were operating divisions within a larger corporation on the model of the operating divisions of the Ford Motor Company, the previous home of Secretary of Defense Robert McNamara. This hypothesis reinforces the Lieberson notion of close contact between a certain segment of industry and the Defense Department and provides a mechanism through which coordination can be seen to have been maintained.

The most interesting theoretical convergence with Lieberson can be seen in the work of Lowi (1964). He, too, is dissatisfied with both pluralist and elitist models. While he states that these two models *do* provide an accurate analogy to the real operation of forces *in certain "arenas of power,"* he believes that there is a third model of power relations which operates under certain conditions.

Lowi feels that the classic pluralist model of relatively open competition and coalition formation applies in the "arena of regulatory decisions." In the case of such decisions, the competing groups are fighting for limited resources which cannot be infinitely broken down into smaller and smaller packages so that each can receive something. A group either receives the license for a particular TV channel or it does not. The frequency cannot be split into two parts so each may receive something. There is a confrontation of winner and loser, privileged and deprived. In this situation, Lowi maintains that coalitions are formed on the basis of mutual interests in order to present the strongest power position in the fight for the limited rewards available.

He feels that the traditional elitist model operates in what he terms the "arena of redistribution." The decisions in this arena involve the taking of property from one large-scale social group like a social class (the "haves") and giving it to another large-scale group or class (the "have-nots"). Lowi notes (1964: 707):

> Issues which involve redistribution cut closer than any others along class lines and activate interest in what are roughly class terms. If there is ever any cohesion within peak associations, it occurs on redistributive issues, and rhetoric suggests that they occupy themselves most of the time with these.

It appears that the arena of redistribution is something of a special case of the arena of regulation in which the groups making coalitions happen to be elite societal elements.

There is a third model which closely ressembles Lieberson's formulation in his discussion of the compensating strategies idea. When decisions are made regarding "distribution"—i.e., short-term dispersal of assets without regard for limited resources, rather than "redistribution" or "regulation"—Lowi maintains that parties adopt a live-and-let-live "log-rolling" or mutual non-interference strategy. "Pork barrel" programs, defense expenditures, and patronage are examples of areas within the distributive arena of power. These kinds of programs can be broken down so nearly everyone can "get a piece of the action."

Since our tax system is only very slightly redistributive, the Federal budget might be seen as something of an arena of distribution. Since it is possible to pacify most major interest groups in the Federal budget-making process—if not through defense spending then through agricultural subsidies or harbor construction—it is tempting for Congress to use this method and view the process as one in which all groups should be kept happy if possible. This method allows the politicians in Congress to avoid making enemies unless absolutely necessary. As Lieberson suggested, each party will concentrate his strength in his own area even to the point of taking small losses in other areas. In short, under this model, industries would be expected neither to conspire to produce certain policies (e.g., high levels of defense spending) nor to democratically compete to produce them. Rather, they would simply ignore each other under the assumption that each would be better off if fighting were avoided and each simply looked after his own interests.

Figures in this study show (1) that there is very little relationship between defense spending and foreign policy voting, and (2) that almost all congressmen vote for defense expenditures. Under our hypothesis derived from the military-industrial complex thesis, it would be expected that congressmen from defense-dependent areas would be more likely to vote for jingoistic foreign policies and high levels of defense expenditures. Conversely, it would be expected that those congressmen from regions not dependent on defense spending would be less likely to vote in this manner. The Lieberson hypothesis of compensating strategies and the Lowi idea of the different arenas of power can be utilized to provide a possible explanation of these unexpected patterns.

In the first place, it can be conjectured that the issues that make up our foreign policy voting scale are somewhat remote from the "practical" concerns of the electorate, including that part of the electorate we call the military-industrial complex. By this reasoning, it could be said that members of the electorate simply did not care enough about these particular issues to exert pressure on the congressmen from their district as long as their basic interests were being met. As Lieberson has stated, they will ignore small losses in other areas in order to concentrate their forces in areas more relevant to their concerns. In this particular case, one might conjecture that defense industry and military constituents are ignoring what might be termed "psychological" losses (at most) incurred when a congressman votes against foreign policy issues dear to them. They might be seen to be concentrating their forces in the more relevant area of defense appropriation voting.

But even if one assumed that this is why all congressmen from dependent districts do in fact vote for appropriations measures, it still leaves unanswered the question of why congressmen from non-dependent districts also vote for high levels of defense appropriations. We conjecture that a congressional behavior pattern—"log-rolling" or "back scratching"—and a fact about post-World War II American politics—the absence of a "peace lobby"—account for this lack of variance. Matthews (1960: 99-100) shows that there is a norm of reciprocity in the Senate. That is, senators vote for bills sponsored by other senators in the expectation of the favors being returned on their pet bills. It is likely that this norm also holds in the House and that one representative will vote for a bill favored by another in the expectation that the favor will be returned. It is assumed that the vote will not harm the representative. Rose (1967) points out that there have been no stable forces working in the political system against high defense budgets in post-war years.[8] Almost no one has had what might be termed a "vested interest" in stopping or reducing defense expenditures in the way that members of the military-industrial complex have had an interest in increasing them.

As a result, we have a situation which closely resembles the arena of distribution discussed by Lowi. There is a high level of interest on the part of the segment of American business which is closely connected with defense manufacturing and a lack of interest on the part of the rest of American industry. These other industries concentrate their efforts on improving government programs which will benefit them more directly: farmers with farm policy, highway contractors with highway policy, etc. No elitist association of peak groups is working to keep defense spending high. There is no need for such imposition of control since those who do not benefit by defense spending do not fight it but rather ignore it in the expectation that they will be rewarded in their own areas.

Therefore, looking at our hypothesis from one point of view, the Department of Defense does not have to reward and punish congressmen on foreign policy issues, since the needed appropriation votes are already provided by the mechanism of the hypothesis of compensating strategies.[9] From the other point of view, congressmen do not have to gear votes on foreign policy issues to the ideological demands of their constituents since their constituents are satisfied with appropriate votes on the appropriations measures. Those congressmen who do not have heavy defense complexes in their districts are none the less working to provide for the material interests of their districts by voting for a defense appropriations measure in that it may encourage other congressmen from dependent districts to vote for special legislation which benefits their own districts.[10]

NOTES

1. As we shall note below, discussions of domestic economic considerations in the decision-making process are not meant to exclude other factors in that process such as real or perceived foreign threats.

2. The necessity of using several scales of defense spending points up the fact that the accuracy of information we have is not optimal. Due to problems like sub-contracting of prime contracts to unknown locations, many of our indices do not reflect as precisely as we might wish the actual area in which funds are spent. Better data exist on sub-contracting, for example, but have been classified by the Pentagon on grounds of security and because they are proprietary information of the companies involved.

3. A tau of .12 is significant with 100 cases while a Pearson product-moment correlation must attain the level of .197 to be significant (at the .05 level) with 100 cases.

4. A prime contract is the original award of a contract to a private firm (usually a manufacturing concern). That firm may, and usually does, sub-contract out part of the job to other firms or subsidiaries. Prime contracts covered include only those $10,000 or larger.

5. There is also some possibility of error in that the spending data are based on fiscal 1964 while the voting data are from 1965. This should not represent a major source of difficulties.

6. The use of tests of significance does not imply an intent to generalize to any population greater than the sample. In this case, our sample is almost identical with the population. The use of tests of significance here is justified as a method of comparing these results with results that might be obtained by chance had these senators been rated on the two variables by random methods (Russett, 1970a: 240).

7. Strictly speaking, the unit of analysis is the state. However, there was little turnover between 1965 and 1967 so the unit may meaningfully be thought of as the senator.

8. This represents something of a break with our past (Ekirch, 1956).

9. The exception is senior, powerful members whose votes and influence are apparently so important as to require special attention.

10. This discussion should not be taken to disparage the impact of the actions of other nations which appeared to reasonable men of the period to be quite threatening to the security of the nation.

REFERENCES

BOLTON, R. E. [ed.] (1966) Defense and Disarmament. Englewood Cliffs, N.J.: Prentice-Hall.

BUEHLER, Col. V. (1967) "Economic impact of defense programs." Statistical Reporter, 68, 1 (July): 1-9.

COBB, S. A. (1973) "The United States Senate and the impact of defense spending concentrations," pp. 197-224 in S. Rosen (ed.) Testing the Theory of the Military-Industrial Complex. Lexington, Mass.: Lexington.

––– (1972a) "Defense spending, foreign policy voting, and the structure of the U.S. House of Representatives," read at 1972 meetings of the Southern Sociological Society at New Orleans, Louisiana.

––– (1969)) "Defense spending and foreign policy in the House of Representatives." Journal of Conflict Resolution 13, 3 (September): 358-69.

COHEN, J. (1965) "Some statistical issues in psychological research," pp. 95-121 in B. B. Wolman (ed.) Handbook of Clinical Psychology. New York: McGraw-Hill.

COOK, F. J. (1962) The Warfare State. New York: Collier Books.

EKIRCH, A. A. (1956) The Civilian and the Military. New York: Oxford Univ. Press.

GRAY, C. and G. W. GREGORY (1968) "Military spending and Senate voting." Journal of Peace Research 1: 44-54.

LENS, S. (1970) The Military-Industrial Complex. Philadelphia: Pilgrim Press and the National Catholic Reporter.

LIEBERSON, S. (1971) "An empirical study of military-industrial linkages." American Journal of Sociology 76, 4(January): 562-585.

LOWI, T. J. (1964) "American business, public policy, case studies, and political theory." World Politics (July): 677-715.

MATTHEWS, D. R. (1960) U.S. Senators and Their World. New York: Vintage.

MELMAN, S. (1970) Pentagon Capitalism. New York: McGraw-Hill.

MILLS, C. W. (1956) The Power Elite. New York: Oxford Univ. Press.

ROSE, A. (1967) The Power Structure. New York: Oxford Univ. Press.

RUSSETT, B. (1970a) What Price Vigilance? The Burden of National Defense. New Haven: Yale Univ. Press.

--- (1970b) "Communication to the editors." Journal of Conflict Resolution 14, 2 (June).
TURNER, J. (1951) Party and Constituency: Pressures on Congress. Baltimore: Johns Hopkins Univ. Press.

Chapter 6

ECONOMIC INTERESTS AND AMERICAN FOREIGN POLICY ALLOCATIONS, 1960-1969

JOHN W. ELEY
JOHN H. PETERSEN

Department of Government
Western Kentucky University

INTRODUCTION

In recent years behaviorally-oriented students of foreign policy have devoted an increasing amount of attention to the explanation of foreign policy behavior. They have focused on foreign policy as a dependent variable to be accounted for by reference to a diverse set of independent variables generally grouped together in clusters which Rosenau (1966) has labeled systemic, governmental, societal, and individual. The central purposes of these research efforts are to provide statistically-based measures of relationships between indicators of foreign policy behavior and indicators of the variable clusters, and to develop generalizations which will account for variation in foreign policy behavior.

Most of the empirically-oriented research has grown out of the comparative approach to foreign policy research. Empirical studies of the foreign

AUTHORS' NOTE: *The authors wish to express their appreciation to the Western Faculty Research Committee for financial support provided for this project, and to the Office of Research and Computer Service which provided technical and data-processing assistance.*

policy behavior of single actors have been in very short supply, as most of those who have concerned themselves with single actors have followed traditional research methods.

The field of American foreign policy in particular is almost totally lacking in research products which are the result of behavioral and scientific methodology. As Eley (forthcoming) has shown, reliable generalizations based upon quantitative methodology and precise and rigorous data analysis are very rare.

One of the purposes of this paper is to demonstrate the possibilities for developing more reliable and precise generalizations on American foreign policy. The other purpose is to examine the relationship between one set of independent variables, i.e., economic interests, and U.S. foreign policy behavior.

This substantive concern is prompted by our concern with and interest in the popularity of the Marxist or neo-Marxist interpretation concerning the importance of private economic interests as causal factors operating on American foreign policy. This theory, which posits a causal connection between the interests and concerns of the dominant corporate sector and American foreign policy behavior, has gained many new adherents in the wake of substantial opposition to what many view as the quintessence of an imperial war. It offers a large number of scholars and concerned citizens a ready answer to the disturbing question: Why Vietnam?

The following excerpts from leading spokesmen of this school provide a useful introduction to the thesis:

> (1) The diplomatic, financial, and if need be, military facilities of the imperialist power are rapidly and efficiently mobilized to help private enterprise in distress to do the job (Baran, 1957: 198).

> (2) A substantial portion of the huge military machine, including that of the Western European nations, is the price being paid to maintain the imperialist network of trade and investment in the absence of colonialism (Magdoff, 1970: 240).

> (3) The relationship between the objectives of foreign economic policy and direct political and military intervention therefore has been a continuous one and an intimate one, indeed, very often an identical one (Kolko, 1969: 81).

> (4) The resulting analysis of the available facts shows that there is a close parallel between, on the one hand, the aggressive United States foreign policy aimed at controlling (directly or indirectly) as much of the globe as possible, and, on the other hand, an energetic and expansionist policy of U.S. business (Magdoff, 1969: 12).

These general statements are supplemented by specific references to the precise needs of the corporate sector for raw materials, markets, and investments. The following brief excerpts illustrate the thrust of these arguments:

> (5) It must be the conscious and primary aim of American foreign policy to ensure that the flow of raw materials from the Third World is never interrupted ... American dependence on foreign supplies makes it necessary for her to maintain regimes in power that are under her total control (Dean, 1970: 145).

> (6) More generally, because the expansion of commodity exports, as well as capital exports, generates even more surplus in the future ... the United States is increasingly compelled to follow the policies of a militant, expansive imperialist power, all in the name of the economic development for the underdeveloped countries (O'Conner, 1970: 64).

It is clear from the above that the model employed in this approach sees policy outcomes as results of forces brought to bear on the political system from its socioeconomic environment which cause the system to make particular responses. These forces arising from the environment are seen as the determinants of both the nature of the political system and its outputs. Thus, the political system and its outputs are seen as the dependent variables to be explained by reference to the environmental variables.

While this theory attempts to account for the range of American foreign policy undertakings around the world, and attributes imperialistic motivations to American foreign policy on the global scale, there is a considerable amount of attention focused on the relationship between the United States and the developing or underdeveloped nations of Africa, Latin America, and Asia. The nations in these regions are seen as very vulnerable to American economic and foreign policy penetration and exploitation. The theory posits a close and continuing relationship between corporate interests and foreign policy behavior throughout the Third World nations.

This explanation applies the theories of Lenin and Hobson on the relationship between capitalism and colonialism to the contemporary international political system. As stressed by O'Conner (1970), the contemporary adherents of this earlier interpretation view capitalism as producing a pattern of neo-colonialism which is marked by substantial capitalist-imperial penetration and exploitation of the politics and economics of the developing nations without the imposition of direct rule by the dominant developed nations along the lines of classic colonialism.

The bulk of the exponents of the "imperialism" thesis rest their case largely on the logic of Marxist-Leninist doctrine. At the extreme these arguments become polemical, supported only by the emotional fervor of the author. The theory is presented as revealed truth which no student of politics should seriously question.

More recently, however, there have been efforts by neo-Marxists to add empirical content to studies of imperialism. These include extended delineation of the growth of the international economic involvement of United States citizens and corporations (Magdoff, 1969), identification of members of the "corporate elite" in key government decision-making roles (Domhoff, 1969), and case studies of various U.S. foreign involvements (Fann and Hodges, 1970). But while they show, on the one hand, that U.S. private capital is widely invested in the world and that the U.S. trades heavily in raw materials and manufactured goods, and on the other hand, that the U.S. has exercised power and influence through its foreign policy, they fail to provide adequate empirical evidence on the relationship between specific economic interests and foreign policy actions. A central purpose of this paper is to work toward this latter goal.

It is clear from the quotations presented here that the neo-Marxist theory does not limit itself to the argument that there is a positive relationship between economic interests and foreign policy behavior. They contend that the relationship is such that one finds a one-to-one relationship between economic considerations and variation in the pattern of foreign policy behavior by the United States.

The adequacy of this theory has been questioned by some scholars (Nelson, 1968; Walters, 1970; Hovey, 1965; Kaplan, 1967; Gilbert, 1970) who view American foreign policy as essentially political in purpose and design. They regard the protection of American security and the perceived requirements of the cold war as the primary factors influencing the recent course of American foreign policy behavior. Accordingly, these analysts draw fundamentally different conclusions concerning the role of economic factors as causal forces.

In this paper we (1) select appropriate indicators of both economic and foreign policy variables; (2) examine the logic of the two major theses concerning the relationship between economic interests and foreign policy behavior; (3) generate testable hypotheses regarding the relationship between indicators; and (4) test these hypotheses through correlational analysis.

THE MEASUREMENT OF FOREIGN POLICY BEHAVIOR

Foreign policy behavior encompasses the entire range of actions undertaken by the government and directed at some entity (nation-state, political party, international organization, individual) beyond the legal jurisdiction of the government. This behavior may be viewed as continuous transactions aggregated at appropriate time periods, as recurrent sequential behaviors—i.e., strategies, designs, and so on, or as discrete acts of limited duration, i.e., events.[1]

Without passing judgment on the merits of these approaches, we have chosen to focus our analysis on transactional behavior. Specifically, we are concerned with the allocation of economic assistance, military assistance, and diplomatic personnel. These activities are among the foreign policy indicators deemed most relevant to private economic interests by the neo-Marxist theory, which presents the most complete analysis of the relationship between economic interests and foreign policy. Moreover, these are widely recognized as important foreign policy activities.[2]

These indicators share the following characteristics: (1) Each indicator can be measured in aggregate form with comparable data available for virtually all target nations. (2) The methods of reporting the data for each indicator provide the researcher with a fairly substantial degree of confidence concerning the reliability of the data. (3) Each indicator taps an important dimension of foreign policy behavior from the perspective of the theories with which we are concerned. (4) Finally, these indicators represent relatively separate dimensions of foreign policy activity, as shown in Table 1.

Economic Assistance as a Dependent Variable

In the entire period since 1948 the transfer of economic resources from the U.S. to other nations has been one of the principal means by which the U.S. has sought to protect and promote certain foreign policy objectives. Each successive administration in power since 1948 has made it quite clear that it regarded the economic assistance program as very closely related to interests and objectives regarded as vital and fundamental by the dominant decision-making elites. In the Kennedy and Johnson administrations, in particular, the spokesmen (e.g., Kennedy, 1961; Rusk, 1965) defended

TABLE 1
INTERCORRELATIONS* OF FOREIGN POLICY VARIABLES, 1965

	All Nations Military Assistance	Diplomatic Personnel
Economic assistance	.37	.32
Military assistance		.40

*Kendall's Rank Order Tau.

economic assistance programs as the most important component of American policy toward most of the nations in the so-called Third World.

Thus, there is considerable reason to believe that an analysis of the distribution of foreign economic assistance in all its various forms will shed important light on the interests and objectives shaping post-war policy.

Foreign economic assistance takes many forms, ranging from "Food for Peace" to multi-million dollar loans for heavy industrial developments. Faced with this situation, we have chosen to focus on one general measure of foreign assistance: namely, the total AID commitments to each country for any given fiscal year. The data include totals for development loans, supporting assistance, technical cooperation, and contingency funds. This is the total dollar amount of economic assistance committed by the U.S. Agency for International Development for the given fiscal year.[3] Economic assistance is also measured in per capita figures to take population of recipient nations into account.

Military Assistance as a Dependent Variable

Foreign military assistance likewise constitutes an important component of American post-war foreign policy. Designed to serve a variety of specific military needs, this assistance has been provided to allies and neutrals throughout the world. As in the case of economic assistance, military aid has been given in accordance with established foreign policy objectives in these countries. For the purpose of this paper, we have defined foreign military assistance as the total dollar value of the funds committed by the United States under the military assistance program for any given fiscal year. This total dollar figure has also been adjusted to a per-capita figure in order to control for the impact of population and is measured at this level as well.

Diplomatic Personnel as a Dependent Variable

In order to exert influence over the decision-making processes of other international actors the United States must have the capability of communicating its desires to the official decision-makers of these actors. Although there are several important channels through which this may be accomplished, the use of formal diplomatic channels is perhaps the most important. Formal communication may be channeled through existing procedures and structures or through ad hoc irregular channels. The bulk of diplomatic and informational communication of a routine non-crisis nature is carried on through formal regularized diplomatic channels through the persons of American foreign service personnel assigned on a continuing basis to the embassies and other posts within each actor with whom diplomatic relations are maintained and through USIA personnel. A measure of the importance of any actor to the United States may thus be ascertained from an analysis of the pattern of distribution of these personnel among the various nations. Since the United States does not have an unlimited number of such personnel at its disposal, the decision-makers must allocate them in accordance with the general principle of allocation discussed above.

The distribution of diplomatic personnel[4] refers to the pattern by which two principal types of personnel are assigned to the various national actors with whom diplomatic relations are maintained. These types are as follows: (a) regular foreign service personnel attached to the Department of State, and (b) United States Information Agency personnel assigned to the various USIS posts in the nations with whom diplomatic relations are maintained. As in the case of the other two foreign policy variables these totals are adjusted to take population into account.

ECONOMIC INTEREST VARIABLES AND INDICATORS

In the selection of appropriate economic variables we were guided by the proponents of the economic determinist theory who list the following factors as most important: (1) the expansion of markets for U.S. exports, (2) the promotion and protection of private corporate investment, and (3) the preservation of access to imported raw materials.[5] These three variables were selected as the ones to be included in our analysis. The indicators used for each of these variables were the dollar value for the U.S. of the exports to each country for the year, the total dollar value of private investments held by all corporations, and the total dollar value of all imports from each country. Data on these variables were gathered for the period 1960-69.

Various writers have emphasized the central importance of one or the other of these factors in explaining foreign policy behavior. In light of this, we have treated each factor as a separate variable in the following analysis. The intercorrelations among these variables are reported in Table 2.

TABLE 2
INTERCORRELATIONS* OF ECONOMIC INTEREST VARIABLES, 1965

	All Nations Imports	Investment
Exports	.68	.36
Imports		.35

Kendall's Rank Order Tau.

RELATIONSHIP BETWEEN FOREIGN POLICY ALLOCATIONS AND ECONOMIC INTERESTS

Economic Interests and Economic Assistance Allocations

The literature on the relationships between economic interests and economic assistance offers two distinct interpretations or theories of their direction and strength. These, which shall be considered in turn, may be referred to as the neo-Marxist and the political strategic theories.[6]

Neo-Marxist Theory: The neo-Marxist theory has been considered in some detail above and need not be examined again. Suffice it to say that the theory offers a straightforward proposition on this relationship which, stated simply, holds that the allocation of economic assistance resources will be influenced by and associated with the distribution of private economic interests. This view leads to the hypothesis that *there is a positive relationship between the distribution of economic interests and the allocation of economic assistance.* [7]

Political-Strategic Theory: The alternative or rival school of thought, which we have designated as the political-strategic theory, regards economic interests as of virtually no importance in the allocation of foreign policy economic assistance resources. This interpretation, which is offered by Kaplan (1967), Walters (1970), Liska (1960), and Nelson (1968), focuses on political and strategic variables relevant to the cold war as the factors underlying American economic assistance allocations. Among the important variables cited by this school of thought are: (1) the containment of communism; (2) competition with the Soviet and Chinese assistance programs; (3) the promotion of economic development; (4) the strengthening of the forces of international stability; and (5) the enhancement of military security.

Moreover, this approach explicitly rejects the argument of the importance of economic considerations. It stresses the minimal level of economic interest in most of the nations to whom economic assistance is allocated and argues that this level is simply too inconsequential to be of even secondary importance. For example, Kaplan (1967: 179) contends that "neither in its professed objectives nor in its allocation of funds has the U.S. foreign assistance program demonstrated a primary concern with the furthering of the interests of its private investors."[8]

A comparable argument is made by Robert Walters (1970: 18) who contends that

> the distinctly secondary economic importance of the less developed countries to the West and the United States makes it unlikely that the economic benefit for the donor is a strong motivating factor in the aid program.

While these two statements make explicit reference to the economic assistance program, their general analyses of the pattern of American interests and objectives in the developing nations suggest that they regard foreign policy behavior toward these nations as based upon non-economic considerations to the almost total exclusion of the very factors regarded as central by the neo-Marxists.

This interpretation suggests the following hypothesis: *There is no relationship between the distribution of American economic interests and economic assistance allocations.*

Military Assistance and Economic Interests

In the area of the allocation of military assistance the neo-Marxist and political-strategic theories offer conflicting views concerning the importance of economic interests. As is clear from the preceding discussion, the neo-Marxist view stresses the importance of the private economic interests as the central concern of policy makers allocating military assistance. As in the case of economic assistance allocations, the theory leads to the hypothesis: *There is a positive relationship between the distribution of private economic interests and the allocation of American military assistance.*

The political-strategic theory, on the other hand, is marked by an almost total disregard of economic interest variables as important for the military assistance program. This theory, which is reflected in Hovey (1965), Walters (1970), and Gilbert (1970), relates the military assistance allocations to the basic strategic security interests of the United States as defined in the context of the necessity of strengthening other nations threatened with aggression from the Communist world. Military assistance is also seen as providing partial payment to those nations granting American base rights, and as protecting certain historical relationships. Economic interests are conspicuously absent from these explanations.

This interpretation leads to the following hypothesis: *There will be no relationship between patterns of distribution of economic interests and patterns of allocations of military assistance.*

Diplomatic Personnel and Economic Interests

The third pattern of allocation to be related to private economic interests is the allocation of diplomatic personnel. In this regard we found no explicit theory concerning the variables associated with the allocation of such personnel. Given the fact that we regard this as an important resource, we have carried the logic of our analysis of the two other resources into this area as well.[9]

The neo-Marxist theory posits the existence of a close relationship between foreign policy behavior and economic interests. As we interpret this theory there should likewise be a relationship between economic interests and diplomatic personnel allocations. The alternative view which appears most consistent with the explicit statements concerning the other two allocations is that there should be no relationship between these variables.

Thus we suggest two alternative hypotheses: *There will be a positive relationship between the distribution of private economic interests and the allocation of diplomatic personnel. There will be no relationship between the distribution of private economic interests and the allocation of diplomatic personnel.*

THE RESEARCH DESIGN

In this paper we are interested in determining the relationship between economic and foreign policy activities. Accordingly, we have focused on the relationship between the variables for all nations with whom the United States interacts economically through the operations of exports, imports, and investment, and/or politically through economic assistance, military assistance, and diplomatic personnel.

We gathered data for each of our foreign policy and economic interest variables for those nations with whom at least some economic or foreign policy interaction had taken place for the period 1960-69. While the number and identity of the nations in the "sample" for each year varies, every year-by-year sample has a very high percentage of all the nations in the world.

The relationships between the distribution of economic assistance and private economic interests were examined for three groups of nations with which the United States maintains foreign relations. These included the total sample of national actors, i.e., 122 cases; the Third World nations, i.e., 87 cases; and the developed non-Communist nations, i.e., 24 cases.

In this exploratory study we have limited our analysis to correlation in hopes of presenting a clear account of the pattern of association between the variables. Given the problem of skewness, we transformed our data by changing the level of measurement from interval to ordinal. Accordingly, the statistical analysis consists of use of the Kendall rank-order correlation tau.[10] In each sample the tau relationships were computed for each year of the ten-year period 1960-69. A mean tau for the decade was also computed.

The existence of these conflicting interpretations concerning the relationship between private economic interests and foreign policy allocations raises an important question concerning appropriate criteria for the rejection or acceptance of the competing hypotheses. The central problem is to specify statistical measures of the relationship which will provide a reliable indicator of strength and direction and provide a decisional rule for categorizing relationships.

In the absence of accepted non-arbitrary rules for deciding if a given value of tau supports the political-strategic or the neo-Marxist theses we have employed the basic test of statistical significance to each of the observed taus. This test is useful in that it provides evidence of the existence or non-existence of a relationship which is of sufficient strength to have occurred other than by chance, a possibility which Winch and Campbell (1969) regard as important in studies of both samples and populations. Clearly, the minimum condition of the existence of a statistically significant relationship must be met if the neo-Marxist thesis is to be accepted. The issue of whether or not a significant relationship is weak or strong is not considered in this paper. Thus, in this paper we are carrying out a weak test of the neo-Marxist thesis. We believe that a more rigorous test requires the demonstration of a relationship which is significant, positive, and strong. This test must await the execution of a multivariate analysis of the relationship between foreign policy allocations and multiple independent variables.

Using the test of significance of taus as the benchmark for accepting or rejecting the two theories, we raise the following questions concerning each of the correlation coefficients: (1) Is the correlation statistically significant? (2) If significant, is the correlation positive or negative?

The neo-Marxist thesis is accepted if the correlation is significant and positive. On the other hand, the political-strategic thesis is accepted if the correlation is non-significant or significant and negative.

ANALYSIS OF RELATIONSHIPS

Economic Assistance and Economic Interests

Economic Assistance and Exports: The relationships between economic assistance and exports are reported in Table 3 below. The vast majority of the economic assistance-exports coefficients are not significant for all three groups of nations. The per-capita economic assistance-exports relationships are likewise not significant. There is some evidence, however, of a trend in the direction of significant positive relationships in the Third World. The early non-significant negative correlations gradually move, in the course of the decade, to significant positive coefficients of .36 (1968) and .28 (1969).

Economic Assistance and Imports: The coefficients between economic assistance and imports are significant and positive for the all-nation and Third

TABLE 3
ECONOMIC ASSISTANCE AND ECONOMIC INTERESTS, 1960-69

Year	All Exports	All Imports	All Investment	Third World Exports	Third World Imports	Third World Investment	Developed Non-Communist Exports	Developed Non-Communist Imports	Developed Non-Communist Investment
1960	−.08	.22*	.10	−.13	.27*	.10	−.07	−.08	−.12
1961	−.11	.18*	.11	−.05	.36*	.17	−.17	−.24	−.28
1962	−.08	.22*	.05	−.13	.39*	.14	−.21	−.33*	−.36*
1963	−.02	.26*	.10	−.04	.36*	.10	.00	−.27	−.19
1964	.04	.28*	.07	.01	.38*	.14	−.14	−.32*	−.34*
1965	.01	.22*	−.02	.00	.31*	.09	−.16	−.32*	−.37*
1966	−.14*	.15*	−.09	.00	.33*	.00	−.28	−.20	−.31*
1967	.01	.17*	−.12*	.10	.41*	.04	−.20	−.18	−.27
1968	.06	.09	−.09	.36*	.41*	.00	−.20	−.22	−.20
1969	.16*	.06	−.09	.28*	.37*	−.07	−.23	−.21	−.26
Mean	.00	.19	.00	.04	.37	.07	−.17	−.24	−.27

*significant at the <.05 level

TABLE 4
PER-CAPITA ECONOMIC ASSISTANCE AND ECONOMIC INTERESTS

	All			Third World			Developed Non-Communist		
Year	Exports	Imports	Investment	Exports	Imports	Investment	Exports	Imports	Investment
1960	−.07	.09	−.03	−.10	.12	−.02	−.26	−.31*	−.22
1961	−.11	.03	.00	−.01	.22*	.05	−.32*	−.39*	−.43*
1962	−.14*	−.01	−.03	−.05	.20*	.03	−.39*	−.35*	−.48*
1963	−.06	.09	−.01	.06	.14	.08	−.19	−.34*	−.30*
1964	−.06	.10	.01	.04	.20*	.11	−.35*	−.51*	−.42*
1965	−.11	.04	−.05	.00	.21*	.05	−.31*	−.29*	−.41*
1966	−.19	.01	−.06	.00	.27*	−.03	−.12	−.05	−.07
1967	−.08	.07	−.13*	.01	.30*	.05	.04	.11	.01
1968	−.00	.02	−.07	.21*	.27*	−.01	−.04	.01	−.01
1969	.11	−.04	−.09	.23*	.32*	−.07	.01	.05	−.06
Mean	.07	.04	−.05	.04	.22	.02	−.19	−.20	−.24

*significant at the <.05 level

[173]

World groups and have decade means of .19 and .37. The coefficients are generally insignificant and negative in the developed non-Communist group. The pattern changes markedly for the per-capita economic assistance-import coefficients in the all-nation group, with all the coefficients being non-significant. The overall pattern of significant and non-significant coefficients for the per-capita relationships in the Third World and developed non-Communist groups remains essentially unchanged, although there are some year-by-year changes for both groups.

Economic Assistance and Investment: The correlations between economic assistance (including per-capita) and investment are generally not significant, with 13 significant and 47 non-significant coefficients. Moreover the significant coefficients are all negative, with the exception of the .14 and .17 values for the Third World in 1961 and 1962.

The political-strategic thesis is supported by data on the following relationships: (a) economic assistance and exports (all three groups); (b) per-capita economic assistance and exports (all three groups); (c) economic assistance and investment (all three groups); (d) per-capita economic assistance and investment (all three groups); (e) economic assistance and imports (developed non-Communist); (f) per-capita economic assistance and imports (all nations, developed non-Communist). Viewing each set in terms of the number of groups to which it applies we see that the political-strategic thesis is supported by 15 relationships.

The neo-Marxist thesis is supported by the data on 3 relationships: (a) economic assistance and imports (all nations, Third World) and (b) per-capita economic assistance and imports (Third World).

Military Assistance and Economic Interests

Military Assistance and Exports: The relationships between military assistance and private economic interests are shown in Tables 5 and 6. The military assistance-export relationships are significant and positive among all nations with a mean tau for the decade of .22. In the Third World group of nations these correlations reach positive significant levels in four of the last five years of the decade. On the other hand, the developed non-Communist nations show an opposite trend from significant positive correlations in the first years of the decade to negative correlations at the end of the period. The per-capita correlations follow essentially similar patterns.

Military Assistance and Imports: The military assistance-import correlations are positive and significant for nearly all the years of the decade in both the all-nation and Third World groups. The mean tau for all nations is .35 and the mean for the Third World is .41. In the developed non-

Communist nations these correlations did not reach significance during the period. No clear trends emerged over the decade among these correlations, although there was some evidence of a change from positive to negative coefficients in the developed non-Communist group as seen in Table 5. No substantial differences in the correlations appeared for per-capita military assistance and export relationships.

Military Assistance and Investments: The military assistance-investment correlations show a varying pattern for the decade. Among all nations the correlations are significant and positive for the first six years of the period but become non-significant for the last four years. The mean tau for the decade is .17. Significant positive correlations also appear in five of the first six years among the Third World nations, with a mean tau for the period of .15. When per-capita figures are employed, the Third World correlations all become non-significant. The military assistance-investment coefficients in the developed non-Communist nations are all non-significant although there is again some evidence of a trend from positive to negative values.

The neo-Marxist thesis is supported by 6 of the relationships, i.e. (1) military assistance and exports (all nations); (2) military assistance and imports (all nations, Third World); (3) per-capita military assistance and exports (all nations); (4) per-capita military assistance and imports (all nations, Third World).

The political-strategic interpretation is supported by 6 relationships as follows: (1) military assistance and imports (developed non-Communist); (2) military assistance and investment (developed non-Communist); (3) per-capita military assistance and exports (developed non-Communist); (4) per-capita military assistance and imports (developed non-Communist); (5) per-capita military assistance and investment (Third World, developed non-Communist).

The remaining relationships showed a mixed pattern of support for the two theses. In some years the data support the neo-Marxist thesis and in other years they support the political-strategic thesis.

Diplomatic Personnel and Economic Interests

Diplomatic Personnel and Exports: The correlations between diplomatic personnel and exports are significant and positive throughout the decade for all three groups of nations, as shown in Table 7. This is clearly the most consistent pattern of relationships among the sets of variables included in this study. These data prompt one to suggest that the two variables are closely related. This conclusion is challenged by the marked reversal in the pattern when the factor of population is introduced and the per-capita diplomatic representation-exports correlations are examined in Table 8. The correlations

TABLE 5
MILITARY ASSISTANCE AND ECONOMIC INTERESTS

Year	All Exports	All Imports	All Investment	Third World Exports	Third World Imports	Third World Investment	Developed Non-Communist Exports	Developed Non-Communist Imports	Developed Non-Communist Investment
1960	.22*	.41*	.30*	-.02	.33*	.19*	.30*	.27	.25
1961	.29*	.47*	.31*	.13	.38*	.25*	.33*	.26	.21
1962	.17*	.37*	.20*	-.03	.41*	.26*	.27	.19	.10
1963	.23*	.39*	.20*	.06	.46*	.16*	.21	.09	-.02
1964	.21*	.44*	.19*	.10	.35*	.13	.07	.01	-.13
1965	.33*	.48*	.26*	.23*	.49*	.21*	.18	.02	-.04
1966	.22*	.31*	.01	.09	.39*	.10	.03	-.10	-.08
1967	.21*	.31*	.06	.34*	.48*	.12	-.14	-.21	-.15
1968	.31*	.30*	.05	.41*	.41*	.09	-.15	-.21	-.10
1969	.25*	.14*	-.04	.35*	.35*	.01	-.18	-.19	-.23
Mean	.24	.36	.15	.17	.41	.15	.09	.01	-.02

*significant at the < .05 level

TABLE 6
PER-CAPITA MILITARY ASSISTANCE AND ECONOMIC INTERESTS

Year	All Exports	All Imports	All Investment	Third World Exports	Third World Imports	Third World Investment	Developed Non-Communist Exports	Developed Non-Communist Imports	Developed Non-Communist Investment
1960	.21*	.37*	.21*	-.02	.28*	.09	.12	.12	.05
1961	.23*	.34*	.23*	.13	.35*	.13	.22	.21	.11
1962	.15*	.26*	.15*	.01	.33*	.08	.09	.07	-.03
1963	.18*	.29*	.11	.08	.26*	.08	-.06	-.12	-.22
1964	.21*	.36*	.10	.10	.27*	.05	-.01	-.03	-.17
1965	.25*	.37*	.16*	.17*	.42*	.18*	.00	-.08	-.17
1966	.20	.27*	.00	.09	.40*	.08	-.02	-.11	-.03
1967	.21*	.27*	.01	.29*	.44*	.10	.04	.04	.02
1968	.26*	.25*	.05	.41*	.42*	.10	-.08	-.08	-.05
1969	.25*	.07	-.01	.38*	.41*	.06	-.10	-.06	-.17
Mean	.21	.29	.10	.16	.35	.10	.02	.06	-.06

*significant at the <.05 level

for these variables are non-significant in the all-nation group, and only part of them remain significant in the Third World group. In the developed non-Communist group the correlations remain significant but change direction from positive to negative. The sharp reversal in the pattern of correlations when per-capita figures are used raises serious questions concerning the nature of the relationships.

Diplomatic Personnel and Imports: As shown in Table 7, the correlations between diplomatic personnel and imports are significant and positive for all three groups of nations throughout the decade, with mean tau for the decade of .51, .44, and .45. As was the case above, these data point to the existence of a relationship between the variables. Once again, however, the introduction of control for population through the use of per-capita diplomatic personnel produces a marked change in the pattern of correlations. These correlations are insignificant in the all-nation group, and significant and negative in the Third World and the developed non-Communist groups, as Table 8 shows.

Diplomatic Personnel and Investment: The correlations between diplomatic personnel and investment follow the pattern observed in the relationships just described with the exception of the Third World group in which correlations are non-significant. When the absolute diplomatic figures are used the correlations for the all-nation and developed non-Communist groups are significant and positive, while the use of per-capita figures produced correlations which are insignificant and/or significant and negative.

The preceding discussion of the correlations would suggest that the neo-Marxist thesis is supported by the data on the following 8 relationships: (1) diplomatic personnel and exports (all three groups); (2) diplomatic personnel and imports (all three groups); (3) diplomatic personnel and investment (all nations, developed non-Communist).

The political-strategic thesis is supported by the data on the following 8 relationships: (1) per-capita diplomatic personnel and imports (all three groups); (2) per-capita diplomatic personnel and exports (all nations, developed non-Communist); (3) per-capita diplomatic personnel and investment (all three groups).

The remaining 2 relationships, diplomatic personnel and investment (Third World) and per-capita diplomatic personnel and exports (Third World) do not consistently support either thesis.

In summary it is clear the relationships between imports and foreign policy allocations are more supportive of the neo-Marxist interpretation than are the exports and/or investment-foreign policy allocation relationships. Ten of these relationships are consistent with this thesis as opposed to 8 which support the political-strategic thesis. Among the exports-foreign policy allocations relationships, 5 support the neo-Marxist thesis and 9 support the political-strategic thesis, while 4 are inconclusive. Among the investment-foreign policy allocations relationships 12 support the political-strategic thesis, 3 support the neo-Marxist thesis, and 1 is inconclusive.

Relationships by Groups

If this total group of 54 relationships is considered on a group-by-group basis, the following findings emerge: (1) Eight of the 18 relationships in the all-nation group are supportive of the political-strategic thesis and 8 are supportive of the neo-Marxist thesis, while 2 of the relationships are supportive of neither. (2) Seven of the Third World relationships support the political-strategic thesis, and 6 support the neo-Marxist thesis, and 4 relationships do not support either thesis. (3) Fourteen of the developed non-Communist relationships support the political-strategic thesis, 3 support the neo-Marxist thesis, and 1 is inconclusive. This suggests that the neo-Marxist thesis has its greatest validity for the all-nation and Third World groups but that for both groups it does no better than the poltical-strategic thesis.

Consideration of Partial and Lagged Correlations

In order to provide additional perspective on the nature of the relationships discussed above we carried out two additional tests, namely partial and lagged correlations. The results of these analyses should be considered briefly at this point.

We carried out partial correlations for our data for 1965 and 1969 in order to determine the extent to which our bivariate relationships were affected by the intercorrelations among variables in a multivariate context. In this analysis we examined the relationships between each of our independent and each of our dependent variables when controlling for one of the other independent variables at a time. This analysis for 1965 resulted in no consistent patterns of change in our original bivariate correlations. In some cases no change occurred in any correlations. In other cases all correlations were slightly reduced.

Comparable results were obtained from the partial correlations in 1969. The only significant difference was in the depressing impact of exports on the strength of the relationship between imports and some of the foreign policy variables.

These results suggest that, on the whole, the economic interest and foreign policy allocation relationships are substantially non-spurious even though, as stressed above, many of them are not significant. Clearly, there is no

TABLE 7
DIPLOMATIC PERSONNEL AND ECONOMIC INTERESTS

Year	All			Third World			Developed Non-Communist		
	Exports	Imports	Investment	Exports	Imports	Investment	Exports	Imports	Investment
1960	.18*	.29*	.39*	.00	.17*	.16*	.40*	.42*	.42*
1961	.33*	.45*	.23*	.24*	.43*	.21*	.34*	.29*	.44*
1962	.32*	.50*	.27*	.11	.43*	.17*	.53*	.45*	.54*
1963	.37*	.48*	.27*	.19*	.40*	.10	.57*	.45*	.53*
1964	.42*	.55*	.28*	.26*	.44*	.18*	.56*	.48*	.55*
1965	.44*	.58*	.25*	.24*	.46*	.13	.50*	.43*	.50*
1966	.44*	.63*	.20*	.37*	.51*	.08	.68*	.45*	.51*
1967	.54*	.55*	.16*	.40*	.51*	.03	.64*	.52*	.48*
1968	.58*	.56*	.17*	.56*	.53*	.04	.67*	.55*	.46*
1969	.62*	.53*	.16*	.57*	.54*	.01	.65*	.50*	.36*
Mean	.42	.51	.23	.30	.44	.11	.55	.45	.48

*significant at the <.05 level

TABLE 8
PER-CAPITA DIPLOMATIC PERSONNEL AND ECONOMIC INTERESTS

Year	All Exports	All Imports	All Investment	Third World Exports	Third World Imports	Third World Investment	Developed Non-Communist Exports	Developed Non-Communist Imports	Developed Non-Communist Investment
1960	.05	−.09	−.01	.18	−.14	−.08	−.29*	−.14	−.21
1961	.10	−.05	.04	.16*	−.02	.02	−.33*	−.27	−.27
1962	.16*	.00	.05	.26*	.01	−.02	−.26	−.10	−.02
1963	.09	.02	.00	.23*	−.15*	−.02	−.50*	−.43*	−.32*
1964	.07	−.01	.01	.19*	−.05	.00	−.47*	−.38*	−.26
1965	.00	.01	−.04	.13	.06	.01	−.57*	−.39*	−.26
1966	−.01	.00	−.02	.05	.05	−.01	−.49*	−.34*	−.32*
1967	.01	.02	−.06	.02	.04	−.10	−.39*	−.29*	−.33*
1968	.05	.05	−.04	.06	.09	−.11	−.35*	−.27	−.27
1969	.03	−.04	−.05	.06	.11	−.07	−.43*	−.38*	−.33*
Mean	.06	.00	.01	.14	.00	−.05	−.41	−.30	−.25

*significant at the <.05 level

TABLE 9
PATTERNS OF SUPPORT FOR THE NEO-MARXIST AND POLITICAL-STRATEGIC THEORIES BY GROUPS AND VARIABLES

	Economic Assistance	Per-Capita Economic Assistance	Military Assistance	Per-Capita Military Assistance	Diplomatic Personnel	Per-Capita Diplomatic Personnel
All Nations						
Exports	P	P	M	M	M	P
Imports	M	P	M	M	M	P
Investment	P	P	O	O	M	P
Third World						
Exports	P	P	O	O	M	O
Imports	M	M	M	M	M	P
Investment	P	P	O	P	O	P
Developed Non-Communist						
Exports	P	P	O	P	M	P
Imports	P	P	P	P	M	P
Investment	P	P	P	P	M	P

M = support for neo-Marxist thesis
P = support for political-strategic thesis
O = no clear support for either thesis

discernible pattern in the partial correlations which would permit one to conclude that one of the economic variables is of greater importance than the others, and that it alone contributes substantially to the relationships between economic and foreign policy variables.

In addition to our cross-sectional analysis which compared economic interests and foreign policy allocations on a year-to-year basis, we examined the correlations between the lagged variables so that economic interests at time t were correlated with foreign policy allocations at time $t+n$. This procedure produced little or no change in the overall patterns of correlations which were revealed in the cross-sectional analysis. Comparable results were obtained when the foreign policy allocations were held constant and the economic interests were viewed at time $t+n$.

SUMMARY AND CONCLUSIONS

In this paper we have considered two of the major conflicting interpretations on the relationship between American foreign policy behavior and private economic interests. We offered a test of the two theories based upon a correlational analysis of the relationships between three central economic interests, exports, imports, and investment, and three important foreign policy activities, the allocation of economic assistance, military assistance, and diplomatic personnel.

We concluded that the relationships between economic interests and foreign policy allocations are less straightforward and consistent than either of the two major theses suggest. The overall pattern across all groups and variables is mixed and complex. The neo-Marxist thesis had its greatest applicability in the all-nation and Third World groups and in the imports-foreign policy allocations relationships and its weakest applicability in the developed non-Communist group and export-foreign policy allocations relationships. Conversely, the political-strategic interpretation has its greatest applicability in those groups and variables for which the neo-Marxist thesis had its least applicability. These findings are summarized in Table 9.

The neo-Marxist thesis clearly overstates the relationships between economic interests and foreign policy allocations. At the same time, however, it does appear to have applicability for certain groups of nations and for certain economic interests and foreign policy relationships. Concurrently, the political-strategic interpretation underestimates the overall relationships among the variables, especially in the area of the imports and allocations.

The theory which seems most appropriate is one which suggests that the relationship between foreign policy allocations and economic interests is complex and variable. The rather simple interpretations considered in this paper should be dropped or revised in favor of a thesis which posits the existence of a set of mixed relationships whose existence, direction, and strength vary across groups and variables. This can be explored more adequately through a complex multi-variable model the development of which must await future research and analysis.

In conclusion, we wish to emphasize the exploratory and tentative nature of this analysis as well as our recognition of the fact that we are far from presenting a definitive test of the two contending theories considered in this paper. We have done little more than provide descriptive statistics on the nature of the relationships between selected economic and foreign policy variables. Nonetheless, we believe that this analysis and others like it are essential in laying the foundations of a theory of American foreign policy. We hope that others will join in this effort to confront some of the major controversies surrounding the nature and origins of American foreign policy within a framework of the scientific study of foreign policy.

NOTES

1. For analysis of the problems of the identification and measurement of foreign policy output, see Hermann (1972), Morse (1972), Blake (1969), and Azar et al. (1972).

2. In focusing on these three indicators of foreign policy behavior we are not suggesting that these are the only indicators which might be selected. Other behaviors such as communications (protests, threats, warnings, etc.), troop deployments in foreign bases, and specific discrete actions (boycotts, embargoes, interventions, etc.) may also be appropriate indicators of foreign policy interest and attention. They have not been included in this analysis both because of our concerns over the reliability and accessibility of data on these variables and the difficulty of relating discrete *ad hoc* behaviors to continuous transactions. In subsequent investigations we hope to overcome these problems and to include these additional indicators.

3. The sources of these data and information on their measurement are contained in the Appendix.

4. In this paper we will refer to diplomatic and informational personnel as simply diplomatic personnel even though some people might find this usage somewhat confusing. In our early work on this problem we treated these personnel separately until we realized that the relative magnitude of the numbers in each category remained fairly constant from country to country. Thus we decided to present a single measure of this activity.

5. These are the economic interests considered most important by most of the scholars. While other indicators of these interests, e.g., holding of foreign bonds, are cited as important, most analysts concur that exports, imports, and investment constitute the major components of private economic activities abroad. For useful discussions of these activities and interests, see Kindleberger (1970), Whitman (1965), Mikesell (1962).

6. In this paper we draw inferences from the available literature in order to generate testable hypotheses concerning the relationship between private economic interests and American foreign policy. In each case we have tried to develop an explicit hypothesis concerning the relationship even when explicit statements are not made by the various authors. It is possible, of course, that some of the scholars cited may disagree with our inferences and regard our tests of their theories as inappropriate, given our understanding of the most appropriate explicit hypothesis.

7. In general, the various scholars considered in this paper are not explicitly concerned with phenomena which they conceptualize as variables. They make no explicit reference to variation in the pattern of foreign policy behavior. Moreover, they generally refer to the matter of the factors associated with decisions on assistance to particular countries on a country-by-country basis. The concept of a pattern of allocation within which there is considerable variation that can be described and explained is implicit in the bulk of analyses of the problem. The study by Wittkopf (1971) is a conspicuous exception to this general tendency to disregard variation.

8. Kaplan (1970: 75) qualifies this general statement with the caveat that it does not apply to Latin America. In this region he sees some relationship between the levels of aid and increases in exports.

9. The only explicit reference to the relationship between diplomatic activity and economic activity of which we are aware is in Terrell (1972: 170). He finds that trade and diplomatic activity cluster together on the dimension or factor which he labels political involvement. This leads him to conclude that trade and the flag go together with the former expanding the level of the latter. Since this is not concerned with our basic problem, however, we do not regard this as directly applicable to our analysis.

10. The correlation coefficients correspond to tau_a or tau_b depending upon the number of tied ranks. The program employed for these computations computes the appropriate statistic automatically.

REFERENCES

AZAR, E. A., S. H. COHEN, T. H. JUKAM, and J. M. McCORMACK (1972) "Making and measuring the international event as a unit of analysis." University of North Carolina Studies of Conflict and Peace Report 3 (January).

BARAN, P. (1957) The Political Economy of Growth. New York: Monthly Review Press.

BLAKE, D. H. (1969) "The indentification of foreign policy output: a neglected but necessary task." Presented at the annual meeting of the Midwest Political Science Association, Ann Arbor.

COHEN, B. (1972) "U.S.-U.S.S.R. in developing countries." Bulletin of Atomic Scientists 28 (February): 22-28.

DEAN, H. (1970) "Scarce resources: the dynamic of American imperialism," in K. T. Fann and S. C. Hodges (eds.) Readings in American Imperialism. Boston: Porter Sargent.

DOMHOFF, G. W. (1969) "Who makes American foreign policy, 1945-1963," in D. Horowitz (ed.) Corporations and the Cold War. New York: Monthly Review Press.

ELEY, J. (forthcoming) "The study of American foreign policy: a critical review of the literature, 1961-1970," in W. O. Chittick (ed.) The Analysis of Foreign Policy Outputs.

GILBERT, S. (1970) "Soviet American military aid competition in the developing world." Orbis 13 (Winter): 1117-37.
GREEN, P. (1968) "Necessity and choice in American foreign policy," in L. Howe (ed.) A Dissenter's Guide to Foreign Policy. Garden City: Doubleday Anchor.
HERMANN, C. (1972) "Policy classification: key to comparative foreign policy," in J. N. Rosenau, V. Davis and M. East (eds.) The Analysis of International Politics. New York: Free Press.
HOVEY, H. (1965) United States Military Assistance. New York: Praeger.
KAPLAN, J. (1967) The Challenge of Foreign Aid: Policies, Problems and Possibilities. New York: Praeger.
KENNEDY, J. F. (1961) "Message to Congress on the foreign assistance program." Department of State Bulletin 44 (May 22): 507-514.
KINDLEBERGER, C. P. [ed.] (1970) The International Corporation. Cambridge: MIT Press.
KOLKO, G. (1969) The Roots of American Foreign Policy. Boston: Beacon Press.
LISKA, G. (1960) The New Statecraft: Foreign Aid in American Policy. Chicago: Univ. of Chicago Press.
MAGDOFF, H. (1970) "Militarism and imperialism." American Economic Review Papers and Proceedings 60 (May).
--- (1969) The Age of Imperialism. New York: Monthly Review Press.
MIKESELL, R. (1962) [ed,] U.S. Private and Government Investment Abroad. Eugene: Univ. of Oregon Press.
MORSE, E. (1972) A Comparative Approach to the Study of Foreign Policy: Notes on Theorizing. Princeton University Center for International Studies Research monograph 36.
NELSON, J. (1968) Aid, Influence and Foreign Policy. New York: Macmillan.
O'CONNER, J. (1970) "The meaning of economic imperialism," in Fann and Hodges (eds.) Readings in American Imperialism. Boston: Porter Sargent.
ROSENAU, J. N. (1966) "Pre-theories and theories of foreign policy," in R. B. Farrell (ed.) Approaches to Comparative and International Politics. Evanston: Northwestern Univ. Press.
RUSK, D. (1965) "Statement before the Senate Committee on Foreign Relations." Department of State Bulletin 52 (April 5): 747-51.
TERRELL, L. (1972) "Patterns of international involvement and international violence." International Studies Quarterly 16 (June): 167-86..
WALTERS, R. (1970) Soviet and American Aid. Pittsburgh: Univ. of Pittsburgh Press.
WHITMAN, M. (1965) Government Risk Sharing in Foreign Investments. Princeton: Princeton Univ. Press.
WITTKOPF, E. (1971) "American, British and German foreign aid: a comparative study of recipient state attributes and aid received." Presented at the annual meeting of the International Studies Association, San Juan, Puerto Rico.
WINCH, R., and D. CAMPBELL (1969) "Proof? No. Evidence? Yes. The significance of tests of significance." American Sociologist 4 (May): 140-43.

APPENDIX

The Data

The six primary variables used in this study, plus population, were derived from the following sources:

(1) The economic interest variables exports and imports were operationalized through data summarized on an annual basis in official U.S. government publications. Since transfers of goods, services, and capital under foreign aid programs are included in published export totals, we have subtracted such aid to arrive at the adjusted export figures used for this study.

The investment variable was operationalized as the total book value at year end of U.S. foreign direct investments. Both published and unpublished government sources were employed.

Sources: U.S. Department of Commerce, Bureau of the Census (1960-1969), Foreign Commerce and Navigation of the United States. Washington, D.C.: Government Printing Office.

U.S. Department of Commerce, Office of Business Economics (1960-1969), Survey of Current Business. Washington, D.C.: Government Printing Office.

(2) The three foreign policy variables were operationalized through compilations of published U.S. government sources. Economic assistance consists of total of commodities, loans, grants, and services supplied by the U.S. to each foreign country for each fiscal year. Military assistance consists of military arms as well as technical and financial aid given under the Military Assistance Program for each fiscal year. The diplomatic personnel variable is based on the total number of official non-military government personnel stationed in each foreign country.

Sources: U.S. Department of State, Agency for International Development (1960-1969), The Foreign Assistance Program: Annual Report to the Congress. Washington, D.C.: U.S. Government Printing Office.

U.S. Department of State (1960-1969), Foreign Service List, Washington, D.C.: U.S. Government Printing Office.

Chapter 7

FOREIGN POLICY CONFLICT AMONG AFRICAN STATES, 1964-1969

RAYMOND W. COPSON
Holy Cross College

International conflict is a matter of serious concern for the developing countries. War, which is a constant danger for some developing states, may bring the loss of essential human and material resources. Where war is not an immediate possibility, international conflict may still persuade states to divert resources from vital development tasks to armaments. Even apparently petty disputes consume the energies of overburdened elites, and they may enhance the local influence of interested great powers.

A relatively new technique in the study of foreign policy known as "events data analysis"[1] provides a method for the investigation of important questions about conflict in the developing areas. Two questions receive particular attention in this study. First, are there variables in several social domains which enable us to explain or predict conflict? Success in finding such variables would, of course, considerably improve our analysis of conflict in the developing areas. Variables in the domains of military power, economic development, domestic politics, and international politics were tested in this essay. Second, in view of the general acceptance of the idea that international conflict is dysfunctional for developing states, can any trend toward the resolution or termination of conflict be discerned? If the developing countries have shown some ability to resolve their differences peacefully, there may be important implications in modern world politics.

We will approach these questions by focusing on the independent African states in the years 1964-69.[2] Although there may be some question about the criteria which define a "developing," "underdeveloped," or "less developed" state, surely the African states are less developed by nearly all standards. The gross national product of most African states falls in the $.5 billion to $5 billion range, and only in South Africa does GNP exceed $10 billion. In no African country does annual per-capita income exceed $1,000 (United Nations, 1968: 823). Rates of illiteracy are high. Industrialization and urbanization have only begun in most areas.

This is not to say that the African countries are typical in all respects of developing countries elsewhere. The mean national income of African states is lower than the mean income of states in Asia and Latin America.[3] African states, with the exception of Egypt, are also weaker militarily than many developing states outside Africa—for example, Cuba, Indonesia, and Philippines.[4] African states are generally far less densely populated than Asian countries,[5] and they do not suffer from the agrarian discontent common in Asia and Latin America. Such differences may well dictate differences in the form, intensity, and duration of conflict, and they may mean that the underlying causes of conflict are also different. Nevertheless, since the African states constitute such a large proportion of the developing states (indeed they compose nearly a third of the states represented at the U.N.), the study of international conflict in Africa is surely important in the study of conflict in the developing areas generally.

RELIABILITY AND CLASSIFICATION OF EVENTS DATA

An events data collection is compiled by the use of current events sources to build up a file of events of the sort in which one is interested. Researchers have typically relied on such sources as *The New York Times, The New York Times Index,* and *Deadline Data on World Affairs* (Rummel, 1963: 6; Tanter, 1966: 43). So that the events collected may be counted in a meaningful way, they must be classified according to some logical scheme (Holsti, 1969: 94) which the researcher may borrow or invent for himself. The categories in this coding scheme should reflect the interests of the researcher. Moreover, the scheme should be exhaustive, so that no event falls into more than one category (Holsti, 1969: 95).

There are several questions which might be raised about this research method. How accurately does published news reflect the character and frequency of events as they really occurred? Official censorship, together with inefficiency, limited resources, and restrictive concepts of newsworthiness on the part of news gathering agencies, limits the reliability of news sources. Cross-cultural barriers to communication and understanding also limit reliability, particularly in using Western sources for events in distant, less developed areas (Galtung and Ruge, 1965; Smith, 1969).

Questions can also be raised about the data-gathering and classification process. How reliably has the researcher or his assistants collected events data from the sources, and how consistently have they coded that data? If other investigators cannot replicate the events data collection with considerable accuracy, surely the results of a study based on the data are of dubious value. Does the classification scheme provide a valid representation of the concepts under investigation? If the coding categories do not conform to the interests of the researcher, the study can hardly help to answer his research questions.

Doubts about events data collections may never be finally laid to rest, but some steps have been taken here to respond to the questions just outlined. On the problem of unintended selection processes in news reporting, three detailed news sources devoted exclusively to African affairs were used. Secrecy, oversight, and cultural blinders may still limit reliability,[6] but when several sources are used, and when the editors of these sources have made a clear effort to be exhaustive in their reporting, this limit has been considerably reduced. By far the most complete source (contributing about 80 percent of the events in the data collection) was the *Africa Research Bulletin,* which has been published monthly since 1964. The collection was supplemented by the *African Recorder* and by *Africa Diary.* The use of these sources for the 1964-69 period generates a rather large collection of 854 events. The size of the collection encourages one to hope (but offers no guarantee) that the frequency of events in each coding category is roughly proportional to the frequency of events which occurred in reality.[7]

The problem of reliability in the coding of events has been dealt with by the adoption of a very simple tripartite coding scheme. The various coding schemes which have been proposed to date typically place a considerable burden on the codifier by requiring that numerous, and sometimes rather subtle, distinctions be made among events (e.g., Rummel, 1966). The multiplication of coding categories, however, multiplies the chances of coding error, and it may complicate the interpretation of results.

All conflict events in this collection, including international acts and intergovernmental communications, were placed in one of the following categories: (1) unfriendly interactions, (2) interference interactions and (3) force interactions (Table 1). Under the first heading are counted all those unfriendly exchanges between states which do not in themselves involve questions of territorial integrity or political independence, nor intervene in

TABLE 1
CONFLICT CLASSIFICATION CATEGORIES, WITH TYPICAL EVENTS

1. Unfriendly interactions:
    expel ambassadors
    expel citizens
    close border
    break diplomatic relations
    mistreat foreign nationals
    seize foreign-owned property
    arrest or detain foreign officials
    advance a territorial claim, without threatening assertion by force
    denounce behavior of a state toward a third state

2. Interference interactions:
    denounce domestic policies of a foreign government
    recognize a secessionist movement
    accuse a foreign state of harboring or training rebel forces
    complain to the O.A.U. or U.N. of guerrilla infiltration
    extend material or verbal support to domestic opposition elements in a foreign state

3. Force interactions:
    protest alleged aggression
    threaten forceful acts
    conduct military maneuvers in a period of tension
    mobilize military forces
    commit a border violation with military forces
    launch an armed attack

domestic affairs. Breaks in diplomatic relations or seizures of property owned by foreigners are common examples of this kind of conflict. "Interference interactions" are all those which involve some sort of intervention short of force in the domestic affairs of foreign states. These events range from criticism of political events in a foreign state to attempts to subvert a foreign government by supporting rebels against it.

Special note should be made here that by "interference interactions" we mean not only acts but also protests, accusations, denials, and other communications related to interference. Often we cannot know (and states themselves may be unsure, untruthful, or mistaken) that an act of interference has occurred, but the fact that communications about interference are exchanged demonstrates that this mode of conflict is a matter of concern to the states involved. The frequency of such interactions must roughly index the intensity of their concern, and changes in the frequency of interaction must show changes in the importance of interference to them.

The same is true of "force interactions," which are all events having to do with the use, or the threat of use, of regular armed military forces. Events related to force are clearly an important mode of international conflict, and this is true not only of acts of force which are confirmed by independent reports (confirmation which is often lacking in Africa) but also of hostile communications which deal with questions of force.

Tests suggest that data gathering and coding according to this scheme can be done reliably.[8] But an equally important advantage of the scheme is that it validly reflects our research interests: the discovery of correlates of conflict and of significant trends in conflict. Each mode of interaction distinguished here has its own particular importance. Force interactions are those which may most seriously disrupt development. Interference interactions have caused serious concern in the Third World because of ideological differences among developing countries. Both force and interference interactions may lead to great-power intervention. Unfriendly interactions are an index of international divisions on ideological or other issues, and they may provide warnings of more serious conflict to come.[9] Thus, if relationships or trends involving these three modes of conflict could be found, the findings would be of some importance in the study of conflict in the developing areas. Moreover, the simplicity of the scheme, and its correspondence to distinctions often drawn by analysts working in more traditional analytic styles, may give the study a somewhat wider appeal than would a more complex typology.

Proponents of the more detailed classification schemes might argue that this scheme imposes three dimensions on the data before statistical analysis has begun. A major goal of their use of factor analysis, after all, was the discovery of a few underlying dimensions among many very basic measures of conflict (Rummel, 1969: 220-221). But the purposes of this study are different, and since the coding scheme is valid for these purposes, there is little reason to employ a more complex scheme.

DOMESTIC POLITICAL INSTABILITY AND FOREIGN CONFLICT BEHAVIOR

In the search for underlying explanations of conflict, or at least for tentative indications of where those explanations might lie, variables which might be correlated with conflict events frequencies have been sought in diverse social domains. The results of these attempts to find correlates of conflict, however, have usually not been encouraging (see Rummel, 1968: 213; but also Wilkenfeld, 1968, 1969). Very few correlates of African international conflict were found in this study, but some interesting findings in two social domains can be reported.

If states are treated as cases, then conflict interaction scores can be attributed to states. A state can be characterized by a certain aggregate conflict events frequency on each conflict variable just as it is characterized by a certain aggregate income or population.[10] When this is done, several simple (product-moment) correlation coefficients above the .30 level suggest that there may be links between the foreign conflict behavior of states and political instability within states. Table 2 shows some association between each mode of conflict and indices of the incidence of civil war,[11] of numbers killed in domestic political strife,[12] and of the frequency of anti-government plotting.[13] Table 3, which displays intercorrelatons among these variables calculated for three time periods, indicates that it is conflict in the 1964-65 period which is most associated with domestic political instability.[14]

In the 1964-65 period, the Congo (Leopoldville), under the premiership of Moise Tshombe (July 1964-October 1965) was perhaps the clearest case in which foreign conflict behavior was linked to domestic political instability. Tshombe was regarded as an enemy of African freedom in many African capitals because in leading the Katanga secession he had shown a willingness not only to destroy the unity of a major African state but also to cooperate with forces, including Belgian financial interests and South African mercenaries, which were regarded as threatening to African independence.[15] This intense hostility toward Tshombe provoked several African governments to lend support to a domestic revolution in the northeastern Congo. Evidence strongly suggests that Algeria, the U.A.R., Kenya, Uganda, Burundi, Congo

TABLE 2
SIMPLE CORRELATIONS: FOREIGN CONFLICT BEHAVIOR AND DOMESTIC POLITICAL INSTABILITY[a]

	All[b]	U.I.[c]	I.I.[d]	F.I.[e]
Civil war	.44	.27	.38	.55
Domestic killed	.34	.24	.30	.37
Anti-government plotting	.20	.31	.11	.16

a. Kenya, Ethiopia, and Somalia excluded because of the distorting effects of their extreme conflict scores.
b. Total conflict interactions.
c. Unfriendly interactions.
d. Interference interactions.
e. Force interactions.

TABLE 3
SIMPLE CORRELATIONS: FOREIGN CONFLICT BEHAVIOR AND DOMESTIC POLITICAL INSTABILITY, OVER TIME[a]

	1964-65			1966-67			1968-69		
	U.I.	I.I.	F.I.	U.I.	I.I.	F.I.	U.I.	I.I.	F.I.
1964-65									
Civil war	.26	.44	.34	.12	.16	.20	.39	−.14	.18
Domestic killed	.56	.63	.78	.06	.14	−.02	.34	.04	.30
Anti-government plotting	.39	.54	.35	.18	−.08	.03	.21	−.20	−.15
1966-67									
Civil war	.30	.46	.46	.04	.17	.25	.39	.18	.52
Domestic killed	.07	.25	.06	.21	.07	.28	.31	.16	.12
Anti-government plotting	.44	.35	.56	.03	−.12	−.14	.18	−.17	.01
1968-69									
Civil war	−.04	.18	.02	.05	.19	.45	.02	.31	.36
Domestic killed	−.12	.10	−.05	−.02	−.01	.30	.11	.21	.16
Anti-government plotting	.05	.17	−.03	.10	−.08	.10	.04	−.14	−.11

a. As in Table 2, Kenya, Ethiopia, and Somalia excluded. Abbreviations as in Table 2.

(Brazzaville), Sudan, and perhaps other states extended, in varying degrees, aid and shelter to the revolutionaries (Wallerstein, 1967: 80; Hevi, 1967: 56; also many references in Africa Research Bulletin, 1964, 1965).

Tshombe was, of course, angered by the aid extended his domestic opponents and he vehemently denounced his foreign opponents on many occasions. Moreover, tensions along the Congo's borders, arising because of the infiltration of rebels from neighboring states, led to several brief military confrontations with Brazzaville, Uganda, and Burundi (Recorder, 1965: 1045). Thus, civil strife in the Congo was related to the frequency of both interference and force interactions. Hostility toward Tshombe naturally also gave rise to a number of events in the category of unfriendly interactions.

This case and others suggest several ways in which, according to the particular circumstances, domestic instability may in part explain foreign conflict behavior. Domestic instability may provoke a government into taking unusual repressive measures, and these measures can cause conflict with those governments which for ideological, humanitarian, or other reasons are sympathetic to the repressed. Leftist support for the Congo rebels, and the humanitarian concern expressed by a very few governments for the Biafran secessionists in Nigeria, exemplify this pattern. A regime will be most vulnerable in a period of domestic instability, and its foreign opponents may be encouraged to seize the apparent opportunity to weaken or destroy it by cooperation with domestic rebels. The intervention against Tshombe may illustrate the temptation that domestic unrest poses to foreign enemies. It is also conceivable (though rarely discussed) that support for Biafra was motivated in part by a desire to weaken one of Africa's potential great powers.

When a new regime comes to power in a coup d'etat, it will probably draw criticism from friends of the old regime, and this provides another link between domestic instability and foreign conflict. The Ghana government, for example, in the unstable period after the military coup in 1966, was subjected to criticism and threats by governments which had been friendly to Nkrumah. Defensive steps were taken against Guinea, Nkrumah's principal supporter (Bulletin, 1966: 483). For the domestic regime, internal instability naturally gives rise to a sense of insecurity, which in turn may lead to accusations of interference against foreign governments. The conservative government of Niger complained for many years of subversion by leftist states in league with domestic rebels (Zartman, 1966: 134), although the external threat was probably not serious. Chad, Sudan, and Ethiopia have been plagued by violent secession movements, and several international incidents, some involving military contingents, have arisen because each state fears outside support for the rebels. As we shall note below, however, there is evidence here, too, that the foreign danger was exaggerated.

The correlations linking domestic political instability and foreign conflict behavior are consistent only for the 1964-65 period, so too much should not be made of the relationship as an explanation of African international conflict. Later in the paper we shall discuss a marked general decline in the frequency of conflict interactions in Africa. It would appear that this explanation has become less important as foreign conflict behavior itself has become a less frequent phenomenon. However, in particular instances, the explanation still seems important, as in the fighting which broke out between Tanzania and Uganda, as well as in the criticism directed toward Uganda by Sudan following the overthrow of Uganda's president, Milton Obote, in 1971.

In the domain of international politics, the only finding of interest was a negative correlation between close association with France and foreign conflict behavior (Table 4).[16] In this study, the French associates were defined as those former French colonies still closely tied to the metropole by treaty arrangements, including accords on defense, foreign policy, technical assistance, military assistance, or general cooperation (Ligot, 1964).[17] It is true that these associates are generally among the poorest and weakest states

TABLE 4

SIMPLE CORRELATIONS: FOREIGN CONFLICT BEHAVIOR AND FRENCH ASSOCIATION[a]

	All	*U.I.*	*I.I.*	*F.I.*
Fr. Association	−.51	−.46	−.45	−.41

a. As in Table 2, Kenya, Ethiopia and Somalia excluded. Abbreviations as in Table 2.

in Africa,[18] but since indices of economic development and military power are not themselves associated with conflict at this level, such characteristics alone cannot explain the indication of pacificity.

Perhaps a better explanation is the French protection which extends to the associates. Partly because of their weakness and poverty, nearly all these states have reached explicit defense accords with France.[19] Nearly all receive technical military assistance. France maintains troops in some of the associated states, and in France forces designated for intervention in Africa are kept in readiness. France has twice demonstrated its African military capabilities by intervention in civil strife—to revive the fallen Mba government in Gabon in 1964, and to put down the secessionist movement in Chad. Consequently, the protection which comes from association with France may make other states reluctant to engage the associates in conflict (Minges, 1966: 37), and it may give the governments of the associates enough security to allow them to remain insensitive to dangers and opportunities which might move others to conflict.

REGIONAL FACTORS AND THE COURSE OF CONFLICT

Conflict events data need not be used solely in the search for correlates of conflict. By simply counting the events which occur in particular time periods, events data can be used to chart the course of international conflict over time. If African conflict events are counted for each year in the period under study, a most interesting pattern can be seen (Figure 1). A distinct flare-up in African conflict occurred in 1965, when several conflicts—the disputes involving Somali irredenta, the crisis connected with Rhodesia's unilateral declaration of independence, conflicts involving alleged Ghanaian subversion, and conflicts involving Tshombe's Congo—were quite active. Since that year there has been a steady yearly decline in the frequency of international conflict events. This decline is evident even when the rather exceptional events in the Somali conflict and the 1965 Rhodesia crisis are

[198]

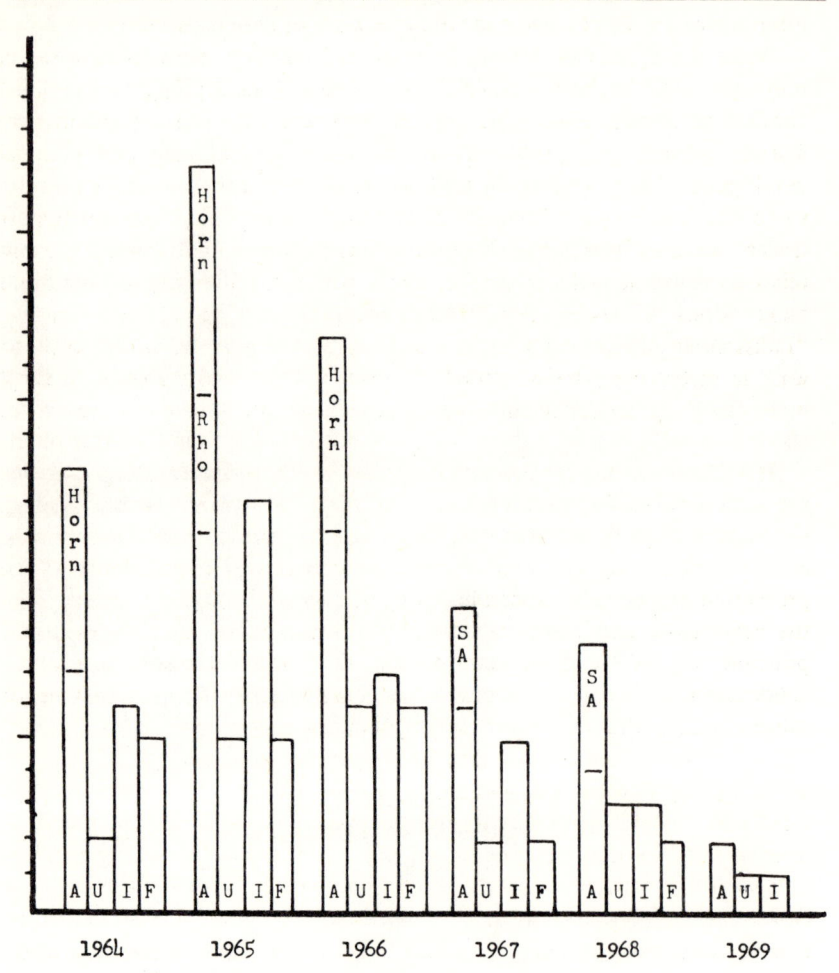

^aIncludes intra-arena and extra-arena conflict (see text). The frequency of all conflict interactions (A), as well as of unfriendly interactions (U), interference interactions (I), and force interactions (F) are shown. Frequency of interactions in the Horn and the frequency of interactions involving South Africa (SA) and Rhodesia (Rho) shown in years of interest.

Figure 1: AVERAGE MONTHLY INTERNATIONAL CONFLICT INTERACTION FREQUENCIES IN AFRICA, 1964-69[a]

excluded. Moreover, the decline is most apparent in those interactions—interference and force—which involve questions of national security.

While the decline in African international conflict seems to have set in only after 1965, African statesmen had for some time deplored international conflict as dysfunctional. The general view was that conflict would only distract African governments from the tasks of economic and political development while opening the way for great-power intervention. Opposition to conflict was a major factor in the call for African "unity," by which most leaders seem to have meant little more than a disposition toward friendly relations aimed at avoiding conflict while, perhaps, promoting economic and other forms of cooperation. Thus, Julius Nyerere (1963) has written: "Indissoluble African unity is the stone bridge which would enable us all to walk in safety over this whirlpool of power politics, and enable us to carry more easily the economic and social loads which now threaten to overwhelm us."

The Charter of the Organization of African Unity dedicates that body to the achievement of a "better life for the peoples of Africa" (Article II), and in accordance with the view that international conflict would prevent the achievement of this goal, the Charter also contains provisions aimed at the prevention of aggression and subversion. The Charter establishes "respect for the sovereignty and territorial integrity of each State" as a fundamental principle of the organization (Article III), and expresses "unreserved condemnation, in all its forms, of political assassination as well as of subversive activities on the part of neighbouring States or any other States." The principle of respect for territorial integrity was strengthened against states such as Morocco and Somalia, which held territorial claims with some ethnic or historic justification, by a 1964 resolution pledging O.A.U. members to "respect the borders existing on their achievement of national independence" (Resolution 16, First Assembly of Heads of State and Government). Yet while a doctrine which held international conflict to be dysfunctional for African states had existed for some years, and while prohibitions against aggression and subversion had existed since the founding of the O.A.U. in 1963, the decline in the frequency of conflict interactions became apparent only after 1965. Clearly some governments, despite doctrine and prohibition, must have regarded international conflict as useful to their ends.

An explanation of the decline of African international conflict may be developed through a survey of conflict in each region of Africa. While there are some states such as Egypt and Algeria, which have been important actors in international conflict throughout Africa, most conflict does occur within regions in Africa. It is only natural that there should be more issues—boundary disputes, political rivalries among leaders, fears of subversion, and the like—and that conflict on these issues should be more intense among states within a region than between states within a region and states without. This is especially so on a continent where the capacity of states to affect other states at any distance is so limited. Even though President Nyerere came to feel, for example, that the bloodshed in the Nigerian civil war ought to be halted and Biafra given its independence, there was little he could do from across the continent to advance the Biafran cause Thus, the level of conflict between Nigeria and Tanzania remained low, even though Nyerere had called the unity of Nigeria into question by recognizing Biafra.

The criteria which define a region usually include geographic proximity as well as historic, ethnic, or economic ties among the members (Cantori and Spiegel, 1970),[20] and on the basis of such criteria concepts of African regions such as "West Africa" and "North Africa" are commonly held. There are some African states which do not participate in conflict in the regions to which they are typically assigned, and in one region, East Africa, no significant conflict occurred between 1964 and 1969. In analyzing international conflict, therefore, it is convenient to think in terms of "conflict arenas" corresponding only roughly to the usual African regions, and composed of states which interact on certain basic conflicted issues. The membership of an arena is determined by comparing the membership of African regions ordinarily based on other criteria and including or excluding states so as to maximize the events frequency within the arena while minimizing the frequency of events involving states outside the arena. Using this procedure, the conflict arenas shown in Table 5 can be established.[21] The yearly frequency of events in each arena is shown in Table 6.

West Africa

In West Africa,[22] the decline in the number of conflict events can be attributed largely to the relaxation of international tensions following the military coup in Ghana in 1966.[23] The socialist regime of Kwame Nkrumah had been regarded as "radical" in African international politics, and several of the "conservative" West African governments were extremely sensitive to the danger of subversion from Ghana. These fears had been acute in 1963, when Ghanaian responsibility for the assassination of President Olympio of Togo was suspected (Thompson, 1969: 311),[24] and again in 1965, when a team of subversives apprehended in Niger was widely thought to have come from Ghana. After the fall of Nkrumah, West African tensions remained high for a time because of the fear that Guinea, in which Nkrumah

TABLE 5
AFRICAN CONFLICT ARENAS, AS SHOWN BY INTERNATIONAL CONFLICT EVENTS DATA, 1964-69

	Intra-Arena Events	Extra-Arena Events		Intra-Arena Events	Extra-Arena Events
West Africa			*East and Central Africa*		
Guinea	65	4	Congo (Kinshasa)	74	45
Ghana	63	24	Sudan	41	16
Ivory Coast	38	1	Burundi	34	0
Niger	20	0	Rwanda	32	4
Dahomey	15	1	Congo (Brazzaville)	32	5
Nigeria	10	16	Uganda	31	6
Upper Volta	9	0	Chad	24	2
Senegal	8	1	Central Africa Rep.	10	8
Togo	8	1		278	86
Mali	4	8			
Sierra Leone	2	0			
	242	56			
North Africa			*Southern Africa*		
Tunisia	17	3	Zambia	103	15
Morocco	15	0	Rhodesia	71	44
Algeria	14	17	Malawi	54	12
U.A.R.	13	27	Tanzania	45	18
Mauritania	5	3	South Africa	25	15
	64	50		298	104
The Horn					
Somali Republic	248	5			
Kenya	155	14			
Ethiopia	93	15			
	496	34			

had taken refuge, would undertake some military or subversive action to restore Nkrumah to power. As these fears proved illusory, however, and as no new challenger to the established order arose, the decline in the frequency of events in the arena began.

It is interesting that the coup in Ghana can be partially attributed to the view in the Ghana military that international conflict was dysfunctional and futile for Ghana. One goal of the officers executing the coup was the termination of the various fruitless conflicts in which Ghana had been engaged. Just after the coup, General Ankrah, the first military chief of state, proclaimed an end to Ghana's disputes with its neighbors, announcing (Bulletin, 1966: 467-468): "The leaders of the (National Liberation) Council

TABLE 6
CONFLICT INTERACTION FREQUENCIES IN AFRICAN CONFLICT ARENAS, 1964-69

	1964	1965	1966	1967	1968	1969
West Africa	16	41	36	16	5	7
North Africa	2	14	,9	7	0	0
The Horn	67	70	74	36	0	1
E. & C. Africa	41	37	33	1	21	6
Southern Africa	7	37	14	37	46	8

and myself are pledged to honour the Charter of the O.A.U. and abide strictly by the O.A.U. resolutions on political refugees and subversion. The days of harbouring political refugees to subvert other states are over." Ankrah's successor, General Afrifa (1966: 65-74, 104-105), attributed his own disgust with the Nkrumah regime partly to the disparity between Ghana's military capabilities and Nkrumah's adventurism in foreign policy.[25]

Afrifa's assessment of Ghana's capacity does not seem unduly modest, since with an army of 14,000 men and with generally quite limited national resources, Ghana was probably not capable of carrying out military offensives abroad or of supporting substantial guerrilla operations. Nkrumah might train small numbers of guerrilla agents, but these agents never proved effective at overturning foreign regimes. To instigate and support major insurrections abroad would have required a developed logistics capability, especially against such periodically hostile states as Niger, Nigeria, and Dahomey, which were located at some distance from Ghana's borders. With its limited military forces, Ghana simply did not have this capability.

Limited capabilities also limited other West African conflicts. It was never really possible that Guinea, with an army of 3,000 men, could, as threatened (Recorder, 1966: 1331), launch an attack 300 miles or more across Ivory Coast or other states against Ghana after the military coup. It is thus not surprising that the Ghana-Guinea conflict faded rather quickly. Guinea and Ivory Coast, old ideological opponents, bickered until recently over trawler seizures, airplane seizures, and other incidents, but since each had insignificant military forces neither could seriously endanger the security of the other. This may explain the desultory character, despite continuing ideological differences, of this conflict in recent years. Indeed, leaders of the two countries have now begun to speak of a rapprochement (Bulletin, 1970: 1921), and as in other West African conflicts, an era of relatively good relations has set in.

North Africa

In North Africa, as Table 6 shows, conflict has been at a low ebb throughout the 1964-69 period. Indeed, since Algeria and Egypt were both more active outside the arena than within,[26] the region does not stand out clearly as a conflict arena. If the data collection extended back to 1963, however, the arena could be more clearly distinguished, since in that year Moroccan irredentist claims, rooted in the historic religious authority of the Sultan of Morocco over a wide section of North Africa (Reyner, 1963: 196; Kapil, 1966: 664), were more insistently pursued. In October 1963 brief fighting broke out between Algeria and Morocco in a region particularly rich in minerals, and the U.A.R. extended military assistance to Algeria in the struggle (Mansfield, 1969: 92; Wild, 1966: 25). Since the border war, the most active dispute in the arena set Tunisia at odds with the U.A.R. over President Bourguiba's criticism of Nasser's belligerent stance toward Israel. Other disputes have centered on Moroccan claims to sovereignty over the territory of Mauritania and Tunisian claims to a section of Algerian territory in a region of oil fields. But few events have been recorded in any of these disputes.

It is interesting to note that no conflict events were recorded in North Africa after 1967, the year of the Arab-Israeli war. This coincidence of dates suggests that one reason for the low level of conflict in the arena may be an enhanced sense of Arab solidarity. Certainly the absence of events in the Tunisia-U.A.R. dispute after 1967 can be explained by the inappropriateness of Tunisian criticism of Egypt in its time of trial. Perhaps other North African governments have been influenced to seek harmonious relations with their neighbors because of the confrontation with Israel.

But distant Israel poses no threat to the Maghreb states of northwestern Africa, and these states are hardly compelled to forgo all prior claims by the Middle Eastern tensions. Thus it may be that the futility of conflict in the Maghreb, demonstrated by the stalemate in the Algeria-Morocco border war, is also a factor explaining the decline in the frequency of conflict events. In the border war the participants quickly suffered counterbalancing defeats, and within a few months each side had agreed to withdraw from occupied territory. Certainly neither side had demonstrated an effective offensive capability. Yet with very large armies—45,000 men in Morocco and 53,000 in Algeria—and with ample supplies of modern imported weapons, each country remains capable of countering an attack by the other. Consequently, there is little profit to be had in renewed conflict. Moreover, neither Morocco nor Algeria can risk turning against other states in the area because of the danger that its rival would take countermeasures in a moment of distraction.

Since conflict has gained nothing for states in the Maghreb, it is not surprising that a new era of cooperation has begun there. Algeria's President Houari Boumedienne, who came to power in a military coup in 1965, has proven to be a skillful diplomat, and it is he who has arranged the detente. With the discovery of rich phosphate deposits in Spanish Sahara, some dispute arose among Algeria, Morocco, and Mauritania over true sovereignty in the colony. Boumedienne was able to end this conflict and to organize a common front of the three countries aimed at forcing Spanish withdrawal. Presumably terms have been reached on territorial arrangements after decolonization. Algeria and Morocco have reached an agreement on the common exploitation of mineral deposits along their frontier (Bulletin, 1970: 1748), while Morocco has renounced its territorial claims against both Algeria and Mauritania (Recorder, 1970: 2479). In a separate development, Algeria and Tunisia have signed an accord which ostensibly settles all points at issue in their border dispute (Bulletin, 1970: 1663). Had experience shown international conflict to be more useful for states in the arena, these reconciliations might not have been possible.

The Horn

In the horn of Africa (named for the shape of the coastline) one might expect international conflict to be especially persistent because the principal disputes in the region involve the homeland of the Somali people, one of the few true nations in Africa (Lewis, 1970). The Somali nation shares a common history of nomadic expansion, a common language, and a common religion (Islam). International conflict arises because the borders of the Somali Republic do not coincide with the limits of Somali habitation, and large numbers of Somalis live in adjacent sections of Kenya and Ethiopia.[27] However, while the strength of Somali nationalism may be responsible for the intensity of international conflict in the arena, where more events are recorded than in any other arena, even here a decline in the frequency of conflict events has occurred. Indeed, virtually no fighting occurred in 1968 and 1969. Somalia has entered into agreements with Kenya and Ethiopia by which the parties have agreed to take steps to avoid conflict,[28] and the infrequency of events in recent years suggests that these agreements have been successfully implemented.[29]

Yet there is little doubt that in the years after 1963 Somalia lent moral and material support to guerrilla activity in Kenya and Ethiopia in the hope of forcing these states into a revision of boundaries. Ethiopia resisted this guerrilla activity with its powerful army and air force, reportedly going so far as to attack Somali frontier posts and to carry out air raids against frontier towns (Diary, 1964: 1648, 1729). This resistance made it clear that Somalia could accomplish little without risking major war, and major war was surely to be avoided in view of the clear military superiority enjoyed by Ethiopia.[30] Kenya's resistance was also firm, and with the assistance of some Ethiopian troops (Bulletin, 1967: 817) it too was able to stimy the guerrilla drive.

A major factor in bringing the fighting to a close was the election in 1967 of a Somali prime minister, Mohammed Egal, who was convinced that his country could no longer afford the heavy military expenditures which the conflict required (Castagno, 1970: 26). Although a military government seized power in 1969, it has shown no inclination to resume the fighting. Thus again the futility of conflict seems to have led to a reduction in the frequency of conflict events.

East and Central Africa

In East and Central Africa, the link between domestic political instability and foreign conflict behavior is striking. Indeed, international conflict in the arena has nearly always been connected with civil unrest—in particular with the civil wars in the Congo (Leopoldville), Sudan, Chad, and Burundi.[31] The Congo has been by far the most active participant in arena conflict. Most of the events in its conflict score accumulated during the Tshombe period, when, as we have seen, many African states cooperated against the Premier. Tshombe, however, proved quite capable of obtaining outside aid against the insurgents,[32] and none of his African opponents was able to counter this support. Thus, even before the fall of Tshombe[33] a sharp drop in the frequency of conflict events was noticeable,[34] and the Congo was moving toward an accommodation with Sudan and Kenya on an end of aid to the insurgents (Recorder, 1965: 1012; Bulletin, 1965: 361).

President Mobutu, who came to power in 1965, is another of those second-generation African leaders who seems intent on avoiding foreign conflict, and he has been generally successful in maintaining good relations with neighboring states.[35] However, relations with the Brazzaville Congo have been sporadically troubled. Perhaps it is inevitable that the Marxist regime in Brazzaville and the Kinshasa government, which has been a favorite of Washington, should be suspicious of one another. Crises seem to occur whenever one government begins to suspect that there is a plot afoot against it. Recently, there was a period without incident following a reconciliation complete with a mutual presidential embrace in 1970, but interference interactions resumed just over a year later.

In the events arising out of the civil wars in Sudan and Chad, there is little evidence that neighboring states intended to subvert either government. Instead of prolonged hostilities, there were frequent meetings between conflict participants to set up investigative panels and border control commissions, or to take other steps to prevent further conflict. After incidents did occur, compensation, apologies, and assurances against recurrence were often extended.[36]

The basic problem in these conflicts seems to have been the difficulty that less developed states with relatively small armies may have in policing their borders. Here, this difficulty was enhanced by the presence of troublesome border populations—black refugees from Sudan residing in Uganda, and Moslem tribes straddling the border between Chad and Sudan. The upsurge in the frequency of events in this arena in 1968 (Table 6) was due primarily to conflict between Sudan and Uganda on the refugee problem. Similarly, conflict has arisen between Sudan and Ethiopia because of the presence of refugees from rebellious Eritrea in Sudan and of southern Sudanese refugees in Ethiopia. But since states have shown no interest in pushing incidents to warfare in the past,[37] one would expect any future crises to ease in due time. Moreover, the occasion for conflict may be passing, since there are signs in the recent reconciliation between the Sudanese rebels and the central government, and in French troop withdrawals from Chad, that domestic political stability is being restored.

The remaining significant dispute in this arena, between Rwanda and Burundi, also involved the movement of rebels across permeable international frontiers. In this case, refugees of the Tutsi tribe infiltrated Rwanda to overthrow the government, which was controlled by members of the Hutu tribe.[38] One may suspect official complicity in this infiltration because of the intense ethnic hatred between the governments. This hatred arose because of the overthrow in 1959-60 of the Tutsi aristocracy in Rwanda by the Hutu majority, acting with Belgian assistance. In Burundi the Tutsi still ruled, and vengeful Tutsi tribesmen sought refuge there. Rwanda proved capable of controlling the infiltration from Burundi, however, since both the military and the popular responses to the Tutsi rebels were quite violent. The conflict ended, at least temporarily, with the overthrow by the army of the traditional monarchy in Burundi in November 1966, although the government continued to be dominated by Tutsi. President Mobutu was able to arrange a formal reconciliation in March 1967 (Bulletin, 1967: 674). Indeed, Mobutu was also able to arrange for the signing of a mutual security pact involving Rwanda, Burundi, and the Congo (Kinshasa) in 1968—no small diplomatic accomplishment in view of past conflicts among these states.

Southern Africa

In the conflicts discussed so far, the frequency of conflict interactions has usually declined as existing governments have lost interest in continued futile struggle or as internal changes have brought new governments, opposed to the old foreign quarrels, to power. In the southern arena, the intensity of feeling on the racial issue raises some doubt as to whether conflict will fade in the usual African pattern. Certainly no clear pattern of declining conflict interactions is yet apparent (Table 6). Some observers—and participants—see a grave world crisis developing in southern Africa, as racial turmoil deepens and as great powers among the developed states involve themselves on one side or the other (Reed, 1967: 1; Kaunda, 1967: 13).

The conflict interaction scores of most actors in the arena (Table 5)[39] are not unusual compared to the scores of major actors in other arenas, and this suggests that the predicted shattering racial conflict has not yet developed. Even Zambia's high score does not result solely from the racial conflict, since it includes events in a minor dispute with Malawi on non-racial issues. The score of South Africa is surprisingly low, even though that country is buffered to some extent by the absence of a long common border with one of the more powerful black African states.[40] With its great power and obvious interest in regional order, South Africa would surely be more active if an international racial war were underway. Tanzania, which is regarded by some South Africans as the greatest potential threat to the security of their state,[41] is also not as active as it would be in such a confrontation.

Events in the conflict between Zambia and Rhodesia, however, have been rather frequent.[42] These events have arisen partly from Zambia's fear that its economic ties with South Africa—ties which have brought Zambia most of its electric power and provided it with rail connections for the export of its copper (Austin, 1966)—would be cut in retaliation for U.S. sanctions or hostile O.A.U. actions before alternative arrangements could be made. But most events, occurring in 1967 and 1968, were connected with the infiltration of armed guerrillas from Zambia into Rhodesia.

Zambia, which has a long common border with Rhodesia and a short common border with South-West Africa, is the only black African state from which guerrilla strikes can be launched, and it is also the state which would bear the brunt of white retaliation should the fighting intensify. Already there have been incursions, perhaps accidental, by South African air and ground forces, which demonstrate the retaliatory capability of the white regimes. A South African air base near the Zambian border generates uneasiness in Lusaka as do overflights of high-altitude reconnaisance aircraft

(Hall, 1969: 186). In the present situation, then, one could expect Zambia, which in the past has denied aiding, sheltering, or encouraging guerrilla forces, to continue to be cautious in its policy toward the infiltrators. To date, in any event, the guerrilla bands crossing the border have been quite small, and white Rhodesia, with the assistance of some South African forces, has had no difficulty in defending itself.

Meanwhile, black African governments generally have grown discouraged with the prospects for liberation in Rhodesia and South Africa, and their support for the liberation movement has dwindled (Hoskyns, 1967: 170; Gupta, 1967: 58-59). A few black governments, indeed, have begun to advocate a "dialogue" with South Africa in the stated belief that peaceful contacts over the long run might do more to promote the cause of the southern blacks than ineffective hostility. One may doubt, of course, that peaceful pressures will ever persuade the southern whites to relinquish their dominant position, just as one may suspect that governments interested in a dialogue are also interested in the economic benefits of friendship with Africa's wealthiest and most industrialized country. All the same, considering South Africa's capacity to produce its own essential weapons (Leiss, 1965: 142; Howe, 1969: 155; Gutteridge, 1964; 113), its ability to mobilize 250,000 armed whites in an emergency (Leiss, 1965: 141), and its evident determination to aid Rhodesia, where the small size of the white population once made revolution seem likely,[43] there is certainly reason for discouragement about the prospects for liberation.

Only a deterioration of the domestic order in Rhodesia and South Africa might enhance the prospects for successful guerrilla action. There is no sign of such a deterioration at present, and the tight control exercised by the white regimes over their black populations constitutes a formidable barrier to any future deterioration. Pass laws, the white monopoly on firearms ownership and weapons training, the banning of dangerous foreign publications, the segregation of blacks in isolated districts, and draconian police tactics are measures which may well continue to inhibit revolutionary activity.

Thus, it seems altogether possible that the low level of conflict observed in this arena in 1969, comparable to the level of conflict before Rhodesia's unilateral declaration of independence in 1965, will persist. Not only are there sound reasons for a continuing low level of guerrilla infiltration but the economic sources of conflict are also becoming less important as Zambia disentangles itself more and more from Rhodesia.[44] Instead of a race war the immediate future may bring a period of disengagement.

The high conflict score of Malawi in this arena is the result of its involvement with Tanzania and Zambia over certain territorial claims and over the alleged infiltration of subversives into Malawi. None of these states has an army of significant size, however, and the chances that these disputes could lead to a major confrontation are remote. President Banda made his first charges of subversion in 1964, when he claimed that some dismissed government ministers, suspected of left leanings, were launching expeditions against him from Tanzania and Zambia. There is no evidence that these two countries actually supported subversion, and both offered official assurances that they were not doing so (Diary, 1965: 2144; Bulletin, 1965: 348). However serious the threat once was, it has evidently passed since no new charges have been made since 1967.

The territorial dispute was initiated by President Nyerere in May 1967, when he announced that he would no longer respect the colonial border in Lake Nyasa, which ran along Tanzania's shore, but instead would respect only a border in the center of the lake. Dr. Banda countered with a claim extending some 100 miles into Tanzanian territory and advanced a further claim to a sizable strip of Zambian territory as well.[45] But such weak states could surely not attempt to fulfill these claims by force, and it is not surprising that by 1969 this issue, too, was fading in importance. The improvement of relations was signified in 1970 by the opening of full diplomatic relations between Malawi and Zambia (Bulletin, 1970: 1862).

Dr. Banda continued to arouse the hostility of governments throughout Africa, however, because of the economic and diplomatic links that he has forged with South Africa, and it is possible that an intensification of the racial conflict might someday subject Banda's government to more serious threats from abroad. On the other hand, as some black leaders begin to speak of a dialogue with South Africa, Dr. Banda appears less the renegade, and his immediate international position improves. While the racial conflict remains quiet, in any event, international conflict poses little threat to Malawi.

CONCLUSIONS

While unique regional factors may be partly responsible for the decline in the frequency of conflict interactions in Africa, certain general factors also seem to be at work. What is most striking is that those countries which apparently did initiate conflict to accomplish foreign policy ends were in every case frustrated. Nowhere has territory permanently changed hands following a resort to force, nor does it appear that governments have fallen as a result of subversion. The futility of African conflict is, of course, firmly rooted in the weakness of most African states. Even the more powerful governments, with the possible exception of South Africa, seem capable only of defensive, rather than offensive, action.

It may be that a learning process has taken place in African international relations. In the new independence situation, some governments with unfulfilled territorial ambitions or with ideological grievances did use force, threaten force, or engage in subversion. But as these governments learned the limits of their power, it became necessary for them or for their successors to adjust their behavior. Adjustment may have been hastened in several cases because foreign conflict came to be seen as contrary to national development goals. As a result of this learning process, the international behavior of the African states in 1969 conformed much more closely to the terms of the O.A.U. Charter than in 1964 and 1965.

For the immediate future, at least, one might expect conflict to remain infrequent in Africa since no major changes in absolute or relative power are apparent. Only in southern Africa does it seem possible that governments, motivated by the passions of the racial issue, might cast caution aside and engage in major fighting. But even in southern Africa present indications are that caution still reigns. The links between foreign conflict behavior and domestic political instability suggest that brief crises may arise when governments are overthrown or threatened from within. Indeed, recent conflicts involving Uganda with Tanzania and Sudan after the Uganda coup demonstrate the continued relevance of these links. But as domestic crises ease, the international crises, as in this recent case, will probably also fade.

For the long run, of course, the picture is less clear. Certainly it is possible that powerful states will emerge in Africa and that these states will be capable of engaging in conflict to accomplish their political and territorial ends. South Africa, which already possesses a modern army and air force, might someday, in the wake of civil unrest or increased guerrilla activity, claim the necessity of military action against Zambia. In the more distant future, other states such as Nigeria or Algeria may acquire an effective offensive capacity and be tempted to impose their will abroad. If so, then African unity and African brotherhood will be put to the test. For the present, however, the African determination to avoid conflict, to limit conflict, and to resolve conflict is most impressive.

NOTES

1. For discussions and representative applications, see Azar (1970), McClelland (1968), McGowan (1969), Rummel (1963, 1968, 1969), and Singer (1972).

2. The states included in this study were Algeria, Burundi, Cameroon, Central African Republic, Chad, Congo (Brazzaville), Congo (Kinshasa), Dahomey, Ethiopia, Gabon, Ghana, Guinea, Ivory Coast, Kenya, Liberia, Libya, Malagasy Republic, Malawi,

Mali, Mauritania, Morocco, Niger, Nigeria, Rhodesia, Rwanda, Senegal, Sierra Leone, Somali Republic, South Africa, Sudan, Tanzania, Togo, Tunisia, Uganda, United Arab Republic, Upper Volta, and Zambia. Since, with but minor exceptions, this list includes all African states, tests of statistical significance, appropriate where population samples are drawn, do not appear.

3. Using 1963 figures (United Nations, 1968), the mean national income of African countries was only about $.8 billion, while the comparable figure for Asian countries, excluding Japan was $3.5 billion. If India were excluded also, the Asian figure was $2.1 billion.

4. Algeria and Morocco, with the largest regular armies outside the U.A.R., have armies of 53,000 and 45,000 men respectively (ISS, 1970). The three states mentioned in the text have armies of 200,000 men or more.

5. Africa has 11 inhabitants per square kilometer, while Asia has 69. These are 1967 estimates (United Nations, 1969: 26).

6. These objections may be especially pertinent in regard to the former French colonies, since censorship is unusually severe there (Levine, 1965: 58-59) and since we have used sources compiled in English-speaking countries. However, international conflict events occur before an international audience, and it seems unlikely that information on such events could have been systematically kept from or ignored by sources which report on African politics with such care as those used here.

7. However, if one calculates the overlap in reporting in the most complete source and each of the other sources, the figures are less impressive. For the ratio:

$$\frac{\text{number of events reported in common by } \textit{Africa Research Bulletin} \text{ and the other source}}{\text{total number of events in the other source}}$$

one finds a 42 per cent overlap between *African Recorder* and *Africa Research Bulletin* and a 47 per cent overlap between *Africa Diary* and *Africa Research Bulletin*. Thus, in drawing events for publication from the universe of actual events, the less complete source drew the same events as the most complete source somewhat less than half the time. This would imply that the universe of actual events is considerably larger than the use of *Africa Research Bulletin* alone would indicate. Nonetheless, the figures are high enough to allow one to hope that a good portion of African international conflict is included in the collection, especially when events from the supplementary sources are added in.

8. Two experiments were conducted. In one, the subject identified and classified events in the first three pages (where most conflict events are reported) of ten randomly selected issues of *Africa Research Bulletin*. Using the formula for the coefficient of reliability (Holsti, 1969: 140):

$$\text{C.R.} = \frac{2M}{N1 + N2}$$

where M is the number of coding decisions on which the judges are in agreement and N1 and N2 refer to the number of decisions made by judges 1 and 2 respectively, we find that the subject reproduced the events data collection with a reliability score of .79. This subject used only written instructions. A second subject, using both written and verbal instructions, identified and classified events from the first three pages of five randomly selected issues with a C.R. of .87.

9. When individual states are treated as cases (see text), the product-moment intercorrelations among the conflict variables are as follows: unfriendly interactions-interference interactions, .56; unfriendly interactions-force interactions, .41; interference interactions-force interactions, .68.

10. These cases may be contrasted to dyadic cases, which are pairs of states. Dyadic cases allow us to treat conflict as a relationship between states rather than as an attribute of states. Preliminary exploration of this data using dyadic cases, however, has not been rewarding.

11. Civil war was scored dichotomously (1 if present, 0 if absent). This was necessary because in most countries where civil war has occurred, official secrecy about events has rendered any sort of events count impossible. As defined for this project, civil war included wars of secession, guerrilla warfare, and mass terrorism.

12. A modified logarithmic scale was used in scoring broad estimates for this variable. Estimates were obtained from the events data sources and from various secondary works.

13. Events counted in this variable included attempted and successful coups d'etat, palace revolts, military revolts, and attempted or successful assassinations of heads of state or other prominent officials.

14. Collins (1967), using somewhat different variables, found relationships between domestic strife and foreign conflict behavior in the 1963-65 period.

15. In 1960 Nkrumah cabled Tshombe in Katanga (Mazrui, 1967: 38): "You have assembled in your support the foremost advocates of imperialism and colonialism in Africa and the most determined opponents of African freedom. How can you, as an African, do this?"

16. This finding tends to confirm the classification by McGowan (1969: 216), using quantitative data, of most of the former French colonies as "Inactive-Dependent" states. Indeed, all but two of the 14 states in his category are former French colonies. See Note 6 on reliability of data from French-speaking countries.

17. The states counted here as French associates on the basis of data given by Ligot (1964) were Cameroon, Central African Republic, Chad, Congo (Brazzaville), Dahomey, Gabon, Ivory Coast, Malagasy Republic, Mali, Mauritania, Niger, Senegal, Togo, and Upper Volta.

18. Some of these states—Ivory Coast, Gabon, and Senegal in particular—are well off from the point of view of per-capita income, but none has an unusually large national income, a large population or a sizable army.

19. Only Mali and Upper Volta lack bilateral defense accords with France (ISS, 1970: 47). Upper Volta, however, does have an agreement calling for technical military assistance.

20. The attempt by Russett (1967: esp. 182-186) to develop quantitative criteria for establishing the existence of regions and subsystems excluded sub-Saharan Africa, for lack of socio-cultural data, from most of the analysis. He felt, however, that the states of former French Africa might have met all criteria had full data been available. North African states were grouped in an Afro-Asian region on a large number of indices, not including conflict.

21. As can be seen in Table 5, three states—the U.A.R., Algeria, and Mali—participated in more conflict outside their arena than within it. Strictly speaking, if extra-arena conflict is to be minimized, these states should be excluded from the arenas to which they are assigned. However, their extra-arena interactions involved far distant states,

particularly Tshombe's Congo, Rhodesia, and South Africa, and this would have made their inclusion in any other arena most inconvenient in an analysis of regional conflict. States such as Gabon or Liberia, which have been assigned to no region, participated in 0 or 1 interactions in the regions to which they might be assigned.

The reader should note that when intra-arena actor scores are calculated, a single event within the arena adds to the score of two arena actors. A single extra-arena event adds to the score of only one arena actor. Thus the intra-arena event score might be considered inflated by a factor of two.

22. Liberia is the most conspicuous absentee in the list of West African conflict actors. Although Liberia has participated in African conflict by criticizing the white regimes in Rhodesia and South Africa, its only recorded West African interaction was the criticism in 1967 of the detention by Ivory Coast of the Guinean U.N. delegation. This is in accord with the analysis of Liberian foreign policy by Liebenow (1962: 383-384; 1969: 196-204). According to Liebenow, the settler oligarchy seeks to avoid undue foreign pressure by maintaining a good reputation in pan-African causes and by avoiding conflict with nearby states, particularly Guinea, a potential ideological opponent.

23. Eight of the twenty dyadic conflicts in this arena include Ghana under Nkrumah. Four more include states participating in events which arose in the immediate aftermath of the coup.

24. It is now recognized that the assassination was carried out by disgruntled soldiers in the Togo army who had recently returned from the French colonial wars (Howe, 1967: 9).

25. Afrifa felt that Ghana's army had been quite unprepared for dispatch to the Congo (Leopoldville) in 1960, and that it was even less prepared for Nkrumah's planned invasion of Rhodesia.

26. The rather high extra-arena scores of these two actors index their importance as leaders in African leftist causes. Libya does not appear on the list of North African actors because it was inactive in the 1964-69 period. Its inactivity has come to an end under the new military regime.

27. Charlier (1966: 310) estimates that there are 850,000 Somalis in the Ogaden and Haud regions of Ethiopia. About 240,000 Somalis are thought to reside in Kenya's northeastern region (Drysdale, 1964: 28). Since the 1967 population of the Somali Republic was estimated at 2,600,000, it can be seen that a considerable portion of the Somali ethnic group resides outside the boundaries of the Republic.

28. In March 1964 at Khartoum, Ethiopia and Sudan agreed to a cease-fire along the border, to the mutual withdrawal of troops from the border region, and to the cessation of hostile propaganda (Bulletin, 1964: 37). There were some incidents after this agreement, but in 1967 only five events are recorded. In 1968 the Khartoum agreement was reaffirmed, and joint commissions of local officials were established to handle border incidents (Bulletin, 1968: 973). Kenya and Somalia jointly agreed to take steps to maintain peace in the border region in an agreement signed at Arusha, Tanzania, in October 1967 (Recorder, 1967: 1828).

29. An exchange of gunfire on the Ethiopia-Somalia border in 1969 led not to escalation but only to urgent consultations aimed at easing tensions (Bulletin, 1969: 1461).

30. Somalia has about 10,000 troops while Ethiopia has about 40,000. The Ethiopian air force is well armed with weapons from the United States and its men have been trained by instructors from the U.S. and Sweden (ISS, 1970; Greenfield, 1965: 358-359).

31. Gabon, a typically inactive French ally, is a Central African state which is not a significant conflict actor in the arena.

32. Tshombe hired white mercenaries from many countries. He also obtained assistance from the United States, including, in August 1964, the loan of four transport planes and their crews. The joint U.S.-Belgian paratroop rescue mission to Stanleyville, in November 1964, was conducted in coordination with government and mercenary forces so that the heart of the rebel territory was penetrated and the rebellion broken.

33. Tshombe was dismissed for internal reasons in October 1965 after the rebels had been effectively suppressed. President Kasavubu may have feared the consolidation of Tshombe's power at this time (Recorder, 1965: 1204; Colvin, 1968: 207-214).

34. Tshombe made no charges of subversion against Burundi after November 1964, none against Sudan after December, and none against Uganda after March 1965. During the rest of 1965 he leveled only one charge of subversion against Brazzaville.

35. Mobutu was involved with Rwanda in 1968 in a dispute over the extradition of a mercenary force which had entered the Congo from Angola and seized Bukavu before fleeing into Rwanda. In the same year there was a dispute with Brazzaville over the execution by the Kinshasa government of Pierre Mulele, a former rebel leader who had been induced to leave Brazzaville under a false guarantee of amnesty.

36. For example, after Sudanese troops had crossed into Uganda in 1968, Sudan offered apologies and assured a Uganda delegation that incidents would not recur. The two states agreed to establish a ministerial commission to meet twice yearly to resolve differences (Bulletin, 1968: 1145). A joint border commission was also agreed upon by Chad and Sudan (Diary, 1965: 348), and the two states later reached an agreement on compensation for incidents (Bulletin, 1967: 860, 902).

37. As noted in the Sudan-Uganda dispute, however, troops have crossed borders. In 1965 the Central African Republic alleged that Sudanese troops had crossed its borders to fire on refugees (Bulletin, 1965: 257). In 1966 Sudan charged that Chad troops had occupied a border village (Bulletin, 1966: 208), and in 1967 Sudan charged Ethiopia with attacking border villages near Eritrea (Bulletin, 1967: 735). These and other incidents may result from inadvertence in a region of poorly defined borders, or from a design to cripple guerrilla operations and inspire more effective police efforts in the neighboring state. Only small numbers of troops have been involved in these incidents, and the incursions have always been brief.

38. In 1963 a large force of Tutsi guerrillas from Burundi was defeated, with great loss of life, by the Rwanda military. In 1964 Rwanda linked this conflict to the radical-conservative political contest in Africa, because Burundi was at that time apparently cooperating in Chinese assistance to the Congo rebels (Bulletin, 1964: 7). The conflict flared again in 1966, however, with border crossings alleged on both sides, long after Burundi's cooperation with China had ended.

39. Botswana, Lesotho, and Swaziland, largely or wholly dependent on South Africa, were not included in this study. Also not included, because they are not African states, were the Portuguese colonies—Angola and Mozambique. Very little is known of what is happening in the racial struggle in these colonies, and reliable events data collection is not possible. However, this exclusion means that a certain amount of conflict involving African states which are included in the study, particularly South Africa, Zambia, and Tanzania, is not analyzed. On the fighting in Angola and Mozambique, see Howe (1969).

40. As noted below, Zambia and South-West Africa do share a short common border, but it lies in a desolate region far from South African population centers.

41. See the remark to this effect by the South African Deputy Minister of Police (Bulletin, 1968: 974). Tanzania may be so regarded because its population, at over 12,000,000, is three times greater than the population of Zambia (although Tanzania is only slightly wealthier). Moreover, guerrilla training camps in Tanzania, which has no common border with South Africa, are relatively secure from attack. Further, President Nyerere has agreed to host the O.S.U. Liberation Committee in Dar-es-Salaam, and he has forged close ties with the People's Republic of China.

42. Sixty-three events in the intra-arena conflict scores of Zambia and Rhodesia result from their mutual conflict.

43. Although no formal alliance has been announced, Prime Minister Vorster has said (Bulletin, 1967: 845): "We are good friends with both Portugal and Rhodesia, and good friends do not need a pact. Good friends know what their duty is if their neighbor's house is on fire. I assure you that whatever becomes necessary will be done." According to Howe (1969: 155), there are 2,700 white South Africans now serving in Rhodesia.

44. The severance of economic ties with Rhodesia is being facilitated by the construction of a hard-surfaced road to Dar-es-Salaam, and of the Tan-Zam railroad which, with Chinese assistance, should be completed in 1974. An oil pipeline already links Zambia and Tanzania. According to a recent report, Zambia will soon be fully independent of power from the Kariba power station in Rhodesia (New York Times, September 28, 1970: 2).

45. Banda feels, on ethnic grounds, that these borders were unfairly determined in the colonial period (Bulletin, 1968: 1178).

REFERENCES

Africa Diary. New Delhi: Africa Publications (India).
Africa Research Bulletin. Exeter, England: Africa Research Ltd.
African Recorder. New Delhi: M.S.R. Khemchand.
AFRIFA, A. (1966) The Ghana Coup. London: Cass.
AUSTIN, D. (1966) "Sanctions and Rhodesia." World Today (London) 22 (March): 106-113.
AZAR, E. (1970) "Analysis of international events." Peace Research Reviews (Oakville, Ontario) 4 (November).
CANTORI, L. and S. SPIEGEL (1970) "The international relations of regions." Polity 2 (Summer): 397-425.
CASTAGNO, A. (1970) "Somalia goes military." Africa Report 15 (February): 25-27.
CHARLIER, T. (1966) "A propos des conflits de frontière entre la Somalie, l'Ethiopie et la Kenya." Revue Française de Science Politique 16 (April): 310-319.
COLLINS, J. (1967) "Foreign conflict behavior and domestic disorder in Africa." Ph.D. Dissertation. Northwestern University.
COLVIN, I. (1968) The Rise and Fall of Moishe Tshombe. London: Leslie Frewin.
DRYSDALE, J. (1964) The Somali Dispute. New York: Praeger.
GALTUNG, J. and M. RUGE (1965) "The structure of foreign news." Journal of Peace Research 2: 64-91.
GREENFIELD, R. (1965) Ethiopia, a New Political History. London: Pall Mall.
GUPTA, A. (1967) "The Rhodesian crisis and the Organization of African Unity." International Studies (New Delhi) 9 (July): 55-64.

GUTTERIDGE, W. (1964) "The strategic implications of sanctions against South Africa," pp. 107-115 in R. Segal (ed.) Sanctions Against South Africa. Baltimore: Penguin.
HALL, R. (1969) The High Price of Principles: Kaunda and the White South. London: Hodder & Stoughton.
HEVI, E. (1967) The Dragon's Embrace. New York: Praeger.
HOLSTI, O. (1969) Content Analysis for the Social Sciences and the Humanities. Reading, Mass.: Addison-Wesley.
HOSKYNS, C. (1967) "Trends and developments in the Organization of African Unity," pp. 164-178 in The Year Book of World Affairs, 1967. London: Stevens.
HOWE, R. (1969) "War in southern Africa." Foreign Affairs 48 (October): 150-165.
--- (1967) "Togo." Africa Report 12 (May): 6-12.
Institute for Strategic Studies (1970) The Military Balance, 1970-1971. London: ISS.
KAPIL, R. (1966) "On the conflict potential of inherited boundaries in Africa." World Politics 18 (July): 656-673.
KAUNDA, K. (1967) "Crisis in southern Africa." African Forum 2.
LEISS, A. (1965) Apartheid and United Nations Collective Sanctions. New York: Carnegie Endowment.
LEVINE, V. (1965) "The course of political violence," pp. 58-79 in W. Lewis (ed.) French Speaking Africa. New York: Walker.
LEWIS, I. M. (1970) "The tribal factor in African politics," pp. A12-A16 in C. Legum and J. Drysdale (eds.) Africa Contemporary Record, 1969-1970. Exeter, England: Africa Research Ltd.
LIEBENOW, J. (1969) Liberia, the Evolution of Privilege. Ithaca: Cornell Univ. Press.
--- (1962) "Liberia," pp. 325-394 in G. Carter (ed.) African One Party States. Ithaca: Cornell Univ. Press.
LIGOT, M. (1964) Les Accords de Cooperation entre la France et les Etats africains d'Expression française. Paris: La Documentation Française.
McCLELLAND, C. (1968) "Access to Berlin: the quantity and variety of events, 1948-1963," pp. 159-186 in J. Singer (ed.) Quantitative International Politics. New York: Free Press.
McGOWAN, P. (1969) "The pattern of African diplomacy: a quantitative comparison." Journal of Asian and African Studies 4 (July): 202-221.
MANSFIELD, P. (1969) Nasser's Egypt. Baltimore: Penguin.
MAZRUI, A. (1967) Towards a Pax Africana. Chicago: Univ. of Chicago.
MINGES, C. (1966) Military Aspects of International Relations in the Developing Areas (Report no. P-3480). Santa Monica: RAND.
NYERERE, J. (1963) "A United States of Africa." Journal of Modern African Studies 1 (March): 1-6.
REED, D. (1967) The Battle for Rhodesia. New York: Devin Adair.
REYNER, A. (1963) "Morocco's international boundaries: a factual background." Journal of Modern African Studies 1 (September): 313-326.
RUMMEL, R. (1969) "Dimensions of foreign and domestic conflict behavior: a review of empirical findings," pp. 219-228 in D. Pruitt and R. Snyder (eds.) Theory and Research on the Causes of War. Englewood Cliffs, N.J.: Prentice-Hall.
--- (1968) "The relationship between national attributes and foreign conflict behavior," pp. 187-214 in J. Singer (ed.) Quantitative International Politics. New York: Free Press.

--- (1966) "A foreign conflict behavior code sheet." World Politics 18 (January): 283-296.

--- (1963) "Dimensions of conflict behavior within and between nations." General Systems Yearbook 8: 1-50.

RUSSETT, B. (1967) International Regions and the International System. Chicago: Rand McNally.

SINGER, J. (1972) "The 'correlates of war' project: an interim report." World Politics 24 (January): 243-270.

SMITH, R. (1969) "On the structure of foreign news: a comparison of the New York Times and the Indian White Papers." Journal of Peace Research 6: 23-35.

TANTER, R. (1966) "Dimensions of conflict behavior within and between nations, 1958-1960." Journal of Conflict Resolution 10 (March): 41-64.

THOMPSON, W. (1969) Ghana's Foreign Policy. Princeton: Princeton Univ. Press.

United Nations (1969) United Nations Statistical Yearbook, 1968. New York: United Nations.

--- (1968) Yearbook of National Accounts Statistics, 1967. New York: United Nations.

WALLERSTEIN, I. (1967) Africa, the Politics of Unity. New York: Random House.

WILD, P. (1966) "The Organization of African Unity and the Algeria-Moroccan border conflict." International Organization 20 (Winter): 18-36.

WILKENFELD, J. (1969) "Some further findings regarding the domestic and foreign conflict behavior of nations." Journal of Peace Research 6: 147-155.

--- (1968) "Domestic and foreign conflict behavior of nations." Journal of Peace Research 5: 56-69.

ZARTMAN, I. (1966) International Relations in the New Africa. Englewood Cliffs, N.J.: Prentice-Hall.

Chapter 8

NATIONAL ATTRIBUTES AND FOREIGN POLICY PARTICIPATION: A PATH ANALYSIS

JAMES G. KEAN
Bowling Green State University

PATRICK J. McGOWAN
Syracuse University

INTRODUCTION

The purpose of the research reported in this paper is to determine the extent to which the national attributes of size and modernization account for selected patterns of foreign policy participation. By cross-classifying these two attributes of nations, we have also produced a useful typology of national foreign policy actors which ranges from large-modern states to small, less-modern countries. Our research should be of interest to scholars in international studies because concepts like size, modernization, economic development, and national power have traditionally been thought to be important determining factors of the external behavior of states. More recently, specialists in the comparative study of foreign policy have proposed alternative typologies of nation-states in an effort to isolate basic types of foreign policy actors.

AUTHOR'S NOTE: *Although they are alone responsible for the present contents of this chapter, the authors are indebted to the critical advice received from Professors Jeanne Laux, Lynn Mytelka, Michael K. O'Leary, Jonathan Wilkenfeld, and Eugene Wittkopf.*

In perhaps the best known previous effort to develop a typology of national actors, James N. Rosenau (1966) employed the three variables of size, wealth, and political accountability to create eight basic types of nations ranging from large, rich, open states to small, poor, closed nations. A considerable amount of recent research testing aspects of the Rosenau typology has reported finding strong relationships between foreign policy behavior and the attributes of size and wealth.

In order to accomplish the objectives outlined above, we shall briefly review the relevant literature regarding the relationship between foreign policy and national attributes. We then clarify the nature of our variables and operationalize them. The rationale for selecting size and modernization as typological variables is given next and we explain why these variables are thought to be major determinants of foreign policy. Following this theoretical justification, we evaluate a causal model linking the attribute variables to foreign policy participation. The technique of path analysis is employed to test the model's fit with the data on the 114 countries included in the study and on four subsets of countries. Finally, we make a case for the acceptance of our theory on the grounds that it provides an explanation for the demonstrated statistical relationship between national attributes and foreign policy behavior, and we indicate areas for further research employing our typology in the comparative study of foreign policy.

ATTRIBUTE-BASED FOREIGN POLICY ANALYSIS

One of the most widely used approaches to foreign policy analysis has been to focus on the attributes of states. In the literature this approach is often represented by focusing on a state's "power" (Morganthau, 1960) or its "capabilities" (Sprout and Sprout, 1962). Although these concepts are rarely explicitly defined and operationalized, they generally include the attributes of physical size, population, level of economic development, and military capability. Foreign policy analysis based on such individualistic conceptions of power and capability are characteristically unsystematic, but nevertheless they have had a central place in traditional international relations literature.

Acceptance of the view that power is a basic determinant of foreign policy is also reflected in recent studies of the behavior of "small powers"–i.e., the unpowerful states (Vital, 1967, 1971; Rothstein, 1968; Schou and Brundtland, 1971; Singer, 1972). These case studies and comparative studies of the behavior of small powers in specific functional areas support the generally accepted view that there are significant differences in the behavior of large and small states and that these differences are principally due to differences in power.

Systematic empirical research employing the national attribute approach to foreign policy analysis has been greatly assisted by the work of Sawyer (1967) and Rummel (1969b). Rummel factor analyzed 236 national characteristics for 82 nations and found size and wealth to be the major attribute dimensions of the nations examined. He (1969b: 135) also reported high correspondence between his findings and those of earlier national attribute analyses by Cattell, Berry, and Russett.

Foreign policy analyses focusing on the attributes of nations were further stimulated by the analytical framework produced by James Rosenau (1966) in which size, level of economic development, and political accountability were dichotomized to produce eight "genotypic" nations. The implicit hypothesis underlying this typology is that these three genotypic attributes are the most significant factors affecting foreign policy behavior.

Empirical research testing the relationship of these variables to foreign policy behavior has used a variety of data sources and statistical techniques. It is fortunate for the purpose of comparing findings that much of the research stimulated by the Rosenau typology has relied upon the work by Philip Burgess (1970) for the operationalization of the variables and for partitioning them into dichotomies. This research has consistently produced findings of significant relationships between size and foreign policy, and lesser but still notable relationships between wealth and foreign policy behavior. The most significant relationships across different data sets are found between size and frequency of activity (East, 1970: 6, 1973; Rummel, 1969a: 232; Salmore and Herman, 1969: 22; Rosenau and Hoggard, forthcoming). Wealth has also repeatedly been found to be related to frequency of activity when WEIS (World Event Interaction Survey) data are used, although the relationship is generally found to be of less magnitude than that between size and frequency of activity (Salmore and Herman, 1969: 22; Rosenau and Hoggard, forthcoming). Based on his analysis of the DON data, Rummel (1969a: 23) concludes that size and wealth jointly account for variation in the participation level of nations in the international system.

Although the apparent effects of size and wealth on frequency of activity are quite impressive, the effects of these attributes decline sharply when more specific patterns of foreign policy behavior are used as the dependent variable. The reported findings are inconsistent and sometimes contradictory.

East (1970: 8; 1973), working with two different data sets, finds that size discriminates well for the type of resource used in foreign policy behavior, but that it does not discriminate for friendly/hostile behavior (1970: 9; 1973). This supports the findings of Rummel (1966: 212-213; 1968: 205), who concluded that conflict behavior was not related to domestic attributes, and more specifically, that the wealth dimension could not account for as much as ten percent of the variation in any of the forms of foreign conflict measured in the DON (Dimensionality of Nations) data (Rummel, 1968: 204). The findings of other studies however suggest caution in accepting the above conclusions.

Rosenau and Hoggard (forthcoming), using WEIS data, found that three of the four "large" genotypes engaged in more conflict behavior than did any of the "small" genotypes and that all of the "large" genotypes engaged in more cooperative behavior than did any of the "small" genotypes. Rosenau and Hoggard (forthcoming) also found that all four "rich" genotypes had more cooperative behavior than did their "poor" counterparts.

The Feierabends (1969: 147), working with their own data set, found moderately high correlations for both the most modern and least modern states and the foreign policy variables of aggression and amity. They also found a consistent relationship between amity and the attributes of area and population, but found neither of these attributes consistently related to aggression (Feierabend and Feierabend, 1969: 149).

Salmore and Herman (1969: 22-23), using WEIS data, found that neither size nor development account for significant variation in any of 22 specific categories of foreign policy behavior derived from the WEIS coding scheme. Size generally accounted for less than ten percent of the variance and development never accounted for as much as eight percent of the variance in frequency with which states engaged in any specific category of behavior.

David Moore (1970: 38-40), using his own transactional measures, has found the attributes of size, wealth, and accountability to be more important than any of six other governmental and societal variables as determinants of seven selected foreign policy variables. Moore's findings, however, do not permit him to conclude which of the attributes is the most important determinant (Moore, 1970: 43-44).

On the basis of this survey of the comparative research on the relationship of size and wealth to foreign policy behavior, we conclude that these variables account primarily for frequency of activity—the persistent finding being that the larger and wealthier nations participate more in international affairs. Whether or not these attribute variables can also account for more discrete patterns of foreign policy behavior is not entirely clear since little research has been completed in this area and because the findings to date vary across different data sets.

Unfortunately, the repeated confirmation of the statistical effects of size and wealth upon participation has not been accompanied by adequate explanations for this finding. This is indeed a serious omission since a fundamental purpose of classification is to make possible the construction of explanations which account for variations in observed phenomena. Classification, leading to explanation, is essential to the ultimate goal of scientific research—the development of empirical theory (Kalleberg, 1966).

For these reasons we have developed an alternative framework for foreign policy analysis based on the attribute variables of size, modernization, resources, and needs. The theoretical explanation of the relationships among these variables and between them and foreign policy behavior is presented in the section of this chapter entitled "The Path Model," below. First, we must define and operationalize each of our concepts.

NATIONAL ATTRIBUTES

The national attributes of size and modernization are the basis for the framework employed in this research. They have been selected for both substantive and methodological reasons. On a substantive level, we know that these two variables are basic attributes of nations in the contemporary world which sharply distinguish different types of states (Rummel, 1969b; Sawyer, 1967). Moreover, neither the size nor the level of modernization of a nation is likely to change very rapidly. They thus provide relatively invariant points of reference, comparable and relatively stable criteria (all states manifest some degree of size and modernization), that can be used for the purposes of classification, hypothesis testing, and explanation (Sjoberg, 1970). This is our methodological reason for preferring size and modernization to more volatile typological concepts such as political accountability (Rosenau, 1966) which can change in a matter of days or weeks. Moreover, we believe that by including a set of intervening variables, needs and resources, our theory can explain the frequently observed relationships between size, modernization, and foreign policy. But in order to do this we must first of all have clear-cut conceptual definitions of our basic variables and reasonable operational definitions of them as well.

Size

Since everything which we are aware of is perceived by human minds, the size of nations is ultimately a social-psychological variable. Scholars and policy-makers refer to countries as diverse as the United States, China, India, the Soviet Union, and Nigeria as "large" or "big" states and others such as Israel, Peru, Sweden, and Togo as "small" or "mini" powers. The problem is that both scholars and policy-makers tend to include a number of more or less related factors such as area, population, gross national product, and military capability when they make these mental classifications. Now, while area and population tend to go together, neither is necessarily related to wealth or military power. Israel is a rather "powerful" small state, whereas India and Nigeria are relatively "poor" large countries.

In our view, then, confusion can be avoided by using size just to refer to the number of members in a given national society. Chinese "society" under the jurisdiction of the People's Republic government has some 750 million members, whereas nomadic bushman bands nominally under the jurisdiction of the government of Botswana can be as small as 50 people. Size, conceived of as the number of members of a national society, is a national attribute that is not necessarily related to the nation's level of modernization, its wealth, or its usable military power. Moreover, this concept can be adequately operationalized by reference to widely reported demographic data on "national populations" in 1963 (see this chapter, appendix item 1, for our actual source).[1] Our use of population to index size is also consistent with previous national attribute studies (Rummel, 1969b; Burgess, 1970).

Modernization

The selection of modernization as our second major attribute springs from our view that it is a basic discriminatory dimension of nations even though it has not been used as frequently as size and wealth in foreign policy research (but see Feierabend and Feierabend, 1969; Morse, 1970). Modernization and economic development are empirically related, but conceptually distinct. Thus, "economic development" involves the modernization of the economy, whereas "modernization" involves changes in every institutional sphere of the society. Modernization is therefore the more inclusive concept and in our view more appropriate than wealth for a typology of national societies.

Support for the view that modernization is a basic discriminatory dimension of nations is found in the widespread attention the phenomenon has received in recent social science literature, especially that dealing with the new states. The works of Lerner (1958), Deutsch (1961), McClelland (1961), and Eisenstadt (1966) are representative of different conceptualizations of modernization employed in the various social sciences. However, the variety and even inconsistency of previous usage does not detract from the importance of the concept.

We conceive of modernity as a "cluster of goods" which increases people's abilities to control their social and natural environments. Modernization, on the other hand, is the process by which institutions are created or adapted for the purpose of "producing" modernity (McGowan and Nyangira, 1972: 14; Black, 1966: 9-34). The process of modernization is taking place in all present-day national societies, but of course at different rates. The cluster of goods which comprises modernity includes such things as educational opportunity, urban amenities, political participation, industrial and service employment, access to media, and medical and transportation facilities (McGowan and Nyangira, 1972: 13). The availability of modern goods is what distinguishes relatively modernized societies from relatively less modern nations. Even the most highly modern societies can become still more modern and the least modern societies have some amounts of the cluster of goods by which modernity is defined. Societies can therefore be compared along a modernity continuum.

Among the most notable characteristics of the more modernized societies is their reliance upon inanimate sources of power and the nature of the tools used by members of these societies—the computer versus the abacus. Levy (1966; 1972) has used these characteristics to operationally define the concept of modernization and to construct a continuum of more or less modernized societies. Morse (1970: 372-373), in an essay with a foreign policy focus, has referred to these indicators to identify societies which have reached high levels of modernization.

We have focused on the modernized society's use of inanimate sources of power to operationalize the concept of modernization. This is acceptably measured by "per capita energy consumption" in 1963 as reported by the United Nations (see appendix item 2 for the actual source). An additional advantage in operationalizing modernization in this manner is the stability of the indicator. Changes in the rate of use of inanimate sources of energy occur relatively slowly and are likely to proceed only in the direction of increasing usage (severe energy crises can blunt this trend).

> Among the members of relatively modernized societies uses of inanimate sources of power not only predominate, but they predominate in such a way that it is almost impossible to envisage any considerable departure in the direction of the uses of animate sources of power without the most far-reaching changes of the entire system (Levy, 1966: 35).

We should also note that since estimates of both population and energy consumption in Western societies are available for the past 150 years, it is possible to produce foreign policy analyses using these attributes for historical periods other than the present.

Resources

International relations literature reflects the attention that has been devoted to the attribute of resources as a determinant of foreign policy. An excellent survey of the literature representing the "resources-as-a-basis-of-power" thesis is contained in Sprout and Sprout (1962: 365-391). The possession of resources, or lack thereof, and the problems of access to resources continue to be a major concern of scholars in international studies (Sprout and Sprout, 1965; Choucri, Laird and Meadows, 1972). This concern is particularly notable among those who focus on "power" to explain foreign policy behavior.

The concept of "power" generally includes some combination of human and material resources, attributes which when combined are then used to refer to "great" or "large" and "weak" or "small" powers. This is most unfortunate, for what difference is there then between the concepts of size and power? On both a conceptual and operational basis, we shall try to keep distinct our attributes of size and resources.

We believe that resources represent a state's potential capability to influence its external environment. The greater the national society's resources, the greater its potential impact upon external events and the greater the range of events it may affect. Conversely, limited resources produce weak states that do not have much potential to affect external events. There is general agreement in the literature that variation in resources contributes to variation in foreign policy behavior. However, there is little agreement as to the specific behavior patterns affected by resources, as East (1973) demonstrates in a survey of propositions on the consequences of inadequate resources for the foreign policy of small states.

The resources variable has been operationalized by using the state's "Gross Domestic Product" (GDP) for the year 1965, where possible. GDP was selected over GNP because it is a more valid cross-national indicator of national capabilities, especially with respect to the centrally planned economies of Eastern Europe.

Needs

Needs are defined as the degree to which a society must interact with its environment in order to maintain its economic, political, social, and cultural institutions. The availability of domestic resources necessary for maintaining these institutions varies among states, thus creating variation in the need to interact with the environment.

A second source of variation in needs is that needs are positively related to level of modernization. The most highly industrialized countries consume a disproportionate share of all types of resources, and as a direct result of their advanced development have resource needs which they cannot meet domestically because of either cost or unavailability (Choucri et al., 1972:

1-23). Recent works by Cooper (1972) and Pearson (1972) stress the importance of the economic needs of the more highly industrialized states for their foreign policies. These authors persuasively argue that the growing economic interdependence among the industrialized countries is making it increasingly necessary for these states to attempt to affect the international political-economic environment simply in order to control or regulate their own domestic economies.

Thus, we see needs as directly affecting foreign policy behavior. The level of a national society's need to interact with its environment is itself determined by its resources and level of modernization. All other factors being equal, modernization promotes needs while resources locally available inhibit the need to interact. Although economic needs are certainly not the only type of needs that affect foreign policy, economic needs are widely recognized as an important source of a state's international behavior. This variable is therefore operationalized by the "per capita dollar value of the nation's total trade" in 1965, as described in the appendix.

To summarize, we are working with four national attributes in this paper: size, modernization, resources, and needs. Size represents the number of members of a national society and it is measured with 1963 population data. Modernization represents the process whereby societal institutions are created or adapted to produce modern goods. It is measured by 1963 per capita energy consumption. Resources are the national society's capability to influence its external environment, as measured by 1965 Gross Domestic Product. Finally, needs are defined as the degree to which a society must interact with its environment to maintain its basic institutions. This has been operationalized by using the 1965 per capital dollar value of the state's total trade.

In a replication of our study, Lopez (1973: 8-12) used principal components factor analysis as an index construction technique and found that size could be indexed by *population* and area; modernization by *energy consumption per capita,* telephones per capita, passenger cars per capita, newspaper circulation per thousand, and physicians per capita; resources by *GDP,* percentage of GDP originating in industrial activity, protein grams per capita, and university students per capita. His findings represent further evidence of the construct validity of our selected indicators of these three concepts. Lopez (1973: 11-12) also found, however, that our indicator of needs (per capita dollar value of total trade) and a plausible alternative, trade as a percentage of GDP, were unrelated. He was unable to arrive at a conceptually adequate composite index of the needs concept, indicating that the operationalization of this variable needs further work.

FOREIGN POLICY BEHAVIOR

The present analysis is concerned with explaining the repeatedly observed strong and positive relationships between aspects of foreign policy behavior and the national attributes of size and modernization. We have used four measures of foreign policy in this paper; international involvement, regional involvement, organizational involvement, and foreign policy focus. We did not select available data on cooperative or conflict activity because these variables are themselves highly intercorrelated with international involvement—i.e., nations which participate most frequently in international affairs also engage in the most cooperative and conflict behavior. Moreover, as Coplin, Mills and O'Leary (1973) persuasively argue, highly aggregated studies of conflict and cooperation behavior are misleading due to the fact that conflict and cooperation exchanged between states varies by issue area; it is not uniformly distributed across all issues upon which states interact.

The four aspects of foreign policy behavior we shall examine in this paper all relate to the concept of participatory behavior. In a factor analysis of the WEIS data, McClelland and Hoggard (1969: 716-718) found that the most important dimension of external behavior, in terms of the number of event types related to it (80%) and the amount of variance it accounted for (56%), was a pattern of participatory behavior they called "cooperation and collaboration" which "suggests routine international behavior" (1969: 717). Their basic pattern is clearly participatory in form (Brody, 1972: 55). While foreign policy conflict has been the focus of a great deal of research, we are persuaded that an attempt to explain what appears to be *the basic dimension of foreign policy behavior* is a theoretically justifiable exercise. Moreover, as we have seen in our review of the literature, national attributes have already been found to be related to levels of foreign policy activity (participation), and we wish in this paper to maximize the replicability of our research with previous efforts.

International Involvement

A basic issue, option, or decision that must be made by the leaders of national societies is the extent to which they will participate in international politics by engaging in official foreign policy behaviors. There are clearly differences among states with respect to this issue. For a variety of reasons, states as diverse as China, Burma, Finland, and Switzerland have at times chosen to limit their official involvement in the international system. On the other hand, states as diverse as the United States, France, South Africa, and Egypt have followed foreign policies of high involvement in international politics. We have operationalized aggregate participation by using the total number of event interactions undertaken by each state between January 1966 and August 1969 as collected by the World Event Interaction Survey (WEIS) and as listed in McGowan and O'Leary (1971: 42-45).

Regional Involvement

Even if a state does not choose to play an active role in the entire international system, it can still choose to participate in the affairs of its own geographical region. Many Latin American states as well as a number of African and Asian states are quite involved in regional foreign policy matters, but relatively uninvolved in the great issues of the international system as a whole. Changes of government in Ghana and Indonesia caused both states to involve themselves less with the world scene and more with events in West Africa and Southeast Asia. We have again operationalized this foreign policy variable by use of the WEIS data as recoded by McGowan and O'Leary (1971: 42-45).

Organizational Involvement

This variable concerns the extent to which leaders have decided to participate in international organizations. Foreign policy participation can take place in a variety of arenas. Today, the settings provided by international governmental organizations (IGOs) and international nongovernmental organizations (INGOs) are increasingly important in this regard. We have measured this foreign policy issue by recording the number of headquarters and subsidiary offices of IGOs and INGOs located in each state in 1970, as stated in appendix item 5. Since states compete to have IGO and INGO headquarters and branches located on their territory, we feel this operationalization reasonably indicates their interest in international organization as arenas for the conduct of foreign policy.

Foreign Policy Focus

An important dimension of foreign policy behavior, related to the notion of participation, is the degree to which it is concentrated on a few or many targets. Egypt, for example, appears to have three main targets—Israel, the United States, and the Soviet Union. The United States, on the other hand, directs its official behavior toward many states and international organizations. Countries with great participation, but spread over many targets, are clearly conducting a different type of foreign policy from states whose activity is focused on just a few key targets. Our measure of focus is the number of targets toward which each state directed five or more event interactions as reported by WEIS between January 1966 and August 1969. These data were compiled by Kegley (1971: 204).

General Considerations

In this paper we have chosen to create three of our measures of foreign policy participation by using World Event Interaction Survey (WEIS) data, despite their well-known validity problems. Our reasons for this decision are the following. First, only WEIS contains data on the external behavior of all states during the late 1960s. Other available data sets, including our own, either cover a more restricted set of cases or, like the DON data, are collected on a different time period—i.e., the late 1950s. Second, in this paper we wish to maximize the comparability of our findings with the earlier studies summarized in the second section of this chapter. Several of these (Salmore and Herman, 1969; Rosenau and Hoggard, forthcoming) used WEIS data to measure their foreign policy concepts. Moreover, since we are concerned with explaining four aspects of participatory behavior, the use of WEIS is appropriate, for it was the WEIS-based research of McClelland and Hoggard (1969) that identified participation as the primary pattern of foreign policy behavior.

Our other reasons relate to the face validity of the WEIS data collection with respect to the uses we are making of it. Gurr (1972: 44) defines face validity as "a theoretically and substantively plausible argument that spells out how and why an indicator represents a significant aspect of a conceptual variable." We note that the most and least participatory countries as reported by Alger and Brams (1967) based upon diplomatic exchange data are the same as the most and least participatory states reported by McClelland and Hoggard (1969) based upon the frequency of event interactions. Finally, as reported in still unpublished research by the WEIS project, three years of events coded from the *Times* of London agree very closely with the original WEIS data based upon the *New York Times*. To be sure, this is a degree of convergent validity that is limited to the elite press of the English-speaking world. Nevertheless, it suggests that *as a source of indicators of relatively aggregate behavior*, the WEIS data are not as invalid as many scholars have argued. For our purposes in this paper we conclude that selecting indicators of participation from the WEIS data is reasonable, but we also urge that our analysis be replicated with other data sets since WEIS is not perfect and has never claimed to be such.

To summarize, in this paper we are using four foreign policy behavior patterns: international involvement, regional involvement, organizational involvement, and foreign policy focus. Each is conceptualized as an aspect of participatory behavior faced by all foreign policy-makers: How much to participate in the international system? How much to participate in affairs of one's geographical region? How much foreign policy activity to devote to international organizations as an arena of foreign policy? And how many or how few targets to direct one's behavior toward? Each aspect of participatory behavior has been measured by use of data sources reported in the appendix for the period 1966 to 1970. The time sequencing of our eight variables is important, because temporal ordering is basic if causal inference techniques, such as path analysis, are to be used. Thus, size and modernization have been measured for 1963; resources and needs for 1965; and the foreign policy variables cover the period 1966 to 1970. Our cases are the 114 countries included in the McGowan and O'Leary (1971) volume.

THE PATH MODEL

In this section we shall develop our theoretical argument as to why size and modernization have been so frequently found to be related to measures of foreign policy. But first, let us examine the bivariate relationships among our eight variables as presented in Table 1. The relationships among the national attribute variables are as expected. Size and modernization are not related (r = .08). In our view it is important to have typological variables that are independent of each other so that their independent and additive impact on dependent foreign policy variables can be statistically determined. Size and modernization are both positively related to resources, while only modernization is related to needs—again as we expected. Resources is independent of needs (r = .05), whereas we had predicted that it would be negatively related to needs. We shall say more about this relationship when we present our path model.

TABLE 1
CORRELATION MATRIX[a]

Variable	1	2	3	4	5	6	7
1. Size							
2. Modernization	08						
3. Resources	40	55					
4. Needs	−12	65	05				
5. IO involvement	11	52	45	40			
6. Focus	50	53	93	−01	44		
7. INT. involvement	44	52	94	00	42	98	
8. REG. involvement	31	25	33	−06	14	54	59

a. Entries multiplied by 100 to remove decimals. With an N of 114 in a two-tailed test r ⩾ .18 is significant at the .05 level and r ⩾ .24 is significant at .01.

The relationships between the national attribute variables and the foreign policy variables are also largely as predicted. Modernization is significantly related to each foreign policy issue, while size is related to three but not to international organization (IO) involvement. Resources manifests the strongest relationships of any national attribute variable with two of the foreign policy measures, r = .93 with focus and r = .94 with international involvement. Finally, the foreign policy measures are themselves moderately related except for the almost perfect relationship (r = .98) between focus and international involvement. This is interesting, for there is no necessary reason why the nations with the most behavior send these actions to the largest number of targets, but this is indeed the case as reported by the WEIS data. Clearly, since focus and international involvement are so closely related, any national attributes that account for one should also account for the other.

The bivariate relationships among our eight variables provide additional evidence for the construct validity of our operational indicators (see also Lopez, 1973, as previously discussed). Among the national attribute measures, every relationship is as expected except for the independence of resources and needs. Gurr (1972: 47) notes that "our theories and hypotheses often suggest how a variable ought to be related to other variables. If an indicator of a variable proves to be related to measures of other variables in the predicted ways, our confidence in its validity increases." This technique for assessing the empirical or construct validity of an indicator is called "criterion validation," perhaps the most satisfactory evidence of validity (Gurr, 1972: 48). The first three attribute variables are positively related to three of our participation measures as predicted. We have also argued that each measure of foreign policy taps an aspect of participatory foreign policy behavior, and we find that they are all positively related to each other as this argument would lead us to expect. The only evidence in the correlation matrix which calls into question the construct validity of any of our indicators is the failure of needs as measured by per capita total trade to correlate positively with the three WEIS-based measures of participation. Need does, however, correlate as expected (r = .40) with international organization involvement.

We shall now present our conception of why the national attributes of size and modernization have so consistently been found to be related to foreign policy activity. Our theoretical explanation of this recurrent finding is presented in the path diagram of Figure 1.

As the diagram illustrates, size and modernization are treated as exogenous variables whose "causes" are not examined in this paper. In any theory, something must be taken as given, and we take as given the national scores of

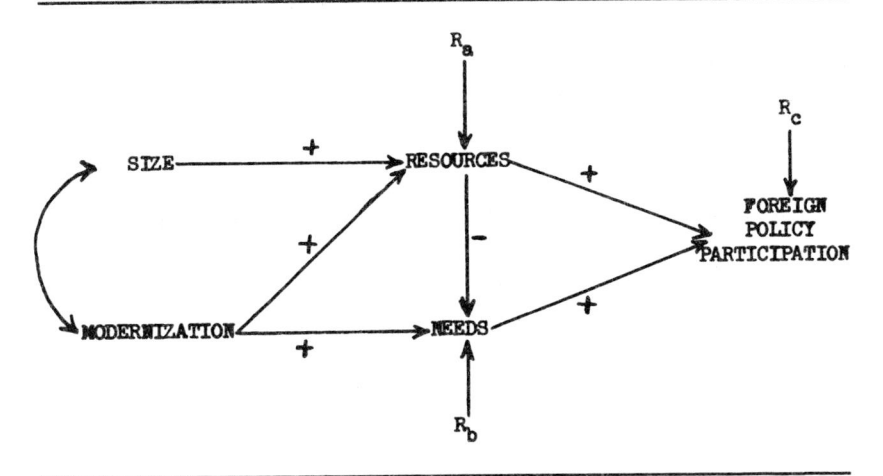

Figure 1: PATH DIAGRAM OF THE RELATIONSHIP OF NATIONAL ATTRIBUTES TO FOREIGN POLICY PARTICIPATION

the 114 states on the attributes of size and modernization. In effect we are saying that these two national attributes are the products of "history." The size of a country as measured by population is both a consequence of historical population growth patterns, including immigration and emigration, and a consequence of past foreign policy as this has affected the population and the territorial boundaries of some states. In a similar fashion, modernization as measured by per capita energy consumption is a consequence of past efforts to apply scientific technology to the control of the social and natural environment of the society. The curved, two-headed arrow represents our theoretical assumption that the size and modernization of national societies are independent of each other. As Table 1 showed, for these 114 states and this data set, their association is only $r = .08$.

Our basic hypothesis is that size and modernization have been found to be related to foreign policy because of the effects of two intervening variables that are determined by size and modernization and which in turn directly affect foreign policy. These two intervening variables are resources and needs. Thus, our path diagram has three endogenous variables—resources, needs, and foreign policy—and two exogenous variables—size and modernization—that do not depend upon other variables in the system.

The causal linkages of the diagram can be expressed in the following path model:

RESOURCES = p_{31} SIZE + p_{32} MODERNIZATION + $p_{3a}R_a$
NEEDS = p_{42} MODERNIZATION + p_{54} RESOURCES + $p_{4b}R_b$
FOREIGN POLICY = p_{53} RESOURCES + p_{54} NEEDS + $p_{5c}R_c$

where p_{ij} refers to the path from the jth independent variable to the ith dependent variable. Resources is thought to be a consequence of the interaction of "raw materials" (size) and the state's capacity to organize human manpower into usable national capability (modernization). A nation's capacity to affect its external environment is therefore jointly caused by its size and level of modernization.

In a similar fashion, a state's need to interact with its environment to maintain its basic patterns of national life is a consequence of both its level of modernization and its available resources. The more modern the state, the more complex its society and the more likely it is to interact with the environment to gain valued goods out of these interactions. Available resources are negatively related to needs, since the domestic environment can produce a greater proportion of the goods valued by members of the society. Size should have no direct independent effect on a state's need to engage in foreign policy activities, but it may have an indirect effect via its impact on resources. That is, size leads to greater resources, making less probable a state's need to secure resources through foreign policy activity.

Finally, we see foreign policy participation as not being directly affected by either a state's size or its level of modernization. These attributes may affect foreign policy indirectly through the intervening variables of resources and needs, both of which are thought to have a significant, direct impact on foreign policy.

The relationship of resources to foreign policy is somewhat complex. Resources are seen to be directly and positively related to foreign policy activity since the greater a state's absolute level of resources, the greater its capacity to engage in foreign policy activity. All other things being equal, great capabilities lead to grand designs and an active foreign policy posture. On the other hand, resources may indirectly depress a state's foreign policy activities. We have argued that a state's need to interact with its environment is reduced by the possession of great resources. Although this may be confusing to the reader, we are simply making the theoretical argument that both resources and needs are directly and positively related to foreign policy activity but that they are themselves negatively related—i.e., resources has a negative effect on needs, as has been illustrated in the path diagram in Figure 1 and in the second equation of the path model.

In summary, our theory as to why size and modernization, or its economic development variant, have consistently been found to be positively related to foreign policy participation is that size and modernization increase the resources available for the conduct of foreign policy and that modernization increases the need to interact with the environment to maintain basic societal patterns. This theory, when one has a set of cases as we do (114 states) and a set of observations for each case on each variable (size and modernization, 1963; resources and needs, 1965; and foreign policy activities, 1966-1970), permits one to make the specific prediction that the direct paths from size and modernization to foreign policy will not be as large as the direct paths from resources and needs. Indeed, the direct paths from the two exogenous variables may be so weak as to be not significantly different from zero and therefore capable of being eliminated, as the path diagram and the path model indicate.

FINDINGS

The hypothesized relationships among the variables in the path diagram of Figure 1 have been tested by the technique of path analysis, a variant of multiple regression analysis (Blalock, 1971: 73-151). Path analysis is appropriate for our research since the assumptions of the technique have been met: (1) we conceive of the relationships among our variables as being additive, and an examination of bivariate scattergrams has confirmed that they are linear; (2) the relationships in the theory are conceived to be asymmetric, and the operationalization of each variable conforms to the time sequence implied by our theory—thus we are working with a simple recursive causal model; and (3) the variables have all been measured on interval scales.[2]

Path analysis is a flexible tool because by repeated applications it permits researchers to eliminate weak or spurious links among variables as in the so-called Simon-Blalock technique (Blalock, 1971: 1-71) and at the same time to secure comparable estimates of the magnitudes of the strong or nonspurious paths linking variables in the model. The general procedure that we have followed with each of the four foreign policy issues is to first estimate all possible linkages by means of separate regression analysis of each fully determined equation in the model. As a second step, we eliminated from each model the paths that were not significant at the .05 level and then reestimated each remaining path by a second regression analysis, thus creating a more parsimonious model.[3]

A principal concern of this paper is to examine the effect of grouping states according to their size and level of modernization, our basic typological variables. We therefore created four subgroups of states by dichotomizing these two variables at their median, giving large states, small states, modern states, and less modern states. For each of these subgroups we repeated the first step of our path analysis—the estimation of all possible linkages via a separate regression analysis of each equation in the model. Tables 2 and 3, displayed later in this chapter, report the results of the complete model estimation for the four subgroups and for all 114 states.

As the reader will recall, we have predicted that the paths from size and modernization to the foreign policy variables will not be significant. If our explanation of the relationship of size and modernization to foreign policy is correct, in Table 2 we should find the direct effects (paths) of the intervening variables to be stronger than the direct effects of size and modernization. Moreover, the direct effects (paths) of size and modernization on foreign policy should be weaker than their net indirect effects (indirect paths plus correlation due to common or correlated causes).[4] Finally, in Table 3, the intervening variables of resources and needs should account for the major portion of the "explained" variance in each of the foreign policy issues.

International Organization Involvement as the Foreign Policy Issue

Figure 2 contains all possible asymmetric linkages between the variables in the path model when international organization involvement is the foreign policy issue. As had been expected, neither of the direct paths from size and

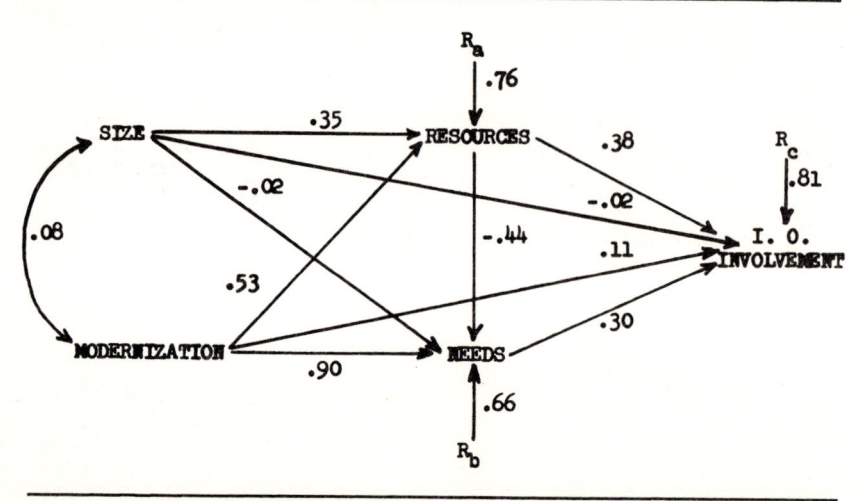

Figure 2: PATH DIAGRAM OF THE RELATIONSHIP OF NATIONAL ATTRIBUTES TO I.O. INVOLVEMENT

modernization to IO involvement is significant at the .05 level (p ⩾ .18), whereas both the path from resources to IO involvement and the path from needs to policy are significant at the .01 level (p ⩾ .24). As Table 2 shows, the net indirect effects of both size and modernization are greater than their direct paths to international organization involvement. Table 3 demonstrates that needs and resources account for 34% of the 35% variance in policy explained by the four attribute variables. Also as predicted, the path from size to resources and the paths from modernization to both resources and needs are all significant; but the path from size to needs (−.02) is not large, as expected. Our prediction of a negative effect by resources on need is also supported since the path is −.44, although their correlation is only .05.

The path analysis of international organization involvement obviously supports our theory that the variables of size and modernization are not directly related to foreign policy, but that these variables indirectly affect foreign policy through the intervening variables of resources and needs.

Four paths can be eliminated from the model since our analysis has shown them to be either very small or spurious. Removing these paths permits the estimation of a simpler revised model in which all paths are significant at the .01 level, as presented in Figure 3. The revised model, estimated through a second independent regression analysis, is identical to our theoretical expectations presented in Figure 1. Although the relatively small percentage

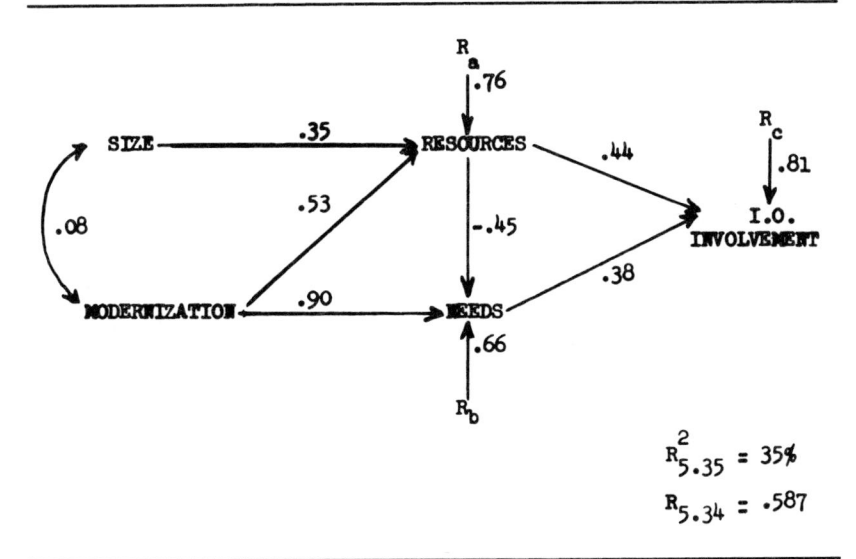

$R^2_{5.35} = 35\%$

$R_{5.34} = .587$

Figure 3: REVISED PATH DIAGRAM OF THE RELATIONSHIP OF NATIONAL ATTRIBUTES TO I.O. INVOLVEMENT

TABLE 2
DIRECT AND INDIRECT EFFECTS OF NATIONAL ATTRIBUTES[a]

Attribute and Policy	All States 114		Large States 57		Small States 57		Modern States 57		Less Modern States 57	
IO involvement										
1. Size	−02	(13)	−04	(09)	−11	(35)	−05	(11)	−147	(223)
2. Modernization	11	(41)	−18	(71)	−71	(105)	09	(36)	03	(16)
3. Resources	38	(07)	51	(−06)	95	(−25)	41	(00)	224	(−145)
4. Needs	30	(10)	61	(−06)	47	(−07)	28	(02)	−08	(−03)
Focus										
1. Size	16	(34)	15	(31)	03	(16)	16	(37)	85	(−26)
2. Modernization	17	(36)	11	(45)	73	(−64)	09	(38)	55	(−29)
3. Resources	78	(15)	84	(11)	14	(02)	81	(13)	−39	(99)
4. Needs	−13	(12)	−07	(13)	−80	(74)	−13	(−06)	−44	(29)
INT. involvement										
1. Size	08	(36)	08	(33)	−12	(19)	08	(39)	44	(06)
2. Modernization	10	(42)	06	(50)	72	(−66)	06	(42)	47	(−24)
3. Resources	86	(08)	91	(06)	18	(−08)	87	(08)	−05	(56)
4. Needs	−10	(10)	−05	(11)	−86	(78)	−09	(−07)	−38	(26)
REG. involvement										
1. Size	23	(08)	32	(07)	−17	(20)	17	(11)	99	(−64)
2. Modernization	40	(−15)	35	(−05)	72	(−65)	22	(−11)	61	(−30)
3. Resources	03	(30)	13	(30)	19	(−10)	08	(22)	−78	(114)
4. Needs	−29	(−23)	−19	(20)	−86	(79)	−33	(06)	−38	(36)

a. Decimals have been removed. Direct effects, or direct paths are listed first for each grouping of states. Net indirect effects are given in parentheses, where NIE = $r_{ij} - P_{ij}$.

of variance accounted for is somewhat disappointing, the perfect fit of Figure 3 with our theoretical model is encouraging.

An examination of Tables 2 and 3 shows that our path model works as well for three of the four subgroups of states as for all states. The best results, with 58% of the variance in international organization involvement accounted for, is with the small states. The one instance where the model does not work is with respect to the less modern states. Here we account for 67% of the variance in IO involvement, but it is size acting negatively that is almost alone responsible—i.e., the smaller the less modern state, the greater its international organization involvement.

Focus as the Foreign Policy Issue

Applying the same analytic procedures to focus as the foreign policy issue produces somewhat different results. As reported in Table 2 for all states when the complete model is estimated, only the path from resources to focus is significant. Nevertheless, this finding is partially consistent with our theoretical expectations. It is the intervening variable of resources that accounts for 63% of the very large 89% variance explained in focus as a policy issue. In addition, the direct effects of both size and modernization as reported in Table 2 are less than their indirect effects. Thus, we continue to find support for our prediction that the direct effect of the intervening variables is greater than the direct effect of the exogenous variables, and for our theory that size and modernization affect foreign policy behavior indirectly through intervening variables.

A more parsimonious model for focus as the foreign policy issue can be constructed because needs can be eliminated from the original model and because the paths from size and modernization to focus are not significant. The diagram of the revised path model for focus, Figure 4, looks quite different from our original path model. However, the path coefficients indicate that the essential element of our theory is supported. Size and modernization have no direct effect on this foreign policy issue. The path from resources to focus has increased in strength and is now .93. The three national attribute variables remaining in the model still account for 86% of the variance in focus. Resources, as an intervening variable, plays the role predicted for it by the theory.

When we examine Tables 2 and 3 to see the effects of replicating this analysis on the four subgroups, we see that the results for all states are repeated by the large states and the modern states. The model does not fare well at all for small states where only 15% of the variance in focus is accounted for by all four national attribute variables. The model does

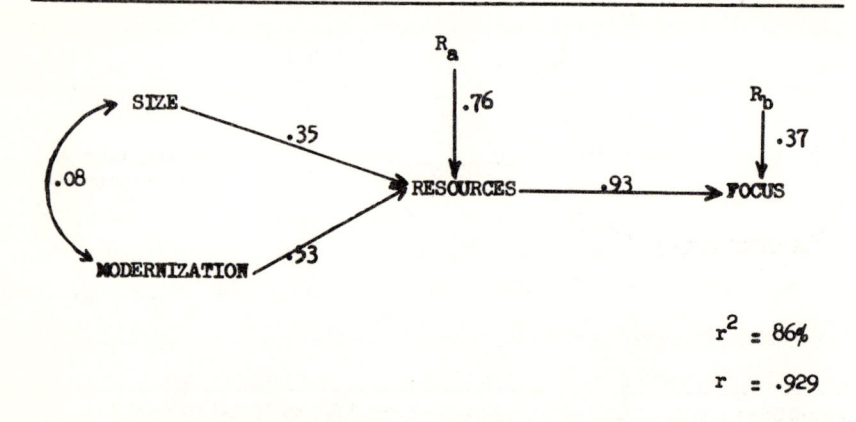

Figure 4: REVISED PATH DIAGRAM OF THE RELATIONSHIP OF NATIONAL ATTRIBUTES TO FOCUS

somewhat better for the less modern grouping of states with 48% of the variance accounted for, but it is size and modernization that together account for 46% of the variance, not the intervening variables as predicted. Possible reasons for this poor performance are given in Table 4. There we see that for both the small and less modern groupings, the average number of targets toward which five or more event interactions were initiated between January 1966 and August 1969 is only one and that the standard deviation for this variable is only two targets. Thus, for both small and less modern groupings of states there is little variation in focus to covary with the national attribute variables.

To summarize, we recognize the differences between the revised path model for focus as the foreign policy issue and our original theoretical model. Nevertheless, the findings support our proposition that size and modernization are not directly related to foreign policy. Our original model does not fit because needs does not have the effect on focus that we had expected. However, the effect of resources is exactly as expected.

International Involvement as the Foreign Policy Issue

Because international involvement and focus are so highly intercorrelated, $r = .98$, our results for the international involvement variable are in all respects substantially similar to what we have just reported for focus (see Tables 2, 3, and 4). Again, the direct paths from size and modernization to international involvement are not significant at the .05 level and are eliminated from the model.

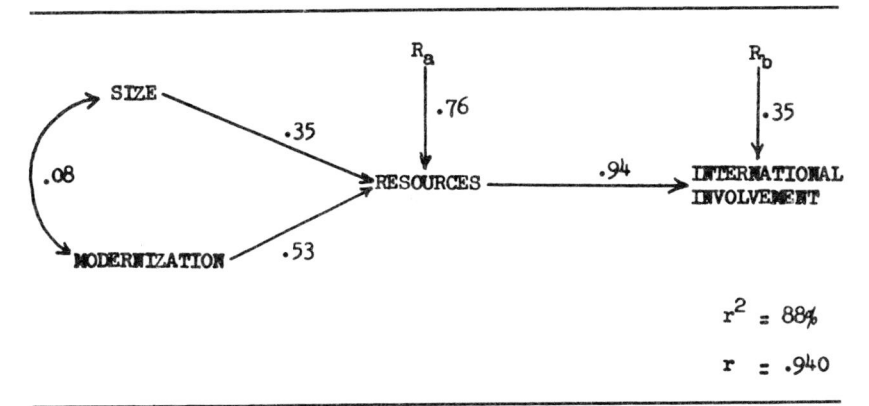

```
        Rₐ                    R_b
SIZE                           
    ＼.35  ↓.76           ↓.35
.08    ↘RESOURCES ──.94──→ INTERNATIONAL
    ↗.53                    INVOLVEMENT
MODERNIZATION
```

                                    $r^2 = 88\%$
                                    $r = .940$

Figure 5: REVISED PATH DIAGRAM OF THE RELATIONSHIP OF NATIONAL ATTRIBUTES TO INTERNATIONAL INVOLVEMENT

As when focus was the foreign policy issue, large and modern states are similar to all states, with resources accounting for the major share of variation in international involvement. The model does not fit well the small and less modern groups of states. Again, as in the prior case of international organization involvement, for less modern states it is size that accounts for the major portion of the variance explained by the model.

Regional Involvement as the Foreign Policy Issue

In the results of the path analysis for regional activity we have, for the first time, findings which are largely inconsistent with our explanation of the relationship of size and modernization to foreign policy issues. As shown in Table 2, the direct paths from the two exogenous variables are both significant. Moreover, the paths from the intervening variables to regional involvement do not agree with our expectations. Resources is just not related to regional involvement (p = .03). Needs is related, but negatively! There is also a reversal between the direct and indirect effects as compared to the other three foreign policy issues. Finally, all four national attribute variables account for an average of only 21% of the variance across the five groupings of countries (see Table 3). Clearly, variables other than the four national attributes are responsible for most of the variation in regional patterns of foreign policy involvement.

An analysis of the complete system of paths again indicated that several could be dropped in a revised model, which is presented in Figure 6. First, although this model accounts for only 20% of the variance in regional involvement, all of the paths are significant. The main differences between Figure 6 and the previous revised models are as follows:

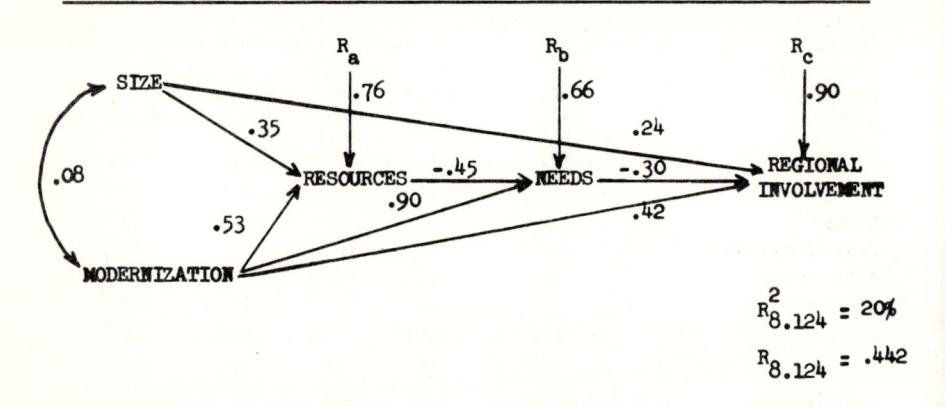

Figure 6: REVISED PATH DIAGRAM OF THE RELATIONSHIP OF NATIONAL ATTRIBUTES TO REGIONAL INVOLVEMENT

(1) there is no direct link between resources and foreign policy behavior;

(2) the impact of needs on regional activity is negative, not positive as predicted; and

(3) modernization is the most potent direct influence on the frequency of regional activity.

The results of our analysis of regional involvement suggest that it is a form of participation different from the first three studied. In retrospect, our other foreign policy issues relate to how national actors participate in the international system as a whole: (1) how involved with international organization; (2) how involved with the entire system via event interactions; and (3) how many targets out of the system to interact with frequently. Regional activity, on the other hand, relates to the geographically defined subsystem to which the actor belongs. Patterns of regional involvement are not well accounted for by any of the national attribute variables. Perhaps national attributes make a difference when foreign policy participation relates to the entire system, but not with respect to regional matters where needs, resources, and level of modernization tend to be similar because of historical and geographical diffusion.[5] For example, could it be that national attributes account for variation in the relations of African states with non-African states in the context of the international system, but that they do not help one account for intra-African relations at the level of the African subsystem? This certainly deserves further investigation.

TABLE 3
SOURCES OF EXPLAINED VARIANCE[a]

Attribute and Policy	All States 114	Large States 57	Small States 57	Modern States 57	Less Modern States 57
IO involvement	R^2 = 35%	47%	58%	29%	67%
1. Size	01	00	06	00	58
2. Modernization	00	01	08	00	00
3. Resources	17	15	26	18	08
4. Needs	17	31	19	11	00
Focus	R^2 = 89%	92%	15%	91%	48%
1. Size	25	20	04	28	35
2. Modernization	01	00	08	00	11
3. Resources	63	69	03	62	02
4. Needs	00	02	00	01	00
INT. involvement	R^2 = 89%	95%	13%	91%	35%
1. Size	19	17	01	22	25
2. Modernization	00	00	08	00	08
3. Resources	69	76	04	68	02
4. Needs	00	02	01	00	00
REG. involvement	R^2 = 20%	28%	12%	18%	27%
1. Size	10	15	00	08	12
2. Modernization	05	03	08	02	14
3. Resources	05	09	04	04	01
4. Needs	00	01	01	04	00

a. Totals not exact due to rounding.

SUMMARY AND CONCLUSIONS

Our explanation of why size and modernization have consistently been found to be related to various measures of foreign policy participation was tested using the technique of path analysis. We have argued that the relationships observed in other studies between these two national attributes and foreign policy are spurious and that, if the intervening variables of resources and needs are introduced in the analysis, the direct links between size and modernization will disappear. As with any research technique, path analysis tells the researcher only whether the results of the analysis are consistent with his theory. The researcher then must decide whether to accept, modify, or reject his model. We find the results of this analysis generally consistent with our theoretical expectations.

TABLE 4
MEANS AND STANDARD DEVIATIONS FOR ALL VARIABLES

Grouping and Measure	Size	Modernization	Resources	Needs	IO	Focus	INT.	REG.
Means								
1. All states	27058	1112	10937	228	30	4	134	31
2. Large	50993	1538	32373	197	47	6	221	42
3. Modern	35185	2125	31760	391	54	6	219	46
4. Small	3124	686	1053	259	12	1	47	20
5. Less modern	18931	99	2115	64	5	1	49	16
Standard Deviations								
1. All states	81001	1649	65244	321	84	8	347	55
2. Large	109863	1986	89990	276	107	11	462	52
3. Modern	95848	1841	90017	385	114	11	472	68
4. Small	1841	1083	2552	360	46	2	123	56
5. Less modern	62595	79	6272	68	7	2	75	31

Our predictions of the interrelationships among the national attribute variables themselves have been strongly supported. Size and modernization are independent of each other. As we expected, resources is positively dependent upon both size and modernization. Needs is independent of size, positively dependent upon modernization, and negatively dependent upon both size and modernization. Needs is independent of size, positively dependent upon modernization, and negatively dependent upon resources when modernization and size are controlled.

It is encouraging to have been able to sort out the interrelations of these four basic and conceptually distinct attributes of nations. More important, however, are the relations of the attribute variables with our measures of foreign policy participation. In three cases out of four, our theory fits the data well. Our results for international organization involvement were identical to our theoretical expectations. In the cases of focus and international involvement, which are conceptually distinct but highly intercorrelated in the WEIS data set, our model must be modified. The intervening variable of resources accounts for the major share of the variance in these two issues, the links between size and modernization being not significantly different from zero. Needs does not perform as expected for focus and international involvement. Finally, the model as a whole does not fit for the foreign policy issue of regional involvement.

Thus, as far as this limited study permits us, we would argue that our basic point is valid. Correlations between size, modernization, and foreign policy participation are spurious because the intervening variables of needs and resources, or resources alone, are the direct link to this aspect of foreign policy. Because our model did not fit at all for regional involvement, we are led to consider its modification. Our findings suggest to us that the national attribute approach to the comparative study of foreign policy may be valid for foreign policy issues of worldwide scope where countries do differ on these attributes. However, when the issue is regional in scope, as is much conflict behavior for example, states in the same region tend not to differ greatly except for size, and therefore the national attribute approach is less useful.

A second modification of our initial model is also perhaps in order. The needs variable really worked as expected only in the case of the foreign policy issue of international organizational involvement. This variable was included in our original model because of the very persuasive arguments recently made on behalf of its growing importance as a determinant of foreign policy behavior (Cooper, 1972; Morse, 1970; Pearson, 1972). Moreover, needs are clearly dependent upon modernization and resources, as our analysis has shown. We believe that this national attribute is worthy of further analysis which could well begin by trying out alternative operationalizations of this variable, such as trade as a percentage of GDP (but see Lopez, 1973). Its relationship to other measures of foreign policy should also be investigated. It may well be that the negative impact of great absolute resources on needs is so strong as to cause needs to relate negatively or not at all to participatory foreign policy behavior.

Our subgroup analysis of large, small, modern and less modern states also produced interesting findings. Our results are generally the same for all states and for the two groups of large states and modern states. To some extent this finding may be the result of outlier effects produced by countries such as the United States, the Soviet Union, and China, which are heavily represented in the WEIS data set. What is more important from a theory-building point of view are the differences found for both the small and less modern states. Our model did not fit well in both cases. In a replication of this paper, using 32 black African states that are all less modern and that are mainly small, Green (1973) found that the attribute variables of size and resources mainly account for intra-African variations in participatory foreign policy behavior. In addition, the average explained variance was low, only 20%, whereas for all states this paper accounts for an average of 58% explained variance across four measures of participation.

We would suggest that although most theorizing in international relations and in the comparative study of foreign policy purports to be general, and therefore applicable to all states, it is implicitly modeled on the behavior of "great" powers. The particular behavioral patterns of smaller states are only now beginning to get the attention they deserve from theorists in foreign policy studies (East, 1973; Rothstein, 1968; Schou and Brundtland, 1971; Vital, 1967, 1971; and Singer, 1972). On the other hand, very little systematic thinking on the foreign policy behavior of less modern states in a world dominated by already modern states has been accomplished. The few scholars working in this area generally share a Marxist or neo-Marxist orientation (e.g., Frank, 1970; Green and Seidman, 1968; Magdoff, 1969). This is probably a correct orientation to the question, for the foreign policy problems of the less modern states—neocolonialism, intervention, penetration, dependence—can perhaps best be understood in the context of political economy. But certainly more work is needed, whatever the ideological orientation.

On the basis of the research reported in this paper, we believe that a typology of national actors for comparative foreign policy analysis based on the attributes of size and modernization is potentially very useful. As Figure

	MODERN STATES	LESS-MODERN STATES
LARGE STATES	Great Resources Moderate Needs U.S.A.[a] U.S.S.R.	Moderate Resources Little Needs NIGERIA CHINA
SMALL STATES	Moderate Resources Great Needs BELGIUM SINGAPORE	Little Resources Little Needs JORDAN BOLIVIA

a. States are merely illustrative examples.

Figure 7: TYPOLOGY OF NATIONAL ACTORS

7 suggests, size and modernization are important because of their effect on resources and needs.

We think that our proposed typology is superior to existing ones in our field for several reasons. First, by relating size and modernization to needs and resources, we have provided a theoretical justification for why grouping states in this fashion should make a difference to their foreign policy behavior. Second, our two-variable typology is simpler than others which use three or more basic variables. Third, the attributes of size and modernization are stable points of reference for which there is adequate data going back well into the nineteenth century. Finally, our findings in this paper suggest that our typology and, we think, perhaps any typology based on national attributes, is useful for explanatory purposes when states from different cells are in interaction. That is, national attribute typologies will aid in

[248]   FINDINGS

understanding and explaining foreign polciy issues of worldwide or interregional scope. But we think that our typology or any other general framework will not be very helpful in situations where most of the states fall in one cell—i.e., in intraregional foreign affairs, such as in the African or Latin American subsystems.

NOTES

1. National population data are often inaccurate by as much as 100%. Thus, before its first census Liberia was thought to have over two million citizens, whereas only 1.001 million were enumerated! Nevertheless, for our purposes Liberia is a "small" national society whether its "true" population is one or even three million. The point is that more accurate data on the populations of less developed countries would not markedly change the rankings of countries on a scale of size measured in this fashion. The same point applies to our indicators of the other national attributes.

2. In order to estimate without bias the path coefficients in the equations of the path model by means of ordinary least squares regression procedures applied separately to each equation, additional assumptions must be made about the residual terms (R_a, R_b, and R_c). These residuals (a) cannot be correlated with each other; (b) they cannot be correlated with variables that determine the dependent variable in the equation in which they appear; and (c) they are assumed to be normally distributed with a mean of zero. One or more of these assumptions are probably not met by our data, as is usually the case in social research. Our estimated path coefficients may therefore be biased.

3. An F test was used to determine the significance levels of the path coefficients, where

$$F = \frac{P_{ij}^2 (N-2)}{1 - P_{ij}^2}$$

When N = 114, p ≥ .18 is significant at the .05 level and p ≥ .24 is significant at the .01 level.

4. Readers should be warned that the path coefficients of Table 2 are not comparable between subgroups of states—i.e., the path of .61 between needs and IO involvement for large states is not necessarily twice as big as the .29 path between these variables for modern states. Path coefficients are standardized regression coefficients, or $p_{ij} = b_{ij}(s_j/s_i)$. The path coefficient is thus a weighted proportion of the standard deviations of the dependent (*i*) and independent (*j*) variable respectively. If the variances and therefore the standard deviations of the dependent variable (s_i) in two different subgroups are different, the paths between any variables *i* and *j* are not comparable. In Table 2 the paths are comparable only within each subgroup for each dependent variable only; they cannot be compared across dependent variables or across subgroups. We do not make such comparisons in this paper and our readers should not either. Comparability can be achieved by calculating path regression coefficients, but this runs into problems of units of measurement and so forth (see Schoenberg, 1972, for a thorough discussion).

5. Among anthropoligists, this is known as "Galton's problem." Traits of nations, such as their level of modernization, diffuse through time and over space—e.g., as one

moves in a southeast direction from London to New Delhi, there is a general and gradual decline in modernity. Thus, most regions are relatively more homogeneous with respect to modernization, resources, and needs, at least in comparison to the entire world "region."

REFERENCES

ALGER, C. F. and S. J. BRAMS (1967) "Patterns of representation in national capitals and international organizations." World Politics 19 (July): 646-663.

BLACK, C. E. (1966) The Dynamics of Modernization. New York: Harper & Row.

BLALOCK, H. M., Jr. [ed.] (1971) Causal Models in the Social Sciences. Chicago and New York: Aldine-Atherton.

BRODY, R. A. (1972) "International events: problems of measurement and analysis," pp. 45-58 in E. Azar, R. A. Brody, and C. A. McClelland, International Events Interaction Analysis: Some Research Considerations. Beverly Hills and London: Sage Professional Paper in International Studies 02-001.

BURGESS, P. M. (1970) "Nation-typing for foreign policy analysis: a partitioning procedure for constructing typologies," pp. 3-66 in E. H. Fedder (ed.) Methodology in International Regions. St. Louis: University of Missouri Center for International Studies Monograph Series.

CHOUCRI, N., M. LAIRD, and D. L. MEADOWS (1972) Resource Scarcity and Foreign Policy: A Simulation Model of International Conflict. Cambridge: MIT Center for International Studies.

COOPER, R. N. (1972) "Economic interdependence and foreign policy in the seventies." World Politics 24 (January): 159-181.

COPLIN, W. D., S. MILLS, and M. K. O'LEARY (1973) "The PRINCE concepts and the study of foreign policy," pp. 73-103 in P. J. McGowan (ed.) Sage International Yearbook of Foreign Policy Studies I. Beverly Hills: Sage.

DEUTSCH, K. W. (1961) "Social mobilization and political development." American Political Science Review 55 (September): 493-514.

EAST, M. A. (1973) "Size and foreign policy behavior: a test of two models." World Politics 25 (July).

--- (1970) "Small states in international politics: some empirical findings." University of Denver Graduate School of International Studies. (mimeo)

EISENSTADT, S. N. (1966) Modernization: Protest and Change. Englewood Cliffs, N.J.: Prentice-Hall.

FEIERABEND, I. K. and R. L. FEIERABEND (1969) "Level of development and international behavior," pp. 135-188 in R. Butwell (ed.) Foreign Policy and the Developing Nation. Lexington: University of Kentucky Press.

FRANK, A. G. (1970) Latin America: Underdevelopment or Revolution. New York: Monthly Review Press.

GREEN, J. E. (1973) "National attributes and the foreign policy of Black Africa: a path model." Syracuse University Department of Political Science seminar paper (April).

GREEN, R. H. and A. SEIDMAN (1968) Unity or Poverty? The Economics of Pan-Africanism. Harmondworth: Penguin.

GURR, T. R. (1972) Politimetrics: An Introduction to Quantitative Macropolitics. Englewood Cliffs, N.J.: Prentice-Hall.

International Associations (1972) "The geography of international associations." Number 3: 173-175.
International Monetary Fund (1969) International Financial Statistics. Volume 22 (October): 32-35.
--- (n.d.) Direction of Trade Annual, 1962-1966.
KALLEBERG, A. L. (1966) "The logic of comparison." World Politics 19 (October): 69-81.
KEGLEY, C. W., Jr. (1971) "Toward the construction of an empirically grounded typology of foreign policy output behavior." Ph.D. dissertation, Syracuse University.
LERNER, D. (1958) The Passing of Traditional Society: Modernizing the Middle East. New York: Free Press.
LEVY, M. J., Jr. (1972) Modernization: Latecomers and Survivors. New York: Basic Books.
--- (1966) Modernization and the Structure of Societies, Vol. I. Princeton: Princeton University Press.
LOPEZ, G. A. (1973) "A reconsideration of national attributes as determinants of foreign policy behavior." Syracuse University Department of Political Science seminar paper (May).
MAGDOFF, H. (1969) The Age of Imperialism. New York: Monthly Review Press.
McCLELLAND, D. C. (1961) The Achieving Society. Princeton: Van Nostrand.
McCLELLAND, C. A. and G. D. HOGGARD (1969) "Conflict patterns in the interactions among nations," pp. 711-724 in J. N. Rosenau (ed.) International Politics and Foreign Policy. New York: Free Press.
McGOWAN, P. J. and N. NYANGIRA (1972) "Relative modernization and the comparative study of national integration in Black Africa." Presented at the Northwestern University Program of African Studies Workshop on National Integration in Africa, Evanston, Illinois (February).
McGOWAN, P. J. and M. K. O'LEARY (9171) Comparative Foreign Policy Analysis Materials. Chicago: Markham.
MOORE, D. W. (1970) "Governmental and societal influences on foreign policy: a partial examination of Rosenau's adaptation model." Ph.D. dissertation, Ohio State University.
MORGENTHAU, H. J. (1960) Politics Among Nations. New York: Knopf.
MORSE, E. L. (1970) "The transformation of foreign policies: modernization, interdependence, and externalization." World Politics 22 (April): 371-392.
PEARSON, C. W. (1972) "The nexes among economic policies." SAIS Review 16 (Winter): 20-30.
ROTHSTEIN, R. L. (1968) Alliances and Small Powers. New York: Columbia University Press.
ROSENAU, J. N. (1966) "Pre-theories and theories of foreign policy," pp. 27-92 in R. B. Farrell (ed.) Approaches to Comparative and International Politics. Evanston, Ill.: Northwestern University Press.
--- and G. D. HOGGARD (forthcoming) "Foreign policy behavior in dyadic relationships: testing a pre-theoretical extension," in J. N. Rosenau (ed.) Comparing Foreign Policies. Beverly Hills: Sage.
RUMMEL, R. J. (1969a) "Some empirical findings on nations and their behavior." World Politics 21 (January): 226-241.
--- (1969b) "Indicators of cross-national and international patterns." American Political Science Review 63 (March): 127-147.

--- (1968) "The relationship between national attributes and foreign conflict behavior," pp. 187-214 in J. D. Singer (ed.) Quantitative International Politics. New York: Free Press.
--- (1966) "Some dimensions in the foreign behavior of nations," Journal of Peace Research 3 (Number 3): 201-223.
SALMORE, S. A. and C. F. HERMAN (1969) "The effects of size, development and accountability on foreign policy." Peace Research Society Papers 14 (Ann Arbor Conference): 15-30.
SAWYER, J. (1967) "Dimensions of nations: size, wealth and politics." American Journal of Sociology 73 (September): 145-172.
SCHOENBERG, R. (1972) "Strategies for meaningful comparison," pp. 1-35 in H. L. Costner (ed.) Sociological Methodology 1972. San Francisco: Jossey-Bass.
SCHOU, A. and A. O. BRUNDTLAND [eds.] (1971) Small States in International Relations. New York: John Wiley.
SINGER, M. R. (1972) Weak States in a World of Powers. New York: Free Press.
SJOBERG, G. (1970) "The comparative method in the social sciences," pp. 25-38 in A. Etzioni and F. L. Dubow (eds.) Comparative Perspectives Theories and Methods. Boston: Little, Brown.
SPROUT, H. and M. SPROUT (1965) The Ecological Perspective on Human Affairs, with Special Reference to International Politics. Princeton: Princeton University Press.
--- (1962) Foundations of International Politics. Princeton: Van Nostrand.
Statistical Office of the United Nations (1970) United Nations Statistical Yearbook–1969. New York: United Nations.
--- (1969) United Nations Demographic Yearbook–1968. New York: United Nations.
--- (1968) United Nations Statistical Yearbook–1967. New York: United Nations.
VITAL, D. (1971) The Survival of Small States. London: Oxford University Press.
--- (1967) The Inequality of States. Oxford: Oxford University Press.

APPENDIX:
Sources Used to Operationalize Variables

(1) Size = 1963 Population. Source: United Nations Demographic Yearbook, 1969 (New York: United Nations, 1970).
(2) Modernization = 1963 energy consumption per capita. Source: United Nations Statistical Yearbook, 1967 (New York: United Nations, 1968).
(3) Resources = 1965 Gross Domestic Product.[ab] Source: United Nations Statistical Yearbook, 1969 (New York: United Nations, 1970).

   (ab) Exceptions due to absence of GDP data in UN Statistical Yearbook.
   (a) 1967 GDP used for Bulgaria, Czechoslovakia, German Democratic Republic, Hungary, Poland, Rumania, USSR. Source: Economic Survey of Europe in 1969, Part I (New York: United Nations, 1970).
   (b) 1966 GNP used for Albania, Yugoslavia, Cuba, Chinese People's Republic. Source: P. J. McGowan and M. K. O'Leary, Comparative Foreign Policy Analysis Materials (Chicago: Markham, 1971).

(4) Needs = 1965 dollar value of total trade per capita. Source: International Monetary Fund, International Financial Statistics 22 (October 1969).
(5) IO Involvement = the number of headquarters and subsidiary offices of international organizations located in the country in 1970[a]. Source: International Associations, "The geography of international associations," (No. 3) 1972. Number (3) excludes EEC and EFTA international nongovernmental organizations.
(6) Focus = the number of targets toward which a state directed five or more acts during the period January 1966–August 1969. Source: Data compiled from World Event Interaction Survey by C. W. Kegley, Jr., "Toward the construction of an empirically grounded typology of foreign policy output behavior" (Ph.D. Dissertation, Syracuse University, 1971).
(7) International Involvement = the total number of foreign policy acts by a country in the period January 1966 to August 1969. Source: Compiled from the World Event Interaction Survey by P. J. McGowan and M. K. O'Leary, Comparative Foreign Policy Analysis Materials (Chicago: Markham, 1971).
(8) Regional Involvement = the total number of foreign policy acts directed toward states in the same continental region as the actor in the period January 1966 to August 1969. Source: Compiled from the World Event Interaction Survey by P. J. McGowan and M. K. O'Leary, Comparative Foreign Policy Analysis Materials (Chicago: Markham, 1971).

PART FOUR

APPRAISALS

Chapter 9

PUBLIC OPINION AND FOREIGN POLICY IN WEST GERMANY

RICHARD L. MERRITT
University of Illinois at Urbana-Champaign

Along with the United States and Japan, West Germany is doubtless the most "surveyed" country in the world. Only hours after American tanks rumbled eastwards in 1945 came social psychologists with their questionnaires. By the fall of that year permanent surveying operations had been set up in the American zone of occupation and, not long afterwards, in the British and French zones as well. Topics of interest included attitudes toward Nazism and denazification, reactions to actual and projected occupation policies, and, increasingly, the cold war (Merritt and Merritt, 1970; A. J. Merritt, forthcoming). The success in limited areas of these early efforts spawned purely German public opinion surveying agencies, either indigenous offshoots of the U.S. Army program itself set up by American-trained researchers, or by others, such as Elisabeth Noelle, who were foresighted enough to see the potentialities for businessmen and politicians of this new research technology (Noelle, 1940; Noelle and Neumann, 1956-67; Noelle

AUTHOR'S NOTE: This paper was presented originally at the thirteenth annual convention of the International Studies Association, Dallas, Texas, March 15-18, 1972. The author is indebted to the Institute of Communications Research of the University of Illinois at Urbana-Champaign for financial support of this study, and to Karl F. Johnson for helpful comments.

and Neumann, 1967; Institut für Demoskopie, 1949-present). By now there are at least a half-dozen nationally-known agencies conducting political and other types of surveys, in addition to research units at some universities and a plethora of market-research firms (EMNID, 1949-).[1]

The extent of surveying operations since 1945 and the availability of their data about West Germans pose an embarrassment of riches for academic analysts of public opinion, particularly those concerned with its role in foreign policy processes. A glance at the major works on this topic nonetheless reveals almost complete dependence upon studies conducted in the United States or, occasionally, foreign studies commissioned and sometimes even carried out by American research units. Attempts to escape this parochial bias have been only partially successful. And yet, to develop anything like a cross-nationally valid model of the interaction between public opinion and foreign policy requires close attention to data from other countries. The purpose of this essay is to suggest some dimensions of the problems that this endeavor is likely to encounter.

PUBLIC OPINION ON FOREIGN POLICY

Microanalysis

Public opinion analysts have developed a number of interesting propositions, some of them at least partially verified, about public behavior regarding and attitudes toward foreign policy issues. Many of the phenomena noticed in American public opinion are discernible in Germany as well. This is particularly true at the microanalytic level. In both countries the well-educated, urban, and upper socioeconomic status groups, as well as individual men, are more knowledgeable about public events, and more likely to have opinions, than are women, the less well educated, the rural, and the poor (Table 1). People are more likely to have opinions than information about foreign policy issues. The closer an issue is to the daily life of the respondent, the more likely he is to have an attitude on it: In mid-1955 West German respondents were more than twice as likely to have no opinion on the Austrian state treaty (51%) as on West German foreign policy matters (25%). There is a clustering phenomenon identified by analysts of cognitive consistency, with the salience of individual images varying directly with the number of other images that are dependent upon them. Thus, of respondents who thought that Western Europe could defend itself from Soviet military attack without West German military forces, 55 per cent opposed the creation of a West German military; among those who thought that Western Europe could not defend itself without such a German contribution, 65 per

TABLE 1
WEST GERMAN KNOWLEDGE OF AND ATTITUDES TOWARD FOREIGN POLICY

Demographic Variable	Percentage Knowledgeable[a]	Percentage with Opinions[b]	No. of Cases
Sex			
Male	81	87	303
Female	52	63	323
Educational Level			
Elementary school	60	71	512
Beyond elementary	87	87	114
Monthly Income			
Up to 149 DM	48	56	76
150 to 299 DM	53	67	161
300 to 399 DM	69	82	147
400 to 499 DM	77	79	94
500 DM and more	78	84	118
Socioeconomic Status			
Upper classes	87	92	17
Middle classes	73	78	308
Lower classes	55	69	300
City Size			
Up to 1,999	57	72	170
2,000 to 24,999	59	68	208
25,000 to 99,999	74	76	54
100,000 and over	76	83	194
Total Sample	65	74	626

a. Average of 5 questions asking awareness of specific issues.
b. Average of 31 questions asking opinions on specific issues.
SOURCE: American Embassy (1955: 50-123).

cent favored setting up West German military forces (American Embassy, 1955: 26). Mass opinions tend to be associated with elite views. And, more generally, we find long-term stability in attitudes along with short-term fluctuations about a secular curve.

Macroanalysis

More intensive analysis of German public opinion can also tell us something about its relationship to public policy and international events. Preliminary studies suggest that such public views are responsive to specific events, but that the swings from the secular trend (shown in linear form in Figures 1a and 1b) are generally not very great and tend to balance out each

[258]   APPRAISALS

$$\text{Strength index} = \frac{\text{Western stronger}}{\text{Western stronger + Communist stronger}}$$

Source: Deutsch and Merritt (1965: 175).

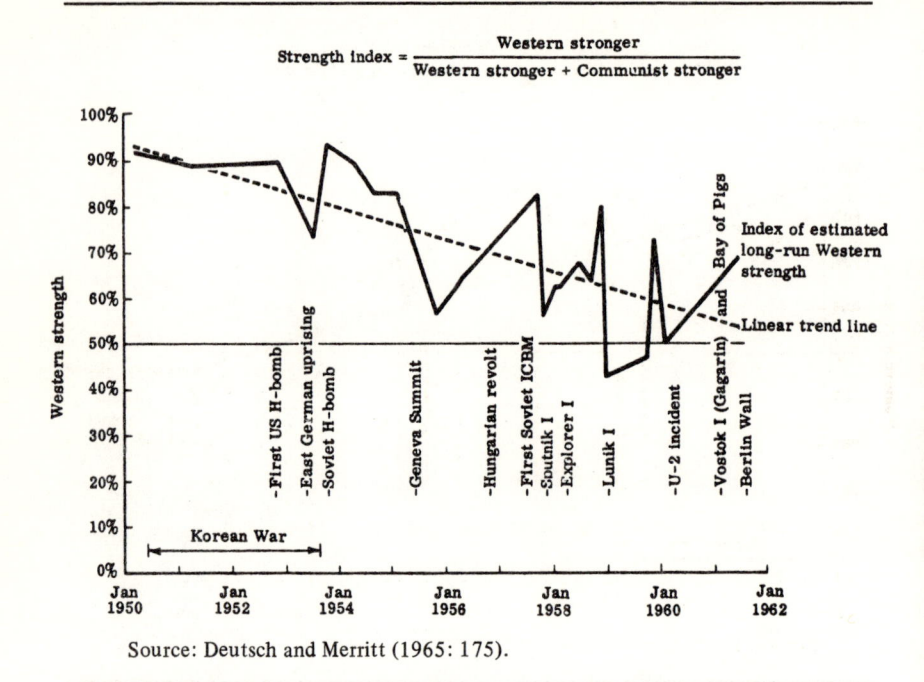

Figure 1a: WEST GERMAN ESTIMATES OF ULTIMATE SUCCESS OF THE COMMUNIST AND WESTERN POWERS IN THE COLD WAR, 1950-1961

other (Deutsch and Merritt, 1965: 175-176). Other research has found that attitudes toward certain countries are correlated at low levels with governmental actions, and are responsive rather than precedent to the latter (Abravenel and Hughes, 1973). (This relationship appears to be less strong for West Germany than for France and Britain.) An alternative hypothesis, also based on public opinion analysis, is that a changing public mood contributes to policy reorientation: Changing public attitudes toward problems of eastern policy (relations with the Soviet Union, acceptance of the Oder-Neisse boundary between Poland and Germany, recognition of the German Democratic Republic, relations with countries that recognized formally the German Democratic Republic, nullification of the 1938 Munich Agreement) certainly preceded and may even have set the political climate in which statesmen felt that changing long-standing principles would not be tantamount to political suicide.[2] Still other studies have revealed considerable congruence in West Germany with regard to issues of European unification among indicators at various levels: public opinion, the views of elites and the

$$\text{Strength Index} = \frac{\text{Western stronger}}{\text{Western stronger + Communist stronger}}$$

Source: Deutsch and Merritt (1965: 176).

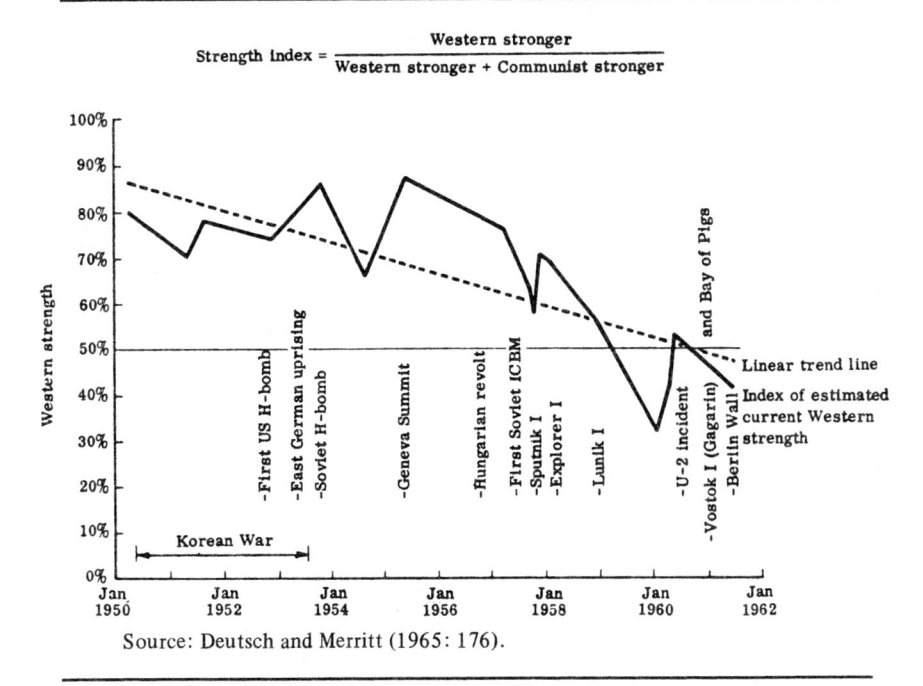

Figure 1b: WEST GERMAN ESTIMATES OF CURRENT STRENGTH OF THE COMMUNIST AND WESTERN POWERS IN THE COLD WAR, 1950-1961

more prestigious newspapers, and transaction flows such as trade, postal and student exchange, and migration (Deutsch et al., 1967: 213-290. Puchala, 1970). Clearly, however, these studies are mere beginnings. Much remains yet to be done on the macroanalytic level before we can state with confidence much of anything about the empirically observed relationship between opinion on the one hand and, on the other, public policy, nation-state behavior, and events.

The Communication Process

West German data can, finally, tell us much about the principles underlying efforts to influence public opinion, and hence certain categories of political outcomes. This is clearest, as is also true in the United States, with respect to electoral behavior. German political parties—particularly the Social Democratic Party (SPD) since Willy Brandt took charge in the late 1950s—have expended considerable sums for image studies which later served as a basis for electoral campaigning. In the same vein, German political analysts have generated much heat and some light on the question of how published poll results influence the electoral process itself (Hennis, 1957; Bauer, 1965; von Dohnanyi, 1965; Hartenstein, 1969; Diekershoff and Kliemt, 1968). In the foreign policy realm, it is difficult not to believe that the extensive propaganda conducted by Adenauer's government in favor of closer ties with the other states of the European Economic Community had an effect upon the increasingly positive attitudes held by West Germans about France and Italy. And someday when the debate is over and the data are released, we shall learn much about the process of opinion formation and change from the 1972 dispute over ratification of the Moscow and Warsaw treaties.

In short, data from the Federal Republic can go some distance toward bolstering or modifying what we think we know about public opinion itself. But is this what we want to know? Yes, of course—at least in part. Such studies can surely help to fill gaps in our theorizing about individual and mass behavior. As political scientists, however, we want to know something more than that. Can we develop a model that explains the interaction between public opinion and public policy? What is the function of mass opinion in the policy-making process? Or, stated more boldly, what do we really know about the political processes of a country when we can specify the parameter of public opinion as indicated by survey data? A second concern, but one that I shall touch upon only briefly here, is normative: What role should public opinion, however defined, play in the foreign policy formulation process? Implicit in this question is the notion of different "publics" with varying degrees of interest, knowledge, and influence. It also raises the crucial problem of how a society can create the type of relationship it desires between public opinion inputs and official responsiveness (Dahrendorf, 1967a). This second concern, then, goes to the very heart of democratic theory.

THE FUNCTION OF PUBLIC OPINION IN THE FOREIGN POLICY PROCESS

When we turn from microanalytic and macroanalytic studies to the actual role played by scientifically surveyed public opinion in the policy process, we find ourselves quite at sea. In the United States, for instance, we have discovered that there is little if any relationship between the foreign policy attitudes of congressmen and those of their constituents (Miller and Stokes, 1963). State Department officials, although paying lip-service to the significance for their own decisions of "public opinion," mean by the term not the results of sample surveys but rather the expressed views of congressmen, a handful of key newspapers, and a few relevant "others" in the personal and professional lives of the decision-makers (Cohen, 1970). And, although the American government for more than two decades has been sampling systematically the views on substantive issues of foreign populations, it is by no means clear what its officers do with these data. Standing as a classic statement of one viewpoint is the remark attributed to John Foster Dulles (cited in Free, 1965; see also R. L. Merritt, 1968): "If I so much as took into account what people in other countries are thinking or feeling, I would be derelict in my duty as Secretary of State." Such findings are indicative of great white areas on our cognitive maps relating surveyed opinion to the processes by which public policy is formed. So frequently, it seems, the phantom-like relationship simply slips through the fingers of the most capable and well-intentioned scholars.

The Paucity of Relevant Research

Unfortunately, studies to date of German political processes make little concrete contribution to our understanding. American specialists on Germany have by and large nodded in the direction of a putative relationship, but without spelling out its dimensions. Alternatively, they have slipped facilely from a discussion of German policy-making processes into a set of statements about the actual distribution of public attitudes on some specific set of issues, such as rearmament or reunification, implying that these distributions are somehow important in public policy-making. Some analysts see public opinion as a limiting condition for foreign-policy makers: officials examine relevant data to see if they have mass support or must override the public temporarily (Deutsch and Edinger, 1959: 115). Or else they offer a partial model, such as the "explanation" that public feelings are less decisive than the preferences of the leadership and the resonance of a particular issue (e.g., Richardson, 1966: 344). German writers describing governmental operations have by and large ignored the opinion-policy relationship even more (an exception is Schmidtchen, 1959). What accounts for this?

There are several possible explanations, the first of which has to do with the sociology of empirical social research in postwar Germany. The Nazi episode was disastrous for German science—disastrous not only because of the wartime disruption of scientific careers and destruction of research facilities but far more serious for the fact that it led numerous first-rate scholars to flee or go into an "internal emigration." Their departure, in itself bad enough, also meant a gap in the training of new scholars, particularly in the social sciences. Not until the mid-1950s did empirical social scientists—trained for the most part in the United States—begin producing major studies, and another decade passed before they began to move into permanent academic positions at such universities as Cologne and the Free University of Berlin. The structure of the universities themselves and the prevailing system of rewards did little to hasten this process: the small number of universities, the limited number (at least until recently) of academic positions guaranteeing scholarly independence to the researcher, the reluctance to recognize as worthy of scholarly attention such new fields as political science, and the domination of such traditional departments as sociology by adherents of an older school. Then, too, German scholars did not have the funds for systematic research, which frequently entails extensive and expensive team efforts, that were available to American social scientists during the late 1950s and throughout the 1960s. All these conditions point to the fact that it simply took time to build the institutional and intellectual foundation for any quantitative research whatever. And it is not surprising, especially given their training in American schools emphasizing electoral research and given the immediate pay-off of such studies in terms of relevance to ongoing political processes, that few West German scholars turned to the thornier issues of public opinion in the policy-formation process.

A second reason is what the German sociologist (and in the Brandt-Scheel coalition ambassador to the European Economic Community) Ralf Dahrendorf termed the anti-empirical bias of German society at large and academicians in particular (1967b; see also R. L. Merritt et al., 1971). The traditional classical-humanist education of German schools, with their emphasis upon Greek notions of idealism (which led, in the words of an eminent English literary critic [Butler, 1935], to "the tyranny of Greece over Germany"), was not conducive to the probabilistic concepts that underlie modern empirical social research. Whether or not this cultural element is the "cause," it remains a fact that German scholars have focused much more upon the idea of "publicness" (*Offentlichkeit*) than upon means to measure its dimensions.[3] Now, of course, a concern with the "essence" of publicness is in the tradition of many American commentators as well (Lippmann, 1922; Rogers, 1949); and "empiricists" would agree with "traditionalists" when they lament an overconcentration on empty-minded measurement based upon fuzzy conceptualization. (Abraham Kaplan [1964: 28-29] has called this the "law of the instrument": A small boy who has been given a hammer, he said, will quickly find that everything needs to be pounded!) The postwar American situation, however, differed from the German in its degree of research pluralism which, together with the availability for a long while of abundant financial resources, facilitated the development and refinement of public opinion concepts and measurement techniques.

Still a third reason, and one of increasing importance, verges on the ideological. Knowledge, an old cliché has it, is power. Some critics of the Federal Republic's political system are openly hostile toward any form of research that could conceivably help to stabilize (or entrench) this system. The notion of value-free research they hold as chimerical, if not downright pernicious. Knowledge about how people behave permits the "power elite" to manipulate them. Thus, they point out, the introduction of surveying techniques into electoral campaigns has led to a substitution of image-making for serious discussion of issues, producing in effect a numbed and ultimately dumb population that cannot effectively criticize or expel those in power (Rytlewski, 1965; Pausewang, 1966; Resch, 1968; Vogt, 1969). That there is an element of truth to these arguments is without doubt, even if they are frequently shortsighted. That is not the point here. Rather, what the argument means for those of us who are interested in learning about political processes is that our research efforts encounter hostility precisely in those circles—most specifically, professors, students, and other intellectuals—where we ordinarily expect none, and that considerable time and energy are spent justifying what we are trying to do rather than in doing it.

The Information Gap

Finally, there is still another and very practical reason for the relative lack of research in West Germany on the role of public opinion in foreign policy formulation processes: the absence of truly useful information. In what circumstances is an American president likely to use or discount public opinion data? We can all remember a recent President who, during his first few months of office, seemed forever to be waving poll results in front of newsmen's noses but who, when events later took an adverse turn for him, was more inclined to express skepticism about the entire polling process. And who among us has not encountered a policy advocate who has been willing to use poll results, provided only that they supported the policy he was advocating? As Wilhelm Hennis (1957: 59-60) has wryly noted, "the independent counsel of science is desired when it can serve as support for one's own political claims." This type of behavior has produced considerable cynicism among public officials and newspaper readers alike, and it has scattered red herrings in the path of analysts seriously interested in policy formation processes.

Similar situations have occurred in postwar German politics. The most well-known example occurred in the early 1950s: Despite poll data persistently reporting adverse reactions to his plan to rearm Germany, Chancellor Konrad Adenauer equally persistently pursued it. In part by ignoring mass opinion as revealed by surveys, and in part by "educating" the German public to the need for an army (in many instances by overemphasizing the Soviet "threat" and thereby helping to create the very condition against which the Federal Republic ostensibly needed protection), Adenauer accomplished his goal—and also raised his party's share of the popular vote from 31 per cent in 1949 to 45 per cent four years later, and in 1957, after the creation of the Bundeswehr, to over 50 per cent (Baring, 1969: 11-12). Adenauer's economic adviser and subsequent vice-chancellor, Ludwig Erhard (1962: 8), commented:

> With regard to German policy in the past 12 years, I would like to say quite frankly that, in my opinion, it has proved successful only because it had the *courage to be unpopular*. It pursued aims and solved problems with which no cheap votes could be won; actions and decisions were determined by a sense of political responsibility.

Adenauer's opponents, by the same token, termed his behavior a high-handed disregard of the very basis of democracy.

In fact Chancellor Adenauer's behavior was far from atypical. Erhard (1962: 12), who succeeded him in 1963, announced his views on this issue in advance. Speaking in 1961 to an international conference of public opinion experts (WAPOR), he said:

> I am not one of those who let their actions be determined by a test. I prefer to ask questions at the beginning, in order to be sure of my facts—but not necessarily in order to act accordingly to those facts, for there are too many varying viewpoints involved.

"Quantitative evidence alone is insufficient," he added. In early 1955, during the parliamentary debate about rearmament, a young and relatively unknown Social Democratic representative from West Berlin rose to speak in opposition. Regardless of what one thinks about public opinion polling, he said (cited in Schmidtchen, 1959: 142), it has proved to be relatively accurate for describing certain developments. Attitudes toward rearmament, he noted, were a case in point:

> Two surveys conducted by one of the largest agencies ... show that the dividing line among the adult population ... cuts right through the middle of the nation. That reveals a very serious problem, and [the government] cannot simply ignore it by saying that the opposition [in parliament] comprises only a third of the votes.

Later that same man, Willy Brandt, when he became Federal Chancellor, proved equally capable of responding to equally divided public opinion results on such issues as the eastern treaties by pursuing equally steadfastly his own foreign policy course.

Compounding the analytic problem that statesmen formulating policy use survey results as only one desideratum—and far from the most important at that!—is another problem of which we are all painfully aware but which bears brief mention here anyway. Partisan pollsters can sometimes, and often quite unconsciously, bias the results of a survey by the questions they ask. In a survey resting upon an admittedly small sample (N = 600) in May 1971, the CDU-oriented Institut für Demoskopie asked a series of questions that elicited a rather gloomy evaluation of Chancellor Brandt's eastern policy (Table 2). The results were duly reported on nationwide television. The questions, however, I would argue, were calculated to produce this pessimistic forecast. This was revealed very sharply in a survey conducted in fall 1971 for the same television station by the EMNID-Institut (1971: 6-7, A1-A2). Asking a national sample of 2,000 adult respondents whether they were for or against Brandt's eastern policy, 63 per cent answered positively, and less than half that number (30%) responded negatively. Putting the two sets of survey findings together suggests that the West German public, although somewhat disappointed about the terms of the eastern treaties and aware that the Soviet Union might be using them to their own advantage, was by and large inclined to accept them anyway. Such a finding, of course, did not help much in predicting whether or not the Federal Parliament would ratify the Moscow and Warsaw treaties of 1970, not accomplished until May 1972.

What all these points suggest is that, if it is difficult to assess the role of public opinion in American foreign policy processes (and we know that it is!), then it is even more difficult in the Federal Republic. Does this mean that we are facing a hopeless task? Not at all. There are several approaches that can help in building theory with cross-national validity.

SOME TASKS FOR RESEARCH

Filling the Information Gap

A number of these possible approaches are sufficiently obvious as to need only brief discussion here. The first deals with foreign-policy attitudes themselves, that is, the microanalytic level. In the case of West Germany, as noted earlier, there is a wealth of public opinion surveys and evaluations potentially available for analysis. An initial task would be to survey these surveys in order to determine what we already know, so that we may more

TABLE 2
SOME WEST GERMAN ATTITUDES ON EASTERN POLICY, MAY 1971[a]

a. In the last twelve months the Federal Government has conducted talks and negotiations with the Soviet Union, Poland, Czechoslovakia, and the German Democratic Republic. What is your impression: Are you pleased or disappointed with these developments to date?

Pleased	30%
Disappointed	43
Undecided	27
	100%

b. Do you believe that the Russians are positively inclined to let the Berlin negotiations reach a conclusion that is also satisfactory for the Federal Republic, or do you not believe that?

Russians are positively inclined	18%
I don't believe it	66
Undecided	16
	100%

c. If it were left up to you, should the Moscow Treaty (with the USSR) come into effect only after a satisfactory regulation of the Berlin question, or should one not make that dependent upon Berlin?

	March 1971	May 1971
Only after progress in Berlin	62%	63%
Should not make it dependent upon Berlin	18	17
I am totally against the Moscow Treaty	4	7
Undecided	5	6
No opinion	11	7
	100%	100%

d. The Moscow Treaty must of course be ratified by the Bundestag. Do you think that the Bundestag in Bonn will ratify the treaty in the coming months, or do you not think so?

Think it will	26%
Do not think it will	52
Undecided	22
	100%

e. Do you believe that Federal Chancellor Brandt, in his negotiations with the East, has correctly or incorrectly evaluated the Russians?

Correctly	33%
Incorrectly	43
Undecided	24
	100%

[a] Sample sizes: 2,000 in March 1971; 600 in May 1971.
SOURCE: Institut für Demoskopie (1971).

quickly turn to the task of determining what else we need to know. This will not be a simple project—and not only because of the plethora of data. Many of the most useful data files appear to be less than completely accessible to German or other scholars, since they are in the hands of private firms, governmental agencies, and political parties. In other cases a demonstrated lack of cooperation between data archives has kept useful information out of circulation. And, of course, even if the data were freely available there would be the immense and expensive job of gathering the card-decks and tapes, storing them, and developing adequate computer routines for retrieving what the individual scholar needs. Work on other aspects of our problem must continue even though the most desirable data bases and facilities are not available.

Another task would be to utilize existing data to develop and test propositions about West German attitudes on foreign policy and international affairs. A starting point might be the replication of some of the findings in the literature based upon American data. It would be useful, for instance, to learn more than we already know about foreign-policy moods and mood swings among the West German public; the relationship of age, sex, partisan identification, and clustering of views on particular sets of issues; the relation between foreign policy attitudes and such political behavior patterns as voting or participation in demonstrations. Clearly, however, scholars with training in the German educational system will have different perspectives that may help us move beyond such propositions in ways that can then be fed back into American analyses of public opinion on foreign policy. It is a commonplace which nevertheless bears restating that only such interaction of conceptualizations and measurement procedures can lead us to any valid and nontrivial cross-national generalizations.

Next, we shall have to pay closer attention to people—the holders of attitudes on foreign policy issues. Numerous scholars have stratified total populations according to the amount of interest they have in foreign affairs, their knowledge about what is happening in the world and at home, and the potential influence that they can bring to bear upon political processes. We have come to accept the notion that perhaps one in twenty adults truly "participates" in the political system. Yet we have learned that the others can sometimes play a key role, too. I am not thinking merely of anomic outbursts of violence aimed at, let us say, the East German government for having built the Berlin wall in August 1961, or the Amerika-Haus in West Berlin as a demonstration against American activities in Vietnam. We have also seen dockworkers tie up shipping to an extent that it affects a nation's export program and balance of payments. Furthermore, as Erwin K. Scheuch (1965:

207-209) reminds us, the mere fact that the masses (in West Germany, if not elsewhere) are passive during times of political stability is no reason to expect them to remain equally passive when orderly processes of government weaken or break down. The effects of such occurrences in the not-too-distant past are burned deeply into Germans' political consciousness. What we need to learn more about are the circumstances in which different aggregates and strata—in West Germany as well as the United States and elsewhere—will behave in particular ways. Survey research provides one means to get at this type of question.

Another concern lies in macroanalysis. Only recently have we begun to correlate attitudes within a system with the whole system's behavior in the international arena. We have learned that there are pitfalls in finding indicators of such "syntality" variables: Official statistics published by national and international agencies may contain intentional or unconscious biases or simply have a margin of error that renders them useless for most analytic purposes; "event statistics" gathered from such publications as the *New York Times Index* or *Facts on File* are only partially complete and tend to stress certain countries and types of events to the virtual exclusion of others; and the use of transaction-flow analysis raises as many questions as it answers. Yet each type of indicator, whatever its limitations in terms of reliability and validity, can serve as a first approximation for generating and testing hypotheses in a crude way. More refined analysis on a country-by-country basis will doubtless yield still richer data and hypotheses, which may then be integrated on a cross-national basis.

Finally, more intensive studies are needed of the West German policy-making process itself. Thanks to scholars like Bernard C. Cohen (1970) and others (e.g., Chittick, 1970), we are beginning to get a fairly good idea of how American governmental officials, both elected and appointed, use public opinion both in their day-to-day work and long-range planning. But, except anecdotally, we have little comparable information about the Federal Republic. We know, for instance, that the Adenauer government commissioned polls,[4] and the Chancellor behaved frequently as though he knew what popular attitudes were, as in the case of the rearmament debate. We nevertheless have little idea how the data generated by the polls were used, if at all. Adenauer's memoirs are silent on this point, as are the published works of his closest associates. How typical was his behavior in the rearmament dispute for general policy-making, especially in foreign affairs?

The five points listed above are apparent to us all. The areas in the relationship between West German public opinion and foreign policy in which I have pointed to a need for further conceptualization, data-making, and theory-building are hardly atypical. Similar lacunae characterize research on other countries, including the United States. Bit by bit many of the gaps are being filled; and current research trends can occasionally make even the most pessimistic scholar hopeful. There are other areas, however, that have received less conceptual attention, and where progress seems to be less satisfactory.

AN UNEXPLORED QUESTION: CROSS-NATIONAL STRUCTURAL DIFFERENCES

One of these lies in the relationship between public opinion on foreign policy and the structure of the policy-making system. To make a simple distinction, the American political system includes a President who is elected (somewhat indirectly) by the population at large and who is constitutionally charged with the task of conducting foreign policy; 100 senators and 534 congressmen who in principle at least are elected independently of both each other and the President and who must perform such duties as advising on and consenting to treaties as well as authorizing foreign policy expenditures; and a bureaucracy (Departments of State, Commerce, Defense, and others) comprising both civil servants and appointed officials who are responsible for gathering and evaluating information, making policy recommendations, and implementing policy once it has been formulated. By contrast, in the Federal Republic of Germany a complex electoral system combining single-member constituencies and proportional representation by state produces a Bundestag of about 496 members, who in turn elect the Federal Chancellor; an upper chamber (Bundesrat) comprises delegates sent by the governments of the individual states; and the President serves more in a representative than in a policy-making capacity. The United Kingdom has a parliamentary system (with an extremely weak upper house) based upon elections in single-member districts. France elects its President directly, and utilizes a system of proportional representation to fill its Chamber of Deputies.

Such structural differences have an impact upon the role that scientifically surveyed public opinion can play in the policy-formulation process. Parliamentarians elected on party lists, no less than appointed bureaucrats, may have less of an appreciation of its significance than does the politician who must appeal directly to voters, pay attention to his popular image, and commission his own surveys to aid him in devising electoral tactics. Yet this latter situation can also foster a basic misunderstanding: Surveys are most helpful in understanding an electoral or other plebiscitary situation in which each person's vote counts for just as much as the next person's vote. If there is anything at all we have learned about processes by which policy is formulated, it is that the plebiscitary notion is of no real use. Aggregates must organize to present their interests as a group, or they must find a spokesman like Ralph Nader who can "represent" them. Mass opinion without such an organizational base has little clout. This is even true, contrary to many textbook explanations, at election time: Voters typically cast their ballots for varieties of reasons—some personal, other sociological, and still others issue-oriented—and it has never been possible, as Woodrow Wilson sought vainly to do in 1920, to turn a popular election into a plebiscite on a single issue. Even so, specific issues such as defense spending in local industries may be sufficiently salient for a particular district that such issues color the outcome of that district's voting behavior. Germany, by the way, provides an interesting test case of the proposition that the form of election is related to attitudes toward public opinion, since half its parliamentary members are elected in their own constituencies, the other half from party lists using a modified form of proportional representation.

The relationship between chief executive and parliament also deserves greater attention. In the United States, where in recent years we have frequently had a Congress dominated by a party that is not the President's, public opinion can be an instrument for battle between the executive and legislative branches. In West Germany the Chancellor is elected by and responsible to the Bundestag. A common complaint is that the executive, which is also conterminous with the majority party or parties, controls the information process to the extent that its own members in the Bundestag are left in the dark (Keller and Raupach, 1970; Schatz, 1970). The individual representative seldom has the resource base needed to conduct his own surveys. By the same token, however, the executive that falls out of tune with popular sentiment runs the risk of defections in its own ranks, which could conceivably produce a positive vote of no confidence that would overturn the executive. To date it does not appear that public opinion survey data have played a significant role in such struggles.

Still another structural issue is the composition of parliamentary bodies. Unlike the United States, the list system in the Federal Republic permits important campaign contributers or constituents, such as business concerns and labor unions, to secure direct parliamentary representation for their delegates. Since such delegates may continue drawing their regular salaries from the firm by which they are employed, they are freed from the responsibility that many other Bundestag representatives have of working to supplement their parliamentary incomes. This in turn means that these delegates can devote their entire energies to pursuing policies consonant with the interests of their employers. Hence they tend to be prominent in committee hearings and able to find the backing to perform research and bill-drafting that other members cannot afford. What all this means for present purposes is that such delegates—and there are more than a few—can afford to ignore popular sentiments as represented by public opinion, however defined. They can in effect create faits accomplis by working quietly within the Bundestag's partisan factions and committee meetings.

If we move below the level of formal governmental institutions and processes, then we find still more structural components of the political system to which attention must be paid. Not the least of these is the role of mass media in society. Industrialized countries in the West have fairly elaborate communications systems that, although basically comparable, differ sharply in some respects. In contrast to the United States, for instance, about half the newspapers sold daily in the Federal Republic of Germany come from the conservative publishing concern controlled by Axel Caesar Springer (Müller, 1969); federal states operate the television and radio stations. This degree of concentration can facilitate concerted campaigns on public-policy issues—as Chancellor Brandt found, much to his distress, when the Springer press mounted a full-scale battle against the eastern treaties! A plethora of other cross-national differences is also of potential relevance in explaining the public opinion-foreign policy nexus as it differs from country to country. These include the role of organized interest groups, the representativeness and support of political parties, the means by which elites are recruited, linkages among groups in the political arena, and cultural differences affecting the foreign policy attitudes and behavior of individuals.

The above are intended to be exemplary rather than exhaustive of the type of structural effects that need more careful examination by students of West German (and cross-national) policy-making processes if they would understand the actual as opposed to the putative significance of public opinion. The striking differences between the structures of the West German and American political systems suggest that findings generated for one may not be applicable directly to the other. Moreover, neither set of findings may apply to France, Belgium, or any of the other industrialized countries of Western Europe, not to speak of the rest of the world. The implication is clear: If we want to move beyond the parochial concern with policy formation in the United States in an effort to develop a valid model of such processes in the industrialized world, it will be imperative to focus more upon behavior in other countries. And West Germany, as a country with well-developed surveying facilities and a rich data collection, may well be the place to begin.

NOTES

1. Data from some university and commercial institutes are available at the Roper Center of Williams College in Williamstown, Mass., and the Zentralarchiv für Empirische Sozialforschung at the University of Cologne.

2. In February 1972 83 per cent of a national sample agreed that the West German government should try to improve its relations with the Soviet Union, 78 per cent that the Federal Republic should have diplomatic relations even with those states that recognized the German Democratic Republic (that is, a repudiation of the Hallstein Doctrine), 48 per cent that the Federal Republic should recognize the GDR, 45 per cent that the Federal Republic should repudiate any claim to the Sudetenland as a step toward improving relations with Czechoslovakia, and 42 per cent that the Oder-Neisse line should be recognized as Germany's eastern border (EMNID, 1972: 4).

3. Many note quite correctly that there is not a single but many publics, and hence a multiple public opinion; accordingly, any emphasis on that variety discoverable through sample surveys will of necessity be incomplete and quite possibly misleading, since it distracts us from our quest for an adequate definition of the concept "public opinion" (Hennis, 1957; Habermas, 1962; Otto, 1966; and especially Luhmann, 1970). This issue, which begins from a normative standpoint, has much in common with the empirical perspectives presented in this paper on the question of the actual use of survey data in public policy formulation.

4. Hennis (1957: 5) notes that the budget in the Federal Chancellor's office for sample surveying increased almost threefold from 1954 ($13,000) to 1956 ($38,000); other funds were also available to support "information" efforts, including surveying operations.

REFERENCES

ABRAVANEL, M. and B. HUGHES (1973) "Public opinion and foreign policy behavior: a cross-national study of linkages," pp. 107-133 in P. J. McGowan (ed.) Sage International Yearbook of Foreign Policy Studies I. Beverly Hills: Sage.

American Embassy, Office of Public Affairs, Research Staff (1955) "Sovereign Germany speaks: reactions to sovereignty, Austria solution and coming four-power conference." Report no. 213 (1 July). (mimeo)

BARING, A. (1969) Aussenpolitik in Adenauers Kanzlerdemokratie: Bonns Beitrag zur Europäischen Verteidigungsgemeinschaft. Munich and Vienna: R. Oldenbourg.

BAUER, H. (1965) 'Spiegelt die Demoskopie die öffentlichen Meinung?" Politische Studien 16, 162: 419-427.

BUTLER, E. M. (1935) The Tyranny of Greece over Germany: A Study of the Influence Exercised by Greek Art and Poetry over the Great German Writers of the Eighteenth, Nineteenth and Twentieth Centuries. New York: Macmillan.

CHITTICK, W. O. (1970) State Department, Press, and Pressure Groups: A Role Analysis. New York: Wiley-Interscience.

COHEN, B. C. (1970) "The relationship between public opinion and foreign policy maker," pp. 65-80 in M. Small (ed.) Public Opinion and Historians: Interdisciplinary Perspectives. Detroit: Wayne State Univ. Press.

DAHRENDORF, R. (1967a) "Aktive und passive öffentlichkeit." Merkur 21, 237: 1109-1122.
--- (1967b) Society and Democracy in Germany. Garden City, N.Y.: Doubleday.
DEUTSCH, K. W. and L. J. EDINGER (1959) Germany Rejoins the Powers: Mass Opinion, Interest Groups, and Elites in Contemporary German Foreign Policy. Stanford: Stanford Univ. Press.
DEUTSCH, K. W., L. J. EDINGER, R. C. MACRIDIS and R. L. MERRITT (1967) France, Germany and the Western Alliance: A Study of Elite Attitudes on European Integration and World Politics. New York: Scribner.
DEUTSCH, K. W. and R. L. MERRITT (1965) "Effects of events on national and international images," pp. 132-187 in H. C. Kelman (ed.) International Behavior: A Social-Psychological Analysis. New York: Holt, Rinehart & Winston.
DIEKERSHOFF, K.-H. and G. KLIEMT (1968) "Ideologische Funktionen demoskopischer Erhebungen: kritische Bemerkungen zu einer Umfrage der EMNID-Institute." Kölner Zeitschrift für Soziologie und Sozialpsychologie 20, 1: 62-73.
EMNID-Institut (1949-present) Informationen: Monatlicher Dienst. Bielefeld: EMNID-Institut GmbH & Co.
--- (1972) Informationen 24, 1/2 (January-February): 1-10.
--- (1971) Informationen 23, 9/10 (September-October): 6-7, A1-A2.
ERHARD, L. (1962) Fragen an die Meinungsforschung. Problems Put to Public Opinion Experts. Allensbach and Bonn: Verlag für Demoskopie, Allensbacher Schriften 8.
FREE, L. A. (1965) "The role of public opinion in international relations: the contributions of public opinion research." Delivered at the Edward R. Murrow Center of the Fletcher School of Law and Diplomacy (1 November). (mimeo)
HABERMAS, J. (1962) Strukturwandel der Öffentlichkeit: Untersuchungen zu einer Kategorie der bürgerlichen Gesellschaft. Neuwied am Rhein and Berlin: Hermann Luchterhand.
HARTENSTEIN, W. (1969) "Gesetzliches Verbot von Wahlprognosen." Zeitschrift für Rechtspolitik 2, 9(September): 201-202.
HENNIS, W. (1957) Meinungsforschung und repräsentative Demokratie: Zur Kritik politischer Umfragen. Tübingen: J.C.B. Mohr (Paul Siebeck), Recht und Staat in Geschichte und Gegenwart 200-201.
Institut für Demoskopie (1949-present) Allensbacher Berichte. Allensbach and Bonn: Institut für Demoskopie (thrice monthly).
--- (1971) "Politik der unerfüllten Hoffnungen im Osten." Allensbacher Berichte 14.
KAPLAN, A. (1964) The Conduct of Inquiry: Methodology for Behavioral Science. San Francisco: Chandler.
KELLER, T. and H. RAUPACH (1970) Informationslücke des Parlaments? Wissenschaftliche Hilfseinrichtungen für die Abgeordneten des Deutschen Bundestages und der Länderparlamente. Hannover: Verlge für Literatur und Zeitgeschehen.
LIPPMANN, W. (1922) Public Opinion. New York: Macmillan.
LUHMANN, N. (1970) "Offentliche Meinung." Politische Vierteljahresschrift 11, 1 (March): 2-28.
MERRITT, A. J. (forthcoming) Public Opinion in Semisovereign Germany: The HICOG Surveys, 1949-1955. Urbana: Univ. of Illinois Press.
--- and R. L. MERRITT (1970) Public Opinion in Occupied Germany: The OMGUS Surveys, 1945-1949. Urbana: Univ. of Illinois Press.
MERRITT, R. L. (1968) "The USIA surveys: tools for policy and analysis," pp. 3-30 in

R. L. Merritt and D. J. Puchala (eds.) Western European Perspectives on International Affairs: Public Opinion Studies and Evaluations. New York: Praeger.

――― E. P. FLERLAGE and A. J. MERRITT (1971) "Political man in postwar West German education." Comparative Education Review 15, 3 (October): 346-361.

MILLER, W. E. and D. E. STOKES (1963) "Constituency influence in Congress." American Political Science Review 57, 1 (March): 45-56.

MULLER, H. D. (1969) Press Power: A Study of Axel Springer. London: Macdonald.

NOELLE, E. (1940) Amerikanische Massenbefragungen über Politik und Presse. Frankfurt/Main: M. Diesterweg.

――― and E. P. NEUMANN [eds.] (1967) The Germans: Public Opinion Polls, 1947-1966. Allensbach and Bonn: Verlag für Demoskopie.

――― [eds.] (1956-1967) Jahrbuch der Offentlichen Meinung. Allensbach and Bonn: Verlag für Demoskopie. (four volumes to date, covering the years 1947-1967)

OTTO, U. (1966) "Die Problematik des Begriffs der öffentlichen Meinung." Publizistik 11, 2: 99-130.

PAUSEWANG, S. (1966) "Zur Kritik der öffentlichen Meinung." Gesellschaft, Staat, Erziehung 11, 5 (May): 395-409.

PUCHALA, D. J. (1970) "Integration and disintegration in Franco-German relations, 1954-1965." International Organization 24, 2(Spring): 183-208.

RESCH, H. (1968) "Zum Verhältnis von Demoskopie und Politik." Blätter für deutsche und internationale Politik 13, 11 (November): 1171-1180.

RICHARDSON, J. L. (1966) Germany and the Atlantic Alliance: The Interaction of Strategy and Politics. Cambridge: Harvard Univ. Press.

ROGERS, L. (1949) The Pollsters: Public Opinion, Politics, and Democratic Leadership. New York: Alfred A. Knopf.

RYTLEWSKI, R. (1965) "Versagen der Meinungsforschung: schwarze Nacht der Demoskopen." Der Politologe 6, 18 (December): 21-29.

SCHATZ, H. (1970) Der Parlamentarische Entscheidungsprozess: Bedingungen der verteidigungspolitischen Willensbildung im Deutschen Bundestag. Meisenheim am Glan: Anton Hain.

SCHEUCH, E. K. (1965) "Die Sichtbarkeit politischer Einstellungen im alltäglichen Verhalten," pp. 169-214 in E. K. Scheuch and R. Wildenmann (eds.) Zur Soziologie der Wahl. Cologne and Opladen: Westdeutscher.

SCHMIDTCHEN, G. (1959) Die befragte Nation: Uber den Einfluss der Meinungsforschung auf die Politik. Freiburg im Breisgau: Rombach.

VOGT, G. (1969) "Uber den Umgang mit Wahlprognosen: Demoskopie zwischen wissenschaftlicher Methode und Scharlatanerie." Neue Gesellschaft 16, 5(May): 427-430.

von DOHNANYI, K. (1965) "Die Verführung der Führer: die Meinungsforschung in der Politik." Neue Gesellschaft 12, 5: 860-863.

Chapter 10

THE STEPS TO WAR: A SURVEY OF SYSTEM LEVELS, DECISION STAGES, AND RESEARCH RESULTS

KARL W. DEUTSCH
Harvard University

DIETER SENGHAAS
Goethe Universitaet

SOME TASKS OF THEORY

Within the general theory of international relations, a theory of war and peace would have three tasks. First, it would have to define operationally certain states of affairs as "war" and others as "peace." It might then be useful to subdivide each of these states further by additional operational criteria. Thus, war might be divided into "limited" and "all-out" wars; peace might be divided into a state of "relatively secure peace" and a state of "war danger" (Deutsch and Senghaas, 1970).

A second task of a theory of war and peace would then be to state the conditions and contingencies under which each of these states of affairs would be more or less probable to occur; and then to check these probabilities against relevant reproducible data about the behavior of individuals, groups, nations, and the international system.

A third task of such a theory would be to surmise which of these conditions could be changed or controlled by deliberate political action so as to make the occurrence of war less likely and eventually to abolish war as a significant practice in human affairs.

TWO CONVERGENT APPROACHES

The effort to develop such a theory may be pursued in two directions. One approach is conceptual and deductive. Here one proposes tentatively a relatively simple scheme of a few basic concepts and relations among them. From this scheme one then works out inferences about what facts ought to be observable if the schemes are true, and one then tests these inferences against observations, readjusting the scheme and broadening and refining the observations until an acceptable fit is reached.

The other approach would consist of making preliminary assumptions about what categories or data would be relevant for the problem to be solved; and then collecting such data systematically, analyzing them, and thus testing the original assumptions about relevance and attempting to develop further concepts and propositions by deductions from the data.

It is often possible to use both approaches, the conceptual-deductive and the empirical-inductive one, and to see whether convergent results can be obtained from such a combined approach. If successful, such a procedure might eventually lead us to a theory of war and peace, but not necessarily to a unique or ultimately true one. Insofar as it could be validated by observation and experiment, our theory would contain a great deal of truth. The aggregate of its verified predictions about reality would be called its truth content; and any alternative theory that might later supersede it would have to include within its own terms most or all of the truth content of its predecessor, while going beyond it to additional verifiable predictions in other respects.

At present there is not even one major provisional theory of war and peace meeting these criteria. The task of starting the succession of coherent and relatively comprehensive theories about war and peace with a cumulatively growing truth content, and with increasing possibilities of application, is still at its beginning—in tragic contrast to the urgency of our need for such knowledge.

The task of the present paper will be to present some relevant partial concepts, models, and theories, and to survey some of the empirical research methods (including the new methods of research by means of simulation) and data by which these theories could be tested. In this manner it is hoped to evaluate explicitly or implicitly at least some of the research work done in recent years, to identify some major gaps in theoretical analysis and empirical research; to indicate some desirable changes in research procedures; and to suggest an agenda for some of the next steps toward the development of a theory of war and peace.

A SIMPLE CONCEPTUAL SCHEME

Some Basic Definitions

For the purposes of this study, and following the usage of the survey by Singer and Small (1972), we shall call "war" any series of events that meets the following three criteria:

(1) *Size:* it results in at least 1,000 battle deaths (not counting, therefore, the indirect victims through famine, lack of shelter, and disease).

(2) *Preparation:* it has been prepared in advance, and/or is being maintained, by large-scale social organizations through such means as the recruitment, training, and deployment of troops, the acquisition, storage and distribution of arms and ammunition, the making of specific war plans and the like; and

(3) *Legitimation:* it is being legitimized by an established governmental or quasi-governmental organization, so that large-scale killing is viewed not as a crime but as a duty.

The definition just given would exclude small incidents among organized forces, large but unorganized and/or poorly legitimated and/or transitory riots. It would include, however, many large and sustained civil wars, since the parties to such wars tend to assume quasi-governmental functions in preparing, maintaining, organizing, and legitimating the process of large-scale killing.

"International wars," on which this paper will focus, are a subset of all wars. They consist of those wars that occur among *established states or governments* which are actors in international relations. An approximate operational test might be diplomatic recognition by at least two major powers.

Not all violence is war, just as not every illness is an epidemic. To call every illness a pestilence might be good propaganda for a short period; it would be poor medical science. To call all violence "war" and all injustice and oppression "structural violence" similarly would bring to social science more confusion than assistance.

The definition of war we have accepted implies a minimal definition of peace. We call "peace" any state of affairs in which no large numbers of people are killed in battles organized, prepared, and legitimized by governments or quasi-governments. Such peace may be by no means ideal. As critics of peace have often said, it may resemble sloth, torpor, apathy, resignation, oppression, or intermittent confused small-scale violence. At some times and places, and for some people, war may be preferable to it. This may well be a central issue in the study of revolutions, or even in a much broader range of social sciences, but it is not a central issue of peace research.

Our conception of "peace research" in the present paper is more narrow. The main threats of war and of the destruction of mankind do not come from the struggles of poor peasant guerrillas to overthrow the rule of landlords in some region, nor from the efforts of local landlords to defend their privileges. Rather, the main threats of war come from the clashes among large powers, most often relatively rich and with highly developed weapons of mass destruction. It is on the prevention and abolition of such wars of mass destruction that our interest is concentrated.

A Fundamental Value Orientation

The comparison with medicine should indicate our value orientation. We are on the side of life, not death. We want to use any knowledge we have, or may yet discover, so as to make organized mass killings such as wars less likely, and to bring about their complete abolition. We also desire the abolition of other evils such as starvation, oppression, injustice, and the like, but we think that is more likely to be accomplished if we also see the distinctions between these wrongs, together with the specific conditions which foster each of them, and the specific ways in which each may best be combatted. If we have focused our limited resources primarily upon the problem of international war, we have done so in the hope that other researchers will cover other sectors of the larger problem of the defense of human life.

A Paradigm of Conflict

War may be thought of as the result of a coordination failure in the behavior of two or more actors in regard to a major need of at least one of them.

In the case of international war, the main *actors* are nation states or their functional equivalents such as major guerrilla movements or emerging revolutionary regimes. Cross-national actors such as international governmental or non-governmental actors (IGOs and INGOs), internal parties, churches, and business corporations are likely to play at most a secondary role. Without the aid of national governments they cannot ordinarily create and commit armed forces on a large scale. Similarly, if one or more of these cross-national actors sought to prevent a war or to end a war after it had started, they would ordinarily do so by acting through the existing governments of nation states or by replacing them with new ones.

By a "need" of any acting system—a person, group, organization, or state—we mean an internal disequilibrium large enough to drive the system to act or search—i.e., to keep changing its state so long as this internal disequilibrium is not substantially reduced. A relationship of a system to its environment, such that the system's disequilibrium is thus substantially reduced, is called a "goal-state," or "goal," of the system. In a goal-state the system comes to relative rest. Goal-seeking behavior is likely to be more effective in systems that receive adequate feedback signals about the state of their environment, their own state, and the results of their own earlier goal-seeking actions. Goal-seeking thus implies interdependence between the actor and its environment; goal-attainment implies the successful coordination of the actor's behavior with the relevant processes in its environment so that the goal is reached. If the relevant environment consists of one or more other actors, goal attainment by any one actor requires successful coordination between the behavior of at least two actors, even though the burden of adjustment may be borne wholly by one of them.

From this situation we may derive a paradigm of conflict. "Conflict" in the simplest bilateral case is a situation where two actors are so interdependent that neither of them may reach a major goal without coordination with the other actor, but where—for whatever reason—the two actors have failed to coordinate their behavior in such a way that no major arrangement of either of them is injured and no major goal or need of either of them is frustrated. If their interdependence persists, at least one actor cannot reach or keep his own goals without injuring the organization of the other or frustrating his goals. In elaborate goal-seeking organizations the attainment of one's goals and the preservation of one's integrity are perceived as rewards while damage to one's integrity or frustration of one's goals is counted as a deprivation. In a conflict situation, therefore, the probability of rewards to one of the interdependent actors will covary negatively with the rewards to the other. One actor's reward will then covary with the other actor's deprivation.

If this negative covariance is complete, we are dealing with a situation resembling a "zero-sum game." In a zero-sum game all gains for one party must come from the losses of another. But there can also be conflict situations which resemble "variable-sum games." In such cases, all parties may gain jointly at the expense of a bank or of nature, or all parties may jointly lose. In relation to the bank or nature, the rewards of the players covary positively, giving them a common interest. The rewards still covary negatively, however, in regard to the distribution of these joint gains or losses among them, and possibly in regard to other adverse interests which might even be larger than their common ones. Game models of this kind, both zero-sum and variable-sum, are drawn from a small subclass of conflicts which have been highly formalized. The distinction between fixed-sum and variable-sum games, however, can be extended by analogy to the larger class of conflicts which are otherwise less convenient to analyze. The differences between games and other kinds of conflicts like wars should not be overlooked. In most games the payoffs to all players are made in the same currency, usually money. In other kinds of conflicts, the rewards to one actor and the deprivations to another may covary without being necessarily commensurable. One actor might win cash (territories or new markets) at the cost of another actor's physical or psychic suffering, which need not be susceptible to measurement in monetary terms.

All conflict implies, therefore, some significant degree of interdependence between the effects of the behavior of two actors. Without interdependence of effects there is no conflict in the real world. Conflict can originate, however, without any interdependence in the images and motivations governing the behavior of either of the two actors. Two absent-minded persons can run into each other; so can two absent-minded drivers or governments. What absent-mindedness can do can be accomplished equally or even more intensely by behavior which is autistic or cathectic, or by simple failures of self-control, perception, or mutual coordination.

Anything that increases the interdependence among two actors in regard to the effects of their behavior also tends to increase the potential need for coordination among them, without necessarily increasing their capacity for coordination. Any increase in operational interdependence will tend to increase, therefore, the risk of coordination failure and hence the probability of conflict. As a result, increases in political and economic integration often have also been accompanied by increased risks of conflict and even of civil wars. If such risks are to be reduced or to be avoided, increased capabilities for coordination of behavior must be provided, corresponding to the increase in the coordination load, i.e., to the increasing coordinative performance which the increased levels of interdependence will demand. Whether or not such provision is made, the connection between approach-behavior, increased interdependence, and the increased risk of conflicts seems inescapable.

Increasing frequency of interactions thus leads to increased needs for coordination, or else to increasing frequency and severity of conflicts. Interaction and interdependence thus create systems of coordination or conflict, peace or war.

The first stage of a survey of peace research may well begin with a survey of the different systems levels—both within nation states and in the supranational and international systems surrounding them—at which a peaceful or warlike outcome may be decided. A second stage will then consist of a survey of the stages of decision, primarily within each nation state, by which information is accumulated or excluded so as to increase the probability of a particular or warlike outcome of the interaction of two nation states, and thus indirectly the frequency of wars in the international system.

In the first stage of this survey we shall mainly be content to list significant research studies which have focused on each particular system level. In the second part, we shall follow the stages of the decision process toward peace or war, and we shall try to summarize the actual research results that are relevant to the probability of the outcome at each stage.

Finally, we shall try to say something about the most crucial gaps in the research studies and results which thus far have become available for each system level and decision stage. It is hoped that such a survey may be of some help in orienting our analysis toward the intellectual resources now available and to suggest some of the lines along which future research for peace might be most urgently needed.

Such future research will be able to draw upon a whole range of different sources of reproducible data. These sources will include historical studies of various periods and sectors of the international system as well as of particular cases; survey data on the level of elites as well as of mass opinion; quantitative and qualitative content analysis by various methods; mathematical and statistical models, analyses, and projections; and, last but not least, the increasing field of simulation. Such simulation exercises will include simulation of decision processes by role-playing persons as well as by combined man-computer methods and by dynamic all-computer methods.

The colleciton and analysis of comprehensive evidence from both real-world and simulation data will require a fair amount of time and resources. In the meantime, however, we have at least some partial data on some of the levels of the political system, drawn from a variety of sources and evidence. It is in this more modest context that simulation procedures have until now made their more useful contributions.

WAR-PROMOTING CONDITIONS:
A SURVEY OF STUDIES AT DIFFERENT SYSTEMS LEVELS

The contemporary theories of international relations, as well as the general theory of systems, have made us long familiar with the concept of "system levels."

A simple scheme, illustrating ten possible system levels, is shown in Figure 1.

Whether a system exists; whether one can observe and test the higher degree of interdependence and transaction flows among its components, and a marked decline of both interdependence and transaction at the system boundaries; and whether there are distinct and identifiable system levels, offering a suitable basis for corresponding levels of observation and analysis—all these are empirical questions (von Bertalanffy, 1965; Buckley, 1968; K. W. Deutsch, 1956, 1968, 1970; Easton, 1965; Lieber, 1972, pp. 120-145; Singer, 1961, 1969b; Young, 1968; Miller, 1965, 1971, 1972). What data are available are best suited for each system level, and what questions, methods and findings are applicable across several levels—all these again are questions that are not well answered by a priori reasoning but rather by experience and continuing experimentation. Some of this experience, and some of the recent research attempts, are surveyed in the present paper.

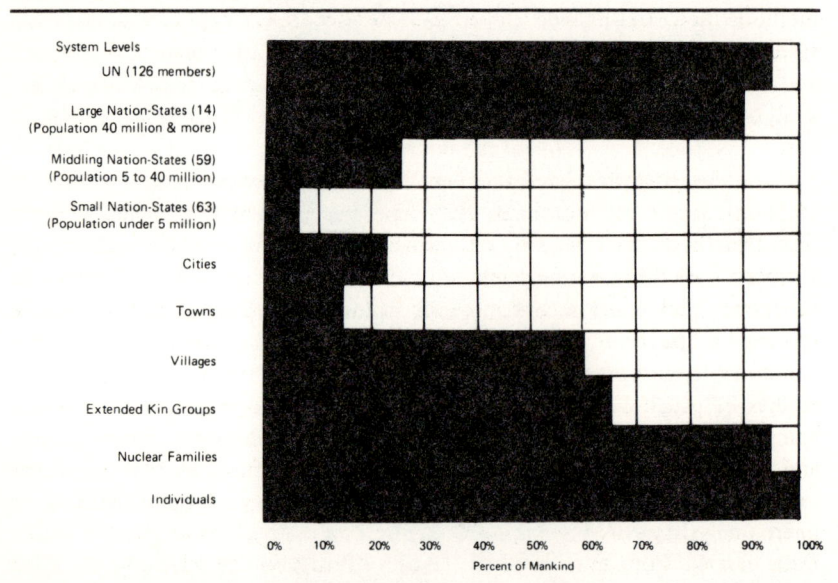

Sources: U.N. Office of Publication, Membership in the United Nations, 1969; Population Reference Bureau Information Service, World Population Data Sheets (Washington, D.C., 1968); K. Davis, World Urbanization, 1950-1970, Vol. 1 (Berkeley: University of California Press, 1969).

Figure 1: A TEN-LEVEL POLITICAL SYSTEM

Whether two actors are on the same system level can be determined by three tests: logical or organization inclusion, population size, and gross power as measured by the probability of prevailing in case of conflict. Actor A is on a higher system level than Actor B if A wholly includes B, but not vice versa; this inclusion may be logical or organizational, or both. In this sense the USA includes Virginia in both respects. The second test is population: A is on a higher level than B if A's population exceeds B's at least by an order of magnitude, i.e., at least by a factor of two, or more usually by a factor of ten. The third test is the probability of prevailing in case of conflict: Actor A "outclasses" Actor B if its probability of prevailing in case of conflict between the two can be estimated operationally (as it can be in many military or economic conflict situations), and if it is larger than 90 or 95 per cent. Usually in international politics all three tests will give the same results, although some exceptions are known.

At each level, particular conditions tend to favor or inhibit the conditions that are likely to propel a nation state toward the outbreak of war. Conditions relevant to the probability of war have been studied at each system level within or above the nation state, or at its own level, either in terms of theoretical analysis, or with the aid of empirical evidence, or by combinations of both theoretical and empirical methods. Recent research developments have been characterized by an increase in the multiplicity of methods used. Methods developed in earlier decades include careful historical studies of particular cases or entire periods, comparative historical analyses, and the systematic macro-economic, macro-sociological, or macro-political analysis of large-scale processes, often with the help of aggregate statistical data.

All these methods have retained their full importance and continue to yield important contributions. They have been joined by a range of more recent methods often dealing with human behavior on a smaller scale, or else with the use of small-scale samples for the better understanding of large-scale processes. Such more recent methods include psychological and psychiatric studies on the level of the individual personality and of its intra-psychic components, and on the level of human behavior in small groups, as well as studies of psychological processes on the level of large groups, mass media and their audience, and entire national societies. Sociology, anthropology, and political science, too, have extended their methods to analysis of the behavior of small groups and individuals; and some of these methods of micro-analysis are now going to be applied to the problems of war and peace. Data derived from micro-analytic studies often have the advantage of being repeatable and reproducible. Macro-analytic studies often deal with cases and situations so large that they are unique. But they have the advantage of including large-scale effects which are often lacking in some small-scale studies and which are particularly relevant in studies on war and peace. A combination of studies at all system levels is likely therefore to be indispensable.

Other methods in addition to sampling and survey research have become available for the exploration of the problems of war and peace. Most notable among these are content analyses, laboratory experiments with individuals and small groups, simulation experiments and gaming exercises, and mathematical models and computer simulations, as well as various combinations of two or several of these methods.

The discussion that follows will survey the availability of studies using these various methods at each system level. A later section will discuss some of the findings from such studies in relation to some possible causal steps on the road to war.

The Level of Intra-psychic Components

The lowest system level relevant for research on war and peace consists of the intra-psychic components of the human individual personality. Classic studies on this theoretical level are the studies by Freud (1915, 1933). This approach was continued by Hopkins (1938) and Strachey (1957). An approach more on the level of learning theory was developed by Durbin and Bowlby (1939), Tolman (1942), May (1943), Dunn (1950), and in the studies edited by Cantril (1950).

The process of *displacement* of hostile feelings within the human psyche onto outside objects as well as other psychological defense mechanisms was emphasized by McNeil (1957, 1961, 1965), Whitey and Katz (1965), and Stagner (1965) in their summaries of many psychological contributions to the study of war and peace published during the last thirty years. For an evaluation of the entire field the studies edited by Kelman (1965) and Zawodny (1966) are most valuable.

A *theory of instincts* on this level of analysis was stressed by Lorenz (1966), and it was critically discussed in the studies edited by Carthy and Ebling (1964), and in several essays in the volumes edited by de Reuck and Knight (1966) and by Fried et al. (1968), and on a more popular level in the volume by Montagu (1968) as well as in a more recent review by Leach (1968). Further theoretical studies can be found in the volume edited by Bramson and Goethals (1968).

Theories of individual and social learning are obviously of major relevance here if we are to understand how the habits of preparing and conducting wars are learned and maintained and how they might be unlearned. But the direct application of learning theory and learning experiments to conflict behavior, and particularly to peace research, is still in its beginnings (Rapoport, 1960; Rapoport and Chammah, 1965). The more recent theories of behavior modification (Skinner, 1971; see also Skinner, 1968) have yet to be tested more fully for their applicability and fruitfulness in a peace research context (for a beginning, see Franck and Weisband, 1971).

Another intrapsychic mechanism, that dealing particularly with *cognitive dissonance,* has been emphasized by Festinger (1957) and in the volume edited by Abelson et al. (1969).

Most of these theoretical studies also make use of empirical cases and data. Primarily empirical studies in this area of personality components relevant to war and aggression have been carried out by Adorno et al. (1950), Levinson (1957), Christiansen (1959), Cooper (1965), and McCloskey (1967). A rather comprehensive collection of both theoretical and empirical studies (including many reports on experiments) has been edited by Zawodny (1966), and a survey of this area has been given by Stagner (1965), Scott (1965), Eckhardt and Lentz (1967), and Eckhardt (1969).

Simulation studies of the effects of personality components on crisis decisions leading to war have been reported by Driver (1965) and Druckman (1968).

The Level of Individual Personality Characteristics

Closely related to the effects of intra-psychic components upon behavior toward war and peace are the effects of the entire personality systems upon such decisions. Here, too, the work of Freud is obviously relevant. Theoretical work in this area has been surveyed by Pear (1950), McNeil (1965), Klineberg (1950, 1964), LeVine (1965), and Scott (1965). Particularly relevant theoretical work has been recently done by Erikson (1958, 1969) and Mitscherlich (1969).

Theoretical and experimental work was combined in the important studies by Dollard et al. (1939) which have been more recently carried further and evaluated by Buss (1961) and particularly by Berkovitz (1962, 1969).

Primarily empirical work on the role of the individual personality in the determination of war-promoting behavior has been carried out and surveyed by Eysenck (1950), and most of it is reported by Eckhardt and Lentz (1967).

Effects of the individual personality in relation to the effects of the mass media and mass opinion have been studied theoretically by May (1943) and Allport (1950). A broad survey of theoretical and empirical work is combined in an article by Rosenberg (1965).

The relationship of personality on conflict behavior in the context of entire tribal or national political systems has been studied by Lasswell (1965), Mead (1940), Malinowski (1941), Mead and Metraux (1965), and in the studies recently collected by Fried et al. (1968, where also further bibliographical references particularly to the anthropological and ethnological literature can be found).

Specific discussion of the relation of highly industrial societies to the promotion of aggressive personalities and behavior of their members was offered by Parsons (1947), A. Plack (1967), Marcuse (1968), Mitscherlich (1969), and Horn (1969).

Biographical studies on crucial decision-makers about war and peace have been published by Alexander and Julie George (1956) and by Rogow (1963).

An empirical study on the actual quantifiable behavior of such a decision-maker was done by Holsti in his piece on John Foster Dulles published in Finlay et al. (1967). Other effects of personality and crisis decision-making were studied theoretically and empirically for the case of the Vietnam war by White (1968) and similar problems were explored in a simulation exercise on human information processing by Schroder et al. (1967).

The Level of Small Groups

Some of the work surveyed by Rosenberg (1965) and Eckardt and Lentz (1967) focuses upon the contribution of small-group processes to the making of decisions about war and peace. Such small-group processes are emphasized in the study of the United States intervention in Korea by Snyder and Paige (1958) and Paige (1968) and in regard to the Japanese decision in 1940 to initiate war against the United States by Maruyama (1962). A particularly recent discussion has been offered by Janis (1972).

Theoretical and empirical studies stressing the facts of dyadic or other small-group relations among actors have been undertaken by Rapoport and Chammah (1965) and Rapoport has surveyed the entire field (1967).

A simulation exercise showing the effects at the small-group level of the adoption of a new national strategy was undertaken by Raser and Crow (1966).

Small-group processes have been studied most thoroughly in their relation to crisis decision-making. A number of theoretical and empirical studies are compiled by Singer (1965). A case study by Paige (1968) is particularly relevant. Simulation studies have been carried out by Hermann (1969) who also surveys the field of crisis decision-making research, and by Robinson et al. (1969). Another simulation study in this area has been carried out and its analyses have been compared with content analysis studies by Zinnes (1966). Substantially the same studies also cover decision-making processes by small groups of high-level executives in the escalation of intergroup and international conflicts.

The Level of Intra-national Interest Groups, Parties, and Mass Media

The next system level is constituted of large interest groups, parties, and mass media. Here the number of persons involved ranges from thousands to millions, and here the contributions of social science change radically. In our provisional survey we found that less than one-fifth of the studies on this level had been done by social psychologists. Only about one-tenth of the scientific studies were contributed by political scientists. The bulk of the work was contributed by economists, historians, and sociologists, and particularly by journalistic writers. It is striking that political scientists, who have done so much work on political parties and interest groups in other respects, have almost entirely avoided the discussion of the role of such large groups in the causation and prevention of war. With the exception of the work on Germany by Kehr (1965), Steinberg (1966), and Brandt (1966), we have not found any major political science study on the role of armament-oriented or war-oriented interest groups; no major study on the "hawks" in Congress or in either of the major parties; no major study of individual senators or congressmen who have publicly urged more warlike policies for the U.S. (such as Senator Henry Jackson or Representative Mendel Rivers); no serious study of the alignment of domestic interest groups in regard to major decisions about arms programs with the exception of Huntington (1961) and Schilling et al. (1962), or about war and peace in such situations as the U.S. decisions to intervene in Korea and Vietnam, the Bay of Pigs enterprise, the limited nuclear test ban of 1963, or the ABM debate of 1968-1969. There seems to be a similar gap in the literature on the role of parties and interest groups in Britain in regard to its decisions to attack in Suez in 1956, or to disengage in India in 1947, and to reduce British commitments east of Suez from the late 1960s on. Nor seems there to be a serious French study with regard to the role of French interest groups in the Algerian war. Doubtless, additional search will reveal a few studies of this kind, but amid the welter of political science research projects and publications about other aspects of political parties and interests groups, the rarity of such work in political science constitutes a non-event which might well be called staggering.

The notion that the most important element in war-promoting behavior is found in large interest groups within the nation state, with special interests distinct from those of the nation and the national elite as a whole, has been pursued in a series of studies ranging over most of the century. These include the works by Hobson (1938), Engelbrecht and Hanighen (1934), Vagts (1937, 1959), Cook (1962), Lapp (1962), Coffin (1964), Kimminich (1964), J. Raymond (1964, 1968), Swomley (1964, and Cochran (1965).

Another group of writings stresses the merging of these special interest groups with the general dominant elites of a nation. Such approaches are often, but not always, class-oriented. Many of these are derived from Marxist ideas, or else from responses to their challenge. Earlier studies of this kind are those of Hilferding (1910), Luxemburg (1912), Lenin (1917, 1939), Schumpeter (1919, 1955), Nearing and Freeman (1925, 1969), Sternberg (1926), Grossman (1929), Mills (1956), Vilmar (1969), and Kolko (1969). Most of the earlier literature has been surveyed in Winslow (1948) and Kemp (1967), and more recent contributions are discussed in Pilisuk and Hayden (1965). More empirically oriented work of this kind has been done by Brandt (1966) and Hallgarten (1967). The role of French interest groups in the 1954 decision to reject a European Defense Community (EDC) has been elaborated in the studies edited by Aron (1958) and Lerner (c. 1957).

Theoretical studies centering their attention on the effect of particular large interest groups, mass media, and parties upon the entire political system are represented by Lasswell's well-known construct of the garrison-police-state (1941, 1962) and by a recent, more policy-oriented contribution by Galbraith (1969) and Melman (1970).

With one partial exception, it should be noted that we have not found a single simulation study explicitly dealing with the effects on war and peace exercised by the activities of particular large interest groups, political parties, and mass media. The partial exception is the most recent version of the World Politics Simulation developed by Coplin et al. (1969), from which no results have as yet become available.

The Level of Nation States and Their Governments

On the next higher system level, that of the nation state as a whole, the theoretical and empirically oriented work by social scientists is much richer. Theoretical studies on the relation between the nation state and large interest groups within it have been done by Ginsburg (1939) and Robbins (1939). Empirical work has been done by Staley (1935), Clark (1936), Rosenbluth (1967), Clayton (1962), and Isard (1962). Collections of relevant studies have been edited by Benoit and Boulding (1963) and by Benoit (1967). Among these studies the work by Leontieff and Hoffenberg in the Benoit-Boulding volume deserves particular attention. A recently published study by Russett (1969) also merits close attention.

Content analyses on the attitudes of dominant national elites as indicated by the content of official communications or elite media have been done by Lasswell (1965), Pool and associates (1952), Angell et al. (1964), Finlay et al. (1967), and Parenti (1969).

A great deal of work has been done on the relationship of mass media and mass opinion to the more or less warlike behavior of nation states. Notable historical studies are those by Fay (1928), Hayes (1926, 1928, 1930, 1948, 1960), and Langer (1935, 1968). Theoretical and empirical studies include Almond (1950), Dahl (1950), Deutsch and Merritt (1965), and the studies edited by Kelman (1965), including notably Kelman's own contribution, and Milton Rosenberg (1967).

Primarily empirical work is offered by Buchanan and Cantril (1953), Roper (1954), Dujiker and Frijda (1960), Bobrow and Wilcox (1966), Deutsch et al. (1967), and Deutsch (1967).

The interplay of the entire national political system, the political culture, and a variety of attributes of each national society with the international behavior of each nation state has been explored in a theoretical article by Katz (1965), and in a number of empirical data collections and studies such as those by Banks and Greeg (1965), Russett et al. (1964), Cattell (1965), Tanter (1964, 1966), Haas (1968), Rummel (1968), Feierabend (1969), Gurr (1969), and Choucri and North (forthcoming).

We have found two simulation studies in this area, with particular comparisons between simulation results and real-world data by Chadwick (1967) and Smoker (1969).

The problem of national strategies adopted by nation states—that is, by national governments more or less with the support of the political system—has been explored largely in theoretical terms. Those theoretical studies include studies by Abel (1941), Bernard (1957), Levi (1960), Rapoport (1960, 1964), Schelling (1960, 1966), Singer (1962), Green (1966), Raser (1966), McNamara (1968), and Senghaas (1969). The studies by Halperin (1967) and by Raser (1966) include a good survey on the discussion of the various theories and doctrines which have dominated most of the field.

Empirical studies of cases of deterrence—or, of its failures—have been undertaken by Russett (1963, 1967), Hosoya (1968), and Naroll (1969).

The deliberate escalation of international conflict by a nation state as a national strategy is discussed by Kahn (1965). The opposite strategy of de-escalation and the facilitating of negotiations is discussed in the theoretical studies by Fromm (1961), Etzioni (1962), Osgood (1962, 1965), Frank (1967), and Fisher (1969).

Crisis decision-making has been studied theoretically and empirically in the example of World War I by North and associates (1963), by Zinnes and associates (1962), by Charles and Margaret Hermann (1967), and by Zinnes (1968), and for the case of the Cuba crisis by Holsti and associates (1964), and most recently by Goulden (1969) on the Tonkin affair.

Descriptive accounts of crisis decision-making by participants have been offered by Dean Acheson (1969), Robert Kennedy (1969) for the Cuba crisis, and by James Thompson (1968) for the Vietnam war. Relevant simulation exercises on crisis decision-making have been reported by Pool and Kessler (1965) focusing on the nation-state level, by Robinson et al. (1969), and by Hermann (1969) and Robinson (1970) with a good survey of the theoretical and empirical literature. Allison (1969) has developed alternative models of crisis decision-making.

Escalation processes and their effects upon the behavior of nation states have been discussed largely in theoretical terms in analyses by K. W. Deutsch (1957), Russett (1962), Boulding (1963), Liebermann (1964), Pruitt (1965), Whitey and Katz (1965), Singer (1969), Morton Deutsch (1969), and Pruitt and R. Snyder (1969).

The effects of the larger international environment—both international reality and economic and technological reality—have been analyzed in terms of theory by Aron (1958), Boulding (1961), and Galtung (1964).

Empirical studies in this area have been carried out by Klineberg (1966) and by Singer and Small (1970); see also Singer (1969) and Singer and Small (1969). Another study is by Choucri and North (forthcoming).

Levels Larger than the Nation State: Regional Systems and International Systems

The highest of our system levels is that above the nation state. For reasons of simplicity we include here both regional systems and the international system as a whole. At this level we have found so far no relevant work at all on any possible effects on war and peace by individual human personalities or by intra-psychic personality components. Nor have we found at this level any work on the effects of mass media and mass opinion, or on national political systems and attributes, or on government organization or bureaucracy. We have found a few studies on large interest groups, such as the international arms trade, by Kemp (1968) and Thayer (1969). Discussions of the possible peace-promoting effects of international corporations have been put forward by Vernon (1969, 1971) and Horowitz (1969), respectively.

A simulation exercise comparing the behavior of international systems with and without such large international corporations has been carried out by Smoker (1968).

The opposite assumption, that large international cartels, corporations and monopolies are likely to promote war, is central to the theory of imperialism by Lenin (1917, 1933), which treats imperialism essentially as a world-wide, rather than as a national, system. More recent theoretical work with this emphasis has been carried out by Baran and Sweezy (1966), and with the use of some empirical data by Magdoff (1969).

A different approach to the succession of international systems related to a change in the character of dominant elites within the component nation states has been worked out by Rosecrance (1963).

The effects of international interaction on the choice of national strategies are the subjects of theoretical, mathematical, and historical analyses by Sloutzki (1941), Saaty (1968), and Huntington (1958), and some effects of the interaction between technological and political change have been discussed by Deutsch (1959).

Empirical work on the neutral impact of crisis decision-making on the international system, with stress on interaction effects, has been done for the Berlin crises by McClelland (1968). More general gaming exercises on similar topics have been reported in the Inter-Nation Simulation (INS) by Guetzkow et al. (1963), Bloomfield and Whaley (1965), in the World Politics Simulation (WPS) by Coplin et al. (1969), and in a comparative evaluation by Alker and Brunner (1969).

Many of the escalation studies, too, emphasize interaction effects on the international level, beginning with the classic theoretical and empirical work of Richardson (1960a). Other theoretical analyses are offered by Boulding (1961), Pruitt (1965, 1969), Caspary (1967), and Gantzel (1969). A mathematical and empirical approach has been pursued by Quincy Wright (1965), Smoker (1966), and Voevodsky (1970). An earlier theoretical and historical study was contributed by Noel-Baker (1958) and a method of simulation has been proposed in the "simple diplomatic game" (SDG) by Benson (1961).

The effects of the international system upon the more or less warlike character of the processes within that system itself were discussed in some of its theoretical aspects by Kaplan (1957), by Deutsch and Singer (1964), and by means of a mathematical model by Wesley (1962). Theoretical and empirical studies were published by Denton (1966) and Denton and Philips (1968), and as part of the results of a major program by Singer and Small (1968) and Singer and Wallace (forthcoming). Substantial simulation studies were carried out by Brody (1963) and in the International Process Simulation (IPS) by Smoker (1968, 1969).

TEN STAGES IN THE PRODUCTION OF WAR

In thinking about the development of political behavior from the actions of individuals to the outbreak of organized violence and war among nations, we may think first of all of the influence of "human nature," i.e., of *individual personalities,* personality structures, and intra-psychic components (e.g., Freud, Dollard, Festinger, Abelson, Zawodny).

A second factor in generating and intensifying international conflicts is the activities of *large interest groups* (e.g., Hobson, Vagts, Benoit, Boulding, Galbraith, Isard).

A third factor may be seen in the coalescence of the leadership of some or all of the major interest groups into a *dominant national elite* and the perceptions and actions of the latter (e.g., Brandt, Lasswell, Lenin, Mills, Schumpeter).

The perceptions and actions of interest groups and elites are amplified and disseminated by the processes of *mass media* and *mass opinion* which thus form a fourth stage or an essential ingredient in the generation of conflict (e.g., Kelman, Fay, Langer, Lasswell, Pool).

Together these four elements influence the *character of the entire national political system and its political culture,* and are in turn influenced by it. They determine the relevant observable attributes of each society and are in turn conditioned by some of these attributes and by the processes which these attributes indicate (e.g., Russett et al., Rummel, Haas, Gurr, Klineberg, Mead, Parsons).

All five of these elements then influence the formal *government and bureaucracy of each country;* and government and bureaucracy, civil and military, in turn produce and conduct most of the *foreign policy and international conflict behavior* of the nation (e.g., Paige, Seabury, Craig and Gilbert, Huntington, A. and J. George, Rogow).

These six elements or factors in the making of a war-promoting or war-preventing situation tend to interact among each other in a variety of feedback patterns. It is characteristic of many feedback processes that the location of the "first" initiative and the exact sequence of subsequent inputs often has less effect on the outcome than do the strength and asymmetry of couplings, the amounts of loss or amplification in regard to energy or information, and other characteristics of the system. In these terms, it is largely a convenience for analysis if we are also calling these factors "stages" and if we are discussing them in a certain sequence.

Yet many studies of innovations and initiatives in human affairs suggest that a decisive combination often has been made first in the mind of an individual or of a very small group of two or three. (For initiatives in the social sciences, see Deutsch, Platt, and Senghaas, 1971.) Presumably, a major initiative toward Islamic culture did come from Mohammed; toward the Reformation, from Martin Luther; toward Mormonism, from Joseph Smith and Brigham Young; toward Marxism, from Marx and Engels; toward classic British imperialism, from Disraeli, Lord Roseberry, and Cecil Rhodes; toward the political culture of present-day India, from Gandhi and Nehru; toward the political system of the Soviet Union, from Lenin, and toward Chinese Communism, from Mao Tse-tung. None of these men, and none of the ideas associated with them, are uncaused causes. They came out of a social environment and had to work in one. Yet the crucial combination or initiative, decisive for the timing of the first "proposals" of the policies then accepted and developed by others, occurred more often in the mind of an individual than at any other level in the social system. This is why the growth of individual predispositions toward war perhaps may be treated legitimately, though provisionally, as a first stage, unless evidence to the contrary is found in a specific case.

Similarly, large interest groups and more or less consolidated cross-interest elites often seem to exercise more influence on a national political culture than the other way around. This, too, however, is a matter of empirical fact, and evidence may modify or reverse this broad assumption.

The same applies in principle to our entire notion of "stages" in the tentative and limited sense in which we are proposing to employ it. We recall from our general familiarity with the international relations field that the movement from peace to war often seems to have followed the pathway and sequence presented in this paper, but we feel sure that this sequence is not the only one possible.

Let us reiterate: even though a certain progression in the formulation of foreign policy and the generation of international conflicts can often be observed through each of these six elements to the next, so that we may in such cases treat them as stages, they are still highly interdependent among each other with a high degree of mutual feedback processes. Furthermore, in principle it is quite possible for them to be relatively isolated from any major inputs from the outside world. In such cases national policies are then almost entirely internally generated and may resemble autistic behavior (Senghaas, 1970). In a relatively open political and social system, by contrast, international processes may already have an effect on each of these six stages. And these effects may then in turn tend to mitigate or intensify war-

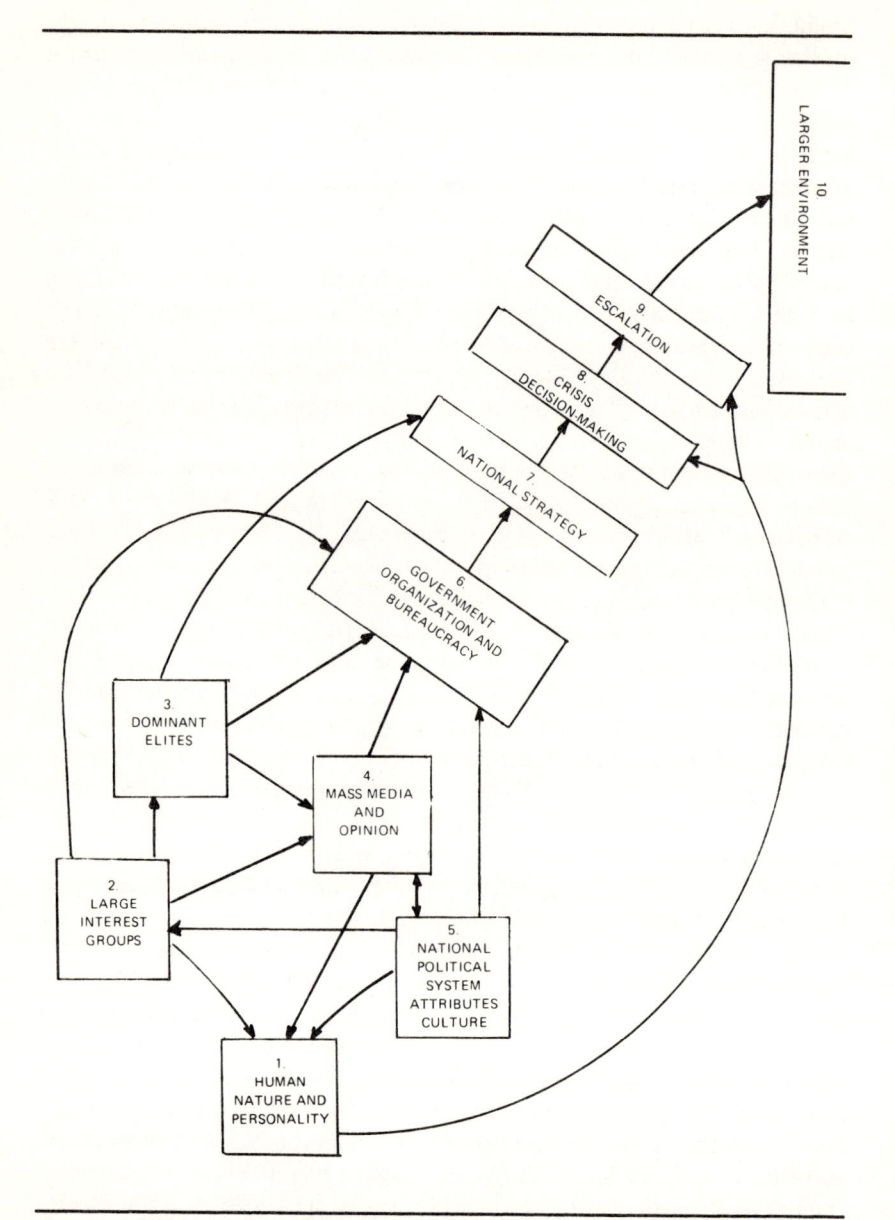

Figure 2: TEN STAGES IN THE PRODUCTION OF WAR. THE EXTREME AUTISTIC CASE. [No major influences from outside world. Only major inside influences shown without feedback]

promoting behavior at each stage. Whether a society is in fact open in this manner is a matter, of course, not of self-perception but of empirical fact.

The seventh stage is the adoption of a *national strategy* in foreign policy matters, including both foreign policy goals and the diplomatic and military methods chosen to attain them. Such strategies may involve a choice between primary emphasis on foreign or domestic goals. Among foreign policy objectives they may involve expansion, containment, or retrenchment. Among diplomatic methods they may involve expansion or reduction of commitments, hegemony or equality, multilateralism or bilateralism, high-risk or low-risk policies. Among military means they may involve high or low levels of armament, greater or lesser reliance on deterrence, choices between nuclear, chemical-biological, and conventional weapons systems, first-strike and second-strike capabilities, and greater and lesser willingness and ability to engage in warfare and to escalate such warfare to higher levels. The choice of such strategies may be almost entirely internally generated, or it may occur in partial response to the actions of other nations and to events on the international level. In either case it will carry national policy into close proximity with actual decisions about war and peace; and it may in fact predetermine the outcome of many such decisions (e.g., Schelling, Rapoport, Singer, Maruyama, Green, Holsti, Senghaas, McNamara, Kissinger).

In the next stage, *crisis decision-making,* such decisions about war and peace are actually made. Their outcome is in part predetermined by the national strategies and capability levels previously chosen, and by the general characteristics of the national governments, bureaucracies, and larger political systems determined at the first six levels. But they are also significantly influenced by small-group processes, by situational pressures in regard to time, fear, stress, and other circumstances, and by the personality characteristics of individuals (e.g., North et al., McClelland, Thompson, White, Hermann, Pool and Kessler, Bloomfield and Waley, Guetzkow et al., Alker and Brunner, and now Jannis, 1972).

Even crisis decisions are made by processes which are primarily intra-national, but the actual consequences of such decisions are likely to depend critically also on the behavior of other nations and of the international system. If this fact was ignored or underrated at earlier stages, in the choice of national strategies and the making of crisis-decisions, its impact now at the stage of *escalation processes* may come as a surprise to some or all of the participants without being any the less serious (e.g., Richardson, Boulding, Quincy Wright, Russett, Pruitt, K. W. Deutsch, M. Deutsch, Etzioni, Charles Osgood, Smoker).

Finally, the conflict process may expand the original escalation sequence

[296]   APPRAISALS

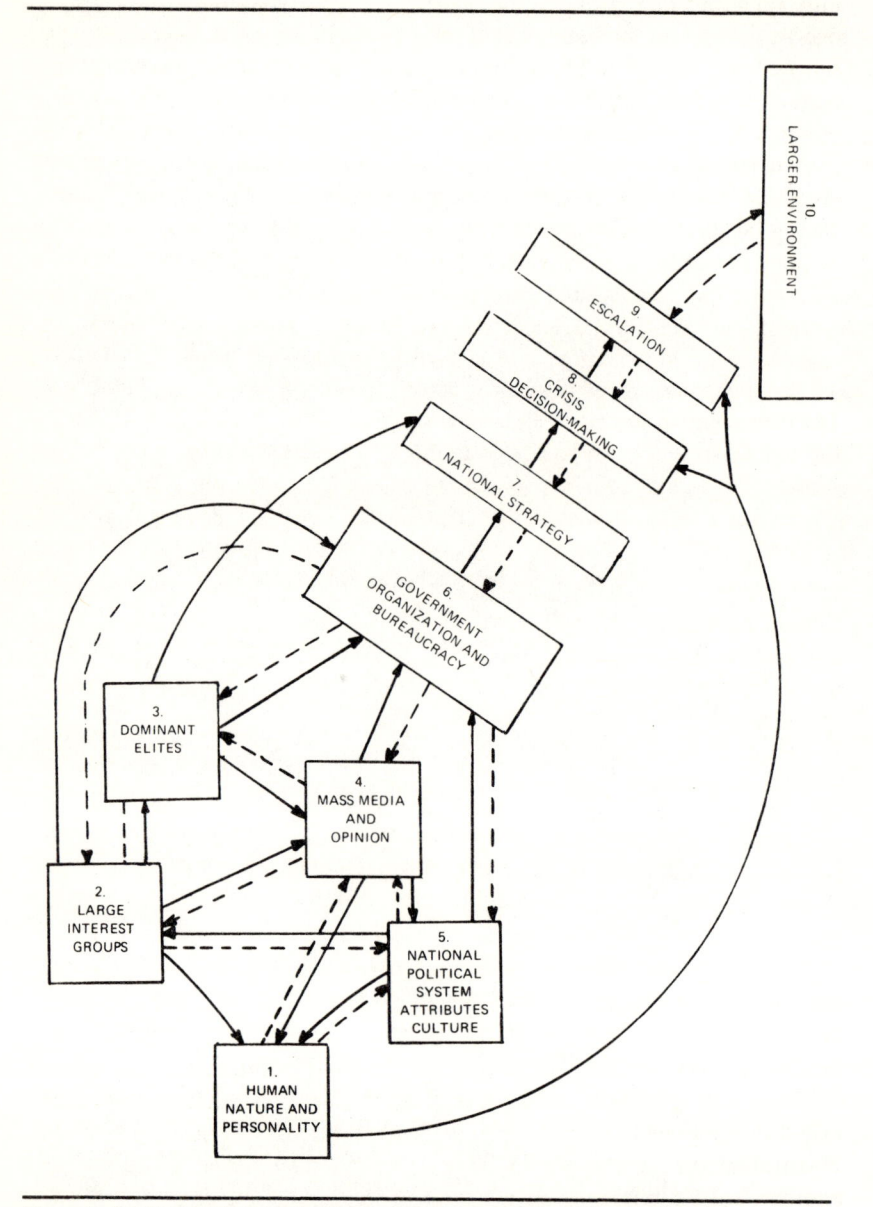

Figure 3: TEN STAGES IN THE PRODUCTION OF WAR [feedbacks shown]

into expanded direct *interaction with the larger environment.* Here there is one last chance of mitigating the conflict and keeping it at a manageable level short of war, or else to expand it further into a war reaching far beyond the original objectives, methods, participants, and consequences envisaged at its origins (e.g., Brody, Singer and Small, Galtung, Kaplan, North and Choucri).

A diagrammatic representation of the ten elements—and often, though not always, stages—in the production of war is given in Figures 2 and 3, and a cross-tabulation of selected studies by stages and system level is given in Table 1.

SOME FINDINGS DISCUSSED BY STAGES IN THE PRODUCTION OF WAR

The Frequency of Cognitive Distortions at the Individual Level

There is an abundance of findings from psychiatry and psychology, comprising both clinical and laboratory data, attesting to the frequency of processes of cognitive distortion and of corresponding failures in the process of reality-testing. Such processes include in the individual the well-known ego defense mechanisms of repression, denial, projection, and displacement. They also include the overemphasis upon images of the prowess and excellence of one's own personality, or group, or nation, and the propensity to correspondingly assertive and conflict-prone behavior.

Freudian psychologists often interpret such observable behavior as a reaction-formation against repressed inner feelings of inadequacy, anxiety, and guilt; followers of the psychologist Alfred Adler used to interpret such behavior in terms of a so-called "inferiority complex." In any case, there is less disagreement about the frequent occurrence of such behavior—and about its effects on the frequency of errors and conflicts in human behavior—than there is about its more abstract interpretation.

There is also massive evidence about the connection between the aggressive behavior of individuals and the frustrations which they are experiencing or have experienced, first highlighted by Dollard et al. (1939). Christiansen's findings (1959) that individuals with higher levels of internal psycho-sexual conflicts were more likely to favor warlike attitudes in international relations, may be interpreted either in Freudian terms or as a special case of the "frustration-aggression syndrome." In either case the observable distortion of international attitudes remains.

There is additional evidence for the tendency of most individuals to become disturbed by high levels of "cognitive dissonance" and to resort

TABLE 1
SIX SYSTEM LEVELS AND TEN STAGES IN THE PRODUCTION OF WAR: DEVELOPED VS. NEGLECTED RESEARCH AREAS

TEN STAGES → SIX SYSTEM LEVELS ↓	1 HUMAN NATURE	2 DOMINANT ELITES	3 MASS MEDIA & MASS OPIN.	4 MASS MEDIA & MASS OPIN.	5 NAT. POL. SYSTEM REGIME & CULTURE	6 GOV. ORGANIZATION & BUREAUCRACY	7 NATIONAL STRATEGY	8 CRISIS DECISION-MAKING	9 ESCALATION	10 LARGER ENVIRONMENT
VI INTERNATIONAL AND REGIONAL							International Relations		Political Science (International Relations)	Political Science
V NATION-STATE		Macro-	Sociology Economics Politics	Social Psychology	Societal Approach	Administrative Bureaucracy Science	Political Science & Societal Approach	Social Psychology		International Relations
IV LARGE INTEREST GROUPS, PARTIES, MEDIA										
III SMALL GROUPS					Socialization Studies	Small Group & Role/ Personality Studies		Small Group Analysis		
II INDIVIDUAL PERSONALITY	Psychology (psycho-analysis)							Psychology		
I INTRAPSYCH. COMPONENTS										

against it to various defense mechanisms, including notably repression and denial as well as reaction-formation in terms of markedly increased activity, which may be proselyting or aggressive (Festinger, 1957). Such behavior is particularly observable after the spectacular failure of a prophecy about the state of the real world, to which the individual earlier had become deeply committed and for which he receives some support from his social group (Festinger et al., 1956). After the failure of any peaceful policy, some pacifists will assert that it should have been tried more thoroughly; after the failure of any war, persons deeply committed to a warlike policy will tend to assert that it should have been fought harder. In either case the process or reality-testing remains largely ineffective.

Related to frequent behavior of this type is the incapacity of many individuals to tolerate ambiguity in a reality situation or in their perceptions of it. Persistent ambiguity may then elicit in such individuals withdrawal behavior or else hostility or rage. The well-known hostility of belligerents against neutrals, or of political extremists against those who hold similar views in more modest form and thus appear to act ambiguously in regard to these values, are cases in point.

Freudian processes, responses to cognitive dissonance, and aggressive responses to frustration, all seem to meet in the case of the "authoritarian personality" which has been found to be highly correlated with attitudes favoring military strength, the ready use of force, and the propensity to engage in inter-ethnic and international conflict, together with the desire for simple "prevailing" by either force or threats in any conflict situation. Persons with such personality structures tend to favor either extreme national isolation from world affairs, or else military intervention in them so as to make the will of one's own nation prevail at all salient points of contact. In either case they find intolerable any process of continuing adjustment to any foreign actor of approximately equal strength (Adorno et al., 1950; Levinson, 1957).

The frequency of persons with a significant degree of such personality structures ranges in modern industrial countries between 10 and 40 per cent, or 25 per cent plus or minus 15, and some highly hierarchical and authoritarian organizations may recruit and promote such personality types in still higher proportions all the way up to decision-making levels (Cantril and Free, 1967).

The effects of most of these processes tending toward cognitive distortions are further reinforced in the case of most individuals by the impact of stress and similar situational conditions, such as fear, perceived hostility, time pressure, fatigue, and other forms of stress—all of which tend to be frequent in international conflict situations on the eve of war. All such conditions, when they are intense, tend to simplify the cognitive elements available for the interpretation of reality and to increase the propensity to perceive hostility in others and to choose more extreme and violent responses. Force is then welcomed, consciously or unconsciously, as a way of making a situation simple and less ambiguous. Findings of this kind have been confirmed both by clinical and laboratory evidence and by simulation exercises, as well as by case studies from the real world (Pruitt, 1965; Schroder et al., 1967).

A final contribution to cognitive distortion in the individual is made by the impact of the smaller or larger group which surrounds him. Substantial cognitive distortions under group pressure have been demonstrated by Asch (1952) and Livant (1965). The results of the latter study should be brought together with those of a recent study by Janis (1972) of group effects in actual decisions about war and peace. The effects of the larger national society with its mass media and political culture upon the cognitive world of the individual have been demonstrated by anthropologists and by the refugee studies by Inkeles and Bauer (1959; but see also Inkeles, 1968).

Together, all this evidence suggests the conclusion that the model of the *rational* individual decision-maker is grossly unrealistic, and that the policy counting upon the continued rational and realistic behavior of one's own side or of one's adversaries in international politics may be more likely to fail than to succeed in the long run. To be safe, a modern traffic system must also be designed for the absent-minded driver, the preoccupied housewife, and the occasional drunk. The avoidance of war in international politics would require an even higher level of explicit provisions for coping with irrational behavior of either or both sides in a conflict among ideologies or nations.

This conclusion is not weakened by the consideration, suggested by Jervis (1968) that, for example, role requirements might constrain national decision-makers to behave rationally even though their personalities and personal experiences might not predispose them to do so. The evidence available at the individual and small-group levels points overwhelmingly the other way. Historical data show, as reported earlier, that between 1815 and 1910 about one-fifth of those wars which have been coded by Singer and Small (1968) were lost by the countries that initiated them, but that from 1911 to 1965 three-fifths of all wars were lost by the initiators. If we should decide to call rational the kind of behavior which initiates a war and then loses it, and which often leads to large destruction in the initiating country and to the overthrow of its government, and often its entire political regime, then it would be in the national interest to discover how such "rational" behavior could be avoided.

There is one element of truth in Jervis' argument. The process of cognitive distortion is usually more complex and subtle than the relatively primitive elements which laboratory procedures are best designed to isolate. Actual statesmen who made decisions which led to war and destroyed their countries usually did pay some attention to aspects of reality warning them away from such courses. They merely underestimated their magnitude and underplayed their salience. Conversely, they overperceived the resources, scientific prowess, and morale of their country and their general chances for success; and they usually overstated the difficulties and penalties of any alternative to war (Russett, 1967). The net result of these subtle distortions is still a gross misperception of reality and the taking of decisions whose outcome is counterproductive and often suicidal for the actor.

A final point on the individual level consists of the relation between possible role-constraints upon irrational behavior and the then-and-there prevailing definition of the role itself. The role of the German Emperor in 1914 was more frequently defined as that of "supreme war lord" (*oberster Kriegsherr*) than as preserver of the peace, and Wilhelm II seems to have shared this prevailing definition. The role of the President of the United States is more ambiguous. He is widely seen as the chief executive responsible for preserving the peace, but also as the commander-in-chief in times of war, which may be seen as recurrent and normal. Since the presidential role also includes a high degree of responsiveness to major domestic interest groups and public opinion, its constraints in themselves do not guarantee the rational perception of international reality.

One popular "folk theory" about warlike behavior has not been confirmed by any of the information we have seen. There is evidence that repression of human impulses may lead to their displacement into aggressive behavior, but there is no evidence that even a substantial increase in sexual permissiveness in a society would necessarily make its behavior more peaceful either on the level of its elites or its masses. Some societies such as imperial Rome, Ottoman Turkey, or the nobility of eighteenth-century France, and other elites which have been highly permissive in sexual matters, were also spectacularly warlike and aggressive for long periods. There is some evidence, on the other hand, that some societies, including some highly industrialized ones, may produce a relatively high level of free-floating aggression among their populations which may then be easily channelled into domestic or international violence (Parsons, 1947; Mitscherlich, 1969; Marcuse, 1968).

The effects of cognitive distortion on the level of intra-psychic components and personality structures are pervasive. They distort perceptions which members of large interest groups have of their own interests. They distort elite perceptions and elite behavior. Catered to by the mass media, and aggregated as mass opinion, they influence the political systems and political cultures of nations and the actions of their governments. They influence the choices of national political and military strategies, the processes of decision-making under crisis conditions, and particularly the processes of escalation. Their effect on the last two stages has been explored by a fair amount of research while their effects at the earlier levels have been relatively neglected. At all stages, however, they tend to make behavior more autistic, less open to reality-testing, and more prone to violent conflict.

The Effects of Large Interest Groups and Dominant Elites

The effects of large interest groups and dominant elites have been explored almost entirely in terms of macro-politics, macro-economics, and macro-sociology—that is, of the levels of large groups, nation states, and the international system—while their relationships to small groups, individual personalities, and intra-psychic components have almost entirely been neglected. On the large-scale levels they have generated many important propositions and hypotheses, but very few items of verified knowledge.

It has, however, been shown abundantly that economic and business groups are working in many countries for higher levels of military expenditures, and that they are aided in this effort by members of the military establishment. It may also be taken as established that such interest groups and elites in some countries predominantly tend to favor national strategies of high military preparedness and deterrence, usually together with the acquisition and development of non-conventional weapons and means for their delivery. Similar groups also favor demands for such weapons and delivery systems in some countries which do not now have them.

The strongest evidence for such relationships in recent years has come from the United States. For many other countries the evidence is weaker, or lacking, or points even in the opposite direction. We may guess, but do not know precisely whether or to what extent, there are similar industrial and military interest groups in the Soviet Union, in China, or in Yugoslavia, North Vietnam, and other Communist countries, and whether these groups favor generally high levels of armaments and national strategies of deterrence. The government of the Soviet Union has accepted a strategy of deterrence at least since the 1960s, but we do not know which interest groups within their country were foremost in producing this result. Some evidence from the Soviet press, indicating differences between defense-oriented and consumer-oriented interest groups, has been cited by Aspaturian (1972; see also Skilling, 1971).

The theory of interest groups also does not account for the failure of Britain to develop intercontinental delivery systems. Empirical studies show that the French elite and French business community were divided about the acquisition of a national nuclear deterrent, and that the overwhelming majority of respondents from the German elite opposed in 1964 a national nuclear deterrent for Germany—as did mass opinion (Deutsch et al., 1967). In regard to the conventional rearmament of Germany, German industry was opposed until around 1956, and it supported Adenauer's policy of delaying German rearmament at that time. Later, German industrial interest favored such armament, and in the early 1960s a majority of German military favored the acquisition of nuclear weapons under European or North Atlantic auspices, as they still may now. According to a recent study, much of German industry now favors the acquisition of advanced weapons systems as a primarily potential source of economically usable technical methods and research results (Brandt, 1966). The strong popular endorsement of the more pacific and anti-nuclear foreign policy of the coalition government of Chancellor Willy Brandt and Foreign Minister Walter Scheel in the 1972 elections may have modified this pattern.

Similar arguments, bolstered by occasional references to the potential threat from China, are now advanced by some military circles in Japan. On the whole, however, the current theories about war-promoting interest groups and "military-industrial complexes," and their elaboration into various theories of imperialism, do not suffice to explain the acquiescence of many former colonial powers in the sweeping process of decolonization between 1945 and 1965 and in their retreat from overt big-power politics and any major competitions in terms of armaments. In developing countries, competitive increases in national armaments have been more frequent, but there the local business communities are not the main driving forces.

What seems well established is the tendency of economic interest groups and high-ranking military and government personnel to form a common elite, primarily through the movements of the same individuals back and forth between government and business and between military and civilian high executive positions (Yarmolinsky, 1969; Pilisuk and Hayden, 1965). There also seems to be some evidence that, despite the partial merger of these elites, major differences among interest groups and within the elite tend to remain (Schumpeter, 1919; Benoit and Boulding, 1963; Boulding, 1966; Galbraith, 1969).

Content analyses have shown that an increase in the symbols of mutual hostility in the elite communications of two countries tends to precede the outbreak of war between them (Lasswell, 1947; Pool, 1952). Elites of rival countries also tend to have a mirror image of each other in many but not all respects (Bronfenbrenner, 1961; Angell et al., 1964).

Mass Media and Mass Opinion

To this extent, then, the members of the dominant elites who are often seen as realistic men of practical experience have in fact their own sources of cognitive distortions. According to the interest group theory, top-ranking business executives and the bulk of the members of the richer strata ought to read the most nationalistic and warlike mass media and hold the most nationalistic and warlike opinions. There is strong evidence for many countries that this belief is false.

The psychological literature would lead us rather to believe that ethnocentric, authoritarian, and warlike views ought to be strongest in those strata whose members were most insecure in terms of income, and even more of status and self-image, and who were most torn by the gap between their aspirations and their achievements. Nationalism and war from this viewpoint would find their main breeding-ground in the lower middle class of most countries and in the mass media, parties, and politicians that cater to it, as well as among those individuals and families who have risen relatively recently from the lower middle class to higher levels of income or power, without having lost as yet their lower middle class images, fears, and resentments. There is strong evidence from many surveys that warlike policies and attitudes are indeed more likely to be supported by the lower middle class than by any other stratum of the population; and that in recent decades rural populations have tended to be more warlike than city dwellers. Skilled workers, rising into the lower middle class, tend to share the latter's ethnocentric and nationalistic attitudes from an early stage onward.

It should be remembered, however, that rural and lower middle class opinions are relatively easily measured by mass survey methods, while the true opinions of the very rich and of the top elite are almost impossible to ascertain in this manner. In this respect the number of members of the elite in the U.S. who favored both the initiation of a bombing strike on Havana in 1962 and the escalation of the Vietnam war in 1965 deserves consideration. Perhaps the most promising line of research hitherto neglected would consist in identifying the conditions when a temporary increase in war-prone attitudes among the dominant elites coincides with the more nearly permanent ethnocentric aggressiveness of the lower middle classes, and when this explosive combination is then fanned to the flashpoint by interest groups, mass media, and the government (Fay, 1966; Langer, 1965).

In general, mass opinion tends to be relatively volatile with up to 40 per cent of the voters, and sometimes even more, changing their attitude on some foreign policy issue after having been exposed to the cumulative impact of a series of messages and spectacular events. Single events, no matter how spectacular, do not ever seem to shift the attitudes of more than 40 per cent of the electorate; and to do even this much their impact must be augmented by the mass media and backed by the authority of the national government (Deutsch and Merritt, 1965). More frequently, single spectacular events shift the attitudes of only between 10 and 20 per cent of the voters, and their impact may wear off completely if the earlier opinions continue to have the backing of relatively stable social groups. Direct personal perceptions of external reality, such as that obtained by visits to foreign countries, tend to be automatically filtered and adjusted by many subjects so as to conform to the anticipated preferences of the home audience to whom they expect to report on their return (Pool, 1965).

In well-integrated countries, differences between age groups, such as those under twenty as opposed to those under fifty, in regard to foreign policy or general politics have tended to be no more than 5 to 10 per cent. A difference of 20 and even 30 per cent, such as was found in the U.S. throughout 1968-72, appears as something new.

Many advanced industrial countries have a nearly permanent sector of 10 to 15 per cent of the voters who favor extreme tactics of repression and race discrimination at home and arms competition and conflicts in international affairs. Such a group was reported in the U.S. by Roper in 1954 and its percentage was only slightly exceeded by the vote for the Wallace-LeMay ticket in 1968. Strongly engaged warlike "hawks" and peace-oriented "doves" were found by a 1967 survey to be not too unequal in strength among American voters, with 18 per cent and 12 per cent, respectively; among the small group of writers of letters to newspapers, however, hawks outnumbered doves nearly two to one (Verba and Nie, 1972: 283). Generally, holders of strongly conservative Republican opinions—who are often more warlike—are far more highly active in politics than any other group of comparable size (Verba and Nie, 1972: 224-228).

In contrast to these specific attitudes, the general lack of information and interest in international affairs by a large part of the electorate has been persistently reported (Cantril and Free, 1967). This evidence of disinterest in foreign matters, so long as it does not become salient, must not be confused with any unwillingness of mass opinion to support a national government during the early stages of almost any dispute with a foreign power after it breaks out and becomes widely publicized. The unwillingness of the majority of voters in a modern welfare state to concern themselves with preventing an international conflict before its outbreak seems only to be exceeded by their willingness to support their national elite after the conflict has started, and for so long thereafter as its cumulative costs do not appear to them prohibitive.

National Political Systems:
Social, Cultural, and Political Attributes

Considerable work has been done on the characteristics of a national political system and its likelihood to engage in domestic or international violence. Some of these studies are based on a combination of theoretical analysis and intuitively selected historical evidence. Societies in deep crisis, it has been plausibly argued many times (Lasswell, 1930; Haas, 1968), are more likely to elevate psychopathological personalities to key decision-making roles, with consequences for the international behavior. Societies which fail to provide security of income and status for large parts of their populations are likely to give rise to extremist political movements, and their rulers may then have to choose between letting the increased aggressive attitudes of these groups explode in domestic strife, or assuaging them by rapid and far-reaching reforms, or channeling them into international conflict—with theory and history suggesting a preference for the third of these responses (Lasswell, 1935).

If this theory of alternative responses to domestic tensions were correct, then foreign conflicts would serve as substitutes for domestic ones. According to the "substitution theory," the frequency of the two types of conflicts ought to be inversely correlated. Unfortunately, another version of the theory predicts the opposite. High degrees of tension ought to create a higher demand both for domestic and for international violence. According to this "joint demand theory," the frequency of the two types of conflict ought to vary together. Finally, a mixed theory would suggest that the effects of substitution and joint demand ought just about to balance each other, and that there should be no observable correlation of any kind between the frequency of domestic and foreign conflict. If anything, it is the last of these three views that seems to be confirmed by the evidence thus far. Rummel (1968), reporting on his analyses, found no correlation in the overall figures for 1955-60 for most of the world. This picture may change, however, in further analysis through the introduction of regional subgroups and discriminating variables.

Another analysis of the correlation of national attribute data and international conflict data suggests that both types of conflicts are related with patterns of social and psychological frustration and aggression in each country. To the extent that the frustration-aggression theory should be applicable at this level, it ought to support the joint demand theory of conflicts which was not confirmed by Rummel's findings. On the contrary, a negative correlation of −.35 between the number of deaths by domestic political violence (1948-1960) with the percentage of military personnel in the population of working age for 74 countries seems to support the substitution theory. Beyond that, countries with high levels of military expenditure relative to GNP tend to be large; this is the opposite of the popular view that small states have to bear a proportionately larger burden of defense. High levels of military expenditure are also positively correlated with higher proportions of expenditures by the central government and by the general government sector. Countries with this grouping of characteristics also have higher levels of linguistic diversity and of Communist votes, and slightly higher levels of industrialization. They have substantially higher levels of marriage rates and emigration, and lower levels of inequality in relation to income and landholdings as well as lower infant death rates. Defense expenditures are closely correlated with the share of military personnel among working-age population, accounting for almost one-half of the variance in military personnel levels. The correlations of the proportion of military personnel with other social characteristics are similar to those of defense expenditures, except that high levels of military participation are somewhat less strongly correlated with marriage and emigration, and more strongly with life expectancy and low birth rates. Military participation is also positively correlated with mass education and the growth of per-capita income, and with capital formation, while levels of defense expenditures are not.

The entire picture suggests that a moderate amount of militarization of a society may be part of a characteristic pattern at intermediate and higher levels of economic and political development (Russett et al., 1964: 269, 270, 294). While participation by the population in military service is correlated with medium- and higher-level incomes, the political intervention by military officers in politics tends to be concentrated in poor, largely illiterate, and dictatorial countries (Banks and Textor, 1963: Table 148). Such military interventions also tend to be associated with semi-modern bureaucracies and also with politically significant activities of the police.

Despite Haas' first promising attempts (1968), a systematic comparison of intrasocial characteristics with the war-and-peace behavior of states remains to be done. The availability of the new war statistics handbook by Singer and Small (1972), and of further data collections on national attributes also in preparation by Singer and Small, will make this for the first time possible.

The Role of Government Organizations, Bureaucracy, and Personnel

In contrast to the obvious importance of the government machinery and personnel for the performance of nations, there is a striking lack of careful study of its effect on the incidence of war and peace. The only systematic studies focusing directly on this relationship are those by Snyder and Paige (1958) and Paige (1968) on the U.S. decision to enter the Korean war, and a more general study of alternative models of such decision processes by Graham Allison (1968). The large literature on civil-military relations does not primarily focus on that problem.

Upon the basis of his studies, Paige (1968) suggests that the decision of the Truman Administration and its top-ranking personnel to intervene in the Korean war in the summer of 1950 was arrived at under the special conditions of crisis decision-making, with its well-known characteristics such as highly selective and limited participation by top-ranking administrative personnel (neither in the decision to enter the Korean war nor during the Cuban missile crisis were there more than fifteen persons involved—a figure which closely resembles the size of the Politburo of the Soviet Union), the limited time available for the consideration of basic alternatives, and the disproportionate importance placed upon selective information derived from memory—particularly with regard to perceived historical precedents at the expense of genuine information search and adequate reality-testing and the exclusion of possibly relevant information provided by seemingly non-involved nations, organizations, or personalities. As a consequence, the definition of the situation and of the values involved developed during the crisis in such a way, as pointed out by Paige, that the decision-makers felt that the values to be served by intervening militarily in Korea outweighed any potential costs.

Unfortunately, there are as yet no other studies available against which these findings from the Korean case could be tested further. The historical studies by Seabury (1954) and Craig and Gilbert (1967), and the biographic studies by the Georges (1956) and by Rogow (1963), do not yield findings in propositional form. They do add, however, some evidence on the very limited realism of top-ranking government personnel when making critical decisions.

The Effect of National Strategies

The discussion about national strategies has produced once again many relevant propositions but few, if any, tested findings. Experimental work by Rapoport and his associates shows that there is a substantial "lock-in effect" in certain types of conflict situations where the two parties have both common and antagonistic interests. In such cases the early initiation of cooperative behavior tends to lead to the early achievement of high levels of mutual cooperation, whereas early non-cooperative behavior tends to have the opposite effect. Unilateral cooperative behavior, if persisted in, tends to make the other side more uncooperative, demanding, and aggressive. Persistent uncooperative behavior has the same effect. The best tactic for inducing cooperation, it was found, consists in opening with cooperative behavior, retaliating to a limited extent for non-cooperation by the other side, and then returning to cooperation; if renewed cooperation is not reciprocated, return again to limited retaliation and then renew cooperation; and continue in this manner until mutual cooperation is established. Personality characteristics have significant effects, albeit less so than lock-in effects. Mutual cooperation among women is 20 per cent less than among men. Displaying prominently the pay-off matrix to both players doubles the frequency of cooperation among them; this would seem to support the notion of "open covenants openly arrived at" (Rapoport and Chammah, 1965).

Rapoport's experiments also show the mechanism of projection; players playing against a hidden computer programmed to respond with random moves tend to impute conscious malice to the unseen opponent. A computer experiment by Macy shows that if two players in such a prisoner's dilemma game are represented by two computers, each programmed to act like a single learning mechanism, they will show the critical lock-in effects similar to Rapoport's human subjects. The critical level for the establishment of cooperative behavior will be 80 per cent cooperation during the early stages of the game. Above this level stable cooperation will be achieved; below this level cooperation will decline to 20 per cent, leaving 80 per cent of the behavior to hostile moves (Macy, 1969).

Such studies suggest quantitative thresholds in the frequency of cooperative moves if they are likely to be reciprocated. Since, however, propositions about deterrence cannot be tested empirically, except by wars at catastrophic costs, the design and the analysis of such limited experiments is of particular importance.

Another way of testing propositions of the deterrence strategy consists in the analysis of historical cases. Statements of deterrence by a big power in the effort to protect the smaller client state are credible less in terms of the threats made than in the actual closeness of economic, social, cultural, and political ties between the protecting power and its clients (Russett, 1963). If a protecting power such as the United States tries to deter a would-be aggressor such as Japan by presenting him with a series of alternatives, all of which appear unacceptable to the latter, then the protector, instead of preventing the attack on his client (China), may merely succeed in precipitating an attack upon himself, despite the attacker's knowledge of the protector's eightfold superiority (Russett, 1967). A sample survey of some periods in history suggests that in the very long run preparations for war do not make peace more likely, but rather have the opposite effect (Naroll, 1969), while increased peaceful economic, cultural, intellectual, or family ties tend to make war less likely.

A simulation study by Raser and Crow showed that an acquisition of an invulnerable second-strike capability tended to make that nation more aggressive in international politics and more inclined to run high risks of war. In an international system in which several nations had such invulnerable deterrents, wars broke out more frequently (Raser and Crow, 1966).

Despite their incomplete character, it seems striking that all empirical research results on deterrence theories seem to contradict the prevailing doctrines of deterrence.

Crisis Decision-Making and Escalation Processes

The adoption of national strategies sometimes occurs under conditions of crisis. In such cases small-group processes may become crucial. Individual members of decision-making committees may then vote against their own conviction for policies which they know will lead to war and disaster for their nation, in order not to have to stand out against the pressure of their group and of the forces behind it (Maruyama, 1963). Other studies find that war-producing decisions are sometimes made incrementally, step by small step, with the opponents of war within the government failing to make a stand at any of these steps in order not to loose their "effectiveness" within its ranks until it is too late (Thompson, 1968). As the crisis intensifies, the impairment of cognitive performance increases. Cognitive complexity deteriorates after a small increase in threat perception. Cognitive performance declines under stress. The capabilities of one's own side as well as those of the potential adversary receive a declining share of attention, while interest becomes focused upon perceptions of the seemingly or actually hostile intent of the adversary. Responses to this perceived intent thus become less calculated and increasingly cathectic—i.e., serving as a release to the actor's inner tensions. Also, as the crisis becomes more acute, the adversary is perceived as more hostile independently from what he actually does (North et al., 1963; Zinnes, 1968; Schroder et al., 1967; Hermann, 1969).

The results found at the level of individuals—that persons with simple cognitive structures are more likely to make decisions leading to war and that persons with authoritarian personalities have the same propensities—are shown by simulation experiments to be particularly relevant at the stage of crisis decision-making (Schroder et al., 1967). Though many of these results are incomplete and some of them are inconclusive (e.g., Robinson et al., 1969) they tend to suggest that the rational response of small decision-making groups to acute threats—an assumption which is central to deterrence theory—cannot, in effect, be relied on.

Insofar as this incomplete evidence permits an estimate, it would be that among adversaries with comparable levels of destructive power, responses to acute deterrence threats would be as likely or more likely to be irrational than not, and that the probability of an irrational response would increase as the threat becomes more intense and credible.

The logical character of deterrence and threat situations may have less of an effect upon their ending in war or peace than the effects of previously held associations, images, and ideologies in the minds of the participants (Senghaas, 1969). A simulation exercise with a high degree of overt "cold war" associations ended in war, while in two comparable exercises couched in more neutral terms, despite the same initial situations, war was avoided (Alker and Brunner, 1969).

There is a fair amount of evidence that escalation processes tend to acquire a momentum of their own, and that their results can be approximated fairly closely by suitable curves or mathematical equations, suggesting a relatively blind and mindless automaton in the process (Richardson, 1960; Rapoport, 1960; Boulding, 1961; Wright, 1965; Smoker, 1966; Caspary, 1967). In addition to demonstrating this tendency for arms races at certain stages, some of the evidence also suggests that a similar automatic process may be at work in the slow escalation of arms levels within a nation state, as in the case of the United States from 1890 to 1969 (Russett, 1969) and for the short-run escalation of United States troop levels in Vietnam (Voevodsky, 1970). Some of these processes may be *autistically* induced by processes within a single country rather than by the interplay of its actions with the responses of its antagonist within the conflict system (Senghaas, 1969; North and Choucri, 1969).

Paralleling to some extent the experimental findings of lock-in effects in conflict experiments under laboratory conditions, some of the analyses of the behavior of states also suggest on theoretical grounds that there may be a point of no return in the conflicts of states (K. Deutsch, 1957; Russett, 1962; Whitey and Katz, 1965; Pruitt, 1965; and M. Deutsch, 1969).

The Effects of the International System

With respect to the effects of the international system, a wave pattern in the observable frequency of war during the last 200 years is reported by Denton (1966) and Denton and Philips (1968), and this is connected by them with the salience of memories of the past wars in the course of successions of human generations.

Singer and Small report a more radical change in the international system since 1910. A first analysis based on the empirical data by Singer and Small (1968) shows that the international system has changed substantially in many respects since 1910, as already reported above.

A substantial early simulation exercise suggests that the proliferation of nuclear weapons from two powers to four powers in an international system tends to change the system from a bipolar to a multipolar system with the two original blocs surviving in loosened form. Awareness in each country of threats from members of the other blocs then declined to about one-half, while the awareness of threats from members of one's own bloc increased, but to a lesser extent, so that the total level of indicators of threat awareness was on the average 25 per cent less than it had been before proliferation (Brody, 1963). This finding accords well with the theoretical prediction that the likelihood of major conflicts in an international system would decline with the transition from a two-power to a four-power or multipower system because of the increasing interaction opportunities and the dispersal of potential hostile attention (Deutsch and Singer, 1966). A four-power system was found to be less war-prone than a two-power system in another simulation exercise in which, however, the four-power world also was characterized by a greater number and activity of international actors (Smoker, 1968, 1969).

CONCLUSION

Our first and necessarily incomplete and provisional survey of the field has shown us far fewer empirical findings than are needed, but more than we initially suspected.

At the same time it has revealed a number of major gaps in the existing research data and activities. Six areas marked as "Gap 1" to "Gap 6" on Table 2 seem relatively empty of usable research. The areas of the main research gaps are:

(1) The larger determinants of "human nature," that is, in our context, of warlike or peaceful individual attitudes and personality patterns.

In particular, the influence of small groups, large interest groups, political parties, and media on such individual attitudes and personalities should be explored more thoroughly.

(2) The effects of small groups, individual leaders, and intra-psychic processes on the attitudes, structure, and behavior of large interest groups, political parties, and dominant elites, in regard to decisions affecting the likelihood of peace or war.

(3) The effects of intra-psychic processes on the structure and behavior of mass media, on the national political culture and regime, and on the government organization and bureaucracy, in regard to matters of war and peace, including particularly the choice of a national strategy.

(4) The effects of small-group processes on the mass media and on the national political culture and regime.

(5) The effects of the larger regional or international environment on the mass media and mass opinion, the national political system, and government organization and bureaucracy.

(6) The effects of large interest groups and political parties on crisis decision-making, escalation, and third-party interventions.

Many positive findings have been discussed in the body of this survey. Here it should suffice to summarize. Already the findings now in hand suggest substantial revisions in international relations in several aspects.

First, the difference between international systems before 1910 and since that time appear so large that the transfer of the conventional wisdom of the earlier period to the later one becomes so dubious as to border on the unacceptable. Systems have substantial effects on the regularity of processes which occur in them. As international systems change, therefore, the realism and practicability of national strategies will change in particular. Far too much of the discussion of foreign policy and national security in the 1970s is conducted against the image of a world susceptible to world hegemony which ceased to exist after 1910, or of a cold war world of two blocs which ceased to exist by 1960. Our lack of understanding of the trends of current international politics is in part due to a lack of other than obsolete intellectual models for comprehending them. Simulation exercises, as pointed out by Smoker (1969), can play a vital role in increasing our intellectual resourcefulness in this respect.

Second, the general assumption of rational behavior in international

TABLE 2
SIX SYSTEM LEVELS AND TEN STAGES IN THE PRODUCTION OF WAR: SPECIFIC STUDIES (See References)

SIX SYSTEM LEVELS \ TEN STAGES	1 HUMAN NATURE	2 INTEREST GROUPS	3 DOMINANT ELITES	4 MASS MEDIA & MASS OPIN.	5 NAT. POL. SYSTEM: REGIME & CULTURE	6 GOV. ORGANIZATION & BUREAUCRACY	7 NATIONAL STRATEGY	8 CRISIS DECISION-MAKING	9 ESCALATION	10 LARGER ENVIRONMENT
VI INTERNATIONAL AND REGIONAL	GAP 1	Smoker (Si) Vernon (T/E) + 3	Magdoff (T/H) Lenin (T/E) + 2	GAP 5			Huntington (Hi)	McClelland (T/E) Guetzkow (Si)	Richardson (T/E) Smoker (T/E) Pruitt (T) + 11	Singer-Small (T/E) Brody (Si) Kaplan (T) + 6
V NATION-STATE		Staley (Hi) Robbins (T) Benoit (T/E) + 4	Angell-Singer (T/E) + 6	Kelman (T/E) Roper (E) + 10	Rummel (T/E) Russett et al (T/E) Hars (T/E) + 8	Craig-Gilbert (Hi) + 2	Schelling (T) Rapoport (T/E) Russett (T/E) Etzioni (T/E) + 12	North et al (T/E) Pool-Kessler (Si) Bloomfield (Si) + 4	K. Deutsch (T) Singer (T) Frank (T/E) + 6	North-Choucri (T/E) Galtung (T) + 5
IV LARGE INTEREST GROUPS, PARTIES, MEDIA		Vegts (Hi) Galbraith (Hi) + 12	Schumpeter (Hi) Kolko (Hi) Mills (T/E) + 13		Lasswell (T) + 2	Raymond (Hi)	Brandt (T/E) Aron (Hi)		GAP 6	
III SMALL GROUPS		GAP 2		GAP 4		Paige (T/E)	Rapoport (Si/E) + 2	Hermann (Si) Zinnes (T/E) + 3		Singer (T/E)
II INDIVIDUAL PERSONALITY	Freud (T) Dollard et al (E) Klineberg (T/E) + 14			Allport (T) Rosenberg (T/E)	Marcuse (T) Parsons (T/E) Mead (T/E) + 5	Georges (Hi) Rogow (Hi)	Holsti, O.	Schroeder et al (Si) White (T/E) + 2	Levinson (T/E) Rosenberg (T/E)	
I INTRAPSYCH. COMPONENTS	Freud (T) Christiansen (E) + 10					GAP 3		Driver (Si) + 2		

KEY: T = Theory; E = Empirical Studies; Hi = Historical Studies; Si = Simulation; M = Mathematical Studies

[314]

politics on the level of high-ranking decision-makers as well as on that of mass opinion is likely to be erroneous in a large proportion of cases. Several mechanisms making for cognitive distortion as well as for the distortion of responses have been identified, including ego defenses, frustration-aggression sequences, cognitive dissonance, intolerance of ambiguity, authoritarian personality patterns, deterioration of cognition and responsiveness under stress and under group pressure, and the more subtle seductions of "group think" on the mutual reinforcement of group members in their erroneous perceptions of behavior. The various sources of cognitive distortion have structural character, in the sense that they often interact and interlock in such a way that even the elimination of one or two of these sources of distortion would not eliminate the joint effect, and that these weakened or eliminated sources of error would soon be restored again. As a result, cognitive distortion is ubiquitous in the lives of individuals and small groups, and persistent and pervasive in each national political system. There seems, also, good reason to doubt the assumption about the rationality of the behavior of large interest groups; and hence, the model of rational interest group behavior, so widely accepted from the days of Karl Marx to the present, may have to be revised. Here, too, is an important field for empirical research which has long been neglected.

Consistent with this major finding that the general theory of the rational decision-maker about war and peace now appears untenable, specific items of research suggest strongly that the theory of deterrence in international politics is seriously inadequate; that large size and defense outlays of a state fail to correlate with any greater likelihood of its remaining at peace; and that the theory of the rationally-acting large interest group now appears no less doubtful. Failures of realistic perception, appropriate response, and mutual coordination of behavior among nation states are more frequent, and are more likely to be interpreted by rulers, elites, and mass opinion in each state as deliberate hostility and malice on the part of some other nation, or of some transnational actor, than the classic rationalist theory of state behavior in international relations would lead us to expect.

In the third place, the behavior of states appears to be more internally determined and potentially more autistic than would appear from the model of nineteenth-century diplomacy. National states act to a significant degree as self-insulating and self-deceiving systems. Interacting with other no less autistic nation states, and prone to interpret any signs of non-coordination or impending collision as evidence of a deliberate hostile intent and attack, each nation state then may be drawn into a larger action-reaction system of mounting latent or manifest conflict, with significant possibilities of mutual lock-in effects into patterns of hostile behavior, and moving toward war beyond some point of no return.

Under these conditions, and in the face of these dangers, it becomes a crucial task to strengthen national and international capacities for self-control. Thus, the effectiveness of various strategies of increasing the reality-testing capabilities of national governments, and of strengthening their collective ego-performance against the blind impact of both internal and outside pressures, becomes a major task in the interest of national security and world peace. The work on peace research that we have surveyed is incomplete, uneven, and scattered among many disciplines, but it shows that an indispensable beginning has been made.

REFERENCES

ABEL, T. (1941) "The elements of decision in the pattern of war." American Sociological Review 6: 853-859.

ABELSON, R. et al. [eds.] (1969) Theories of Cognitive Consistency. Chicago: Rand McNally.

ACHESON, D. (1969) Present at the Creation: My Years in the State Department. New York: Norton.

ADORNO, T. et al. (1950) The Authoritarian Personality. New York: Harper & Row.

ALKER, H. R., Jr. and R. D. BRUNNER (1969) "Simulating international conflict: a comparison of three approaches." International Studies Quarterly 13: 70-110.

ALLISON, G. (1968) "Conceptual models of the Cuban missile crisis." American Political Science Review 53: 689-715.

ALLPORT, G. (1950) "The role of expectancy," pp. 43-78 in H. Cantril (ed.) Tensions that Cause Wars. Urbana: Univ. of Illinois Press.

ALMOND, G. (1950) American People and Foreign Policy. New York: Harcourt, Brace & World.

ANGELL, R., V. DUNHAM, and J. D. SINGER (1964) "Social values and foreign policy attitudes of Soviet and American elites." Journal of Conflict Resolution 8, 4.

ARON, R. (1958) War and Industrial Society. London: Oxford Univ. Press.

ART, R. (1969) The TFX Decision: McNamara and the Military. Boston: Little, Brown.

ASCH, S. (1952a) Social Psychology. New York: Prentice-Hall.

--- (1952b) "Effects of group pressure upon the modification and distortion of judgments," in Swanson, Newcomb and Hartley (eds.) Readings in Social Psychology. New York: Henry Holt.

ASPATURIAN, V. (1972) "Soviet Union," in Macridis and Ward (eds.) Modern Political Systems: Europe. Englewood Cliffs, N.J.: Prentice-Hall.

BANKS, A. and P. GREGG (1965) "Dimensions of political systems: factor analysis of a cross-polity survey." American Political Science Review 59 (September): 602-614.

BANKS, A. S. and R. TEXTOR (1963) A Cross-Polity Survey. Cambridge, Mass.: MIT Press.

BARAN, P. and P. SWEEZY (1966) Monopoly Capital. New York: Monthly Review Press.

BENOIT, E. [ed.] (1967) Disarmament and World Economic Interdependence. Oslo: Universitetsforlaget.
——— and K. E. BOULDING [eds.] (1963) Disarmament and Economy. New York: Harper & Row.
BERKOWITZ, L. [ed.] (1969) Roots of Aggression. A Re-Examination of the Frustration-Aggression Hypothesis. New York.
——— (1962) Aggression. New York: McGraw-Hill.
BENSON, O. (1961) "A simple diplomatic game," pp. 504-511 in J. N. Rosenau (ed.) International Politics and Foreign Policy. New York: Free Press.
BERNARD, J. (1957) "The sociological study of conflict," pp. 33-117 in UNESCO (ed.) The Nature of Conflict. Paris: UNESCO.
BLOOMFIELD, L. and B. WHALEY (1965) "The political-military exercise: a progress report." Orbis 8 (Winter): 854-870.
BOBROW, D. and A. WILCOX (1966) "Dimensions of defense opinion: the American public." Papers of the International Peace Research Society 6: 101-142.
BOULDING, K. E. (1968) "A pure theory of death: dilemmas of defense policy in a world of conditional viability," pp. 112-130 in K. E. Boulding (ed.) Beyond Economics. Ann Arbor: Univ. of Michigan Press.
——— (1966) The Image. Ann Arbor: Univ. of Michigan Press.
——— (1963) "Towards a pure theory of threat systems." American Economic Review 53: 424-434.
——— (1961) Conflict and Defense. New York: Harper & Row.
BRAMSON, L. and G. W. GOETHALS (1968) War: Studies from Psychology, Sociology, Anthropology. New York: Basic Books.
BRANDT, G. (1966) Ruestung und Wirtschaft in der Bundesrepublik. Berlin: Witten.
BRODY, R. (1963) "Some systematic effects of the spread of nuclear weapons technology: a study of simulation of a multi-nuclear future." Journal of Conflict Resolution 7: 663-753.
BRONFENBRENNER, U. (1961) "The mirror image in Soviet-American relations: a social psychologist's report." Journal of Social Issues 17, 3: 45-56.
BUCHANAN, W. and H. CANTRIL (1953) How Nations See Each Other. A Study in Public Opinion. Urbana: Univ. of Illinois Press.
BUCKLEY, W. F. [ed.] (1968) Modern Systems Research for the Behavioral Scientist. Chicago: Aldine.
BUSS, A. (1961) The Psychology of Aggression. New York: John Wiley.
BUTOW, R. (1969) Tojo and the Coming of War. Stanford: Stanford Univ. Press.
CANTRIL, H. [ed] (1950) Tensions that Cause Wars. Urbana: Univ. of Illinois Press.
——— and L. FREE (1967) The Political Beliefs of Americans. New Brunswick, N.J.: Rutgers Univ. Press.
CARTHY, J. and F. EBLING (1964) The Natural History of Aggression. London and New York: Academic Press for the Institute of Biology.
CASPARY, W. (1967) "Richardson's models of arms races: description, critique, and an alternative model." International Studies Quarterly 2: 63-88.
CATTELL, R. and R. GORSUCH (1965) "The definition and measurement of national morale and morality." Journal of Social Psychology 67: 77-96.
CHADWICK, R. W. (1967) "An empirical test of five assumptions in an inter-nation simulation about national systems." General Systems 12: 177-192.
CHOUCRI, N. and R. NORTH (forthcoming) The Determinants of International Violence. San Francisco: W. H. Freeman.

CHRISTIANSEN, B. (1959) Attitudes Towards Foreign Affairs as a Function of Personality. Oslo: Oslo Univ. Press.
CLARK, G. (1936) The Balance Sheets of Imperialism. New York: Columbia Univ. Press.
CLARKSON, J. and T. COCHRAN [eds.] (1966) War as a Social Institution. The Historian's Perspective. New York: Columbia Univ. Press.
CLAYTON, J. L. (1962) "Defense spending: key to California's growth." Western Political Quarterly 15: 280-293.
COCHRAN, B. (1965) The War System. New York: Macmillan.
COFFIN, T. (1964) The Armed Society. New York: Penguin.
COLTON, T. (1969) "The 'new biology' and the causes of War." Canadian Journal of Political Science 2: 434-447.
COOK, F. (1962) The Warfare State. New York: Macmillan.
COOPER, P. (1965) "The development of the concept of war." Journal of Peace Research 2: 1-17.
COPLIN, W. D. [ed.] (1968) Simulation in the Study of Politics. Chicago: Markham.
––– (1966) "Inter-nation simulation and contemporary theories of international relations." American Political Science Review 60: 562-578.
––– C. ELDER, and M. LEAVITT (1969) "World politics simulation." Washington, D.C.: Industrial College of the Armed Forces. (mimeo)
COSER, L. (1956) The Functions of Social Conflict. New York: Free Press.
CRAIG, G. and F. GILBERT (1953) The Diplomats, 1919-1938. Princeton: Princeton Univ. Press. (republished 1967, New York: Atheneum)
DAHL, R. E. (1950) Congress and Foreign Policy. New York: Harcourt, Brace & World.
DEUTSCH, K. W. (1970) Politics and Government. Boston: Houghton Mifflin.
––– (1969) "On methodological problems of quantitative research," pp. 19-39 in M. Dogan and S. Rokkan (eds.) Quantitative Ecological Analysis in the Social Sciences. Cambridge, Mass.: MIT Press.
––– (1968) Analysis of International Relations. Englewood Cliffs, N.J.: Prentice-Hall.
––– (1967) Arms Control and the Atlantic Alliance. New York: John Wiley.
––– (1966a) Nationalism and Social Communication. Cambridge, Mass.: MIT Press.
––– (1966b) The Nerves of Government. New York: Free Press.
––– (1959) "The impact of science and technology on international politics." Daedalus 88: 669-685.
––– (1957) "Mass communication and the loss of freedom in national decision-making." Journal of Conflict Resolution 1: 200-211.
––– (1956) "Shifts in the balance of communication flows: a problem of measurement in international relations." Public Opinion Quarterly 20: 143-160.
––– and R. MERRITT (1970) Nationalism and National Development. An Interdisciplinary Bibliography. Cambridge, Mass.: MIT Press.
––– (1965) "Effects of events on national and international images," pp. 132-187 in H. Kelman (ed.) International Behavior. New York: Holt, Rinehart & Winston.
DEUTSCH, K. W., J. PLATT, and D. SENGHAAS (1971) "Conditions favoring major advances in social science." Science 171: 450-459.
DEUTSCH, K. W. and D. SENGHAAS (1971) "A framework for a theory of war and peace," pp. 23-46 in A. Lepawsky et al. (eds.) The Search for World Order. New York: Appleton-Century-Crofts.
––– (1970) "The fragile sanity of states: subsystem drives, system controls, and

supra-system limitations," pp. 105-163 in M. Kilson (ed.) Essays in Honor of R. Emerson.

DEUTSCH, K. W. and J. D. SINGER (1964) "Multipolar power systems and international stability." World Politics 16: 390-406.

DEUTSCH, M. (1969) "Conflicts: productive and destructive." Journal of Social Issues 25, 1: 7-41.

--- (1958) "Trust and suspicion." Journal of Conflict Resolution 2: 265-279.

DENTON, F. (1966) "Some regularities in international conflict, 1820-1949." Background 9: 283-296.

--- and W. PHILLIPS (1968) "Some patterns in the history of violence." Journal of Conflict Resolution 12: 182-195.

DOLLARD, J. et al. (1939) Frustration and Aggression. New Haven: Yale Univ. Press.

DRIVER, M. J. (1965) "A structure analysis of aggression, stress, and personality in an inter-nation simulation. Lafayette, Ind.: Purdue University. (mimeo)

DRUCKMAN, D. (1968) "Ethnocentrism in the inter-nation simulation." Journal of Conflict Resolution 12: 45-68.

DUJIKER, H.C.J. and N. H. FRIJDA (1960) National Character and National Stereotypes. Amsterdam: North-Holland.

DUNN, F. (1950) War and the Minds of Men. New York: Harper.

DURBIN, E.F.M. and J. BOWLBY (1939) Personal Aggressiveness and War. London: Kegan Paul.

EASTON, D. (1965) A Framework for Political Analysis. Englewood Cliffs, N.J.: Prentice-Hall.

--- (1965) A Systems Analysis of Political Life. New York: John Wiley.

ECKHARDT, W. (1969) "Ideology and personality in social attitudes." Peace Research Reviews 3, 2.

--- and T. F. LENTZ (1967) "Factors of war/peace attitudes." Peace Research Reviews 1 (October).

ENGELBRECHT, H. C. and F. C. HANIGHEN (1934) Merchants of Death. New York: Dodd & Mead.

ERIKSON, E. H. (1969) Gandhi's Truth. New York: Norton.

--- (1963) Childhood and Society. New York: Norton.

--- (1958) Young Man Luther. New York: Norton.

ETZIONI, A. (1968) The Active Society. New York: Free Press.

--- (1962) The Hard Way to Peace. New York: Meridian.

EYSENCK, H. J. (1950) "War and aggressiveness: a survey of social attitude studies," pp. 49-81 in T. H. Pear (ed.) Psychological Factors of Peace and War. London: Hutchinson.

FALK, R. and S. MEDLOVITZ (1966) The Strategy of World Order. New York: World Law Fund. (4 vols.)

FAY, S. B. (1966) The Origins of the World War. New York: Free Press.

FEIERABEND, I., R. FEIERABEND, and B. NESVOLD (1969) "Social change and political violence: cross-national patterns," pp. 606-667 in H. Graham and T. R. Gurr (eds.) Violence in America. New York: New American Library.

FESTINGER, L. (1957) A Theory of Cognitive Dissonance. Evanston, Ill.: Row, Peterson.

---, H. RIECKEN, and S. SCHACHTER (1956) When Prophecy Fails. Minneapolis: Univ. of Minnesota Press.

FINLAY, D., O. HOLSTI, and R. FAGAN (1967) Enemies in Politics. Chicago: Rand McNally.
FISHER, R. (1969) International Conflict for Beginners. New York: Harcourt, Brace & World.
——— [ed.] (1964) International Conflict and Behavioral Science. New York: Basic Books.
FRANCK, T. M. and E. WEISBAND (1971) Word Politics: Verbal Strategy Among the Superpowers. Oxford: Oxford Univ. Press.
FRANK, J. D. (1967) Sanity and Survival: Psychological Aspects of War and Peace. New York: Vintage.
FREUD, S. (1953a) "Thoughts for the times on war and death," pp. 275ff. in Vol. 14 of S. Freud, Works. London: Hogart.
——— (1953b) "Group psychology and the analysis of the ego," pp. 67ff. in Vol. 18 of S. Freud, Works. London: Hogart.
——— (1953c) "Why war?" in Vol. 22 of S. Freud, Works. London: Hogart.
FRIED, M., M. HARRIS, and R. MURPHY (1968) War: The Anthropology of Armed Conflict and Aggression. Garden City, N.Y.: Natural History Press.
FROMM, E. (1961) May Man Prevail? An Inquiry into the Facts and Fictions of Foreign Policy. New York: Anchor.
GALBRAITH, J. K. (1969) How to Control the Military. New York: New American Library.
GALTUNG, J. (1964) "A structural theory of aggression." Journal of Peace Research 1: 95-119.
GANTZEL, K. J. (1969) "Rustungswettlaufe und politische entscheidungsbedingungen," pp. 110-137 in E. O. Czempiel (ed.) Die Anachronistische Souveranitat. Koln and Opladen: Westdeutscher.
GEORGE, A. and J. GEORGE (1956) Woodrow Wilson and Colonel House: A Personality Study. New York: John Day.
GIFT, R. (1969) A Discipline for the Study of War. Lexington: Polemological Studies.
GINSBURG, M. (1939) "The causes of war." Sociological Review 31: 121-143.
GOULDEN, J. (1969) Truth Is the First Casualty: The Gulf of Tonkin Affair—Illusion and Reality. Chicago: Rand McNally.
GRAY, C. et al. (1968) A Bibliography of Peace Research. Eugene Ore.: General Research Analysis Methods.
GREEN, P. (1966) Deadly Logic: The Theory of Nuclear Deterrence. Columbus: Ohio State Univ. Press.
GROSSMAN, H. (1929) Das Akkumulations—und Zusammenbruchs Gesetz des Kapitalistischen Systems. Leipzig: Hirschfeld.
GUETZKOW, H. (1969) "Simulations in the consolidation and utilization of knowledge about international relations," pp. 284-300 in D. Pruitt and R. Snyder (eds.) Theory and Research on the Causes of War. Englewood Cliffs, N.J.: Prentice-Hall.
——— (1968) "Some correspondences between simulations and 'realities' in international relations," pp. 202-269 in M. A. Kaplan (ed.) New Approaches to International Relations. New York: St. Martin's.
——— et al. (1963) Simulation in International Relations. Englewood Cliffs, N.J.: Prentice-Hall.
GURR, T. R. (1970) Why Men Rebel. Princeton: Princeton Univ. Press.

--- (1969) "A comparative study of civil strife," pp. 544-605 in H. Graham and T. R. Gurr (eds.) Violence in America. New York: New Amsterdam Library.
HAAS, M. (1968) "Social change and national aggressiveness, 1900-1960," pp. 215-244 in J. D. Singer (ed.) Quantitative International Politics. New York: Free Press.
HALLGARTEN, G. (1967) Das Wettruesten. Frankfurt/Main: Europaeische Verlagsanstalt.
HALPERIN, M. (1967) Contemporary Military Strategy. Boston: Little, Brown.
HAYES, C. I. (1960) Nationalism: A Religion. New York: Macmillan.
--- (1948) The Historical Evolution of Modern Nationalism. New York: Macmillan. (first published, 1928)
--- (1930) France: A Nation of Patriots. New York: Columbia Univ. Press.
--- (1926) Essays on Nationalism. New York: Macmillan.
HERMANN, C. F. (1969) Crises in Foreign Policy: A Simulation Analysis. Indianapolis: Bobbs-Merrill.
--- (1967) "Validation problems in games and simulations with special reference to models of international politics." Behavioral Science 12: 216-231.
--- and M. G. HERMANN (1967) "An attempt to simulate the outbreak of World War I." American Political Science Review 61: 400-416.
HILFERDING, R. (1910) Das Finanzkapital. Vienna: Brand.
HOBSON, J. A. (1938) Imperialism: A Study. London: Allen & Unwin.
HOLSTI, O., R. NORTH, and R. BRODY (1968) "Perception and action in the 1914 crisis," pp. 123-158 in J. D. Singer (ed.) Quantitative International Politics. New York: Free Press.
--- (1964) "The management of international crisis: affect and action in American-Soviet relations." Journal of Peace Research 1: 170-190.
HOPKINS, P. (1938) Psychology of Social Movements. London: Allen & Unwin.
HOROWITZ, D. [ed.] (1969) Corporations and the Cold War. New York: Monthly Review Press.
HORN, K. (1969) "Politische psychologie: erkenntnis-interesse, themen und materialien," pp. 215-268 in G. Kress and D. Senghaas (eds.) Politikwissenschaft: Eine Einfuehrung in ihre Probleme. Frankfurt/Main: Europaeische Verlagsanstalt.
HOSOYA, C. (1968) "Miscalculations in deterrent policy: Japaneses-U.S. relations, 1938-1941." Journal of Peace Research 5: 97-115.
HUNTINGTON, S. (1961) The Common Defense. New York: Columbia Univ. Press.
--- (1958) "Arms races: prerequisites and results." Public Policy 8: 41-86.
INKELES, A. (1968) Social Change in Soviet Russia. Cambridge: Harvard Univ. Press.
--- and R. A. BAUER (1959) The Soviet Citizen. Cambridge: Harvard Univ. Press.
ISARD, W. and G. KARASKA (1962) "Unclassified defense contracts: awards by county, state and metropolitan area of the United States, fiscal year 1962." Philadelphia: World Friends Research Center. (mimeo)
JANIS, I. L. (1972) Victims of Groupthink. Boston: Houghton Mifflin.
JERVIS, R. (1968) "Hypothesis on misperception." World Politics 20: 454-479.
KAHN, H. (1965) On Escalation. New York: Praeger.
KAPLAN, M. A. (1957) System and Process in International Politics. New York: John Wiley.
KATZ, D. (1965) "Nationalism and strategies of international conflict resolution," pp. 356-390 in H. Kelman (ed.) International Behavior. New York: Holt, Rinehart & Winston.

KEHR, E. (1965) Schlachtflottenbau und parteipolitik 1894-1901: Voraussetzungen des Deutschen Imperialismus. Vaduz.
KELMAN, H. C. [ed.] (1965) International Behavior: A Social-Psychological Analysis. New York: Holt, Rinehart & Winston.
KEMP, G. (1968) "Arms transfers for developing countries." Proceedings of the International Peace Research Association 2: 254-268. Assen, Netherlands: Van Gorcum.
KEMP, T. (1967) Theories of Imperialism. London: Dennis, Dobson.
KENNEDY, R. (1969) Thirteen Days. New York: Norton.
KIMMINICH, O. (1964) Ruestung und Politische Spannung. Guetersloh: Bertelsmann.
KLINEBERG, O. (1964) The Human Dimension in International Relations. New York: Holt, Rinehart & Winston.
——— (1950) Tensions Affecting International Understanding. New York: Social Science Research Council.
KLINGBERG, F. (1966) "Predicting the termination of war. Battle casualties and population losses." Journal of Conflict Resolution 10: 129-171.
KNOBLOCH, E. and D. SENGHAAS (1968) "Ausgewaehlte Bibliographie zur Friedensforschung," pp. 559-589 in E. Krippendorf (ed.) Friedensforschung. Koeln-Berlin: Keipenheuer & Witsch.
KNORR, K. and S. VERBA (1961) "The levels-of-analysis problem in international relations," pp. 77-92 in K. Knorr and S. Verba (eds.) The International System: Theoretical Essays. Princeton: Princeton Univ. Press.
KOLKO, G. (1969a) The Politics of War. New York: Random House.
——— (1969b) The Roots of American Foreign Policy. Boston: Beacon.
KRIESBERG, L. [ed.] (1968) Social Processes in International Relations. New York: John Wiley.
KRIPPENDORF, E. [ed.] (1968) Friedensforschung. Koeln-Berlin: Kiepenheuer & Witsch.
LANGER, W. L. (1965) The Diplomacy of Imperialism. New York: Alfred Knopf. (first published, 1935)
LAPP, R. (1962) Kill and Overkill. New York: Basic Books.
LARSON, A. (1963) A Warless World. New York: McGraw-Hill.
LASSWELL, H. D. (1965a) World Politics and Personal Insecurity. New York: Free Press. (first published, 1935)
——— (1965b) The Language of Politics: Studies in Quantitative Semantics. Cambridge: MIT Press. (first published, 1947)
——— (1962) "The garrison state hypothesis today," pp. 51-70 in S. P. Huntington (ed.) Changing Patterns of Military Politics. New York: Free Press.
——— (1960) Psychopathology and Politics. New York: Viking.
——— (1948) Power and Personality. New York: Norton.
——— (1941) "The garrison state." American Journal of Sociology 46: 455-468.
——— and N. LEITES et al. (1949) The Language of Politics. Studies in Quantitative Semantics. New York: Stewart.
LEACH, E. (1968) "ignoble savages." New York Review of Books 11 (October 10): 24-29.
LENIN, V. I. (1939) Imperialism, the Highest State of Capitalism. New York: International.
LEONTIEF, W. and M. HOFFENBERG (1963) "Input and output analysis of

disarmament impacts," in Benoit and Boulding (eds.) Disarmament and the Economy. New York: Harper & Row.

LERNER, E. and R. ARON [eds.] (c. 1957) France Defeats EDC. New York: Praeger.

LEVI, W. (1960) "On the causes of war and the conditions of peace." Journal of Conflict Resolution 4: 411-420.

LEVINE, R. A. (1965) "Socialization, social structure, and inter-social images," pp. 45-69 in H. Kelman (ed.) International Behavior. New York: Holt, Rinehart & Winston.

LEVINSON, D. J. (1957) "Authoritarian personality and foreign policy." Journal of Conflict Resolution 1: 37-47.

LIEBER, R. (1972) "Interest groups and political integration: British entry into Europe." American Political Science Review 66, 1.

LIEBERMANN, J. (1964) "Threat and assurance in the conduct of conflict," pp. 110-122 in R. Fisher (ed.) International Conflict and Behavioral Science. New York: Basic Books.

LIVANT, W. P. (1963) "Cumulative distortion of judgment." Perceptual and Motor Skills 16: 741-745. Reprinted in J. D. Singer (ed.) Human Behavior and International Politics: Contributions from the Social-Psychological Sciences. Chicago: Rand McNally, 1965.

LORENZ, K. (1966) On Aggression. New York: Harcourt, Brace & World.

LUXEMBURG, R. (1921) Die Akkumulation des Kapitals. Ein Beitrag zur Oekonomischen Erklaerung des Imperialismus. Berlin: Vereinigung Internationaler Verlagsanstalten.

MACK, R. and R. C. SNYDER (1957) "The analysis of social conflict. Towards an overview and synthesis." Journal of Conflict Resolution 1: 212-248.

MACRAE, J. and P. SMOKER (1967) "A Vietnam simulation: a report on the Canadian/English joint project." Journal of Peace Research 4: 1-24.

MACY, M. (1969) "On prisoner's dilemma." Cambridge, Mass. (unpublished)

MAGDOFF, H. (1969) The Age of Imperialism. The Economics of U.S. Foreign Policy. New York: Modern Reader.

MALINOWSKI, B. (1941) "An anthropolitical analysis of war." American Journal of Sociology 46: 521-555.

MARCUSE, H. (1968) "Aggressiveness in advanced industrial society," ch. 8 in H. Marcuse, Negations. Boston: Beacon.

MARUYAMA, M. (1963) Thoughts and Behavior in Modern Japanese Politics. London and New York: Oxford Univ. Press.

MAY, M. A. (1943) A Social Psychology of War and Peace. New Haven: Yale Univ. Press.

McCLELLAND, C. (1968) "Access to Berlin: the quantity and variety of events, 1948-1963," pp. 159-186 in J. D. Singer (ed.) Quantitative International Politics. New York: Free Press.

McCLOSKY, H. (1967) "Personality and attitude correlates of foreign policy orientation," pp. 51-109 in J. Rosenau (ed.) Domestic Sources of Foreign Policy. New York: Free Press.

McNAMARA, R. S. (1968) Essence of Security. New York: Harper & Row.

McNEIL, E. B. [ed.] (1965) The Nature of Human Conflict. Englewood Cliffs, N.J.: Prentice-Hall.

--- (1961) "Personality, hostility and international aggression." Journal of Conflict Resolution 5: 279-290.

――― (1959) "Psychology and aggression." Journal of Conflict Resolution 3: 159-293.
MEAD, M. (1940) "Warfare is only an invention, not a biological necessity." Asia 40: 402-405.
――― and R. METRAUX (1965) "The anthropology of human conflict," pp. 116-138 in E. B. McNeil (ed.) The Nature of Human Conflict. Englewood Cliffs, N.J.: Prentice-Hall.
MELMAN, S. (1970) Pentagon Capitalism. New York: McGraw-Hill.
MILLER, J. (1972) "Living systems: the organization." Behavioral Science 17, 1: 1-182.
――― (1971) "The nature of living systems." Behavioral Science 16: 277-301.
――― (1965a) "Living systems: basic concepts." Behavioral Science 10: 193-237.
――― (1965b) "Living systems: cross-level hypotheses." Behavioral Science 10: 337-411.
MILLS, C. W. (1956) The Power Elite. New York: Oxford Univ. Press.
MITSCHERLICH, A. [ed.] (1969a) Bis Hierher und Nicht Weiter. Ist die Menschliche Aggression Unbefriedbar? Munich: Pieper.
――― (1969b) Die Idee des Friedens und die Menschliche Aggressivitat. Frankfurt: Suhrkamp.
――― (1969c) Society Without Father. New York: Harcourt, Brace & World.
――― (1968) "Aggression und anpassung," pp. 80-127 in H. Marcuse et al., An passung und Aggression in der Industriegesellschaft. Frankfurt/Main: Suhrkamp.
MODELSKI, G. (1969) "The simulation of world politics." Seattle: University of Washington. (unpublished)
MONTAGU, A. [ed.] (1968) Man and Aggression. New York: Galaxy.
NAROLL, R. (1969) "Deterrence in history," pp. 150-164 in D. Pruitt and R. Snyder (eds.) Theory and Research on the Causes of War. Englewood Cliffs, N.J.: Prentice-Hall.
NEARING, S. and J. FREEMAN (1969) Dollar Diplomacy. New York: Modern Reader.
NERLICH, U. [ed.] (1966a) Krieg und Frieden im Industriellen Zeitalter. Guetersloh: Bertelsmann.
――― [ed.] (1966b) Krieg und Frieden in der Modernen Staatenwelt. Guetersloh: Bertelsmann.
NEWCOMB, T. M. (1947) "Autistic hostility and social reality." Human Relations 1: 69-86.
NIEZING, J. (1969) War, Disarmament and Sociology. Rotterdam: University Press Studies in Peace Research.
NOEL-BAKER, P. (1958) The Arms Race. London: Stevens.
NORTH, R. and N. CHOUCRI (1969) "Aspects of international conflict: military prepardedness, alliance commitments, and external violence." (mimeo)
――― (1968) "Background conditions to the outbreak of the first World War." Papers of the International Peace Research Society 9: 125-137.
NORTH, R. et al. (1963) Content Analysis: A Handbook with Applications for the Study of International Crisis. Evanston, Ill.: Northwestern Univ. Press.
OSGOOD, C. E. (1965) Perspective in Foreign Policy. Palo Alto, Calif.: Pacific.
――― (1962) Alternative to War or Surrender. Urbana: Univ. of Illinois Press.
PAIGE, G. D. (1968) The Korean Decision. New York: Free Press.
PARENTI, M. (1969) The Anticommunist Impulse. New York:
PARSONS, T. (1947) "Certain primary sources and patterns of aggression in the social structure of the western world," Psychiatry 10: 167-181.
PAUL, J. and J. LAULICHT (1963) In Your Opinion: Leaders' and Voters' Attitudes on Defense and Disarmament. Clarkson: Canadian Peace Research Institute.

"Peace Research in History." (1969) Journal of Peace Research 6, 4.
PEAR, T. H. (1950) Psychological Factors of Peace and War. New York: Philosophical Library.
PILISUK, M. and T. HAYDEN (1965) "Is there a military-industrial complex which prevents peace?" Journal of Social Issues 21, 3: 67-117.
PLACK, A. (1967) Die Gesellschaft und das Bose. Eine Kritik an der Herrschenden Moral. Munich: List.
POOL, I. S. (1965) "Effects of cross-national contact on national and international images," pp. 106-127 in H. Kelman (ed.) International Behavior. New York: Holt, Rinehart & Winston.
— — — and A. KESSLER (1965) "The kaiser, the tsar, and the computer: information processing in a crisis." American Behavioral Scientist 8: 31-38.
POOL, I. S. et al. (1952) The "Prestige Papers." A Survey of their Editorials. Stanford: Stanford Univ. Press.
PRUITT, D. G. (1969) "Stability and sudden change in interpersonal and international affairs." Journal of Conflict Resolution 13: 18-38.
— — — (1965) "Definition of the situation as a determinant of international action," pp. 393-432 in H. Kelman (ed.) International Behavior. New York: Holt, Rinehart & Winston.
— — — and R. C. SNYDER [eds.] (1969) Theory and Research on the Causes of War. Englewood Cliffs, N.J.: Prentice-Hall.
RAPOPORT, A. (1967) "Games which simulate deterrence and disarmament." Peace Research Reviews 1, 4 (August).
— — — (1964) Strategy and Conscience. New York: Harper & Row.
— — — (1960) Fights, Games, and Debates. Ann Arbor: University of Michigan Press.
— — — and A. CHAMMAH (1965) Prisoner's Dilemma. Ann Arbor: Univ. of Michigan Press.
RASER, J. (1966) "Deterrence research." Journal of Peace Research 3: 297-327.
— — — and W. CROW (1966) "A simulation study of deterrence theories," pp. 146-165 in Proceedings of the International Peace Research Association, Inaugural Conference. Assen, Netherlands: Van Gorcum.
RAYMOND, J. (1968) "Growing threat of our military-industrial complex." Harvard Business Review 46 (May-June): 53-64.
— — — (1964) Power at the Pentagon. New York: Harper & Row.
REUCK, A. and J. KNIGHT [eds.] Conflict in Society. London: Ciba Foundation.
RICHARDSON, L. F. (1960a) Arms and Insecurity. Chicago: Quadrangle.
— — — (1960b) Statistics of Deadly Quarrels. Chicago: Quadrangle.
ROAZEN, P. (1968) Freud: Political and Social Thought. New York: Alfred A. Knopf.
ROBBINS, L. (1939) The Economic Causes of War. London: J. Cape.
ROBINSON, J. A. (1970) "Crisis decision-making: an inventory and appraisal of concepts, theories, hypotheses and techniques of analysis." Political Science Annual 2: 111-148.
— — — , C. F. HERMANN, and M. G. HERMANN (1969) "Search under crisis in political gaming and simulation," pp. 80-94 in D. Pruitt and R. Snyder (eds.) Theory and Research on the Causes of War. Englewood Cliffs, N.J.: Prentice-Hall.
ROGOW, A. (1963) James Forrestal: A Study of Personality, Politics, and Policy. New York: Macmillan.
ROPER, E. (1953-1954) "American attitudes on world organization." Public Opinion Quarterly 17: 405-420.

ROSECRANCE, R. (1973) International Relations: Peace or War? New York: McGraw-Hill.
——— (1963) Action and Reaction in World Politics. Boston: Little, Brown.
ROSENAU, J. N. [ed.] (1969) International Politics and Foreign Policy. New York: Free Press.
ROSENBERG, M. J. (1969) "Attitude change and foreign policy in the Cold War era," pp. 111-159 in J. N. Rosenau (ed.) Domestic Sources of Foreign Policy. New York: Free Press.
——— (1965) "Images in relation to the policy process: American public opinion on Cold War issues," pp. 278-334 in H. Kelman (ed.) International Behavior. New York: Holt, Rinehart & Winston.
ROSENBLUTH, G. (1967) The Canadian Economy and Disarmament. New York: St. Martin's.
RUMMEL, R. (1968) "The relationship between national attributes and foreign conflict behavior," pp. 187-214 in J. S. Singer (ed.) Quantitative International Politics. New York: Free Press.
RUSSETT, B. (1969) "Who pays for defense?" American Political Science Review 63: 412-426.
——— (1967) "Pearl Harbor: deterrence theory and decision theory." Journal of Peace Research 4: 89-106.
——— (1963) "The calculus of deterrence." Journal of Conflict Resolution 7: 97-109.
——— (1962) "Cause, surprise, and no escape." Journal of Politics 24: 3-22.
——— et al. (1964) World Handbook of Political and Social Indicators. New Haven: Yale Univ. Press.
SAATY, T. (1968) Mathematical Models of Arms Control and Disarmament. New York: John Wiley.
SCHELLING, T. (1966) Arms and Influence. New Haven: Yale Univ. Press.
——— (1960) The Strategy of Conflict. Cambridge: Harvard Univ. Press.
SCHILLING, W., P. HAMMOND, and G. SNYDER (1962) Strategy, Politics, and Defense Budgets. New York: Columbia Univ. Press.
SCHLESINGER, A. M., Jr. (1965) A Thousand Days. Boston: Houghton-Mifflin.
SCHRODER, H. M., M. J. DRIVER, and S. STREUFERT (1967) Human Information Processing. New York: Holt, Rinehart & Winston.
SCHUMPETER, J. (1955) "The Sociology of Imperialism," pp. 3-98 in J. Schumpeter, Imperialism and Social Classes. New York: Meridian.
SCOTT, A. (1958) Aggression. Chicago: Univ. of Chicago Press.
SCOTT, W. A. (1965) "Psychological and social correlates of international images," pp. 71-103 in H. Kelman (ed.) International Behavior. New York: Holt, Rinehart & Winston.
SEABURY, P. (1954) The Wilhelmstrasse: A Study of German Diplomats Under the Nazi Regime. Berkeley: Univ. of California Press.
SENGHAAS, D. (1970) "Zur analyse von drohpolitik in den internationalen beziehungen." Aus Politik und Zeitgeschichte B 26/70, 27 (Juni): 22-55.
——— (1969a) Abschreckung und Frieden: Studien zur Kritik Organisierter Friedlosigkeit. Frankfurt/Main: Europaeische Verlagsanstalt.
——— (1969b) "Konflikt und konfliktforschung." Koelner Zeitzchrift fuer Psychologie und Sozialpsychologie 21: 31-59.
SILBENER, E. (1946) The Problem of War in the Nineteenth Century Economic Thought. Princeton: Princeton Univ. Press.

SINGER, J. D. (1969a) "Feedback in international conflict: self-correcting and otherwise." Ann Arbor: Univ. of Michigan Mental Health Research Institute, 245.
——— (1969b) "The global system and its subsystems: a developmental view," pp. 21-43 in J. N. Rosenau (ed.) Linkage Politics: Essays on the Convergence of National and International Systems. New York: Free Press.
——— (1969c) "Modern international war: from conjecture to explanation." Ann Arbor: Univ. of Michigan Mental Health Research Institute, 244.
——— [ed.] (1968) Quantitative International Politics: Insights and Evidence. New York: Free Press.
——— [ed.] (1965) Human Behavior and International Politics: Contributions from the Social Psychological Sciences. Chicago: Rand McNally.
——— (1962) Deterrence, Arms Control, and Disarmament. Columbus: Ohio State Univ. Press.
——— (1961) "The level-of-analysis problem in international relations." World Politics 14, 1(October): 77-92.
——— and M. SMALL (1972) The Wages of War, 1816-1965. New York: John Wiley.
——— (1970) "Patterns in international warfare, 1816-1965." Annals (September): 145-155.
——— (1969) "Formal alliances, 1816-1965: an extension of the basic data." Journal of Peace Research 3: 257-282.
——— (1967) "Alliance aggregation and the onset of war, 1815-1945," pp. 247-374 in J. D. Singer (ed.) Quantitative International Politics. New York: Free Press.
——— (1966) "Formal alliances, 1815-1839." Journal of Peace Research 3: 1-32.
SINGER, J. D. and M. WALLACE (forthcoming) "Large-scale violence in the global system: definition and measurement."
——— (1969) "Inter-governmental organization and the preservation of peace, 1816-1965: a preliminary examination." Yearbook of World Affairs 23.
SKILLING, H. G. (1971) Interest Groups in Soviet Politics. Princeton: Princeton Univ. Press.
SKINNER, B. F. (1971) Beyond Freedom and Dignity. New York: Alfred A. Knopf.
——— (1968) Technology of Teaching. New York: Appleton-Century-Crofts.
SLOUTZKI, N. M. (1941) The World Armaments Race, 1919-1939. Geneva Studies 12: 1-129.
SMOKER, P. (1969) "Simulation for social anticipation and creation." Evanston, Ill.: Northwestern Univ. Press. (mimeo)
——— (1968) "International process simulation: a man-computer model." Evanston, Ill.: Northwestern Univ. Press. (mimeo)
——— (1966) "The arms race: a wave model." Papers of the International Peace Research Society 4: 151-192.
SNYDER, R. and G. PAIGE (1958) "The United States decision to resist aggression in Korea: the application of an analytical scheme." Administrative Science Quarterly 3: 341-378.
STAGNER, R. (1965) "The psychology of human conflict," pp. 45-63 in E. B. McNeil (ed.) The Nature of Human Conflict. Englewood Cliffs, N.J.: Prentice-Hall.
STALEY, E. (1967) War and the Private Investor. New York: Howard Fertig.
STEINBERG, J. (1966) Yesterday's Deterrent: Tirpitz and the Birth of the German Battle Fleet. New York: Macmillan.
STERNBERG, F. (1926) Der Imperialismus. Berlin: Malik.

STRACHEY, A. (1957) The Unconscious Motives of War. London: Allen & Unwin.
SWOMLEY, J. (1964) The Military Establishment. Boston: Beacon.
TANTER, R. (1966) "Dimensions of conflict behavior with and between nations, 1958-1960." Journal of Conflict Resolution 10: 41-64.
――― (1964) "Dimensions of conflict behavior within nations, 1955-1960: turmoil and international war." Peace Research Society Papers 3: 159-184.
THAYER, G. (1969) The War Business. The International Trade in Armament. New York: Simon & Schuster.
THOMPSON, J. C. (1968) "How could Vietnam happen? An autopsy." Atlantic Monthly 221 (April): 47-53.
TOLMAN, E. C. (1942) Drives Toward War. New York: Appleton-Century.
UNESCO [ed.] (1957) The Nature of Conflict. Paris: UNESCO.
VAGTS, A. (1959) A History of Militarism–Civilian and Military. New York: Meridian.
VERBA, S. and N. NIE (1972) Participation in America. New York: Harper & Row.
VERNON, R. (1971) Sovereignty at Bay. New York: Basic Books.
――― (1969) "The role of U.S. enterprise abroad." Daedalus 98 (Winter): 113-133.
VILMAR, F. (1969) Ruestung und Abruestung im Spaetkapitalismus. Frankfurt/Main: Europaeische Verlagsanstalt.
VOEVODSKY, J. (1970) "Quantitative behavior of warring nations." Peace Research Reviews 3, 5.
von BERTALANFFY, L. (1965) "General system theory." General Systems 1: 1-10.
WALTZ, K. N. (1959) Man, the State and War. New York: Columbia Univ. Press.
WEHLER, H. (1969) Bismarck und der Imperialismus. Koeln: Kiepenheuer & Witsch.
WESLEY, J. P. (1962) "Frequency of wars and geographical opportunity." Journal of Conflict Resolution 6: 387-389.
WHITE, R. (1968) Nobody Wanted War: Misperceptions in Vietnam and Other Wars. Garden City, N.Y.: Doubleday.
WHITEY, S. and D. KATZ (1965) "The social psychology of human conflict," pp. 64-90 in E. B. McNeil (ed.) The Nature of Human Conflict. Englewood Cliffs, N.J.: Prentice-Hall.
WIESNER, J. B. et al. (1969) ABM: An Evaluation of the Decision to Deploy an Antiballistic Missile System. New York: New American Library.
WINSLOW, E. M. (1948) The Pattern of Imperialism. A Study in the Theories of Power. New York: Columbia Univ. Press.
WOHLSTETTER, R. (1965) "Cuba and Pearl Harbor. Hindsight and Foresight." Foreign Affairs (July): 691-707.
――― (1962) Pearl Harbor: Warning and Decision. Stanford: Stanford Univ. Press.
WRIGHT, Q. (1965a) A Study of War. Chicago: Univ. of Chicago Press.
――― (1965b) "The escalation of international conflict." Journal of Conflict Resolution 9: 434-449.
―――, W. EVAN, and M. DEUTSCH [eds.] (1962) Preventing World War III. New York: Basic Books.
YARMOLINSKY, A. (1969) "The problem of momentum," pp. 144-149 in J. Wiesner et al., ABM: An Evaluation of the Decision to Deploy an Anti-Ballistic Missile System. New York: New American Library.
YOUNG, O. (1968) Systems of Political Science. Englewood Cliffs, N.J.: Prentice-Hall.
ZAWODNY, J. K. (1966) Man and International Relations; Vol. I: Conflict. San Francisco: Chandler.

ZINNES, D. A. (1968) "The expression and perception of hostility in prewar crisis: 1914," pp. 85-119 in J. D. Singer (ed.) Quantitative International Politics. New York: Free Press.
--- (1966) "A comparison of hostile behavior of decision-makers in simulated and historical data." World Politics 17: 474-502.
---, R. NORTH, and H. E. KOCH (1961) "Capability, threat, and the outbreak of war," pp. 469-482 in J. N. Rosenau (ed.) International Politics and Foreign Policy. New York: Free Press.

PART FIVE

BIBLIOGRAPHY

BIBLIOGRAPHY OF RECENT FOREIGN POLICY STUDIES, 1970-72

JAMES GREEN

Syracuse University

The following criteria were used to compile this bibliography: First and foremost, the study had to be comparative in the sense that it must examine two or more actors or two or more comparable instances of behavior of one actor. Second, the study had to account for the causes and/or consequences of foreign policy or attempt some measurement of foreign policy behavior. In addition, studies were included which discussed general public opinion as a predictor of national foreign policy behavior and as a consequence of events and conditions in the international system. Third, the study had to be empirical or it had to represent a theory which demonstrated real potential for operationalization. "Empirical" in this sense was not rigidly defined as quantitative, but as an effort to undertake controlled data-based investigation. Finally, the study had to have been published between January 1970 and September 1972.

It is the intention of the Editor to include a bibliography of this sort in each edition of the *Yearbook*. Corrections and additions should be addressed to the Editor for inclusion in subsequent editions.

AROSALO, U. (1970) "A model of international interaction in Western Europe." Journal of Peace Research 7: 247-258.
BECKER, A. S. and A. L. HORELICK (1970) Soviet Policy in the Middle East. Santa Monica: RAND.

BENJAMIN, R. W. and L. J. EDINGER (1971) "Conditions for military control over foreign policy decisions in major states: a historical exploration." Journal of Conflict Resolution 15: 5-31.
BONHAM, G. M. (1970) "Participation in regional assemblies: effects of attitudes of Scandinavian parliamentarians." Journal of Common Market Studies 8: 325-336.
BRODIN, K. (1972) "Belief systems, doctrines, and foreign policy." Cooperation and Conflict 7, 2: 97-112.
CASPARY, W. R. (1970a) "The mood theory: a study of public opinion and foreign policy." American Political Science Review 64, 2: 536-547.
––– (1970b) "Dimensions of attitudes on international conflict: internationalism and military offensive action." Peace Research Society Papers 13: 1-10.
CHADWICK, R. (1970) "A partial model of national political-economic systems: evaluation by causal inferences." Journal of Peace Research 2: 121-131.
CLARK, J. F., M. K. O'LEARY, and E. R. WITTKOPF (1971) "National attributes associated with dimensions of support for the United Nations." International Organization 25, 1: 1-25.
COBB, R. W. and C. ELDER (1970) International community: a regional and global study. New York: Holt, Rinehart & Winston.
CUTLER, N. E. (1970) "Generation succession as a source of foreign policy attitudes: a cohort analysis of American opinion, 1946-1966." Journal of Peace Research 1: 33-48.
DOWTY, A. (1971) "Foreign-linked factionalism as a historical pattern." Journal of Conflict Resolution 15: 429-442.
DUNCAN, W. R. [ed.] (1970) Soviet policy in developing countries. Massachusetts: Blaisdale.
EAST, M. A. (1972) "Status discrepancy and violence in the international system: an empirical analysis," pp. 229-316 in J. N. Rosenau, V. Davis, and M. A. East (eds.) The Analysis of International Politics. New York: Free Press.
GAREAU, F. H. (1970) "Cold war cleavages as seen from the United Nations General Assembly: 1947-1967." Journal of Peace Research 32: 929-968.
GEORGE, A. L., D. K. HALL, and W. E. SIMONS (1971) The Limits of Coercive Diplomacy: Laos-Cuba-Vietnam. Boston: Little, Brown.
GLEDITSCH, N. P. (1971) "Interaction patterns in the Middle East." Cooperation and Conflict 6, 1: 15-30.
HANREIDER, W. (ed.) (1971) Comparative Foreign Policy: Theoretical Essays. New York: David McKay.
HILTON, G. (1971) "A closed and open model analysis of expressions of hostility in crisis." Journal of Peace Research 8: 249-262.
HOADLY, J. S. and S. HASEGAWA (1971) "Sino-Japanese relations, 1950-1970: an application of the linkage model of international politics." International Studies Quarterly 15: 131-157.
HOLSTI, K. J. (1970) "National role conceptions in the study of foreign policy." International Studies Quarterly 14: 233-309.
HOLSTI, O. R. (1970) "Individual differences in the 'definition of the situation'." Journal of Conflict Resolution 14: 303-310.
––– and R. C. NORTH (1970) "Perceptions of hostility and financial indicies during the 1914 crisis," pp. 112-132 in N. Rosenbaum (ed.) Readings on the International Political System. Englewood Cliffs, N.J.: Prentice-Hall.

HVEEM, H. (1972a) "Foreign policy opinion as a function of international position." Cooperation and Conflict 7, 2: 65-86.
——— (1972b) International Relations and World Images: A Study of Norwegian Foreign Policy Elites. Oslo: Universitetsforlaget.
——— (1970) " 'Blame' as international behavior." Journal of Peace Research 7: 49-67.
IVERSON, C. (1971) "A note on foreign policy opinions as a function of position in channels of influence and communication." Cooperation and Conflict 6, 1: 56-58.
JACOBSEN, K. (1970) "Sponsorship activities in the U.N. negotiation process." Cooperation and Conflict 4: 241-269.
KEGLEY, C. W., Jr. (1971) "Toward the construction of an empirically grounded typology of foreign policy output behavior." Ph.D. dissertation, Syracuse University.
KEIM, W. D. (1971) "Nations and conflict individuality." Journal of Peace Research 8: 287-292.
LAMBELET, J. C. (1971) "A dynamic model of the arms race in the Middle East, 1953-1964." General Systems Yearbook 16: 145-167.
McGOWAN, P. J. (1970) "Theoretical approaches to the comparative study of foreign policy." Ph.D. dissertation, Northwestern University.
MERKL, P. (1971) "Politico-cultural restraints on West German foreign policy: sense of trust, identity, and agency." Comparative Political Studies 3, 4: 443-468.
MITCHELL, W. C. (1971) "The role of stress in the war in Vietnam: an analysis of U.S. actions and public statements, 1964-1967." Peace Research Society Papers 17: 47-60.
MOORE, D. W. (1970) "Governmental and societal influences on foreign policy: a partial examination of Rosenau's adaptation model." Ph.D. dissertation, Ohio State University.
MUELLER, J. E. (1971) "Trends in popular support for the wars in Korea and Vietnam." American Political Science Review 65: 358-375.
——— (1970) "Presidential popularity from Truman to Johnson." American Political Science Review 64: 18-34.
PATCHEN, M. (1970) "Social class and dimensions of foreign policy attitudes." Social Science Quarterly 51, 3: 649-667.
PELOWSKI, A. L. (1971) "On the use of quasi-experimental design in the study of international organization and war." Journal of Peace Research 8: 279-285.
PHILLIPS, W. R. (1971) "The dynamics of behavioral action and reaction in international conflict." Peace Research Society Papers 17: 31-46.
PORSHOLT, L. (1971) "A quantitative conflict model." Journal of Peace Research 1: 55-66.
PUCHALA, D. J. (1970a) "Integration and disintegration in Franco-American relations, 1954-1965." International Organization 24, 2: 183-208.
——— (1970b) "International transaction and regional integration." International Organization 24, 4: 732-763.
RITTBERGER, V. (1971) "Organized multinational cooperation within regional settings: a preliminary analysis." Peace Research Society Papers 17: 93-118.
ROBINSON, J. P. (1970) "Balance theory and Vietnam related attitudes." Social Science Quarterly 51, 3: 610-616.
ROSENAU, J. N. (1970) The Scientific Study of Foreign Policy. New York: Free Press.
SALMORE, S. (1972) "National attributes and foreign policy: a multivariate analysis." Ph.D. dissertation, Princeton University.

SALMORE, S. and C. HERMANN (1970) "The effect of size, development and accountability on foreign policy." Peace Research Society Papers 14: 15-30.
SIGAL, L. V. (1970) "The 'rational policy' model and the Formosa Straits crises." International Studies Quarterly 14: 121-156.
SINGER, J. D. (1972) "The 'correlates of war' project: interim report and rationale." World Politics 24: 243-270.
——— (1970) "Escalation and control in international conflict: a simple feedback model." General Systems Yearbook 15: 1963-1973.
SIVERSON, R. M. (1970) "International conflict and perceptions of injury: the case of the Suez crisis." International Studies Quarterly 14: 157-165.
SMALL, M. and J. D. SINGER (1970) "Patterns in international warfare, 1816-1965." Annals of the American Academy of Political and Social Science 391: 145-155.
STOESSINGER, J. G. (1970) The United States and the Super Powers: United States-Soviet Interaction at the United Nations. New York: Random House.
TALIKKA, N. (1970) "Economic and power frustrations as predictors of industrial and political conflict strategies." Journal of Peace Research 4: 267-290.
TERHUNE, K. (1970) "From national character to national behavior: a reformulation." Journal of Conflict Resolution 14, 2: 203-263.
TERRELL, L. (1972) "Patterns of international involvement and international violence." International Studies Quarterly 16, 2: 167-186.
——— (1971) "Societal stress, political instability, and levels of military effort." Journal of Conflict Resolution 15, 3: 329-346.
THOMPSON, W. R. (1970) "The Arab sub-system, and the feudal pattern of interaction: 1965." Journal of Peace Research 7: 151-167.
TODD, J. E. (1971) "The 'law-making' behavior of states in the United Nations as a function of their location within formal world regions." International Studies Quarterly 15: 297-315.
VINCENT, J. E. (1971) "Predicting voting patterns in the General Assembly." American Political Science Review 65: 471-495.
——— (1970) "An analysis of caucusing group activity at the United Nations." Journal of Peace Research 7: 133-150.
VITAL, D. (1971) The Survival of Small States: Studies in Small Power/Great Power Conflict. London: Oxford Univ. Press.
WALLACE, M. D. (1971) "Power, status, and international war." Journal of Peace Research 8: 23-35.
WALTERS, R. S. (1971) American and Soviet Aid: A Comparative Analysis. Pittsburgh: Univ. of Pittsburgh Press.
WEEDE, E. (1970) "Conflict behavior of nation-states." Journal of Peace Research 7: 229-235.
WEINSTEIN, F. B. (1972) "The uses of foreign policy in Indonesia: an approach to the analysis of foreign policy in the less developed countries." World Politics 24: 356-381.
WITTKOPF, E. R. (1971) "The distribution of foreign aid in comparative perspective: an empirical study of the flow of foreign economic assistance, 1961-1967." Ph.D. dissertation, Syracuse University.
ZINNES, D. A. and J. WILKENFELD (1971) "An analysis of foreign conflict behavior of nations," pp. 167-213 in W. Hanrieder (ed.) Comparative Foreign Policy. New York: David McKay.